Autobiographical Statements in Twentieth-Century Russian Literature

Edited by
Jane Gary Harris

PRINCETON UNIVERSITY PRESS

PRINCETON, NEW JERSEY

Copyright © 1990 by Princeton University Press
Published by Princeton University Press, 41 William Street,
Princeton, New Jersey 08540
In the United Kingdom: Princeton University Press, Oxford

Library of Congress Cataloging-in-Publication Data

Autobiographical statements in twentieth-century Russian literature /
edited by Jane Gary Harris.
p. cm.—(Studies of the Harriman Institute, Columbia University)
Includes bibliographical references.
1. Russian literature—20th century—History and criticism.
2. Authors, Russian—20th century—Biography—History and criticism.
3. Autobiography. I. Harris, Jane Gary. II. Series: Studies of the
Harriman Institute.
PG3016.A98 1990   891.709′004—dc20   89-24300

ISBN 0-691-06818-6 (alk. paper)

This book has been composed in Linotron Times Roman

Princeton University Press books are printed
on acid-free paper, and meet the guidelines for
permanence and durability of the Committee on
Production Guidelines for Book Longevity of
the Council on Library Resources

Printed in the United States of America by Princeton University Press,
Princeton, New Jersey
10 9 8 7 6 5 4 3 2 1

TO MY MOTHER

whose seemingly endless autobiographical narratives had more to do

with this book than she realizes

Contents

Preface

THE ESSAYS in this book, *Autobiographical Statements in Twentieth-Century Russian Literature*, are intended to move the reader familiar with the accepted canon of Russian literature to explore the extraordinary range and diversity of writing in the autobiographical mode that emerges in the twentieth century. The introductory essay, "Diversity of Discourse," surveys and discusses the issues central to current autobiographical theory and practice in the West and in the Soviet Union. The fourteen essays that follow, selected according to principles of chronology and diversity as well as fundamental interest, illustrate from various critical perspectives the role and complexity of the "autobiographical statement" in twentieth-century Russian literary discourse.

Each of the contributors to this volume was asked to discuss a given author's writings with special reference to his/her use of first-person narrative and, specifically, the autobiographical mode. Hence, each essay treats one or more works of a given author, focusing on the kinds and variety of autobiographical forms and devices employed while attempting to define the place of the given author or work in the context of its contribution to twentieth-century Russian literary autobiographical statements.

The chronological organization of the selections is offered to readers as a "dialogue" between periods and styles, if not always between the authors, presenting first the experimental writings of the early years of the twentieth century (Rozanov, Remizov, and Bely); second, the unusual autobiographical writings of the mid-1920s to early 1940s (Mandelstam, Pasternak, Olesha, and Zoshchenko); and finally, the vast range and vitality of the more contemporary writings of the 1960s through the 1980s (Nabokov and Jakobson, as well as Sinyavsky and Limonov–major émigré writers; and Trifonov, Nadezhada Mandelstam, and Lydia Ginzburg—representatives of the variety of Soviet literary endeavors). Although the majority of the writers represented in this anthology are figures well known in the Russian literary arena, essays on the autobiographical statements of the renowned scholars Lydia Ginzburg and Roman Jakobson were also included, because their lives and writings were so intimately connected with prominent literary circles.

Approximately half of the essays gathered here were written specifically for this collection; the others were culled from various sources and revised for the purposes of this volume. My only regret is that space does not allow for all the fine autobiographical works written during this century to be discussed. However, it is hoped that these essays will provide the reader with a new perspective on twentieth-century Russian literary history and that both the essays and the Select Bibliography will encourage and stimulate further examination of this fascinating realm of narrative discourse. Where available, English translations of the works discussed in the essays are noted in the bibliography.

Furthermore, because we hope that this book will have a readership well beyond the field of Russian literature specialists, the contributors and I have decided to follow a mixed transliteration/spelling system for the names used in the text. Nevertheless, transliterated spellings always pose a problem. For both first and last names, as well as patronymics that have become more or less standard in English-language publications (using -*y* rather than -*i* or -*j*), we have tried not to confuse the reader with new spellings. We have thus chosen to use the more familiar masculine and feminine endings for last names ending in -*sky* (masc.) or -*skaya* (fem.) rather than introduce the seemingly unpronounceable -*skij* or -*skaja*; hence Dostoevsky and Vjazemsky (rather than Dostoevskij and Vjazemskij) and Chukovskaya, Kommissarzhevskaya, and Shklovskaya. Among prominent names included in the text are those of writers Andreyev, Bely, Chukovsky, Dostoevsky, Mayakovsky, Sinyavsky, and Zabolotsky and the musicians Scriabin and Tchaikovsky. First names include Alexander, Evgeny, Korney, Maxim, Nikolay (and the patronymic Nikolaevich), Vasily (and Vasilievich), Yury (and Yurievich), as well as Evgenya, Lydia, Nadezhda, Nadya, Natalya, Sonya, Tanya, and so on. Place names such as Ulyanovsk and Mikhailovsky Square follow the same principle. We have also chosen to use the more pronouncible *kh* instead of *x* in such names as Khlebnikov and Kruchenykh.

However, where the names of persons or places are relatively unfamiliar, or belong predominantly to the realm of scholarship, we have preferred to retain the modified scholarly transliteration system (using *j* instead of *i* or *y*). Therefore, we have kept such spellings as Tynjanov and Pjast as close to the standard transliteration as possible.

On the other hand, the bibliography and notes use the modified scholarly transliteration system (e.g., endings: -*skij* vs. -*sky* or -*skii*; -*skaja* vs. -*skaya* or -*skaia*; and -*j*- is used to represent *i kratkoe*) when referring to Russian Cyrillic-alphabet publications of Russian texts. Latin-alphabet publications are cited with the spellings provided in the given text; thus readers should note that spellings will differ in French-, German-, Italian-, Spanish-, and Swedish-, and English-language citations to the same author.

Acknowledgments

I OWE the idea for this volume to the lively discussions in my NEH Summer Seminars on Russian Literary Autobiography given at Columbia University, in which we frequently bemoaned the dearth of scholarly materials on basic problems of Russian and Soviet autobiography, memoirs, and first-person narrative. It is hoped that this collection of essays will initiate a larger response to this void and suggest the significance of the trend toward first-person narrative in the literature of this century.

I would also like to express my gratitude to IREX, the Kennan Institute, the American Philosophical Society, and the University of Pittsburgh's Russian and East European Studies Program and Faculty of Arts and Sciences Grants Committees for providing much-needed funding at various stages of this project, and I am much indebted to those Soviet and American colleagues who both contributed to the dialogue informing this volume and who helped me to locate the materials mentioned in the introduction and Bibliography.

I am also most grateful to those publishers, journals, individuals, and organizations who gave their permission to print revised versions of the designated texts; *Slavic and East European Journal, Studies in Twentieth-Century Literature*, Mouton de Gruyter, Professor Stanislaw Pomorski, Routledge and Kegan Paul, and G. K. Hall and Co.

Last but not least, I must thank my family for their patience in bearing up under the inevitable strains associated with scholarship and publication. And I want to express my special thanks to my daughter, Maia, for her pertinent suggestions in the editing of the essays and help with the more mundane aspects of typing.

Autobiographical Statements
in Twentieth-Century Russian Literature

Diversity of Discourse: Autobiographical Statements in Theory and Praxis

Jane Gary Harris

DIVERSITY OF FORM has characterized autobiographical discourse since the beginning of the Western literary narrative tradition. One of the consequences of this diversity has been the complexity and confusion plaguing attempts to describe it. Historically, autobiography is classified as one of the oldest forms of narrative, its organizational patterns being associated with the rise of the ancient novel. This close association between the novel and autobiography is perceived as traceable to the earliest examples of narrative: the "series of autobiographical and biographical forms worked out in ancient times [had] a profound influence [on both] European biography and the development of the European novel as a whole."[1] The distinctive characteristics of these early forms have been defined as "biographical time" and the conception of a new "human image," that of "an individual who passes through the course of an entire life," characteristics still fundamental to contemporary definitions of autobiography, whether examined in terms of genre, mode, or discourse.

In his discussion of the earliest forms of autobiography, M. M. Bakhtin discerns three primary patterns: (1) the Platonic scheme, in which the life course of one seeking true knowledge is revealed; (2) the rhetorical pattern, in which the author accounts for himself to the public through normative-pedagogic self-glorification; and (3) the memoir, the most historically oriented form, in which the individual, family, or clan is identified through his fate, fortune, or genius. Nevertheless, Bakhtin also points out that it was not until the Middle Ages that "the private spheres of a man's life" began to be evaluated in literary narrative. Even then "the true laying bare of the 'internal man' came about only with the help of outsiders . . . through some means of exposing the 'internal man,' " allowing his "free and self-sufficient subjectiv-

---

[1] See M. M. Bakhtin, "Forms of Time and the Chronotope," in *The Dialogic Imagination: Four Essays by M. M. Bakhtin*, ed. and trans. J. M. Holquist (Austin: University of Texas Press, 1981), 130–40. This essay is subtitled "Notes Towards a Historical Poetics," and is dated by the editor as 1937–38. The conclusion of the essay, however, dates from 1973. For perhaps the most detailed history of autobiography (as far as it goes), see Georg Misch, *Geschichte der Autobiographie*, 8 vols. (Frankfurt am Main: Schulte und Bulmke, 1949–69). Georg Misch, *A History of Autobiography in Antiquity*, 2 vols. (London: Routledge and Kegan Paul, 1950) is a translation of the first two volumes.

ity" to be perceived.[2] This occurred at first primarily through use of third-person perspective.

Many recent studies of autobiographical narrative have questioned whether modern critics may not be reading autobiographical intention into older works not originally conceived as autobiography. They claim that the differentiation between modern or "true" autobiography and other forms of narrative occurred in conjunction with the emergence of the literary movements of pre-romanticism and romanticism—in particular, with the appearance of the bildungsroman and Rousseau's *Confessions*—at the very earliest, at the end of the seventeenth century or the early eighteenth century.[3] It was only then that the first-person perspective came to dominate the telling of the life story and that authors succeeded in "isolating individual life sequences, characters with interior perspective" who often endeavored to "heal themselves through contact with nature and the life of the simple people."[4]

If modern autobiography emerged amid the flowering of European romanticism, it has also been suggested that the recollective reconstruction of experience was inspired by the poetics of self-consciousness defining romantic lyric poetry as much as by the sentiments, values, and analytic methods of Rousseau's *Confessions*.[5] Autobiography, by employing the device of the self-reflexive narrator to achieve a comprehensive understanding of the self through the poetic reconstruction of experience, is said to have developed along the same lines as the dialectics of consciousness and imagination voiced in such works as Wordsworth's *Prelude*.[6]

[2] Bakhtin, "Forms of Time," 164.

[3] See Elizabeth Bruss, *Autobiographical Acts: The Changing Situation of a Literary Genre* (Baltimore: Johns Hopkins University Press, 1976), 33. Bruss is concerned primarily with English and American autobiography. See also George Gusdorf, "De l'autobiographie initiatique à l'autobiographie littéraire," *Revue d'histoire littéraire de la France* 75 (1975): 957–94. Gusdorf is concerned primarily with French autobiography but touches on earlier European writings as well. In this essay he rejects Philippe Lejeune's arguments in *Le pacte autobiographique* (Paris: Editions du Seuil, 1975) that Rousseau's *Confessions* marks "the beginning of the literary genre of autobiography properly speaking." Gusdorf believes that "modern literary autobiography was born with the desacralization of religious autobiographies" (990), and thus Rousseau represents the culmination not the beginning of a trend; hence the force of his model for the future. See also Eugene Vance, "Augustine's *Confessions* and the Grammar of Selfhood," *Genre* 6, no. 1 (March 1973): 1–28. Vance writes that "Autobiography, as is well known, is a neologism of modern culture that originated with romantic myths of expression at the turn of the last century. As an outgrowth of romanticism, autobiography seemingly rests on the assumption that language can and should serve man as a mode of subjective action" (1).

[4] Bakhtin, *The Dialogic Imagination*, 231.

[5] Harold Bloom, *Romanticism and Consciousness: Essays in Criticism* (New York: W. W. Norton, 1970); André Monglond, *Le préromantisme français*, vol. 2 (Paris: José Corti, 1966), especially chapter 5 on Rousseau's *Confessions* and inner lyricism.

[6] Geoffrey Hartman, *Wordsworth's Poetry, 1787–1814* (New Haven: Yale University Press, 1964); and William Spengemann, *The Forms of Autobiography: Episodes in the History of a Literary Genre* (New Haven: Yale University Press, 1980).

Generally speaking, most scholars of autobiography agree that what is most important thematically and structurally is that the narrator recognizes how the perceived process of his own development parallels the course of his narrative and hence that the structure of autobiographical discourse is based on the parallelism between the narrator's growing consciousness of his experience and the objectification of that experience in the telling. Or, to put it more directly, the narrative structure of autobiographical discourse is grounded in both the author's and the reader's recognition of the interplay or tension between the course of the narrative and what B. J. Mandel termed "autobiographical consciousness"—"Memories do not make an autobiography; they constitute . . . the autobiographical consciousness . . . that consciousness which thinks about itself—its present, past and future."[7] Mandel's observation suggests that the narrator can endeavor either to speak in his own voice about his own life or to speak as a fictitious character. What is most significant for autobiographical discourse is the perceived evolution of attitude or the transformation of mood that emerges through the self-reflective process, not the fictionality of narration or lack thereof. Consequently, it is this transformation that expands the narrative perspective to the extent that the narrator creates, or asserts that he gains, a more comprehensive sense of self based on the perception and reconstruction of his self-development at the time of writing. Ultimately, the narrator may also express a sense of fulfillment and peace of mind reinforced by his achievement of self-consciousness. The addressee or reader may participate vicariously in the process of reflexive recollection presented in this form of retrospective narrative.

On the other hand, as Cyrus Hamlin points out in "The Poetics of Self-Consciousness in European Romanticism,"[8] such fulfillment "is not without a sense of paradox . . . which also corresponds to the theory of self-consciousness." This paradox derives from the recognition of uncertainty with respect to the understanding of recollected experience since "some kind of self-surrender or loss of self-control" is involved, often resulting from the perception that "the self becomes the agent or instrument of a higher power, whose concerns go beyond the life of the self and thus remain for that self ineffable." Nevertheless, it is this very paradox that generated the romantic concept that the act of recollection is identical with the creative process and the concomitant notion that works created through the process of recollection become more than works "about" the growth of the poet's mind; rather, they are taken to reflect or express the creative process itself. This concept was developed still further by the romantic and modernist movements in positing the idea that only poetry can recreate, and thus capture, moments of experience otherwise inef-

[7] B. J. Mandel, "Full of Life Now" in *Autobiography: Essays Theoretical and Critical*, ed. James Olney (Princeton: Princeton University Press, 1980), 49–72.

[8] Cyrus Hamlin, "The Poetics of Self-Consciousness in European Romanticism: Holderlin's *Hyperion* and Wordsworth's *Prelude*, *Genre* 6, no. 2 (June 1973): 142–77.

fable or incomprehensible and that only through the poetic act of recollection can the conscious mind attain such moments of higher intuition. The recollected experiences, usually presented as the climactic moments of the narrator's life, are perceived as comprehensible solely as a result of the creative act of recollection, that is, as a result of the narrative. Thus retrospective narrative, in being the recollection of experiences that go beyond understanding, has affinities with the romantic lyric, which assumes an aesthetic existence of its own removed from both the actual experiences portrayed in the narrative and the recollections themselves. Autobiographical narrative, according to this theory, thereby achieves aesthetic meaning as an autonomous creative act. Spengemann describes the process with regard to Wordsworth: "The self he set out to discover philosophically, he ended up realizing poetically; it could not be abstracted from the words which are its cause and adequate symbol."[9]

Literary history, consequently, seems to indicate that the origins of autobiography are twofold: credence is given on the one hand to a close association with the development of the novel and on the other hand to a close relationship with the development of romanticism and lyric poetry. Failure to take account of the dual nature of this complex literary heritage may have led to much of the confusion as well as the diversity in scholarly studies of autobiography.[10]

The study of autobiography, although dominated by historical research until the last quarter century, has finally come into its own as a subject of theoretical and critical debate. Since George Gusdorf's seminal essay, "Conditions and Limits of Autobiography" (1956) and Roy Pascal's pioneering effort *Design and Truth in Autobiography* (1960)[11] scholars have attempted to define autobiography as a "literary" as opposed to a "non-literary" genre, as a category of writing, or as a mode of narrative perception. The spectrum of study has been vast, ranging from broad theoretical generalizations grounded in a historical and thematic perspective, such as Spengemann's assertion in *The Forms of Autobiography*[12] that *any* work treating the theme of self-realization, including fictional narratives in the manner of Hawthorne's *Scarlet Letter* or

---

[9] Spengemann, *The Forms of Autobiography*, 91.

[10] Among scholars who have emphasized comparisons between the genres of autobiography and the novel, see Roy Pascal, *Design and Truth in Autobiography* (Cambridge, Mass.: Harvard University Press, 1960); Patricia Spacks, *Imagining a Self: Autobiography and the Novel in Eighteenth-Century England* (Cambridge, Mass.: Harvard University Press, 1976); and Georges May, *L'autobiographie* (Paris: PUF, 1979). Among those who have emphasized the source of autobiography in romanticism or concentrated on interpreting Wordsworth's *Prelude* in terms used to define autobiography, see Eugene Vance, "Augustine's *Confessions* and the Grammar of Selfhood," 1–28; Lejeune, *Le pacte autobiographique*; Cyrus Hamlin, "The Poetics of Self-Consciousness in European Romanticism," 142–77; Paul de Man, "Autobiography as Defacement" in *The Rhetoric of Romanticism* (New York: Columbia University Press, 1984), 67–81.

[11] Georges Gusdorf, "Conditions and Limits of Autobiography," in Olney, *Autobiography: Essays Theoretical and Critical*; Pascal, *Design and Truth in Autobiography*.

[12] Spengemann, *The Forms of Autobiography*.

lyric poems such as Wordsworth's *Prelude*, can be included in the genre, to more cautious, indeed conservative, criteria such as Lejeune's concise definition in *Le pacte autobiographique* based on an ideal narrative form as well as thematic considerations: "a retrospective account in prose that a real person makes of his own existence when it stresses the individual life, in particular, the story of his personality."[13] Elizabeth Bruss's more elaborate set of "rules to be satisfied by the text and the surrounding context of any work which is to 'count as' autobiography," presented in *Autobiographical Acts*, stands somewhere between Spengemann and Lejeune. She focuses on the "dual role" of the narrator, and consequently, on the narrative act:

> Rule 1. An autobiographer undertakes a dual role. He is the source of the subject matter and the source for the structure to be found in his text. (a) The author claims individual responsibility for the creation and arrangement of his texts. (b) The individual who is exemplified in the organization of the text is purported to share the identity of an individual to whom reference is made via the subject matter of the text. (c) The existence of this individual, independent of the text itself, is assumed to be susceptible to appropriate public verification procedures.

> Rule 2. Information and events reported in connection with the autobiographer are asserted to have been, to be, or to have a potential for being the case. (a) Under existing conventions, a claim is made for the truth-value of what the autobiography reports—no matter how difficult that truth-value might be to ascertain, whether the report treats of private experiences or publicly observable occasions. (b) The audience is expected to accept these reports as true, and is free to "check up" on them or attempt to discredit them.

> Rule 3. Whether or not what is reported can be discredited, whether or not it can be reformulated in some more generally acceptable way from another point of view, the autobiographer purports to believe in what he asserts.[14]

The most extreme or nontraditional discussion of autobiography in Western literary theory appears in Paul de Man's essay, "Autobiography as Defacement," in which he takes the view that "Autobiography . . . is not a genre or a mode, but a figure of reading or of understanding that occurs, to some degree, in all texts." De Man's deconstructive approach treats autobiography neither as a genre nor mode, but rather as a process of cognition dependent on the reading of the text. This approach is developed in a slightly different direction by Jacques Derrida in his discussion of Nietzsche's *Ecce Homo*.[15] De

[13] Lejeune, *Le pacte autobiographique*.

[14] Bruss, *Autobiographical Acts*, 10–11.

[15] See Jacques Derrida, *The Ear of the Other: Otobiography, Transference, Translation (Texts and Discussions with Jacques Derrida)*, ed. and trans. Christie V. McDonald (New York: Schocken Books, 1985). Originally published as *L'oreille de l'autre* (Montreal: Vlb Editeur, 1982).

Man suggests that the "autobiographical moment happens as an alignment between the two subjects involved in the process of reading in which they determine each other by mutual reflective substitution." Thus, he posits a "specular model of cognition" in which the "two subjects" are defined as a "specular pair" and are identified as "the author *of* the text and the author *in* the text who bears his name." The "autobiographical moment," then, is conceived as a "specular structure" in which a kind of "mirror-like self-understanding" takes place. De Man claims that this "specular structure is interiorized in a text in which the author declares himself the subject of his own understanding, but this merely makes explicit the wider claim to authorship that takes place whenever a text is stated to be *by* someone and assumed to be understandable to the extent that this is the case."[16] While de Man thus denies the existence of an autobiographical genre, Michael Sprinker's deconstructivist reading of autobiography tries to associate it with other "books without authors," concluding that "no autobiography can take place except within the boundaries of a writing where concepts of subject, self, and author collapse into the act of producing a text."[17] In other words, Sprinker seems to accept the possibility of autobiography as a genre but claims, following Derrida, that "the autobiographical self" cannot exist outside the text and that the informing "I" is therefore as insignificant to the autobiographical text as it is to a work of fiction.[18]

[16] De Man, "Autobiography as Defacement," 67–81.

[17] Michael Sprinker, "Fictions of the Self: The End of Autobiography" in Olney, *Autobiography: Essays Theoretical and Critical*, 342.

[18] See, for example, Derrida, *The Ear of the Other*. On "truth" or "intention," Derrida states: "The effects or structure of a text are not reducible to 'truth,' to the intended meaning of its presumed author, or even to its supposedly unique and identifiable signatory" (29); on interpretation: "An interpretive decision does not have to draw a line between two intents or two political contents. Our interpretation will not be readings of a hermeneutic or exegetic sort, but rather political interventions in the political rewriting of the text and its destination" (32); and on the problem of the border: "I can no longer say what an empirical text is, or the empirical given of a text. What I can do is refer to a number of conventions—precisely those conventions which sustain traditional or academic discourse. . . . When we employ such discourses, we think we know what a given text is—a text that we receive in the editorial form of an authenticated corpus, and so on. We also have a number of 'empirical facts' about Nietzsche's life. . . . Nevertheless, the presupposition is . . . that one knows what one means by Nietzsche's 'empirical' life. That is, one assumes that one knows what is at the organizing center of the debate. *If one problematizes things as I tried to do . . . however, the opposition between, for example, the empirical and the non-empirical* (but there are other names for this opposition) *is precisely what becomes problematic. I then no longer know what this experience is that grounds the value of the empirical.* This is the case whether one is speaking of Nietzsche's life or his corpus—his body, if you will—or the corpus called Nietzsche's works. . . . Wherever *the paradoxical problem of the border is posed,* then the line that could separate an author's life from his work for example, or which, within this life, could separate an essentialness or transcendentality from an empirical fact, or, yet again, within this work, an empirical fact from something that is not empirical—*this line itself becomes unclear.* Its mark becomes divided; its unity, its identity becomes dislocated. When this

In a valiant attempt to defend autobiography against deconstruction not only as a genre but as a genre dependent on its human and cultural context, Janet Gunn[19] claims that the "autobiographical situation makes it possible to account for autobiography as a significant human and cultural activity as well as to reinstate its membership in the category of life." Gunn opposes "cancelling that membership when selfhood is circumscribed by textuality or when alienation is taken to be the inevitable price of bringing the self to language" (118). She objects to what she terms views that assume autobiography to be "a private act of the self writing" or to be "part of a reified textual system" because both "overlook the cultural dimension of the autobiography" by failing to account either for "the reading self of the autobiographer" or "the reader we necessarily become when we set out to understand the autobiographical text" (31). In defining autobiography as "a poetics of experience," she claims that "autobiography is a human, cultural, and religious act taking place within [a] context of trust or what Michal Polyani calls the 'system of acceptances' which grounds all of our knowledge, even—and most especially—the knowledge we have of ourselves" (28).

While this debate is probably unresolvable because grounded in semantic and philosophical differences affecting the formulation, and indeed cognition, of such fundamental concepts as "writing" and "genre," and hence "autobiography," the primary concern of this volume is not to formulate a resolution but rather to emphasize the diversity and flexibility of the forms characterizing the phenomenal renewal of interest in autobiographical discourse in the twentieth century and, more specifically, to broaden the reader's awareness of Russian twentieth-century literature and writing about the self.

Explanations of this phenomenon have ranged from the notion that "the autobiographical endeavor has endured, and variety, human variety, may be the secret of its endurance"[20] to the assertion that "the number of autobiog-

---

identity is dislocated, then the problem of *autos*, of the autobiographical, has to be totally redistributed. Finally, if one gets around to wondering . . . about the status of the autobiographical, then one has to ask whether one will understand the autobiographical in terms of this internal border and all the rest, or instead rely on the standard concepts prevailing throughout tradition. Once again, one is faced with a division of the *autos*, of the autobiographical, *but this doesn't mean that one has to dissolve the value of the autobiographical récit. Rather, one must restructure it otherwise on the basis of a project that is also biographical and thanatographical.* And what name shall this redistribution be given in the 'Nietzschean corpus' in general, in 'Nietzsche's thought' in general, in 'Nietzsche's signature,' and so forth? It would all come down to setting Nietzsche's autobiography, or Nietzsche's auto-biographical thought, on the back, so to speak, of some thought of eternal return. *That is, the autobiography is signed by something that arises out of the thought of the eternal return in Nietzsche*" (44–45; my italics).

[19] See Janet Varner Gunn, *Autobiography: Toward a Poetics of Experience* (Philadelphia: University of Pennsylvania Press, 1982).

[20] Bruss, *Autobiographical Acts*, 18.

raphies corresponds to a real social need'' and to a demand for authenticity greater than that provided by the verisimilitude of realist fiction.[21]

The works examined in this collection of essays were intentionally chosen to represent the diversity of formal features and textual strategies present in twentieth-century Russian autobiographical narrative. What these texts have in common is precisely their autobiographical discourse, be they statements that can be classified under the rubric of conventional autobiography or statements found in works difficult to classify or not ordinarily classifiable as autobiography, memoirs, or documentary literature. The focus is on the signs of autobiographical discourse. These may include, for example, thematic patterns—or as de Man expressed it, ''thematic insistence on the subject, on the proper name, on memory, on birth, eros and death, and on the doubleness of specularity''—as well as recurrent forms and styles, representative devices, modalities, mannerisms, and other factors that establish each writer's work unquestionably as a narrative form or a category of writing associated with but possibly differing from traditional classifications of autobiography as encompassed by Lejeune's definition or Bruss's rules.

References to the spectrum of definitions available in the current scholarship on autobiography are given in the essays included in this volume as they pertain to particular texts as well as in the appended selected bibliography. For example, ''autobiographical discourse''[22] may be expressed either through the ''autobiographical act''[23] (that is, autobiography or autobiographical narrative viewed as a traditional but constantly changing genre) or through the ''autobiographical statement'' (a more generic term applied to any expression of autobiographical discourse, including nontraditional forms, that is, forms not automatically classified as autobiography, such as the novel or even a collection of scholarly essays).[24]

The autobiographical act may perhaps be considered as a form of mediation between life and narrative or discourse, where the life includes memory, eval-

---

[21] Janos Szavai, ''La place et le role de l'autobiographie dans la littérature,'' *Acta Litteraria Academiae Scientiarum Hungaricae* (Budapest) 18 (Budapest: Akademiai Kiado, 1976): 398–414.

[22] See Tsvetan Todorov's article ''The Notion of Literature,'' *New Literary History* 5, no. 1 (Autumn 1973): 5–16, in which he suggests ''the opposition between literature and nonliterature [be] replaced by a typology of the various types of discourse.'' He states: ''Instead of the simple notion of literature we now have a number of different types of discourse, each equally deserving of attention'' (16).

[23] See Bruss' definition of *Autobiographical Acts*. She tries to define ''autobiography as an autonomous act with its own peculiar responsibilities'' (6) and rules. Nevertheless, her rules eliminate many of what I would term ''autobiographical statements,'' including the introduction of the autobiographical mode or autobiographical discourse in novels and other fictional works and, indeed, parodies of autobiography. See her rules (10–11), cited above.

[24] For a broad definition of autobiography that includes fictional forms such as the novel, see Spengemann, *The Forms of Autobiography*.

uation, and events and where discourse both selects and orders those aspects of the life and thus ultimately defines, reimagines, and expresses the self-image in a new form, in the autobiographical narrative. "Autobiographical consciousness" (Mandel), which gives impetus to the discourse, is present and active both on the conscious and unconscious levels, invoking conventions of language and literature as well as social, psychological, historical, and spiritual conventions, both factual and fictional. In this way, autobiographical discourse may be considered simultaneously as intentional and subjective as well as invented and objective.

This volume, then, is less concerned with classification or taxonomy per se—that is, with the seemingly endless problematics of whether autobiography or autobiographical discourse should be considered as a mode, genre, or subgenre, or with the concomitant issue of defining the canon and thus determining which works are or are not autobiographies[25]—than with introducing the reader to the range of strategies and approaches involving autobiographical discourse and constituting autobiographical statements adopted by Russian writers over the course of the twentieth century.

Nevertheless, while this volume focuses on the transformation of the individual narrator's experience into autobiographical discourse, on the expression of themes of memory and imagination, and on the role of time consciousness and personal history or the history of the self in time in the formulation of autobiographical narrative, theoretical arguments will be raised and discussed when appropriate. Above all, each of the essays attempts to illuminate problems that a given author of autobiographical narrative encounters in trying to organize and give meaning to actual (or what he perceives to be, or treats as actual) human experience. Hence, among the essays are attempts to ascertain how a "poetics of experience" may define the human, cultural, and spiritual act taking place—its human and cultural dimensions—and to determine what the particular structures or conventions of autobiographical discourse may be that enable particular texts to be meaningful. Certain essays endeavor to show how the autobiographical situation makes it possible to account for autobiography as a "significant human and cultural activity," while others show how selected stylistic or rhetorical devices, tropes, and grammatical cat-

[25] For a number of perspectives on this debate, see: A. M. Clark, *Autobiography: Its Genesis and Phases* (Edinburgh, 1935); Paul de Man, "Autobiography as Defacement"; J. Mehlman, *A Structural Study of Autobiography: Proust, Leiris, Sartre, Levi-Strauss* (Ithaca: Cornell University Press, 1984); Paul Jay, *Being in the Text* (Ithaca: Cornell University Press, 1984); Sprinker, "Fictions of the Self" and Louis Renza, "The Veto of the Imagination: A Theory of Autobiography" in Olney *Autobiography: Essays Theoretical and Critical*; Gunn, *Autobiography: Toward a Poetics of Experience*; and other works cited in this article. See also Alistair Fowler, *Kinds of Literature: An Introduction to the Theory of Genres and Modes* (Cambridge, Mass.: Harvard University Press, 1982), which quite curiously avoids discussing the problems of autobiography and autobiographical forms by almost completely omitting autobiography as a topic. See also the appended selected bibliography.

egories may be viewed as signifying practices peculiar to autobiographical discourse, even though they are not necessarily limited to such narratives. Still other readings discuss how given works may employ, modify, parody, or implicitly comment upon techniques and procedures peculiar to the poetics of autobiographical discourse, while others demonstrate how meaning is produced when a work purposely violates or evades such conventions.

Fundamental problems have faced scholars of autobiography and narrative as well as authors of autobiographical statements when classifying texts as "autobiographical." Of major significance is the most basic philosophical (and psychological) problem of self-knowledge, of whether one can know oneself, and if so to what extent? If not, what is that which is "known" as "the self?" To what extent does one create the self? And in creating a self what is its ontology? How is the self apprehended? Can it be an immediate object of knowledge? Is an author's assertion of truthfulness or his rejection of fiction just a mask, or does it direct the reader to certain meanings in the text? What kind of fictions still permit a writer or reader to regard a work as autobiographical? And what, for example, does Todorov's statement that "verisimilitude is the mask which is assumed by the laws of the text and which we are meant to take for a relation to reality"[26] imply for readers approaching autobiographical texts? Most fundamental, perhaps, can one communicate a sense of oneself to another? If so, what can be communicated, and how can it be communicated? Can one convey one's own experiences or perceived experiences to another? If not, for whom does the self exist? Do the conventions of autobiographical discourse require the same suspension of disbelief as do works of fiction? If not, how do they differ? And what is the purpose or function of autobiographical discourse?

Two prominent literary questions always posed in attempting a theory of autobiography are whether to treat autobiography as a literary or nonliterary genre and whether firm distinctions can be drawn between autobiography and fiction.[27] Such questions have been repeatedly raised with regard to both twentieth-century texts and such classics as Rousseau's *Confessions*. Needless to say, they have not been resolved.

Despite such questions and concerns, de Man's comment that "empirically as well as theoretically, autobiography lends itself poorly to generic definition; each specific instance seems to be an exception to the norm" paradoxically places autobiographical narrative at the center of twentieth-century literary attention by highlighting the essential characteristic of twentieth-century literary movements, namely, the persistent demand for new literary forms appropriate to the problems and perceptions of an age of change and discontinuity.

---

[26] Tsvetan Todorov, "An Introduction to Verisimilitude," trans. Richard Howard, in *The Poetics of Prose* (Ithaca: Cornell University Press, 1977), 83.

[27] See Derrida, *The Ear of the Other*, for his discussion of "borders" and the problematics of the line between our knowledge of what is "empirical" and "nonempirical" fact.

The essays in this volume thus also attempt to demonstrate how quests for new forms of literary expression so often inspired or were satisfied by autobiographical discourse, sometimes fictional, sometimes nonfictional in intention. For example, in his critical essays of the 1920s, "End of the Novel" and "Birth of Plot," the poet Osip Mandelstam denies a role for lyric poetry in the new Soviet state because "poetry itself demanded prose." He posits the "end of the novel" because the new historical era lacks "interest in the human fate of the individual," which he perceives as the "pivot" of the traditional nineteenth-century novel. He also condemns "psychological prose" as discredited by "the growing impotence of psychological motivation in confrontation with the forces of reality" and expresses disdain for sociologically oriented prose focused exclusively on daily life. Instead, on the penultimate page of "Egyptian Stamp," a unique modernist piece of autobiographical discourse, he openly declares his preference for first-person narrative: "What a pleasure for the narrator to switch from the third person to the first. It is just as if, after having had to drink from tiny inconvenient thimblesized glasses, one were suddenly to say the hell with them, to get hold of oneself, and drink cold, unboiled water straight out of the tap."[28] Nabokov some years later, in writing his autobiography *Speak Memory*, also raises the issue of the appropriate moment in a writer's life for turning from fiction to autobiography. Pilling quotes Nabokov's expressed need to write autobiographical narrative: "The man in me rebels against the fictionist."[29]

The renewed and refocused interest in autobiographical discourse witnessed in twentieth-century prose, the concomitant failure to place or to define autobiography as a genre, and the emphasis on its perceived flexibility and diversity as a form acknowledged by both writers and scholars, in Russia and the Soviet Union as well as in the West, may perhaps be taken as evidence of some formidable twentieth-century cultural phenomenon. Expressed equally in traditional and nontraditional autobiographical texts, this phenomenon may well represent the ultimate mode of literary perception for this century, in that it provides the perfect vehicle for what Geoffrey Hartman has called "the unmediated vision." According to Hartman, modern poets having "lost the full understanding of revealed religion, accepted the individual quest for truth and forced by this same quest to seek mediation, sought it neither in Christ nor in tradition but in the very things that caused them to seek: personal experience and sense experience. . . . Personal experience becomes the sole authority and source of conviction, and the poet a new intermediary."[30] If Hartman's explanation is applied to developments in twentieth-century narrative, some under-

---

[28] See "Egyptian Stamp," *The Noise of Time: The Prose of Osip Mandelstam*, ed. and trans. Clarence Brown (San Francisco: North Point Press, 1986), 162.

[29] Vladimir Nabokov, *Speak Memory* (New York: Pyramid Books, 1967), ch. 5, opening paragraph.

[30] Geoffrey Hartman, *The Unmediated Vision* (New York: Harcourt and Brace, 1966), 172–73.

standing of the role of autobiographical discourse in twentieth-century literature becomes possible.

First of all, if theorists of autobiography interpret twentieth-century autobiographical narrative as an aesthetic (as well as philosophical, moral, and
psychological) repudiation of the strictures of canonical genres, the choice of
the autobiographical mode represents a demand to move beyond the conventions of nineteenth-century realism—verisimilitude and concern for the objective rendering of psychological heroes are perceived as inadequate means to
render the demands of the new epoch.

Second, the diverse possibilities of autobiographical writings seem to have
become more apparent as the dual origins of autobiographical narrative have
been observed. The blending and juxtaposition of the two seemingly opposite
directions taken by autobiographical writings have given rise to a variety of
forms. On the one hand, is the confessional form, which delves more deeply
into the psyche than the realist novel and emphasizes the subjective portrayal
of consciousness or the subconscious. On the other hand is the memoir form,
which gives primacy to the cultural dimension of a life by attempting to show
how personal history is an integral part of history proper or how the individual
life is determined by external forces. Indeed, personal history is often shown
to be governed as much by external as internal forces. Although these two
approaches were less frequently combined in the past, they have tended to
merge over the course of the twentieth century, both in the West and in the
Soviet Union, as confession blends with or develops into testimony. The Soviet critic N. K. Konstenchik in her article "Genre and Narrative Structure in
Contemporary Literary Autobiography"[31] observes that "contemporary autobiographical 'confession' is as a rule combined with 'prophecy,' while lyricism is merged with the publicistic and philosophical. Recent autobiographical prose . . . is characterized by the variety of genre forms and
unconventional narrative structures" (133).

Third, while the creation of a new set of canons has been viewed by some
as moving in a direction emphasizing "authenticity," because of the inclusion
in literary works of a wealth of factual data, and by others as taking a more
"lyrical" or "poetic" direction, because of the focus on the subjective perspective, it is clear that both of these tendencies move beyond realism. It is
interesting to note that while western scholars have clung to the term "autobiography," frequently stressing the individual, personal, and confessional
aspect of autobiographical discourse, recent Soviet scholarship has tended to
emphasize the "factualism" or "authenticity" of memoir by coining the term
"documentary literature" to encompass both traditional autobiography and

[31] N. K. Konstenchik, "Zhanr i sjuzhet sovremennoj pisatel'skoj khudozhestvennoj avtobiografii" in Zhanr i Kompozitsija Literaturnogo Proizvedenija, ed. A. M. Garkavi et al. (Mezhvuzovskij sbornik. Vyp. 2. Kaliningrad: Kaliningradskij gos. universitet, 1976), 131–42.

other, newer narratives of "fact." More recently, however, Soviet critics have additionally recognized the lyrical nature of much memoir writing. A fine example is E. A. Balburov's 1985 study of "lyric prose," *Poetika liricheskoj prozy: 1960s–1970s*, which focuses on the relationship between lyric poetry and contemporary nonfictional memoir genres in the works of Bergolts, Soloukhin, and others. In addition, Balburov discusses the penetration of fantastic or fictional elements in the "lyric memoir prose" of Konetsky, Granin, and Kataev.[32]

Fourth, if we look more closely at autobiographical discourse since Rousseau, we also see that the autobiographical mode, unlike any other mode of narrative perception, has allowed the writer to assert himself simultaneously as a man in history *and* as a creative writer or poet by confronting the immediacy of his present consciousness with his own past as a source of human value in history. This time consciousness, which has become such a dominant force in twentieth-century literature, is particularly prominent in autobiographical texts. While on the one hand it is clearly related to what Bakhtin called "biographical time," that is, to the recognition of the sequence of acts or stages in the life course providing support for the perception of the passage of time and its continuity in one's own life and, consequently, its objectification in narrative form, there is also present in autobiographical texts what I prefer to call specifically "autobiographical time." If the "autobiographical act" is initiated by the writer taking up his pen to confront his own experience of history, his consciousness of the moment of writing is complicated by the fact that he is simultaneously attempting to recollect his past while reimagining and restructuring it according to the ideological and aesthetic principles determined by his present experience.

Indeed, it is at this juncture that the writer's choice of form may coincide with a moral or even prophetic act, with an ideological decision to take responsibility for his literary act. Or, to put this another way, for many writers the possibility arises that the autobiographical act may be or become an act of moral testimony. To the extent that the writer's encounter with his culture or with his epoch is confrontational, it may, and often does, involve a significant moral dimension. Thus, while moral responsibility is not necessary or essential to the self-reflexive autobiographical act, the moral dimension may loom large in this form. Gunn defines this moral potential in claiming, "The autobiographical situation makes it possible to account for autobiography as a significant human and cultural activity as well as to reinstate its membership in the category of life." In this way, writers may seize upon the autobiographical act because of its potential for moral commitment.

For most modern autobiographers, experience of the immediacy of his or her temporality serves as both the impulse to create and as the subject of cre-

---

[32] E. A. Balburov, *Poetika liricheskoj prozy: 1960s–1970s* (Novosibirsk: Nauka, 1985).

ation.[33] The autobiographer's subject, then, is not merely the self or the conceptualization of the self but the relationship of that self to time. And in the twentieth century that relationship often takes the form of a dialogue with contemporaneity. Autobiographical time literally incorporates into narrative what the modern writer has perceived as necessity: "The dual truth of invention and memory is as necessary as bread."[34] If this is so, the aesthetic tension of autobiographical discourse is closely bound up with time consciousness, not solely with biographical or biological time but with auctorial and aesthetic time as well—with the moral and psychological potential as well as the aesthetic dimension of autobiographical time.

Nevertheless, in interpreting autobiographical texts, it is equally imperative to stress the analogy between discourse in autobiography and discourse in the novel with respect to what Bakhtin termed "the time-space chronotope." We are reminded that in both instances the author-creator "remains outside the world he has represented in his work." No matter how great the author's consciousness of history, no matter how precisely he represents his "unmediated vision," his experience of a world without an intermediary, through direct authorial discourse, he still remains outside of the world represented in the text:

> Even had he created an autobiography or a confession of the most astonishing truthfulness, all the same he, as its creator, remains outside the world he has represented in his work. If I relate (or write about) an event that has just happened to me, then I as the *teller* (or writer) of this event am already outside the time and space in which the event occurred. It is just as impossible to forge an identity between myself, my own "I," and that "I" that is the subject of my stories as it is to lift myself up by my own hair. The represented world, however realistic and truthful, can never be chronotopically identical with the real world it represents, where the author and creator of the literary work is to be found.[35]

Thus, what is emphasized in Hartman's concept of the "new intermediary," in this discussion of the "chronotope," and in the essays comprising this volume are the unique aesthetic properties of the autobiographical act and the autobiographical statement. The texts considered in this anthology are viewed primarily as works of literature, as created objects, not merely as recollections

---

[33] For a more detailed discussion of this topic, see J. G. Harris, "Between Source and Pattern: The Mediating Function of the Autobiographical Mode in Texts of Joyce, Mandelstam, Schulz" in *American Contributions to the IXth International Congress of Slavists, Kiev, 1983* (Columbus; Slavica, 1985), 201–21. For a suggestive essay on some aspects of this significant topic, see also Burton Pike, "Time in Autobiography." *Comparative Literature* 28 (1976): 326–46. For an interesting essay on the treatment of stages in the life cycle, see Patricia Spacks, "Stages of Life: Notes on Autobiography and the Life Cycle," *Hudson Review* 30 (1977): 29–46.

[34] Osip Mandelstam, "Literary Moscow" in *Mandelstam: The Complete Critical Prose and Letters*, ed. and trans. J. G. Harris (Ann Arbor: Ardis Publishers, 1979).

[35] Bakhtin, *The Dialogic Imagination*, 256. This section dates from 1973.

of empirical reality, factual events, or even experienced truths. The autobiographical narrative itself is perceived as transforming, and thereby creating, both the concept of the self and the self as an autonomous entity. Despite the caveats of Lejeune and Bruss and the doubts of de Man and Derrida, the subject of literary autobiography, or of autobiographical discourse regarded as literary, must be viewed not simply as the author but as an invented, recreated, or "specular" equivalent facing his encounter with time. While that encounter may, and very often does, involve a significant moral dimension, the dilemma of moral responsibility may or may not be much different for the author of such a text than it is for the author of a traditional work of fiction,[36] even though traditional autobiographical forms have normally been accepted by readers as reliable and true.

Hence, studies of autobiography and autobiographical theory over the past twenty-five years have come to wrestle with the "literary" signs of autobiographical discourse, and although little has been resolved, it continues to fascinate both writers and readers. A brief survey of the current Western and Soviet literature on autobiography is in order here to establish its significance and implications for the texts examined in this volume.

While developments in contemporary Western autobiographical theory (primarily French and American) were initiated by the seminal efforts of Gusdorf and Pascal to define traditional autobiography as a literary genre, the studies that followed have been extraordinarily varied in approach, often strongly influenced by the writings and numerous translations of French and Russian literary theorists published in recent years, namely, Tzvetan Todorov,[37] Gérard Genette,[38] and M. M. Bakhtin,[39] to cite but a few of the most prominent figures. While these theorists have not provided definitions of autobiography, they suggest new categories and distinctions for consideration. Perhaps most important for the study and reading of autobiographical narrative is the proposal to examine it in terms of "discourse" rather than "genre" and thus to treat autobiographical narrative not merely as a nonfictional form, but as literary discourse. For example, Todorov's article "The Notion of Literature," translated and published in the influential American literary journal *New Lit-*

[36] For example, Rousseau as both the author and subject of the *Confessions* is no more nor less reliable than Tolstoy as the author of *War and Peace*. And Solzhenitsyn as the author and subject of *Gulag Archipelago* is no more nor less reliable than Solzhenitsyn as the author of *Cancer Ward* or *One Day in the Life of Ivan Denisovich*.

[37] Tzvetan Todorov, "The Notion of Literature," *New Literary History* 5, no. 1. (Autumn 1973): 5–16; idem, *The Poetics of Prose*, originally *La poetique de la prose* (Paris: Editions du Seuil, 1971).

[38] Gerard Genette, *Narrative Discourse: An Essay in Method*, trans. Jane E. Lewin (Ithaca: Cornell University Press, 1977), originally in "Discours de recit," a portion of *Figures III* (Paris: Editions de Seuil, 1972).

[39] See *The Dialogic Imagination*. Also on Bakhtin, see Todorov, "How to Read?" (1969) in *The Poetics of Prose*.

erary History,[40] proposes that "the opposition between literature and nonliterature [be] replaced by a typology of the various types of discourse." Todorov argues that "instead of the simple notion of literature we now have a number of different types of discourse, each equally deserving of attention." This thesis helped make possible Elizabeth Bruss's definition three years later of "autobiography as an autonomous act with its own peculiar responsibilities" (*Autobiographical Acts*, 6) and her assertion that "the diversity of [autobiographical] works alone should be enough to demonstrate that there is no intrinsically autobiographical form" (10). She makes the further point that "the rules for the [autobiographical] act provide [no more than] a field within which the task of self-imaging and self-evaluation is understood to take place, making whatever does take place recognizable as a form of self-evaluation" (13). Nevertheless, while Bruss's rules still eliminate from consideration as autobiographical texts works that Spengemann might treat under his far more inclusive definition of the autobiographical act (any work treating the "theme of self-realization"), her view of autobiography as a "changing genre" moves far beyond Lejeune's more cautious model. Thus, while certain scholars have formulated a more conservative definition of autobiography as a genre (Lejeune, May), others looked to sociology, anthropology, psychology, and philosophy for explanations, focusing on "autobiography as a second reading of experience" (Gusdorf, Starobinski).[41] Still others, in an effort to reevaluate, broaden, and indeed restructure the definition of autobiography as a changing genre or to reinterpret it conceptually as something other than a genre, have made use of structuralist and semiotic constructs or psychoanalytic and deconstructivist approaches available in contemporary French scholarship (de Man, Derrida, Renza, Sprinker et al.).[42]

On the other hand, Soviet studies over the past twenty-five years have focused on what have been termed "documentary prose genres," stimulated by the attempt to understand the developments in Soviet prose of the late 1950s to 1980s. The first Soviet postwar study of autobiographical forms, an article by S. Mashinskij, "The Memoir-Autobiographical Genre," published in the

---

[40] *New Literary History* contains some of the earliest efforts to redefine autobiography, including Francis R. Hart, "Notes for an Anatomy of Modern Autobiography," *New Literary History* 1, no. 3 (Spring 1970): 485–511; Warner Berthoff, "Witness and Testament: Two Contemporary Classics," *New Literary History* 2, no. 2 (Winter 1971): 311–37; and William L. Howarth, "Some Principles of Autobiography," *New Literary History* 5, no. 2 (Winter 1974): 363–81.

[41] See for example the essays by Georges Gusdorf, "Conditions and Limits of Autobiography" and Jean Starobinski, "The Style of Autobiography" in J. Olney, *Autobiography: Essays Theoretical and Critical*. See also Gusdorf's arguments in his later discussion, "De l'autobiographie initiatique à l'autobiographie littéraire."

[42] See for example, the essays in the two volumes of *Genre* devoted to autobiography; Mehlman, *A Structural Study of Autobiography*; Renza, "The Veto of the Imagination: A Theory of Autobiography," and Sprinker, "Fictions of the Self: The End of Autobiography." See also de Man, "Autobiography as Defacement" and Derrida, *The Ear of the Other*.

influential literary journal *Problems of Literature*,[43] appeared in 1960, coincidentally the same year that Pascal's *Design and Truth in Autobiography* was published in the United States. Mashinskij, in calling for a "concrete study of this genre at its various stages of development to define its significance for Soviet literature" (129), essentially initiated the serious study of autobiography and documentary prose in Soviet literary scholarship. Although primarily concerned with describing what he terms the genre of "literary autobiography" ("khudozhestvennaja avtobiografija") in nineteenth-century Russian literature, Mashinskij recognizes that this opens up "unexplored literary possibilities" for writers seeking new forms. He recognizes and classifies contemporary Soviet autobiographical narratives such as Gladkov's trilogy and Paustovsky's tetrology as outgrowths of the nineteenth-century tradition.

Throughout the 1960s, and especially in the latter half of the decade, numerous articles as well as discussions of memoir literature and "documentary prose" appeared in leading literary journals and in the newspaper *Literaturnaja gazeta* (*Literary Gazette*).[44] The topic was thus given high priority in official Soviet literary studies, paralleling the flood of autobiographical and documentary literary writings. By 1971 articles bearing such titles as "Memoir Prose" and "Nonimaginative Prose (Contemporary Documentary Literature)"[45] appeared in books devoted to genre study. The authors of these essays have consciously portrayed the extraordinary rush of autobiographical narratives in the writings of the 1960s as a national and cultural phenomenon. For example, Dikshina discusses the significance of "documentary prose" in terms of the "demand of the age" and views it as "broadening the choice of artistic methods, dictating different tasks to the writer (164)." She defines "documentary prose" as "the broad category of memoir literature" ("obshirnaja memuarnaja literatura") and recognizes additionally the emergence of a new fictional form, the so-called "documentary tale" ("dokumental'naja povest"), as an original development in memoir literature. Kuznetsov states that "Autobiographical prose today boldly informs us of the most complex problems of the age. Writers are seeking a literary structure to allow them to create their new picture of the world." Consequently, autobiographical prose is perceived as a vital, indeed revolutionary new form associated with literary, moral, and spiritual renewal. "Personal experience" is viewed as the "key"

[43] S. Mashinskij, "O Memuarno-avtobiograficheskom zhanre," *Voprosy literatury* 6 (1960): 129–45.

[44] Questionnaire sponsored by *Voprosy literatury* 9 (1966); "Literatura. Dokument. Fakt," a discussion sponsored by *Inostrannaja literatura* 8 (1966); V. Subbotin and L. Lazarev, "Dialog," *Literaturnaja gazeta*, 8 May 1967); "K sporam o khudozhestvennom dokumente," *Novyj Mir* 8 (1968).

[45] See for example the articles by M. Kuznetsov, "Memuarnaja proza" and N. Dikshina, "Nevydumannaja proza (O sovremennoj dokumental'noj literature)" in *Zhanrovo-stilevye iskanija sovremennoj sovetskoj prozy*, ed. L. M. Poljak and V. E. Kovskij (Moscow: Nauka, 1971).

to the secrets of the epoch (127). By 1977 Adolf Urban, in an article entitled "Literary Autobiography and the Document,"[46] names several different forms of contemporary autobiographical prose, including at the lowest level the "dossier autobiography," then the "autobiographical memoir," and at the highest level the "aesthetically conceived autobiography," which he traces back to the nineteenth century, to the tradition of Herzen and Korolenko. He also cites what he terms the "autobiographical tale," in which the author uses his own life as the basis of an imaginative literary work, as well as "a variety of the autobiographical tale in which the names of the author and hero are different," which also may be traced back to the nineteenth century, in this case to Aksakov's trilogy. Finally, in 1985 E. A. Balburov in a study of "lyric prose"[47] focuses on the relationship between lyric poetry and the nonfictional documentary memoir genres. In this work, he also discusses the penetration of fantastic or fictional elements in "lyric memoir prose."

The Soviet literary term "documentary prose," then, is more inclusive than "autobiography" or "memoirs," since it encompasses both under one rubric. N. D. Konstenchik[48] clarifies the use of the term "documentary literature" in a 1976 article that emphasizes its scope as significantly larger than autobiography or memoir literature—hence its widespread use in contemporary Soviet literary terminology. She argues that it makes no sense to distinguish between "documentary" and "biographical-memoir literature" since "memoirists use documents as well," and points out that both are based on "the factual," have a similar aesthetic "orientation toward authenticity," and use documents, personal recollections, and testimony as "structural material."

Jakov I. Javchunovsky's major theoretical work, *Documentary Genres*,[49] published in 1974, sets out to review not only the problematics of contemporary documentary literature, its history and typology, but to discuss in this context "the rise of the role of fact" in the structure of literary works and in the contemporary "literary process." Furthermore, Javchunovsky attempts to define the problems associated with the structure of documentary prose—in particular, the image of the narrator and methods of characterization—providing a rationale for choosing the term "documentary literature" over terms such as "nonimaginary literature," "literature of fact," "literary-documentary literature," or "plotless prose," found in the scholarly literature[50] and affirming the literary as opposed to nonliterary nature of documentary prose.

[46] Adol'f Urban, "Khudozhestvennaja avtobiografija i dokument," *Zvezda* 2 (1977): 192–208.

[47] E. A. Balburov, *Poetika liricheskoj prozy: 1960–1970gg.*

[48] N. D. Konstenchik, "Zhanr i sjuzhet sovremennoj pistel'skoj khudozhestvennoj avtobiografii."

[49] Jakov Isaevich Javchunovskij, *Dokumental'nye zhanry* (Saratov: Saratovskij gos. universitet, 1974).

[50] "Nevymyshlennaja literatura," "literatura fakta," "khudozhestvenno-dokumental'naja literatura," "bessjuzhetnaja proza."

With respect to literary history, he indicates that although many memoirs were not literary in intent, they have influenced the development of literary genres and subgenres because "their aesthetic influence on the literary process was enormous" (17).

He also attempts to describe various subgenres in documentary prose and to distinguish contemporary documentary literature from the "literature of fact" popular in the 1920s. Among documentary prose subgenres, he mentions "the noticeable growth of autobiographical narratives," namely the work of Paustovsky, Ehrenburg, Bergoltz, Soloukhin, Kaverin, and Bek (8–9). He differentiates such "autobiographical narratives," however, from other subgenres that he notes are more concerned with events and facts of the past than with the personal views or experiences of the narrator. The latter emphasize eyewitness testimony, documentation, and objectivity rather than subjectivity. Furthermore, Javchunovsky asserts, a writer of documentary prose does not conceal his sources but openly discusses them as sources of valorization.

Javchunovsky draws further distinctions between documentary literature and journalistic accounts and historical narrative, pointing out that documentary literature is concerned not only with the present or the past but with the relationship of past and present, with the perception or interpretation of the past; therefore, its purpose is broader than journalism and history, for it attempts to provide a "new measure of historical truth in the form of *belles lettres*." Above all, documentary literature, according to Javchunovsky, "has an aesthetic function." In this regard, he recognizes the mobility of the boundaries between literary and nonliterary genres and the complexity of their interrelationship. He also recognizes another trend in contemporary prose: documentary literature has served as a model for numerous works that are "imitations of documentary literature," and in these works "fact" acts as a stimulus to "fantasy," since they often contain both imaginary and factual heroes on an equal footing. A good example is Y. Semenov's "Seventeen Moments of Spring" ("Semnadtsat' mgnovenij vesny").

In summarizing his findings, Javchunovsky recognizes that "documentation is a movement in literature and art, an arena of artistic creation, and that within its confines authors strive to express the truth of the age and of humankind with the support of factual testimony." He points out that "documents and facts not only make up the primary materials or hidden subtext [of documentary genres] but also organize their integral structure" (22). Thus Javchunovsky's discussion of documentary genres like J. Gunn's discussion of autobiography, emphasizes that this type of writing is both a "significant human and cultural activity" as well as an art form.

Consequently, Javchunovsky cautions the reader on the "necessity of recognizing the relationship between the subjective and objective principles in artistic creation," asserting that "different measures of objectivity and subjectivity are accepted in different epochs. Most important, their relationship must be recognized as fundamental to documentary art, and thus this relationship itself must be present in documentary art'' (27). Javchunovsky's focus on the relationship of the narrator to his materials *as a fundamental sign of documentary literature* corresponds to the emphasis on the narrator's dual role in the autobiographical act as opposed to his single role in fiction as pointed out by Bruss. This idea is extremely important to a discussion of documentary literature or autobiographical narrative, because it indicates how empirical facts—although authentic—must inevitably be reimagined and transformed through the narrator's subjective as well as objective presentation. Significantly, this allows us to draw a distinction between documentary literature and fiction based on the role and function of the narrator.

In this context we can read Lydia Ginzburg's astute observation that the special ''dynamic of documentary literature'' is grounded in the peculiar ''dual nature'' of the form, a theory which she posits in an effort to contrast the dynamic of nonfictional, documentary narratives with that of the fictional texts of realism in her discussion of ''documentary genres'' in *The Literary Hero* (1979).[51] This observation essentially moves one step beyond Bruss and Javchunovsky. Ginzburg notes that in a work of fiction, the ''imaginative idea that derives from experience creates a 'second reality,' while documentary literature provides the reader with a dual cognitive response and a dual emotional experience because a feeling for the authenticity of the events of actual life is provided that no art form can reproduce'' (7). In further characterizing documentary literature she recognizes the significance of the interplay or tension between the planes of the life experience and the aesthetic interpretation: ''In documentary literature, it is as if the artistic expression contains the reader's independent knowledge of the depicted subject. The peculiar dynamic of documentary literature is found in the state of equivalence or commensurability produced by the incomplete merger of the two planes—the plane of the life experience and the plane of the aesthetic interpretation'' (7).

Ginzburg thus provides a highly original perception identifying the power of the documentary text to create a dynamic realistic effect, even though she seems to imply that documentary literature (including autobiography) is lower in the hierarchy of literary forms than fiction, as it is ''incomplete'' in contrast to fiction, which creates ''complete'' forms or a ''second reality.'' In this sense, as opposed to Javchunovsky, Ginzburg does not seem to regard the duality of documentary literature as a fundamental aesthetic feature, or at least not as an aesthetic principle.

Consequently, as opposed to most Western theorists of autobiography who for the past twenty-five years have determined to treat autobiography as a literary rather than a historical act, Ginzburg seems to argue here that as a form of documentary literature autobiographical narrative is an ''intermediate

---

[51] Lydia Ginzburg, *O literaturnom geroe* (Leningrad: Sovetskij Pisatel', 1979).

stage" in the formation of potential literary texts: "Documentary literature provides an intermediate stage between the aesthetic properties of social, historical, and psychological concepts and the specific aesthetic characteristics of literary texts" (7).

While it would seem that Ginzburg like Bruss recognizes and identifies the essential duality of autobiographical narrative, unlike Bruss she does not consider the potential aesthetic properties of that duality. This may be due to the fact that Ginzburg's critique is concerned primarily with texts of realistic fiction expressed as part of her studies of the literary hero (*The Literary Hero*) and psychological prose (*Psychological Prose*)[52] and not as part of an analysis of either documentary literature or autobiography; nor is it concerned with twentieth-century texts. In this context, Ginzburg neither assesses the autobiographical mode nor examines the structural functions or textual possibilities of autobiographical discourse to ascertain its particular aesthetic fascination for the twentieth-century writer or reader. Hence, what Bruss observes as the dual role of the autobiographer or, I would add, as a distinguishing feature of autobiographical discourse, Ginzburg perceives merely as a distinctive feature of all documentary literature.

This raises the more general problem of genre study and of the distinctions that can be drawn between literary and nonliterary texts, and therefore the problem of classifying writings that clearly employ elements of autobiographical discourse. Among the works discussed in this anthology are those that no one would dispute as being autobiographical, but there are several that challenge all conventional generic definitions, such as Trifonov's *House on the Embankment* (discussed by Fiona Björling), Lydia Ginzburg's own writings, *Old and New* (treated here as autobiography by Sarah Pratt), and Roman Jakobson's *Dialogues* (discussed by Krystyna Pomorska as a scholar's autobiography). Yet these texts are all autobiographical statements, for autobiographical discourse ultimately determines their unique character.

Yury Tynianov in his essay "On Literary Evolution"[53] proposes that the hierarchy of genres in any given period might differ from the hierarchy in a previous or subsequent period. He also suggests that different genres might embrace or stress particular properties serving different aesthetic purposes and functions in different epochs. The author's choice of genre, then, depends as much on his sense of his own aesthetic requirements at the time of writing as on the reader's expectations, that is, on the reader's acceptance or rejection of available genres, generic features, or modes of perception.

While Ginzburg, in identifying its "peculiar dynamic," clearly recognizes the essential tension of the duality of documentary literature, she does not

---

[52] Lydia Ginzberg, *O psikhologicheskoj proze* (Leningrad: Sovetskij Pisatel', 1971).

[53] Yuri Tynianov, "On Literary Evolution" in *Readings in Russian Poetics*, Matejka, ed. (MIT Press, 1971), 66–78.

evaluate the aesthetic properties of that tension. Rather she juxtaposes it to the aesthetic coherence of the fictional text of realistic literature, which is said to reveal no connections with "the plane of the life experience" because it is an autonomous "second reality." Todorov (1973), on the other hand, by proposing that "the opposition between literary and nonliterary [be] replaced by a typology of the various types of discourse, each equally deserving of attention,"[54] obviates the problem of categorizing texts as fictional and nonfictional raised by Ginzburg. De Man's stance (1979) that "the distinction between autobiography and fiction is not an either/or polarity" takes Todorov's position to its outer limits.[55]

Regardless of how extreme these views may appear to the traditional scholar of autobiography, they do assure a literary as opposed to historical interpretation of autobiographical narrative by focusing on narration or discourse as the major organizing principle of the text. If we accept the idea that discourse organizes the experience or that the plane of the aesthetic experience determines the plane of the life experience in autobiographical narrative, we must reject the more conventional approach to autobiography that regards the subject matter or "truth" of the life story as its organizing principle but has difficulty explaining the imaginative or "fictional" elements in the story telling. This is not, of course, to deny the power of the "feeling for the authenticity of the events of actual life"—either brute emotional truth or the moral dimension—so frequent in twentieth-century autobiographical discourse.

Thus we would like to propose that in works of literary autobiography, viewed here as a subgenre of autobiography, the expression or "aesthetic interpretation" is foregrounded. However, the plane of aesthetic interpretation must be seen as constantly involved in interplay or dialogue with the plane of the life experience or, as Javchunovsky phrased it, "the relationship between the subjective and objective principles of artistic creation . . . must be recognized as fundamental to documentary art. This relationship itself must be present in documentary art." Again we encounter signs of the inherent duality of autobiographical forms and must recognize the writer-narrator as a kind of mediator in the continuing dialogue between objective and subjective principles of art, between aesthetic interpretation and authenticity—actual life experience—between expression and experience, invention and memory. Hence, our hypothesis that the aesthetic coherence of a given autobiographical statement resides in the articulation of the tension created by this dialogue—often expressed in the laying bare of the mediating act—suggested implicitly by Javchunovsky and expanded by Ginzburg. The most literary autobiographies, then, may be viewed as those in which the balance seems to shift toward

[54] Tzvetan Todorov, "The Notion of Literature."

[55] De Man, "Autobiography as Defacement." See also "The Rhetoric of Temporality" in Charles S. Singleton, ed., *Interpretation Theory and Practice* (Baltimore: Johns Hopkins University Press, 1969), 173–209.

aesthetic interpretation; the more commonplace autobiographies—usually not written by creative writers—as those in which the balance tends toward the life experience, memory, or truth as opposed to the discourse. Hence the significance of the reader's interpretation of the autobiographical statement.

In summing up this brief survey of current autobiographical theory and its implications for our understanding of a major twentieth-century literary and cultural phenomenon, I would like to suggest that Ginzburg in her formulation has actually located the organizing principle of autobiographical narrative, that is, its inherent duality as a literary form, while Paul de Man's assertion that ''the distinction between autobiography and fiction is not an either/or polarity'' is equally suggestive of the fundamental aesthetic dynamic of autobiographical discourse. Autobiographical discourse may thus be viewed as the art of mediation between the two planes of experience and interpretation, between ''the autobiographical consciousness'' and the ''autobiographical imagination.'' And with regard to the reader, the autobiographical statement produces a particular ''dual cognitive response and dual emotional experience'' (Ginzburg) that no other literary act can produce. Hence the uniqueness of autobiographical discourse and the source of its aesthetic power. Furthermore, because this inherent duality is ''not an either/or polarity,'' each text emerges as a variable. Each author generates his own statement based on his individual understanding of the dual nature of autobiographical discourse as opposed to, say, realist fiction.

In sum, the dual nature of autobiography is exhibited first of all, as Bruss points out, at the level of the autobiographer's role: choosing himself or his conception of his self as subject, as well as recognizing himself as the source of the structure of his text. Second, as Javchunovsky indicates, the ''relationship between the subjective and objective principles of artistic creation'' is fundamental and ''must be present in documentary art.'' Third, according to Ginzburg, duality is an essential element in the reader's perception of the mode or genre. This is reflected in the reader's ''dual cognitive response and dual emotional experience'' of the text and the enterprise. Fourth, de Man's perception of the absence of an either/or polarity admits of a freedom unique to literary narrative and, perhaps extraordinarily receptive to the twentieth-century consciousness concerned with finding a place, meaning, or identity for the self in a discontinuous, often alien, incomprehensible, and chaotic world. Fifth, the condition of duality is present on the plane of time consciousness (historical, metaphysical, and philosophical), both in the writer's confrontation of the immediacy of his own temporality at the moment of the writing with his retrospective past and in his recognition of the tension generated between the consciousness of his experience of temporality and his quest for artistic timelessness. Time consciousness in the autobiographical mode, then, usually invokes both the experience of change, that is, an awareness of temporality, and a concept of time as an enduring and powerful force affecting human destiny (Bergson's concept of *la durée*). A minimum of two time frames are involved, that of the author-narrator's present, the time of writing, and that of the retrospective memory (time past) recreated both subjectively through the eyes of the narrator-protagonist and objectively by the author-narrator.

And last but not least, the state of duality is perceptible on the thematic plane, in the tension between memory and imagination generated in the creative articulation of the text. Memory, the time of memory as well as the experience and process of memory—"autobiographical consciousnesss"— serves as the raw material for the autobiographical narrative imagination. However, that imagination cannot begin to function without recourse to the experience of memory and time consciousness, for the autobiographical imagination works to reformulate and restructure experience as a conscious act of interpretation. Furthermore, that act of interpretation may be consciously prophetic or may deny or reject moral purpose in the name of the aesthetic.

The dynamic of autobiographical narrative, then, is to be found in the articulation of its dual nature whose tension is resolved in the process of what Gusdorf calls "the second reading"; nevertheless, the articulation of that autobiographical tension must be sought ultimately in the language and patterns of each unique text.

.   .   .

It is now possible to review some of the more specific theoretical propositions, constructs, and signs of autobiographical discourse as represented by the Russian and Soviet authors examined in this anthology.

Jean Starobinski (1971) and Georges May (1979)[56] at the beginning and the end of the 1970s defined autobiography as a form of biography, referring to the genre as a "biography of a person written by himself." The significance of such a definition for several of the texts considered here is twofold. First of all, the term "biography" with its emphasis on *bios* as opposed to *autos*, implies a more distant, objective, and indeed historical approach toward the writer's subject matter of the self.[57] The distance the author attempts to convey in presenting his self suggests that the subjective examination of inner consciousness is not the only means to autobiographical self-reflexion. A writer might choose to establish an objective hero, an alter ego, in lieu of focusing on the immediacy of the psyche, the subjective development of the self. For example, Krista Hanson demonstrates how Zoshchenko takes upon himself the task of reviewing his early years from the objective, scientific vantage

[56] Starobinski, "The Style of Autobiography"; May, *L'autobiographie*.

[57] See James Olney, "Some Versions of Memory/Some Versions of Bios: The Ontology of Autobiography " in *Autobiography: Essays Theoretical and Critical*, 236–67.

point of the principles of Freudian analysis as he understands it. This approach is diametrically opposed to Olesha's more subjective quest to identify and depict his inner self. Although Olesha also seemingly rejects the self he sees by referring to another writer as a source of valorization—Elizabeth Beaujour shows how he is moved to compare himself unfavorably with Proust—Zoshchenko in an apparently serious endeavor opts to apply Freud's reading of personality with the ultimate objective of transforming his own personality.

Second, the concept of poetic distance differentiates the purpose of many twentieth-century autobiographical statements from their eighteenth- or nineteenth-century counterparts in that external environmental, cultural, and historical factors are recognized as having as significant an impact on the psyche as more internal or personal factors. Many writers of literary autobiography have sought and found sources of consciousness outside the psyche as well as outside their immediate family or social environs; those sources have most frequently been located in history or in books. Consequently, Rozanov, for example, writes what Anna Lisa Crone has termed "an autobiography of literature," while Mandelstam defines his adult self-image as that of a "*raznochinets*-writer" seeking his roots in Russia's cultural history. Trifonov's and Sinyavsky's personal tasks are perceived as intimately linked to their consciousness of contemporary history (Björling, Nussbaum), while Limonov's series of self-reflexive "novels" is intricately bound up with his perception of his immediate social or indeed sociological environment (Carden).

Pascal, in his seminal book on autobiographical theory, *Design and Truth in Autobiography*, notes that "autobiography is . . . an interplay, a collusion between past and present; its significance is indeed more the revelation of the present situation than the recovery of the past."[58] Pascal confirms here the significance of the writer's experience of time consciousness at the very moment in which he initiates the autobiographical act. He perceives it as both distinct from and juxtaposed to the experience of acquiring self-consciousness. The implication is that the experience of being conscious and the experience of becoming aware of gaining consciousness, equally present in autobiography, are elicited by different means. This negates Kazin's remark in "Autobiography as Narrative"[59] that the autobiographical act initiates the encounter between the conscious and the subconscious "awareness of oneself being conscious." Rather, the narrative structure generated by the autobiographical mode of perception seems to make possible the *simultaneous representation and juxtaposition* of subjective and objective perspectives pertaining to the experience of consciousness (the moments of being *and* the process of becoming). The "collusion between past and present" is mediated through

[58] Pascal, *Design and Truth in Autobiography*, 11.

[59] Alfred Kazin, "Autobiography as Narrative," *Michigan Quarterly Review* 3 (1964): 210–16.

the controlling consciousness and imagination of the writer who unites subjective and objective narration—the recollective experience of memory and its imaginative recreation (the "second reading")—through the conscious revelation of his own immediate and hence concrete sense of temporality. The union of the subjective and objective consciousness of autobiographical discourse thus occurs in the author's immediate present through the mediation of the autobiographical narrator conscious of his dual role. Or, as Gusdorf presented it several years earlier, "autobiography is a second reading of experience, and it is truer than the first experience because it adds to experience itself consciousness of it."[60]

Significantly, in most of the writings examined in this anthology memorable events and moments in the writer's life and in Russia's cultural history are filtered through the hero's developing imagination and aesthetic consciousness. The attempt to present the process and progress of the hero's developing consciousness as it flows through time or history, may in several instances be traced back to a familiarity with the Bergsonian theory of time as duration extraordinarily popular in Russia during the first quarter of the twentieth century. Bergson's concern is less with the functioning of the individual psyche than with the enduring self "in its flowing through time" or history. In *An Introduction to Metaphysics* (Paris, 1903) he states: "There is one reality, at least, which we all seize from within, by intuition and not by simple analysis. It is our personality in its flowing through time—our self which endures."[61]

Remizov, for example, judges his life in terms of his historical experiences, with particular reference to the Russian revolution (Raevsky-Hughes). Ginzburg's autobiographical statement, on the other hand, emerges through a work dominated by literary history and criticism. Her life is defined by if not subordinate to its place in her reformulation of literary history. She evokes the life of her protagonist through her critical essays, her memoirs, and her recreation of her role as literary scholar and intellectual (Pratt). Similarly, Pomorska perceives Jakobson's "scholarly autobiography" as defined in terms of his "words," his perceptions of himself as a linguist in a given time frame, as part of a movement. And Mandelstam and Sinyavsky, on one level of their texts at least, equate their lives with Russia's cultural history. Mandelstam, in particular, attempts to articulate in his autobiography the Bergsonian concept of the intuitive grasp of time—specifically, that fluid quality of reality, history, or time that represents the awareness of experience as continuous process.

Indeed, like many twentieth-century writers, Mandelstam indicates the importance of redefining individual biography within the context of time or history. The object of the autobiographical act is viewed as the acquisition of a

[60] Gusdorf, "Conditions and Limits of Autobiography," 38.

[61] Henri Bergson, *An Introduction to Metaphysics*, trans. T. E. Hulme (New York: 1949; original: Paris, 1903), 8.

"sense of time" that links the author's individual destiny with Russia's cultural history. This is also a significant factor in the writings of Remizov, Mandelstam, Trifonov, and Sinyavsky, among others. In his essay "End of the Novel" Mandelstam offers an explanation of this problem. Since "biography—the pivot of the novel," he claims, belonged to the nineteenth century, the novel was no longer valid as a twentieth-century genre; twentieth-century man had to seek a new form in order to acquire a twentieth-century "sense of time":

> The sense of time that man possesses in order to act, to conquer, to perish, to love—this sense of time gave the European novel its basic tonality, for, I repeat: the *compositional measure of the novel is human biography.* . . . Today Europeans are plucked out of their own biographies, like balls out of the pockets of billiard tables. . . . *A man devoid of biography cannot be the thematic pivot* of the novel, and the novel is meaningless if it lacks interest in an individual human fate, in a plot and its auxiliary motifs. (*CPL*, 200; *SS*, 2:269)[62]

As men "devoid of biography" in an age of discontinuity, twentieth-century writers sought to create a new sense of self that would nevertheless have an enduring place in history. As writers, they had to find an appropriate form and create an adequate language to articulate that history. The rejection of the novel for autobiography or the novel's transformation through an infusion of autobiographical discourse, then, reflects the new demands, the need to apprehend a form into which their own sense of time both as human beings *and* as writers could be projected, located, and examined.

In *Le pacte autobiographique* Lejeune raises the fundamental question of which aspects of "the individual life" comprise the "story of a personality." Each author represented in this anthology provides a programmatic statement or lays bare his role as mediator, either to define the uniqueness of his approach to the text or to isolate certain moments in his life as symbols of his individual destiny, as impulses or stimuli provoking a change in his perception of the self and/or the universe. Each writer thus provides an entry into his life that informs it with a sense of unity or focuses on particular moments in that life, the sum and sequence of which particularize his autobiographical vision.

For example, Remizov's focus on the "unforgettable moments which shaped his life" allows his "creative memory" to constantly take him "beyond the limits of personal biography" (Raevsky-Hughes), while Bely best defines his self in terms of his fiction (Castellano). Mandelstam's programmatic statement rejects outright a self-image suggesting anything personal or

---

[62] Citations to Mandelstam's prose other than *Noise of Time* refer first to the English translation in J. G. Harris, *Mandelstam: The Complete Critical Prose and Letters (CPL)* (Ardis, 1979) and second to the Russian text in Struve-Filipoff, *Sobranie Sochinenij (SS)*, vols. 1–4 (New York: Inter-Language Literary Associates, 1967–71; Paris: YMCA Press, 1981). Italics are mine unless otherwise noted. Further citations will be to *CPL* and *SS*, respectively.

intimate; rather, he asserts the primacy of memoir, the presentation of the self with reference to historical context, the definition of the self with reference to cultural context. Ginzburg seems to develop this even further, illuminating what is true to her self-definition as a literary intellectual. According to Pratt, she combines what might be called personal memoirs with the distance of impersonal literary criticism, thereby achieving a unique self-portrait. Sinyavsky, according to Nussbaum, provides a dialogue between what he conceives as two actual but distinct selves, the self as a writer and the self as a literary critic. Nussbaum indicates how the images of Sinyavsky and his pseudonym Abram Tertz alternately collide and merge in his series of autobiographical statements. Isenberg suggests that Nadezhda Mandelstam provides yet another concept of self-definition: "She represents her writing as a posthumous continuation of her marriage role: unable to save [her husband's] life, she is determined to save his writings, and her own prose becomes part of that magnificent effort."

Hence, the conventional view of autobiography as the "story of a personality" propounded by Lejeune is expanded and transmuted through the unique and concrete autobiographical statements of the writers discussed in this collection.

Paul Jay in his study of the literature of self-representation, *Being in the Text*, posits that all forms of self-reflexive literature, nonfictional as well as fictional, share the same problem, namely, the "dissimilarity between identity and discourse": "Dissimilarity between identity and discourse is understood as the epistemological context within which the self is produced, and its status as a product is what becomes central. . . . Precisely this dissimilarity is at work in disrupting the smooth transposition of the psychological subject of an autobiographical text (the author) into its literary subject (its protagonist)."[63] While some twentieth-century writers carefully avoid focusing on the psychological subject, concentrating on discourse rather than identity, others choose to emphasize problems of identity by presenting multiple identities, each defined by his own identifiable form of discourse. Rozanov and Sinyavsky, for example, create a dialogue between multiple identities. Rozanov provides no less than eight distinctive personae discoursing with one another (Crone), while Sinyavsky depicts a kind of ongoing dialogue between two personae, the self as author and the self as critic (Nussbaum).

In *Autobiographical Acts*[64] Bruss moves beyond Lejeune's closed formulation based on types of narrative accounts and Jay's interest in the philosophical assumptions behind the text to define autobiography in terms of rules of the authorial act. To Bruss, autobiography is "an autonomous act with its own

---

[63] Paul Jay, *Being in the Text: Self-Representation from Wordsworth to Roland Barthes* (Ithaca: Cornell University Press, 1984), 29.

[64] Bruss, Autobiographical Acts.

peculiar responsibilities," an independent literary genre that generates its own rules. The most significant rule is that "the autobiographer undertakes a dual role": he is both "the source of the subject matter *and* the source of the structure found in the text." The writers under consideration here each provide a version of a life story which accords with this principle of duality. Because these are stories in which the writers are themselves the heroes, the structures and symbolics of the texts are equally determined by their subject matter and their objective stance. The chronological scheme of traditional autobiography, although having at least a skeletal presence in contemporary autobiographical narrative, recedes into the background. Instead particular moments are foregrounded as symbols (Remizov); parallel developments identify the emerging poetic consciousness with Russia's cultural history (Mandelstam); the influences, work, and writer's memories are linked through conceptual as opposed to chronological time and denoted only by their relative space in the text (Ginzburg); and the consciousness of language and its articulation is perceived as determining the direction of a writer's life (Pasternak, Limonov, and Osip and Nadezhda Mandelstam).

Michael Sprinker's statement in "Fictions of the Self" that "The origin and the end of autobiography converge in the very act of writing, as Proust brilliantly demonstrates at the end of *Le temps retrouvé*, for no autobiography can take place except within the boundaries of a writing where concepts of subject, self, and author collapse into the act of producing the text" emphasizes the "act of writing" above all else.[65] Thus Bely, according to Castellano, not only requires three different approaches—three different speakers— for his three successive volumes of memoirs but also has to "reengage himself with his own previous fiction" in order to fully interpret himself, to complete an autobiographical statement.

Nevertheless, it must be noted that this emphasis on expression or discourse does not deny the significance of social context, for autobiographical narrative is always addressed to an implied reader-interlocutor outside of the self or is presented in the form of an objectified self or alter ego. It always implies an effort to present an image of the self in time, which may take the form of a confession, self-affirmation, apology, or even cautionary tale. The writer's quest for an appropriate twentieth-century form thus reflects the social impetus behind the autobiographical statement—the need to find a reader, the desire to communicate a version of the self, or the quest to apprehend the age in terms of one's place in it. While this may be expressed by the conscious inclusion in the narrative structure of internal interlocutors—Rozanov (eight speakers), Sinyavsky (two speakers)—it may also emerge through reference to constructs external to the self perceived as determining the self: for Remizov and Bely, aspects of literature and history; for Rozanov, literature itself; for Mandel-

[65] Sprinker, "Fictions of the Self," 342.

stam, Nabokov, and Sinyavsky, Russian history; for Zoshchenko, Freudian psychology; for Ginzburg and Jakobson, literary scholarship, intellectual discourse, and literature; for Olesha or Pasternak, other writers. It may even appear, as for Limonov, in the speech patterns of a particular world or subculture or for Nadezhda Mandelstam in the rhetoric of a particular way of life.

Consequently, the very act of writing an autobiographical statement may also be viewed as a socializing process geared toward creating and presenting an image of the self in time, be it contemporary history, a specific historical moment in the past, or a moment in literary history. This choice of a literary form with its concomitant socializing process is usually presented as an affirmation of self, although it may take the form of an apology. Indeed, autobiographical statements are most often affirmative, even if paradoxically, they contain statements negating the sense of self. Olesha's denials of self, for example, are countered by his choice of a literary form. The form is affirmative despite the semantic denials it contains.

Moreover, since the focus of autobiography is most often the author's mind and the language expressing that mind, the problems of expression, explanation, definition, and communication are foregrounded through the narrator's rhetoric in the very process of articulating the interplay or tension between the plane of the life experience and the plane of aesthetic interpretation.

Because most twentieth-century writers were consciously seeking new literary forms, either as an escape from what they perceived as the constraints of the canonical genres or because they assumed that the biography providing the focus of the nineteenth-century novel and autobiography was inadequate to the demands of the twentieth century, primary emphasis gradually shifted from concern for subject matter to problems of discourse and form. This is expressed in various ways: for example, Bely's autobiographical works refer to the "facts" of his fiction (Castellano), while Remizov views the first twenty years of his literary life as no more than a search for a literary form that would free him from the constraints of traditional literary genres (Raevsky-Hughes).

Indeed, the motif of the quest is common to autobiographical discourse because by definition it cannot have a finite ending. It may even be regarded as an incomplete form in that its resolution is open to change. The reader may be left with a sense that a process has been initiated, but that the dialogue with the self and with the reader is still open, inconclusive. Knowledge that the author and protagonist may yet be alive may have something to do with the absence of an either/or polarity discussed by de Man. Thus, while the autobiographical text as such is complete as an act of writing, the majority of the Russian authors considered in this anthology have found it necessary to write more than one autobiographical statement.

Twentieth-century writers, then, in choosing to face the challenge of making an autobiographical statement, seem to have viewed the dialogue or tension between the plane of aesthetic interpretation and the chaos or catastrophe of the plane of the life experience as aesthetically significant. Remizov, for instance, first in actively seeking new literary forms and second in choosing deliberately to avoid the chronological in narrating events from his life, compels his "carefully chosen episodes [to] attain special meaning, to become symbols of his life and destiny" (Raevsky-Hughes). Since Remizov's search for self-identification and self-expression coincided with exile and forced travels, that is, with movement, instability, and chaos, it is through the organization of his life as literary material that he finds a way of overcoming or averting that chaos. Rozanov too is portrayed by Crone as ultimately substituting literature for his life by writing an "autobiography of literature." And Ginzburg in her autobiographical statement *The Old and the New* portrays her life as predominantly literary and aesthetic: her life is a life of books; her relationships are relationships with writers and literary scholars; her emotions, thoughts, and values are derived from her aesthetic system. Similar observations may be made with reference to the work of such recent Russian emigré writers as Sinyavsky and Limonov. And Pomorska phrases the problem with reference to Pasternak: "The poet's life is interesting only by virtue of those moments that can 'defend themselves' with the poetic word."

Moreover, the idea of writing as a defense, as an attempt to avert catastrophe, is cast as a principle by Mandelstam in his essay "Badger Hole," where he associates it with poetic culture itself and, in particular, with the methodology of Blok and Dante: "Poetic culture arises from the attempt to avert catastrophe, to make it dependent on the central sun of the system as a whole, be it love, of which Dante spoke, or music, at which Blok ultimately arrived" (CPL, 137; SS, 2:275). Mandelstam's depiction in his autobiography of the "bookcase of childhood" symbolizes his attempt to avert catastrophe by substituting an aestheticized pattern of family relationships for his actual family: the order of the bookshelves serves to overcome the "Judaic chaos." The uppermost shelf, both physically and spiritually, belongs to the Pushkin volume that models Mandelstam's idea of poetry as the vehicle of world culture; it alone is capable of absorbing "everything into itself." Literature and culture are imagined as the means for ordering and thereby overcoming catastrophe.

B. J. Mandel in his essay "Full of Life Now" (1980) reiterates the idea that "an autobiography . . . is an artifact, a construct wrought from words."[66] In assessing the aesthetic coherence of the texts examined in these essays, the literary factor, the "construct wrought from words," is considered of primary significance. Bearing features of both the novel and the lyric, autobiographical narrative throughout the twentieth century has been offered as a new and flexible literary utterance, as an "open" form ready to assimilate change in an age of change and discontinuity. It has been frequently perceived as an anti-

---

[66] Mandel, "Full of Life Now," 49–72.

canonical form whose canons were perpetually undergoing redefinition even as its formal features were subjected to modulation and alteration.

As writers, most of the authors of the texts under discussion have sought and found motivation in language or in the philological impulse. In several of these texts authors invent literary protagonists either totally separate from themselves (Trifonov) or as parts of splintered selves (Remizov, Rosanov, Bely, and Sinyavsky). These authors require a plurality of perspectives or consciousness, inventing for their purposes more than one narrator or hero. For example, Raevsky-Hughes characterizes Remizov as both a "chronicler-scribe and oral narrative singer." Björling presents the voice of Trifonov's hidden narrator as essential to the full understanding of his fictitious hero, and Rozanov and Sinyavsky offer in both dialogue and chorus the several voices of their splintered speakers. Limonov emphasizes language, specifically the jargon, slang, and obscenities of the underworld or the street, as crucial to an understanding of the human personality (Carden), while Nadezhda Mandelstam is master of a clearly definable ironic discourse: "The writer's irony is a rich field for the study of how rhetorical effects can be moves in a contest for authority" (Isenberg).

Furthermore, in twentieth-century literary autobiographical statements the conscious attention to language and speech patterns has broadened the possibilities for literary prose and developed the linguistic potential in a variety of directions. Writers as diverse as Rozanov, Remizov, Mandelstam, Bely, Olesha, Sinyavsky, and Limonov have consciously aimed at revitalizing language as a part of their quest for a new form appropriate to convey twentieth-century consciousness, introducing elements not associated with conventional autobiography. For example, Rozanov's eight speakers differentiate their voices; Sinyavsky's writer-critic and writer-author are distinguished by opposing speech characteristics. Trifonov's autobiographical voice is both merged with and disassociated from his novelistic voice through specific linguistic elements. Limonov's language is filled with slang and jargon intended to shock his readers into reading him in a nontraditional manner. Limonov's poetic or lyric voice, like Bely's, is expanded and extended through the use of first-person narrative, while the prose patterns are deepened and widened through the intensely personal verbalization of the inner voice (Carden, Castellano). Nadezhda Mandelstam, as Isenberg indicates, clearly uses a rhetoric of irony. The choice of language itself represents an ongoing inner dialogue with consciousness, conscience, and externally anticipated speech patterns. But where Bely and Mandelstam are still operating within the range of speech patterns acceptable in the 1920s, expressed through their extraordinarily lyrical prose, Sinyavsky and Limonov incorporate the speech habits and nonstandard language of the 1960s to 1980s into their discourse in a conscious attempt to decanonize or depoeticize it.

Consequently, in the autobiographical statements reviewed in this anthology we perceive the boundary between what is told (the plane of reality, autobiographical consciousness) and the telling (the plane of aesthetic interpretation, the autobiographical imagination) as the central focus of autobiographical discourse. The dialogue, interplay, or tension established between the telling and the told is emphasized, while the process of telling itself is foregrounded, offering the reader another vital sign of the twentieth-century literary autobiographical narrative. What Gusdorf terms the ''second reading of experience'' is viewed as an act of aesthetic interpretation dependent not on the autobiographical consciousness as defined by Mandel but on the narrative—the writer's imaginative recreation of and meditation on his conception of his self or his life in time. Each work discussed here is therefore viewed as a second reading of experience but also as a concrete effort to provide that life experience with a unique or original aesthetic interpretation.

CHAPTER 1

Rozanov and Autobiography: The Case of Vasily Vasilievich

Anna Lisa Crone

ROZANOV'S USE OF THE AUTOBIOGRAPHICAL MODE

In a recent discussion of modern autobiography Paul de Man wrote: "Empirically as well as theoretically, autobiography lends itself poorly to generic definition; each specific instance seems to be an exception to the norm."[1] Nevertheless, Elizabeth Bruss in *Autobiographical Acts* puts forth some general guidelines for autobiography as a genre. Although she stipulates that these may sometimes be violated, she suggests that they provide a basis for generic definition. The essential aspects of her "rules" for autobiography that have relevance for Rozanov's use of the autobiographical mode follow:

Rule 1: The autobiographer is the source of the text's subject matter and structuring. He claims individual responsibility for its creation and ordering, and his existence is assumed to be a verifiable fact.

Rule 2: Information and events reported in connection with the autobiographer are supposed to have happened or to be true. No matter how difficult it may be to verify the events or attitudes mentioned, the claim for their truth is made.

Rule 3: Even if what is reported can be or has been discredited, the autobiographer purports or believes it to be true.[2]

These rules, as we shall see, clearly exclude Rozanov's writings and his protagonist Vasily Vasilievich from the genre of autobiography. Yet Rozanov's relationship to that genre and his use of the autobiographical mode is extremely interesting; its various facets will be explored here.

Where Rousseau had his J.J., Rozanov has his V.V., the fictional character Rozanov fashioned from his "self." He bears most of the author's autobiographical, or seemingly autobiographical, data in his most personal and intimate works—*Solitaria* (*Uedinennoe*, 1911) and *Fallen Leaves: Basketful One* and *Basketful Two* (*Opavshie list'ja. Korob pervyj* and *Korob vtoroj*, 1913–

---

[1] Paul de Man, "Autobiography as Defacement" in *The Rhetoric of Romanticism* (New York: Columbia University Press, 1984), 68.

[2] Elizabeth Bruss, *Autobiographical Acts* (Baltimore: Johns Hopkins University Press, 1976), 10–11.

1915), as well as *The Apocalypse of Our Time* (*Apokalipsis nashego vremeni*, 1917–1919).[3]

In these works the reader is introduced to V.V. through the several literary masks or voices that Rozanov adopts and that I have described elsewhere as the confessor,[4] the homebody,[5] the buffon,[6] and the gossip.[7] There are at least four other voices—the prophet of doom, the mentor, the mystic, and the objective critic—whose discourse is more restrained and elevated than that of the down-to-earth V.V., whose "plain Russian" voice emerges in the crossfire of opinions, ideas, prejudices, and feelings dispersed throughout these works. The polyphonic exchange between the simpler voices of V.V. and the more exalted, intellectual ones introduces a cacophony into the total self portrayed. What is more, the elevated voices contain very little autobiographical material. The presence of this higher self makes it difficult to sense any unity in the first-person narrator in much the same way that it is difficult to grasp a sense of Michel, the self embedded in Montaigne's discussion of myriad topics in his *Essais*.

Solitaria and *Fallen Leaves: Basketful One* and *Basketful Two* constitute Rozanov's trilogy. His *Apocalypse* is often grouped with them as a kind of continuation in form and as a part of the work of the "late Rozanov." The massive amount of autobiographical material in these works is presented most often by a voice that I call the confessor. Moreover, it is usually conveyed in such a way as to seem spurious or contrived. Although the tone of the work is autobiographical, the reader suspects that this confession is pure fiction.

Paradoxically, Rozanov managed in these works to fulfill some of the important functions of modern autobiography, without actually practicing the genre. This is part of the reason why his late works are considered so signifi-

---

[3] Wassilij Rosanow, *Ausgewählte Schriften* (Munich: A Neimanis, 1970). All references to Rozanov texts refer to this edition.

[4] The confessor is described in A. L. Crone, *Rozanov and the End of Literature* (Wurzburg: JAL Verlag, 1978); 37–39, as "the voice which endeavors to justify his personality . . . his art and method. . . . He gives confidential information to the reader, whom he often addresses directly and with whom he chats in an intimate tone. . . . There is an intimate tone but no real intimacy. . . . The Confessor presents Rozanov as a loving, warm individual." His entries can be categorized thus by content: (1) self-apology and self-praise; (2) expressions of guilt; (3) commentary on friends, marriage, and family—autobiographical material; (4) confidential asides to the reader.

[5] The homebody—"a generalized Russian citizen of the lower *meshchanstvo*, and [represents] . . . its language, tastes, prejudices, enjoyments, values, practical know-how, religious sensibilities, and occasionally, its literary preferences." Ibid., 33–34.

[6] The buffoon—this voice is "humorously self-deprecating, indicating the speaker's many shortcomings . . . exposing all 'his' supposed feelings of inferiority and insecurities. It ridicules the self playfully, without the sharp edge of the gossip." Ibid., 35, n. 7.

[7] The gossip "reports all sorts of details behind any . . . event, personality or movement. This wiseacre exposes all the 'dirty linen.' " The voice is cynical and not averse to dealing a low blow. Ibid., 32–33.

cant and why they enjoyed such popularity in their day. (The other reason why these works are still studied is more strictly literary, and its tangential connection with autobiography will be considered in the second part of this essay.) In a sense, it might even be said that Rozanov was attempting not an autobiography of himself but an *autobiography of literature*.

Let us first address ourselves to the character V.V., who seems to possess many qualities of an autobiographer. His obsessive love for everything small, private, homey, and everyday (bytovoj) immediately strikes the reader. There is ample reason to believe that this characteristic was far less central to the empirical personality of Rozanov than it is to this character, although many readers have failed to differentiate between the two. The author chooses to present a character or persona to whom the average reader of *New Times* (*Novoe vremja*)—where Rozanov published several times a week—would be able to relate and in whom that reader would take an active interest. Thus, Rozanov lowers the level of his persona in order to raise the level of self-consciousness in the average Russian city dweller or, in general, any reader. He provides the average reader with an alternative to the unfamiliar models of behavior, modes of expression, and lifestyles encountered in "landowners' literature," a term applicable to many of the Russian classics. By emphasizing his own sense of alienation from the aristocracy, what he calls the social class difference (soslovnaja raznitsa), V.V. expresses his sense of alienation from the authors and characters of many literary works of the nineteenth century as well as from the authors of scholarly and journalistic articles. This professed alienation from high literature—dubious indeed if one applies it to Rozanov the writer—is part and parcel of V.V.'s intimate relationship with the reader. V.V. mirrors the average reader, speaks his language, and thereby leads him to self-reflection, pushing him toward an evaluation of his own individuality. In other words, the reader very often sees himself in V.V., and to the extent that this is true Rozanov performs a service similar to that which Montaigne performed for his fellow aristocrats in sixteenth- and seventeenth-century France.[8]

Of course, many readers preferred tales of the aristocracy, stories of heroes with lives, problems, language, and culture far removed from their own. Many had no desire to break with the heroic or aristocratic models of Russia's literary past. In his *Essais* Montaigne warns the reader who is not open to risk and change to put his book down before starting:

> This is an honest book, reader. It warns you at the outset that in it I have set no goal but a domestic and a private one. I have no thought of serving you. . . . If I had written a book to seek the world's favor, I should have bedecked myself better, and should present myself in a studied posture. I want to be seen here . . . without pose

---

[8] Donald Frame, *Montaigne: A Biography* (New York: Harcourt, Brace & World, 1965), 310–23.

or artifice. . . . So reader, I am myself the matter of my book. You would be unreasonable to spend your leisure on so frivolous a subject.[9]

Rozanov follows suit in *Solitaria*:

Why do I write? For whom? Simply, I need to. Ah, dear reader, I have long since been writing "without a reader," simply because *I like to*. Just as I publish without thought for a reader. . . . I simply like to. And I won't cry or get angry if a writer, who has bought the book by mistake, throws it in the trash basket. . . . So there, reader, I don't stand on ceremony with you—and you don't have to stand on ceremony with me, either:
"Go to hell!"
"Go to hell yourself!"

Among the reading public of Rozanov's day were many who could not stomach Dostoevsky's fiction or Dostoevsky as he presented himself in *The Diary of a Writer* (*Dnevnik pisatelja*). "Dostoevshchina" is still a term for highly scandalous, even criminal life. These facts did not stop Rozanov from creating his V.V. in a Dostoevskian mold, as a Dostoevskian creature come alive and living in St. Petersburg. Few characters sound more like Dostoevsky's underground man than Rozanov's confessor:

It's amazing how I could always accommodate myself to lying. Lies never tormented me. And for a strange reason: "Just what business is it of yours [addressed to the reader or anyone else] to know exactly what I think?" "Just what obliges me to tell you my real thoughts?" My deepest subjectivity . . . made it so that I was always living as if behind a *curtain* . . . that could not be removed or torn. . . . If at the same time, in the majority of cases (even always, it seems to me), I wrote sincerely and honestly, this was not out of love of truth which I not only lacked but "could not even imagine having"—but out of carelessness. To lie you have to "think something up," and "make ends fit together," "to construct something." It's much harder than just telling things as they are. And so I simply put things "as they are" down on paper, which is the essence of my veracity. . . . At times it seems to me that I am the most honest and sincere of all writers. (*Solitaria*, 54)

Here we see the ambiguous V.V. in action: is he a sincerely honest man or a lazy liar? In Rozanov, as in the *Notes from Underground* (*Zapiski iz podpol'ja*) that so influenced him, there is a Bakhtinian backward glance (ogljadka) to the *Confessions* of Rousseau. Rozanov, who has said that he is perpetually "behind a curtain," undertakes to reveal himself by confessing while at the same time explicitly denying that he is confessing at all or that his trilogy contains any self-revelatory intentions.

Despite his disclaimers, it is quite possible that Rozanov turned to the more

[9] Michel de Montaigne, *Essais* in *Oeuvres complètes* (Paris: Louis Canard, 1924), 1:1–3 (my translation).

"private" communication with the reader found in *Solitaria* and *Fallen Leaves* for reasons not unlike those that led Rousseau to take up autobiographical confession at the end of his life. Like Rousseau, Rozanov was one of the most lonely and criticized of writers. His isolation became most acute around 1913, when he was expelled from the Religious-Philosophical Society for his highly idosyncratic position on the Beilis Case.[10] Like Rousseau, Rozanov invited an avalanche of criticism with his extreme iconoclasm and his ideological changeability. Sinyavsky believes that Rozanov courted such criticism on purpose so as to be always ostracized from the various literary camps.[11] Something similar can certainly be said of Rousseau. Yet another parallel lies in Rozanov's insistence on being so different from other men of letters that even those who respected his undeniable talent were forced to disapprove of him much of the time. Rozanov used his new form as a means of direct self-expression, as Rousseau had done in his *Confessions*—to explain himself both to contemporaries interested enough to listen and to posterity. Thus Rozanov in his trilogy and in *The Apocalypse* struck a more personal and intimate note with the reader than he ever had before (except in personal letters and necrologies). But the "personal" element in his work is only partially self-descriptive. The work expresses its personal effect not by rendering the author's own life and thoughts but by evoking an intense personal experience in the reader. With an effect similar to that of Dostoevsky's fiction, Rozanov leaves us somewhere between fiction and autobiography; it is certainly not autobiography as defined by Bruss's rules.

In the trilogy and *The Apocalypse* Rozanov wished to reveal to the literate Russian world of his day a complex, fluctuating, constantly changing and disintegrating, as well as reforming self-in-process. And he wanted to pass off this character, more complex even than Dostoevsky's underground man, as his own self, as the author of many notorious and brilliant articles and books published under the names Rozanov, Varvarin, and other pseudonyms. With these objectives in mind, it is no wonder that he made recourse to spiritual and confessional autobiography and to apology. Indeed, there are many pages in Rozanov's late works that would fit perfectly into a genuine autobiography. For example, Rozanov's appeal to the Jews to forgive him for all he wrote against them (*The Apocalypse*) contains elements of both confession and apology; his "First Love" could be found in a confessional work; while the nu-

---

[10] In the Beilis Case a Jew was accused of the ritual murder of a Christian youth. The case had a resonance in Russia not unlike that of the Dreyfus Affair in France. Rozanov took the unusual position that Beilis had, of course, committed the killing as part of a religious ritual demanded by Judaism. In the context of Rozanov's very positive regard for that religion, some critics have tried to empathize with Rozanov's interpretation of this as an act of a religious zealot, implying that the ritual sacrifice of Christians was part of Jewish religious practice. Most people, however, including the members of the Religious-Philosophical Society, saw it as base anti-Semitism.

[11] Andrey Sinyavsky, *Opavshie list'ja Rozanova* (Paris: Sintaksis, 1982), passim.

merous tales recounting religious experience and faith have caused his works to be compared to Pascal's *Pensées* and Avvakum's *Autobiography* (*Zhitie protapopa Avvakuma*).[12] In Rozanov such passages always break off suddenly or abruptly, however, being interrupted just as the reader is about to settle into them.

The frankness of such passages, as is so often the case with autobiography, is suspect. The honesty and sincerity of Rousseau, Augustine, Montaigne, and Cellini—of almost all autobiographers—have been impugned. Yet in Rozanov there is another problem: the reader must question whether Rozanov had any intention of being or even of appearing to be honest or sincere. Any attentive reader senses that Rozanov lies with as little effort and compunction as he tells truths and that there is no way of distinguishing truth from falsehood, fact from fiction, in his works. It may be that V.V. lies as unabashedly as that most endearing of literary liars, General Ivolgin in Dostoevsky's *The Idiot* (*Idiot*). This embroils the reader in yet another paradox: there may be nothing more honest for the inveterate liar to do in a self-revelatory work than to display amply his own brand of lying. Such a view assumes that the specific nature and content of a man's lies contain important information about him. Of course, there remains the residual possibility that Rozanov, like Ivolgin, may sometimes tell the truth inadvertently or that he may do so out of laziness, for the sake of variety, or by deliberate design. In the latter cases, even though he tells the truth, the reader's confidence in the author's veracity has been so shaken that he will not receive the message as true.

This relativizing of truth and falsehood, the ambiguity that makes it impossible to distinguish between the two in apparently autobiographical statements, led Doestoevsky to point out repeatedly in *The Idiot* that the truth is often much less believable than lies and inventions.

In order to read Rozanov's trilogy without extreme frustration, the reader must relegate questions of truth and falsehood to a marginal or even irrelevant status. This serves two purposes. First, it places a shadow over the entire genre of autobiography and memoir. By accusing the autobiographer of lying, Rozanov seems to be unmasking the genre's past practitioners as liars. For example, one negative reference to Rousseau's most awful confession—that he left several of his illegitimate children on the stairs of a state-run orphange[13]— is consonant with the desire to satirize earlier autobiography and Rousseau in particular. The material about Tolstoy as a man is likewise censorious. Rozanov also echoes the question Heine raised in connection with Rousseau as to whether the truth can be known or told, even when the human subject intends

---

[12] Vladimir Pozner compared Rozanov to Pascal in his essay on Rozanov in *Panorama de la littérature russe contemporaine*. Comparisons with Avvakum are found in Zoreslava Kaulbach, "The Life and Works of V.V. Rozanov" (Ph.D. diss. Cornell University, 1973).

[13] J. J. Rousseau, *The Confessions*, trans. John Grant (London: Dent, 1943), 1:314–17. For the Rozanov citation, see *Solitaria*, 25.

to tell the truth and sincerely believes that he is doing so. The underground man, the clearest model for Rozanov's confessor, directly cites Heine's view. All this skepticism and relativism in modern autobiography goes back to Montaigne's What do I know? ("*Que sçay-je?*"). Indeed, in the very variation of voices in his late works Rozanov presents a self unsure and ignorant of its own contents, its nature, its limits, and its future. Often voices speak out in him the presence of which he is unaware:

> Once I was standing in Vvedensky Church with my three-year-old Tanya. . . . There was no service, but the church was never locked. . . . I liked to come there with Tanya who was thin and especially graceful. . . . We feared she might have meningitis like our first child and that she might not "make it." And there we stood; it was silent—silent. . . . Marvelous . . . when suddenly it was as if a voice whispered: "You *don't belong* here. *Why* have you come? To *whom*? No one *expected* you. And don't go on thinking that you've done something "right," and "comme il faut," coming here together as "father and daughter." . . . When I heard this voice, *perhaps my very own voice, but formulating this thought for the first time* [italics mine], without preparation or warning, as something "sudden," "unexpected," "from somewhere." (*Fallen Leaves*, 2: 260)

This passage gives the impression that Rozanov is intoning voices de profundis, from a deeper level of self, discovering himself in the process of writing. Apparently at least eight personae, each with its own characteristic tone, style, and world view, battle for dominance in the pages of Rozanov's last four works.[14] Some betray an awareness of the others; some are oblivious to the several contending selves. This dynamic form conveys V.V. in the process of grasping for a sense of self, for a suitable vehicle for self-expression, yet the essential self ever eludes the comprehension of a single voice that attempts to define or impose order on it.

The self displayed in this effort changes so much that it appears to be disintegrating; in it "the centrifugal forces of decomposition" exceed by far the "centripetal forces of self-coherence and organization" (to use the terms of personality structure employed by Viacheslav Ivanov and Osip Mandelstam).[15] What remains is a disparate, doubling self, held together only by the use of the pronoun "I." The concept of the weakening of the individual (even the death of individuality) was common in fin-de-siècle Russian letters from Dostoevsky's underground man, its first notable harbinger in 1864, through

[14] See Crone, "Polyphony in the Late Rozanov: The Eight Voices" in *Rozanov and the End of Literature*, 25–45, for a discussion of the values and limitations of this typology.

[15] This conception of the self in terms of center and periphery is seen in Ivanov's metaphors in his articles on Nietzsche and Dionysianism and in Mandelstam's article "End of the Novel" in J. G. Harris, *Mandelstam: The Complete Critical Prose and Letters* [*CPL*] (Ann Arbor: Ardis, 1979), 199–200.

Blok, Bely, Ivanov, Mandelstam, and Rozanov.[16] The spectacle of the disintegration of an individual in Rozanov's work reflects the falling apart of the writer's self. Rozanov associates his loose and fragmentary discourse with modern Russian writers' inability to "hold together."

The sense of a self without cohesiveness is produced by the coexistence in these works of the higher, exalted voices (prophet of doom, mentor, objective critic—the intellectual, analytic voice—and mystic) and the lower, more earthy voices (confessor, homebody, gossip, and buffoon). While the latter four bear most of the "autobiographical" information, all Rozanov does in the end is flirt with the autobiographical mode.

If we consider Rozanov's works in terms of their truth content, this pseudo-autobiography is more suspect than the average autobiography. The well-planned, controlled nature of Rozanov's trilogy makes it seem less sincere than his final, desperate, and prophetic *Apocalypse*. Still, it would obviously be a mistake to take any of these works as pure and honest outpourings of a soul. They are all too consciously crafted. The autobiographical material they contain is copious—Rozanov's childhood with his mother in Kostroma, his gymnasium days attested to in the letters of his friend Kostya Kudravtsev (thirty pages of which are included in the text, though they are impossible to verify), his first love, and so on. Conspicuously absent, however, is the story of his first marriage to Dostoevsky's demonic mistress Apollonaria Suslova. On the other hand, Rozanov includes reams of material on his second marriage to Varvara Rudneva, her prior marriage and child from that marriage, their common children, his second wife's character and friends, and the progression of her illness (especially in the second part of *Fallen Leaves*). Also included are materials on his literary intimates and enemies, his hatred of certain leftists and revolutionaries, a list of reprehensible acts he committed, and positive and negative remarks about himself.

To many of the entries Rozanov adds a notation in parentheses or italics, allegedly to explain where it initially came to him or was jotted down. He further adds second thoughts about the content of the entries. The locations are in many cases obviously contrived to show the contrast between the nature of the thought and the situation in which it arose (for example, "in the W.C.," "at my coin collection," "on the sole of my shoe"). Despite its contrived nature, the constant appearance of this device can suggest to the reader that he is with V.V. in all manner of intimate places. The reader is therefore in constant conflict. If he lets down his guard, these notations make him feel that he

---

[16] This sense of the disintegrating personality is seen in the introduction to Blok's "Vozmez-die" as well as in his articles, in the plight of Dudkin and Nikolay in Bely's *Petersburg*, in Mandelstam's "End of the Novel" and his character Parnok in "Egyptian Stamp," and in Ivanov's many articles, although he is more ready to welcome the collectivist future and feels that individualism must be overcome or taken to a higher stage whence it will be reintegrated into the collective.

is virtually a member of the Rozanov family, eating a watermelon in the kitchen, warming himself at the family hearth, or seeing the sleeping Varvara with her withered hand. The autobiographical spell that Rozanov casts arouses sympathy in the reader, who then recalls the playfulness and contrary nature of the narrator and begins to feel that the author must be toying with him. This dynamic is exactly what Gerard Genette describes in his analysis of Proust's *A la recherche du temps perdu*, which, like Rozanov's works, bridges auto-biography and fiction: "Each example taken from the *Recherche* can produce . . . an endless discussion between a reading of the novel as fiction and a reading of the same novel as autobiography. We should perhaps remain within this whirligig."[17] Rozanov's reader is in a similar whirligig in the late works, and he yearns for the works' resolution as fiction or autobiography. Paul de Man writes of this dilemma: "The distinction between fiction and autobiography is not an either/or polarity. . . . It is undecidable. . . . As anyone who has ever been caught in a revolving door or on a revolving wheel can testify, it is most uncomfortable."[18] The fact that Rozanov may just be spinning false-hoods and passing them off as autobiography (perhaps his wife is not very sick!) tries the reader's patience. To overcome this state and continue reading sympathetically the reader must decide either that the works are to be treated as pure fiction and may indeed be such or that all autobiography contains large doses of pure fiction and that this author is merely unmasking it (the more common resolution of the dilemma).

Montaigne's *honnête homme* and Rousseau's cult of sincerity are thus dem-onstrated as unattainable; Heine's notion that the writer will be untruthful even when he tries to give a faithful account of things is invoked a thousand times. Yet Rozanov tries to extract himself from this whole controversy. He asks: "Just what business is it of yours what I really think?" (*Solitaria*, 54).

Indeed, Rozanov went so far as to claim that there was some truth in all views and ideas, although for him ideas were hardly central. In fact, they were only necessary insofar as he liked to experiment with the verbal espousal of various opinions, political and otherwise. He stated, furthermore, that one could not espouse a point of view without believing in it wholeheartedly at the moment of utterance. These statements provoked the many charges of ideo-logical anarchy and irresponsibility against Rozanov. A similar anarchy and contradiction may be seen in the internal opposition among his various selves in the trilogy. Few contemporaries were able to forgive Rozanov this ideolog-ical volatility, especially where his highly unstable, now pro, now con views on Jews and Christianity were concerned. Mandelstam was one of the few critics to understand that what mattered to Rozanov was language, the music

[17] Gerard Genette, *Figures III*, trans. Paul de Man (Paris: de Seuil, 1972), 50.
[18] De Man, "Autobiography as Defacement," 70.

of words, the unbridled expressiveness of human speech, and man's contrary nature.[19]

ROZANOV'S ACHIEVEMENT AND THE RUSSIAN CONTEXT

The impossibility of honest autobiography in no way prevented Rozanov from using the autobiographical mode, from weaving an autobiographical spell. Indeed, his late works actually achieve some of the instructive effects considered significant in modern biography. Rozanov's work is doubly instructive in that he not only overcomes the suspect nature of autobiography by fashioning a contrived self—V.V.—who calls attention to himself as lie/fiction but he is able to portray that self as it develops over time. What he achieves through V.V. and the other voices is twofold. He enlarges the psychosocial awareness of the more naive, ordinary reader and expands the self-awareness of the sophisticated reader, writer, or critic, as well as literature's awareness of itself. He introduces the notion of literature as something living within the human subject, who is inhabited by numerous literary voices. The subject's awareness of self becomes *his awareness of literature within him*.

We pointed out that the four late works contain a wealth of true or fictional autobiographical materials dispersed throughout a wide variety of entries— essays, poems, prose poems, aphorisms, dialogues, vignettes, short stories, and so on. In my polyphonic analysis of these texts in *Rozanov and the End of Literature* I described the style and voice of the confessor, the homebody, the buffoon, and the gossip—the voices that combine to produce the personality of V.V.[20] The confessor, with the occasional aid of the other three, creates the impression of confessional biography. Yet the very manner in which the autobiographical materials are dispersed prevents the full emergence of autobiography. Furthermore, if the words uttered by these voices, or the words of the confessor alone, are culled from the four works, there is still much material that disqualifies what remains as autobiography or confession. The works are rife with contradiction and paradox, divergent versions of the same thing, while Rozanov's penchant for being different every minute contributes to the constant variability of the narrating ''I,'' the themes, and their treatment.

One of the most important aspects of autobiography in the Western world, as outlined by Karl Weintraub in his thematic history of the genre, is the value placed upon the individual. From the dawn of Christianity, however, there has been a conflict in autobiography between the value placed on the unique, idiosyncratic individual and that placed on the exemplary *model* of the Christian life that early autobiographies often exhort the reader to follow. Weintraub's *The Value of the Individual* documents the slow and zigzagging emergence of

[19] See Mandelstam, ''On the Nature of the Word'' in Harris, *CPL*, 123–25.
[20] See notes 4–7, above.

a highly valued individuality progressively freed from the dominance of external models of behavior from Augustine to Goethe.[21] Lovejoy points out the great change that led to the heightened valuation of the individual in the modern period: "There have been in the entire history of thought few changes more momentous than those which took place when it came to be believed not only that there are diverse excellencies . . . [in human life] . . . *but that diversity is the essence of excellence*" [italics mine].[22] Lovejoy terms this idea "the discovery of the intrinsic worth of diversity" and consequently of the individual qua individual. Jakob Burckhardt showed the emergence of the powerful individual in the Italian city-state, a development that culminated in the cult of individualism of the romantic age.[23]

In Russia, however, the bulk of society was not westernized and remained under the sway of collectivist concepts such as the Slavophile *sobornost'*.[24] This led to less cultivation and less appreciation of the concept of individuality in Russia than in Europe. Nevertheless, that part of Russian society influenced by Western notions of individualism produced some of the most radically individualist figures in all of Western culture, both in literature (in particular, Dostoevsky's heroes Stavrogin, the grand inquisitor, and Raskolnikov) and in life (Bakunin, Savinkov, Tolstoy, and Azef), individuals of truly Nietzschean stature. Dostoevsky, the greatest recorder of such Russian individuals, was simultaneously fascinated and morally appalled by unbridled individualism. He felt that the highest calling and sacred duty of such individuals was to relinquish their free will and *freely* submit to the integrated group consciousness (the Orthodox ecclesiastical community). Thus, the great poet of powerful human wills, whom Nietzsche had admired at first, censured the very individualism he had described, denouncing it as evil unless subjugated to God and Christianity.

Dostoevsky's "Legend of the Grand Inquisitor," the ideological core of *The Brothers Karamazov* (*Brat' ja Karamazovy*) was the subject of Rozanov's second scholarly work, and Dostoevsky continued to exert enormous influence on Rozanov throughout his career. In the "Legend" the aged inquisitor of Seville attempts to force all men to relinquish their individual freedom to him and the Catholic Church, so as to become part of a rationally ordered society. Man, in his view, is a childish rebel happy to exchange his individual freedom

---

[21] Karl J. Weintraub, *The Value of the Individual* (Chicago: University of Chicago Press, 1982).

[22] Arthur O. Lovejoy, *The Great Chain of Being* (Cambridge, Mass.: Harvard University Press, 1973), 293.

[23] Jakob Burckhardt, *Civilization of the Renaissance in Italy*, trans. Irene Gordon (New York: Mentor Books, 1960), ch. 2.

[24] *Sobornost'* is an organic conception of ecclesiastical consciousness, which defines the church internally, not as a center of authority but as a congregation of "lovers in Christ"; the members are "organically united"—faith and religious knowledge or revelation is possible only within the collectivity.

for miracle (mythical belief and magic), mystery (magic), and bread (sustenance). Individual freedom is a terrible burden thrust upon man by a Christ who did not understand the basic weakness of man's nature. The way the inquisitor proposes to relieve man of this freedom and the highly organized society he envisions prefigure the modern totalitarian state. This work has inspired numerous negative utopias pleading for the protection of individualism in the face of monolithic totalitarian threats. Zamyatin's *We*, Huxley's *Brave New World*, and Arthur C. Clarke's *Childhood's End* are but a few novels that bear the stamp of "The Legend of the Grand Inquisitor."

In *Notes from Underground*, written some fifteen years before *The Brothers Karamazov*, Dostoevsky had described man as by nature a rebel who would never allow himself to be regimented in a rationally organized society, especially one based on utilitarian principles. To regiment man in this way reduced him to the level of a piano key or an organ stop. According to Dostoevsky's "underground man," there is a most "advantageous advantage" for man—the assertion of his free will and individuality against any rationally ordained good, even if this rebellion cost him his life.[25] Of course, this underground man is not a hero for Dostoevsky but an antihero. The underground man espouses ideas familiar from the antirationalist Montaigne who centuries earlier had said that man's behavior could not be regulated by reason, that there were no universal standards for human conduct but merely a wide range of habits and customs. The underground man is the same sort of relativist and skeptic. He feels himself constantly changing, as did Montaigne: "There is as much variation between myself and myself as between you and myself."[26] According to these ideas, man will delight in overthrowing and discrediting any attempt to define him, especially any rational model of behavior.

Because Rozanov believed that man was indefinable, he chose to present an underground personality in his trilogy as the vehicle for his self. Unlike Dostoevsky in *Notes from Underground*, however, Rozanov acts like an autobiographer, claiming that his underground character is the real, living Rozanov. Furthermore, he places positive value on the unbridled individualism of this character, reveling in V.V.'s model-exploding self-expressiveness.

V.V. is in part a fictional construct. As I have pointed out, he is of *indeterminate fictionality*; his actual relationship to V.V. Rozanov can not be ascertained. Rozanov made a clear decision to present in these works a defense of the individuality of the small, private person, using a possible or feasible underground character as a mirror of his reader. Dostoevsky too was preoccupied in *Notes from Underground* and later works with presenting "the man of the Russian majority."[27]

---

[25] F. M. Dostoevsky, *Zapiski iz podpol'ja. Sobranie Sochinenii* (Leningrad, Nauka, 1973), 5: 118ff.

[26] Montaigne, *Essais* 321.

[27] Dostoevsky, *Zapiski iz podpol'ja*, 378. The note concerns Dostoevsky's attempt to accom-

Presenting this self-contradictory, at times shocking and disgusting, yet always lively V.V. in the pseudo-intimate manner of these writings, Rozanov endeavored not only to shock the reader but to force him to reflect upon himself and on the fact that there is much in each of us that can shock if described in "plain Russian." Rozanov shocks the reader by breaking certain social taboos and conventions of literary decorum—he discusses sexual desire and feelings, the maternal instinct and some of its psychological particulars, hunger and starvation, the sensual enjoyment of food, bodily odor and functions—since for Rozanov the body is the "flesh of the spirit." Rousseau always prepares his reader for something shocking or despicable that he is about to relate and then confesses something quite inconsequential; Rozanov without any warning and quite abruptly shocks the reader time and again. Ever emphasizing that V.V. is the average Russian, the consumer and lover of life's small pleasures, he challenges the reader to measure himself against the standard set by the character. What is more, many of Rozanov's contemporary readers did see themselves in V.V.; they recognized something of themselves in his language, in his tone, and in certain of his views. As I indicated earlier, this accounts for the claims of Rozanov's extreme "Russianness"—for the fact that he introduced into serious high, as opposed to mass, literature, widespread Russian attitudes, and feelings and that he did so in the language of everyday life, of the kitchen and pantry, the bedroom, and the doctor's office.[28] What might have seemed strange and removed from the reader when encountered in Dostoevsky's extreme characters in Rozanov's work becomes quite down-to-earth and familiar.

For example, Shatov's theory about the inextricable link between Russian nationality and Orthodoxy may seem abstract and exalted in Dostoevsky's *The Possessed (Besy)*, but when Rozanov repeats the same notion in his homely way, the idea seems to merit consideration by the average Russian who is neither a terrorist nor a religious mystic. Dostoevsky's grand inquisitor appears cruel as he rants against Christ; yet in *The Apocalypse* Rozanov attacks Christ on similar and related grounds—for his weakness and failure to demonstrate his power (to do more miracles)—in such a way that a broader readership was forced to consider the inquisitor's point of view and Ivan Karamazov's Antichrist stance in general.[29]

Rozanov's significance in the Russian literature of the Silver Age is partly due to his having made Dostoevsky's writings about the individual and his role in the world an essential part of the self-searching of a broader spectrum

---

plish this in *Notes from Underground* and his sense of satisfaction that he had achieved it in *The Adolescent*.

[28] For a definition of the mass reader and mass literature, see Jeffrey Brooks, "Readers and Reading at the End of the Tsarist Era," *Literature and Society in Imperial Russia, 1800–1914*, ed. William Todd (Palo Alto: Stanford University Press, 1978), 119ff.

[29] See Rozanov's *Apokalipsis nashego vremeni*, 455–58.

of society and so of the period's *Weltanschauung*. As opposed to Count Tolstoy, the great practitioner of the landowner's novel, Dostoevsky (himself a scion of impoverished nobility) dealt with a much larger cross section of Russian society. Mandelstam, a Jew and an intellectual of mixed class (raznochinets), speaks of nonaristocratic scholars and writers in Russian literature as men "in fur coats above their station."[30] Rozanov descends further than any of them in his self-reflexive metaphors and in his metaphors for literature.[31] In the trilogy he goes out of his way to emphasize the class difference he felt between himself and many other writers.

In general, the intellectual of mixed class has more in common with aristocratic Russian writers than with Rozanov's confessor or homebody. Other of his voices or masks, such as the prophet of doom, the mentor, and the critic, are harder to distinguish from the literary man of noble origin. Rozanov, whose mother was of noble lineage, dispensed with all attempts to conform to the style of upper-class literature in the voices of the confessor, the homebody, the gossip, and the buffoon. Although Rozanov could participate on equal footing with almost any writer of the period and had already done so in his earlier writings, in his last four major works he placed unprecedented emphasis on his simplest Russian faces, focusing on the value of the simple Russian man, the Orthodox morality of his wife Varvara, and the traits of V.V., a more complex characterological specimen. Rozanov defends the right of such little men to be active participants in literature, claiming that their personalities are fine subjects for psychological analysis. In this full-valued treatment of the Orthodox urban Russian is something of the orientation of the Native Soil Conservatives who appealed to the upper classes to join with the lower classes in a complete social reconciliation.[32]

Rozanov's main concern, more than total reintegration of Russian society, however, is to defend the right of each quirky and even unsavory individual to have and to voice his opinions and to enjoy all the peculiarities of his multifaceted character. In Rozanov's trilogy the traditional St. Petersburg little man has his longest, although perhaps the most disjointed, monologue.

Having established the little man's right to be the subject of belles lettres as a real person (through the autobiographical mode), Rozanov did much to expand the means by which writers could write about themselves, gossip, confess, offer criticism, and so on, as well as indulge in self-reflexive analysis. No longer did one have to be a poet-idol like Alexander Blok or a Count

---

[30] Mandelstam, *Shum vremeni* in *Sobranie Sochinenii* (New York: Inter-Language Literary Associates, 1967), 2:100–108.

[31] Rozanov constantly emphasizes that literature is his most natural element, his "trousers— he's always in them and there's no point standing on ceremony with them."

[32] Rozanov was much influenced by the Native Soil Conservative movement (Pochvennichestvo) in the persons of such leading members as Dostoevsky and Rozanov's mentor, the historian Nikolay Strakhov.

Tolstoy for one's autobiography or confession to have an interest or educational value for the general reader. Although Rozanov in actual fact had much in common with Blok, Bely, Soloviev, and even Tolstoy, he deemphasized that side of himself in his trilogy, focusing his lens instead on the homely, unmentionable, instinctual parts of human biography and thus expanding the language of autobiography and memoir—using the nicknames and family words that convey private meanings, whispers of intimate life, and allusions to obscenity and to the language of the street, of thieves, and of other members of society's lower echelons. By means of this linguistic variety and by his selection of the simple urban individual as the main vehicle of autobiographical information. Rozanov provided catalysts for the future development of the Russian autobiographical mode. V.V. was a supreme individualist, a man who would not relinquish his selfhood, even if it meant his soul's perdition. Striking in these works is V.V.'s elation over his own unique personality. V.V. is not masochistic like Dostoevsky's underground man; rather, he is decidedly happy with many aspects of his existence.

Rozanov's voluntarily assumed antiaristocratic stance strengthened the importance of the individual as such, regardless of his class status, in a country where collectivist values and ideas still dominated the traditional Orthodox consciousness. Rozanov's V.V. teaches the cultivation of the individual by example, emphasizing tolerance for even the most eccentric individuals. Through V.V. Rozanov fosters self-explanation, self-analysis, and self-knowledge in the reader, helping him to oppose the pressure of the heroic, restrained, and aristocratic models of literary decorum that had been dominant earlier.

Nevertheless, Rozanov invoked the autobiographical mode for another significant reason. After all, his gossip, homebody, and confessor are not entirely new voices for the educated Russian reader. In fact, they all have antecedents in the nineteenth-century literary tradition. What is new is the autobiographical element—these voices are associated with an actual, living individual, whose name and address are supplied in the text.

Each of Rozanov's voices has easily recognizable antecedents: the gossip is known from Dostoevsky and Leskov; the buffon is clearly Dostoevskian; the confessor, as we have pointed out, has much in common with the underground man; the prophet of doom appears in Lermontov and in various aspects of romantic and contemporary poetry. What is different in Rozanov's trilogy is that these literary masks voice claims to reality—they intermittently claim to be Rozanov. Thus, we have here more than the spectacle of the disintegrating modern ego discussed above. The implication is that the disarray of the self demonstrated through the ''I'' of these texts causes or exemplifies the disjunctive, and ultimately disintegrating, character of Russian literature in the second decade of the twentieth century. The self, which once appeared more orderly and contained as expressed in given literary modes, now gropes at all the available modes simultaneously, unable to fit into any single one, to be identified with the language of any particular form. As a result, voices and styles become intermingled—the high and the low, the aristocratic and the plebian; and, what is more, they are juxtaposed in incongruous ways, causing them to clash and destroy each other's effectiveness. This is what Rozanov with his many selves—as different from himself every minute as he is different from another person—shows is happening *to literature*. He demonstrates this process through literature, claiming that it is happening within the writer V.V. Rozanov; within himself literature is witnessing and experiencing its own death, the disintegration of its old selves. Rozanov used the autobiographical mode to project a self composed entirely of disjointed but recognizable literary voices. As Burckhardt emphasized in his essay on the Renassiance, the individual develops most strongly when there are no set rules for him to follow, when the old standards have been overturned and the new not yet instituted. This is exactly the state of the literary genres in the early years of the twentieth century. It is this situation that enabled Rozanov to say:

> Sometimes it seems that the disintegration of literature is taking place in my work, the disintegration of literature's *very essence*. And perhaps that is my role in the world. Perhaps that accounts for my [peculiar] morality and immorality, for my good points and bad ones. I introduced into literature the most petty, fleeting, and invisible movements of the soul, the spiderwebs of life. But it's absolutely impossible to imagine that I could do this because ''I wanted to.'' What actually happened is much more frightening [for me]: it is endlessly frightening and sad. . . . There was never before a case . . . of a person who at the moment when tears were streaming down his face and his soul was torn—felt with the unerring ear of a listener that the tears were flowing literarily, musically, ''if only I could write this down''—and that is the only reason I did. . . . Clearly in me literature had reached a kind of apogee, the height of literariness, of literature's essence as the need to express and reflect. . . . The essence of literature lies *not in thinking things up* but in the need *to lay the heart bare*. And where this is concerned I am the end and I have brought about the end. And I have a strange premonition that I am the *last writer*, after whom literature in general will cease, except for rubbish which will also stop soon enough. . . . This is perhaps why I am conscious of some ''final disaster'' linked with my ''self'' [ego]. . . . ''The self'' is terrible, disgusting, enormous and tragic with the final tragedy, because in my ''self'' the colossal millenia-old ''self'' of literature has somehow dialectically ''dissolved and disappeared!'' (*Fallen Leaves*, 2:220–21)

CHAPTER 2

Alexey Remizov's Later Autobiographical Prose

Olga Raevsky-Hughes

ALEXEY REMIZOV (1877–1957) was a well-established and influential writer by 1917.[1] Although he never enjoyed wide popularity largely due to his non-belletrist manner, unusual style, and "difficult" language, his influence on the younger generation of writers was of such magnitude that for the period from the 1910s through the 1920s one can speak of a "Remizov school" in Russian prose. Boris Pilniak and Alexey Tolstoy, to mention only two of the most prominent names, considered themselves Remizov's disciples.[2] He was a friend of Alexander Blok and Vsevolod Meyerhold; the latter saw in Remizov's dramatic work a new beginning for the Russian theater. But with the wane of ornamentalist prose in the 1930s Remizov was quickly forgotten. In the emigration the fame of his antipode, the classicist Ivan Bunin, was in ascendance, and in the Soviet Union the "return to Tolstoy" all but obliterated the name of Remizov from public memory.[3]

In 1913, at the age of thirty-six and at what would prove to be the peak of his success, Remizov denied having written any autobiographical works and at the same time, rather paradoxically, insisted that everything he wrote was about himself.[4] Coming from a prose writer whose collected works included

[1] A different version of this essay, titled "Volshebnaja skazka v knige A. Remizova *Iveren'*," was published in *Aleksej Remizov: Approaches to a Protean Writer*, UCLA Slavic Studies 16 (Los Angeles: Slavica, 1987).

[2] See for instance Alex M. Shane, "An Introduction to Alexei Remizov," *The Bitter Air of Exile: Russian-Writers in the West, 1922–1972*, ed. Simon Karlinsky and Alfred Appel, Jr. (Berkeley: University of California Press, 1977). See also: Gleb Struve, *Russian Literature Under Lenin and Stalin, 1917–1953* (Norman: University of Oklahoma Press, 1971); Alex M. Shane, *The Life and Works of Evgenij Zamjatin* (Berkeley: University of California Press, 1968); Peter Alberg Jensen, *Nature as Code: The Achievement of Boris Pilnjak, 1915–1924* (Copenhagen: Rosenkilde and Bagger, 1979).

[3] See Vladimir Markov, "Neizvestnyj pisatel' Remizov," *Aleksej Remizov: Approaches to a Protean Writer*.

[4] "Avtobiograficheskikh proizvedenij u menja net. Vse i vo vsem avtobiografija—i mertvets Borodin ('Zhertva')—ja samyj i est', sebja ja opisyvaju, i Pet'ka ('Petushok') tozhe ja." A. M. Remizov, "Avtobiografija, 1913" (Fair copy in the Remizov Archive in the State Public Library, Leningrad: GPB, fond 634, no. 1). I am grateful to Greta N. Slobin for providing me with a copy of this text.

several volumes of short stories and novels[5] this statement is something of a surprise. But with the passing of years it was not the author of narrative fiction but the other Remizov, the one who retold legends and fairy tales and wrote lyric prose, who took over. In his late autobiographical book *Splinter* (*Iveren'*, 1986)[6] he declares himself to be a "singer of songs" not a novelist. This provides a clue to Remizov's prolonged search for his true genre, for the first twenty years of his long professional life can be described as an attempt to discover a literary form that would free him from the constraints of traditional genres.[7] His professed break with traditional form was, without doubt, an expression of the spirit of the times but at the same time had deeper roots in Remizov's opposition to the classical literary Russian tradition and language of Pushkin, Turgenev, and Tolstoy.

Remizov had a natural affinity with writers whose language, both lexically and syntactically, was dominated by oral modes of communication. This inclination was defended by Remizov throughout his life as a conscious and deliberate choice. Among those whom he considered his predecessors are Gogol, Leskov, and, most significantly, Avvakum. In *Splinter* Remizov's belonging to the "minor" line in Russian literature and his conscious opposition to the main, classical line is made explicit in the author's encounter with Briusov, who according to Remizov rejected his prose as too colorful (231–36). Remizov sees this as a rejection by the literary establishment, which is obviously an overstatement since he was part of the literary life of his times and was widely published during the period.

Except for the retelling of fairy tales and legends and the narratives based on his wife's life, Remizov's major output during the last thirty-five years of his life was autobiographical prose.[8] This prose cannot be classified as either memoirs or reminiscences, nor is it autobiography in the narrow sense of the word. It is a "story" of his life, but the narration is deliberately achronologi-

[5] His collection of works in eight volumes was published in 1908–1910. See Hélène Sinany, *Bibliographie des oeuvres de Alexis Remizov* (Paris: Insititut d'études slaves, 1978); see also additions to the bibliography by Horst Lampl in *Wiener Slawistischer Almanach* 2 (1978): 301–26.

[6] Published as volume 7 in the series *Modern Russian Literature and Culture: Studies and Texts* (Berkeley: Berkeley Slavic Specialities, 1986), ed., introd., and commentary by Olga Raevsky-Hughes. Page references to this edition are given in the text. *Iveren'* is a rare Russian word and is defined in the dictionary of Vladmir Dal' (*Tolkovyj slovar' velikorusskogo jazyka*) as "fragment."

[7] He started publishing in 1902; his last book, *Circle of Happiness* (*Krug schast'ja*), appeared in 1957, the year of his death. Several volumes were published during his lifetime.

[8] In "An Introduction to Alexei Remizov," *The Bitter Air of Exile*, Shane divides Remizov's work into two categories, derivative and nonderivative. The derivative consists of folktales and legends of both literary and folkloric origin retold in a particularly Remizovian way; the nonderivative encompasses his long and short fiction, lyric prose, dreams, and biographical and autobiographical narratives.

cal; carefully chosen episodes attain special meaning, becoming symbols of his life and destiny.

Remizov's selectiveness goes beyond the expected "selective memory" of a memoirist; there is a design in the choice of facts narrated, and those details of his life that he chooses to talk about attain disproportionate significance. In the introduction to *With Clipped Eyes* (*Podstrizhennymi glazami*, 1951), the high point of Remizov's idiosyncratic genre, he takes the reader into his confidence—explaining that the choice and meaning of the episodes narrated are not external: "To write a book of 'knots and twists' [of memory] is to write more than one's own life dated according to a birth certificate, such a book is going to be about that 'which I cannot forget.' "[9] Interpretation is far more important than the facts themselves, and factual biography is transformed into fiction.

The prologue to *With Clipped Eyes* is a good example of the variety of material included and the associative process that makes Remizov choose certain facts. It is an account of those unforgettable moments that shaped his life. The sound of Moscow's bells in the city of his birth and childhood blends with an image of destitution in Paris, the city where he lived the last thirty-three years of his life. Traditional liturgical singing in the Kremlin Dormition Cathedral appears side by side with his "all-encompassing fear"—fear of crossing streets and bridges: "I fear automobiles, buses, tramcars, trolleys and horses, which are so rare in Paris."[10] The list continues with fear of fires and of being late, of strangers and acquaintances, and ends on a contrasting note of the incomparable joy of experiencing a storm at sea. Among other "knots and twists" is the memory of leaving Russia the day Blok died[11] and of a bird nesting in a plane tree outside his window in Paris. The litany of the unforgettable moments, introduced with the refrain "How could I forget" ("I razve mogu zabyt' "), ends with an evocation of the names of Avvakum, Gogol, and Leskov, the writers to whose language and style Remizov considered himself an heir.

In the course of the narration his creative memory constantly takes him beyond the limits of personal biography. He is not confined chronologically or thematically but moves freely from the story of his life to a discussion of literature; his friends and acquaintances float in and out of his pages. By switching to his circumstances at the time of writing, Remizov constantly reminds the reader of the temporal perspective.

In his autobiographical prose Remizov ranges from vague personal associations, as in *Along the Cornices* (*Po karnizam*, 1929), to a quite precise ac-

[9] *Podstrizhennymi glazami* (Paris: YMCA Press, 1951), 5.

[10] Ibid., 9–10.

[11] Actually, Remizov and his wife left Russia on August 5, 1921, two days before Blok's death, but Remizov repeatedly and consistently connected his departure with the death of Blok—a good example of reinterpreting biographical facts and assigning symbolic significance to them.

count of a specific period in his life in *Splinter*. Dream sequences, which were an indispensable part of his art from the very beginning, continue to play a major role in his autobiographical prose. In *Russia in a Whirlwind* (*Vzvikhrennaja Rus'*, 1927) the use of dreams reflects the indescribable reality of the revolutionary years in Petrograd. The author's contemporaries and friends, who inhabit the book in large numbers, migrate with great ease from reality to dream and back; some appear only in dreams. In *Along the Cornices* factual reality appears as most distant and unreal. This book provides the best illustration of Remizov's view of the relation of the two: dreams are not to be separated from reality. It is more than a literary device; it is an attempt to convey the author's experience of the interpenetration of dream and reality.[12] Dreams allow Remizov's memory to go through "reincarnations": in *Splinter* his inspired memory ranges from the Arab calligraphers to Boileau. The tribute to his predecessors emphasizes his love of writing, of the art of a scribe who preserves culture, the common memory of the people, from oblivion.

Just as he blends fact and fiction, Remizov brings play into serious accounts. His early *Kukkha* (*Kukkha*, 1923), although written in the form of an address to his close and by then deceased friend the philosopher and writer Vasily Rozanov, is full of mischief.[13] So in a certain sense is *A Flute for Mice* (*Myshkina dudochka*, 1953), despite the fact that its chronological framework encompasses the grim years of World War II and the Nazi occupation of Paris.[14] The time frame for *Kukkha* is the revolution of 1905; the selection of material included is influenced by Rozanov. But Remizov shared Rozanov's predilection for the insignificant and the everyday and, in paying tribute to his famous friend, he manages to tell quite a lot about himself.

Russia in a Whirlwind, published in book form only in 1927, narrates the author's experiences during the years of the Revolution and Civil War in Petrograd. The text blends the specific and subjective with the general and public. Paradoxically, the apparently limited view of his own apartment and the details of the hardships of life during the years of War Communism allow Remizov to penetrate the essence of developments in Russia at the time. Osten-

---

[12] *Martyn Zadeka* (Paris: Opleshnik, 1954), 8.

[13] See L. S. Fleishman, "Iz kommentariev k 'Kukkhe'. Konkrektor Obezvelvolpala," *Slavica Hierosolymitana* 1 (Jerusalem, 1977): 185–93.

[14] Another book to appear in the early 1950s was *In Rosy Shimmer* (*V rozovom bleske*) (New York: Chekhov Publishing House, 1952), a tribute to Remizov's wife Serafima Pavlovna Dovgello, who died in May 1943. This volume includes a section titled "Through the Fire of Sorrows," an account of the war years and his wife's long and incapacitating illness and death. But since Remizov gives detailed accounts of their everyday existence, the somber subject for the most part remains in the background. Descriptions of the evening reading sessions allow him to talk about literature. Daily visitors bring the news of the world beyond the confines of their house and provide a humorous touch. The awesome responsibility and the dreadful loneliness of the spouse destined to survive is depicted through the narrator's communication with a mouse that regularly appears in the kitchen "to help with the dishes."

sibly preoccupied with trivia, *Russia in a Whirlwind* is one of the most profound accounts of the Russian Revolution written by a contemporary. By focusing on the insignificant and unheroic, Remizov is able to show the irreversible change that the Revolution brought to the very fabric of Russian life, not in matters of state and ideology but in the life of each and every individual. A mask of jocosity is only a mask. (How does one talk about everyday chores that are not a matter of choice but a question of survival?)

In *Splinter*, as elsewhere, Remizov is both chronicler-scribe and oral narrator-singer. As a chronicler he registers exact dates and names, trying to fix the past in its most minute details, and as an improvising singer he organizes the text rhythmically, using alliterations and refrains and introducing a lyrical strain.

In a manner similar to Old Russian scribes, Remizov introduces a basic text in different collections and books, often creating new versions to fit new contexts. In this the "scribe" is supported by the "teller of tales" who freely varies—expands and contracts—a given text.

Splinter, Remizov's last autobiographical narrative to be published posthumously, covers the period from 1896 to 1903, the years of the author's arrest and exile for his revolutionary activity as a student.[15] This is also the time when Remizov began to write professionally: he appeared in print for the first time in 1902. Remizov did not succeed in publishing *Splinter* in the 1950s, when it was written. In describing it to one of his correspondents, he called it "the simplest of all my books."[16] This statement, although partly meant to counteract the firmly established view of his books as incomprehensible and hence unpublishable, does describe *Splinter* correctly. Compared with the intricately structured *Russia in a Whirlwind*[17] or thematically and chronologically diverse *Music Teacher, Splinter* appears simpler and more obviously co-

[15] The other two are *Encounters* (*Vstrechi*) (Paris: Lev, 1981), the author's title for which was [*Petersburg Gully*] (*Peterburgskij buerak*), and *Music Teacher* (*Uchitel' muzyki*) (Paris: La Presse Libre, 1983). The first comes closest to "memoirs" in the strict sense of the term, for, although many episodes of the author's experiences as a beginning writer in Petersburg are narrated here, to a large extent it is concerned with encounters with famous personalities. It includes sections on Fedor Shaliapin, Maxim Gorky, Alexander Blok, Sergey Diagilev, and Vasily Rozanov.

The pastiche nature of his autobiographical prose reaches its highest point in *Music Teacher*. The narrator appears under different names and at various points is identified with different fictitious characters. On the composition and history of writing *Music Teacher*, see Antonella d'Amelia, " 'Avtobiograficheskoe prostranstvo' Alekseja Mikhajlovicha Remizova" and "K istorii sozdanija 'Uchitelja muzyki'," *Uchitel' muzyki*, i–xxxiii and 555–67, respectively.

[16] *Natal'ja Kodrjanskaja, Remizov v svoikh pis'makh* (Paris, 1977), 352. Remizov's letters to Kodrjanskaja chronicle his work on the book in the late 1940s and early 1950s. On his attempts to publish *Iveren'*, see his letters of 1953–1954 to Yurij Elagin in Yurij Elagin, *Temnyj genij* (*Vsevolod Mejerkhol'd*), 2nd ed. (London: Overseas Publishing Interchange Ltd., 1982), 419, 420–21.

[17] On the composition of *Vzvikhrennaja Rus'*, see Hélène Sinany-McLeod, "Strukturnaja kompozitsija *Vzvikhrennoj Rusi*" in *Aleksej Remizov: Approaches to a Protean Writer*.

herent, as it covers a well-defined chronological span. But this most obvious aspect of the book is governed by something far more significant for Remizov: a definition of his place in Russian literature. This is not the first time that he treats the subject.

In *Splinter* Remizov reiterates his place in the minor line of Russian literature by sketching his literary genealogy. Through Gogol, Dostoevsky, and Veltman this leads to Bulgarin and Dal as representatives of the natural school. From Gogol he inherits the fantastic and the fairy tale, from Dostoevsky the acute perception of human suffering. In the varied literary output of Veltman, Remizov singles out linguistic and stylistic elements congenial to him.[18] The mention of Dal is not surprising for, like Dal, Remizov defended the "Russian manner" ("russkij lad"), by which he meant word order, and looked for it both in old texts and in colloquial speech.

But that Bulgarin is on the list of literary predecessors comes as a surprise, if not a shock. This, at least partially, is the author's intention. But it is also a testimony of Remizov's unfailing and faithful literary memory. Bulgarin, a writer and a journalist whose name brings to mind not his works but his service in the secret police and his vicious attacks on what was best in the Russian literature of his time, was also the author of "physiological sketches" and the first to use the term "natural school," albeit in the negative sense.[19]

The mention of the natural school gives Remizov a chance to change from author and protagonist into literary character, here a minor Petersburg civil servant. This provides a clue to the relationship of author to character—"an aspiring writer Remizov," he is author and character at the same time. The author looks back at the character from a fifty-year perspective, while the young writer still lives in the aged Remizov.

Frequently the protagonist's thoughts appear to be those of insignificant civil servants like Gogol's Akaky Akakievich or Dostoevsky's Goliadkin, reflecting a desire not to attract attention, to live quietly, and to be on one's own.[20] The author becomes one of the oppressed and the downtrodden: in *Splinter* he is accused of being a police informer and does not defend himself. The autobiographer assumes the role of a fictional character and merges with Dostoevsky's poor clerk. In the end he is exonerated, for his accusers realize their mistake. The ridiculousness of false accusation and his poor-clerk response are made clear at another point in the story when, upon being accused of stealing the silver spoons, he almost feels responsible for their disappearance. The self-denigration of the protagonist of *Splinter* is a consistent and conscious literary position of Remizov the writer. Remizov liked to stress that

[18] Among the features that Remizov shares with Veltman are the mixing of the imaginary and the real, irony and the grotesque, and above all his remarkable knowledge of and dependence on spoken language.

[19] See *Kratkaja literaturnaja entsiklopedija* 1 (Moscow, 1962), col. 770.

[20] *Iveren'*, 31; see also Natal'ja Kodrjanskaja, *Aleksej Remizov* (Paris, 1959), 87.

he was never accepted as an equal by his fellow writers. Emphasizing this nonrecognition, he paradoxically declares that he is not a "real" writer, as opposed to the recognized and the successful.

His literary fate and biography come together in this book as he searches for the first signs of the writer Remizov in the willful young student and exile. He discusses his cultural and literary roots and comments—with passion—on the development of Russian literary language.

Beneath the story of his exile, his beginnings as a writer, and his meeting with fellow exiles[21] is perceived one of Remizov's permanent themes—his musings on the fate of man. Fatalistic acceptance of one's destiny clashes with a desire to live according to one's will (po svoej vole). One of the masks that the narrator uses in *Splinter* is a hero of a fairy tale. The classical attributes of this character will allow Remizov to combine the fate that cannot be changed with free choice.

The title *Splinter* in context refers both to a wayward member of a family and to a writer who does not follow a traditional path but chooses his own. At one point this title was almost abandoned in favor of that of the longest chapter in the book, "Nomad" ("Kochevnik"),[22] which covers the period from Christmas of 1896 to the summer of 1900—Remizov's exile in Penza and his thirteen dwellings in that city. Nomadic existence is indeed what the whole book is about: an exile is homeless by definition. Exiled as a student, he returns as a professional writer, which in Remizov's interpretation makes him homeless by profession.[23] During his forced peregrinations in the Russian north he becomes a permanent nomad. And in a way his early experience of the life of a nomad—an exile—foretells his thirty-six years of emigré life.

Remizov's inclusion of diverse and seemingly unrelated stories in a single book and his practice of publishing individual chapters as separate stories and then incorporating the same material in different books may suggest that the material is arranged randomly. This, however, is far from true. In *Splinter* the organization of material plays a decisive role.[24] In narrating the story of his exile and his birth as a writer, Remizov follows the structure of a fairy tale.[25]

---

[21] Most prominent among those are the future philosopher Nicholay Berdiaev, the famous Socialist-Revolutionary terrorist Boris Savinkov, and future Commissar of Education and Culture in the Soviet Union Anatoly Lunacharsky.

[22] Kodrjanskaja, *Aleksej Remizov*, 87.

[23] Viktor Shklovsky called Remizov a nomad who as an innovative writer is forever homeless: "As a cow eats up the grass, so literary themes are eaten up and literary devices become worn out and threadbare. A writer cannot become a farmer, he is a nomad who moves to new pasture with his herd and his wife." V. Shklovskij, *Zoo, ili pis'ma ne o ljubvi, Sobranie sochinenij v trekh tomakh* (Moscow, 1973), 1:182.

[24] Remizov described the process of composing his books as building: "I am constructing my book" (*stroju moju knigu*). The order of chapters in *Splinter* is carefully reiterated in his letters of the period.

[25] See V. Ja. Propp, *Morfologija skazki* (Moscow: Nauka, 1969); E. M. Meletinskij, S. Ju.

The very appearance of the protagonist is marked by unusual signs. The youngest in the family, he is born on the "magic" night of June 24, the summer solstice and St. John's Eve, the night when according to legend the rare flower of the fern blooms and shows the daring the way to hidden treasure. His magic, "clipped" eyes[26] are open to the hidden and the mysterious, but this gift is offset by his mother's curse, which "casts a dark and bitter shadow over [his] soul" (16).[27]

The hero of a fairy tale usually has rather unprepossessing beginnings and is not distinguished by good looks.[28] The narrator in *Splinter* comments on his own unattractive appearance; his eyes are like buttons, he is nearly a dwarf and a hunchback, and he stutters (12, 52). Other characters also mention his unusual appearance. In the anguished loneliness of his exile his peculiarity is transformed from bad luck or unattractiveness into something loftier: his unusual destiny. Now he begins to see himself as a chosen one, a person with a unique destiny: "I have wandered off so far from the usual world, and what looks rosy to you is neither rosy nor blue to me, it has its own color and flavor, its own fragrance and voice. I live in a different world, and my sorrow and anguish are not yours, I am free from any fetters—'this is permitted' and 'that is prohibited' " (96).

As befits the protagonist of a fairy tale, the narrator has not yet settled on a profession. Not able to make up his mind at the university, he works simultaneously in natural science, philosophy, and law. Before the onset of his wanderings the protagonist is cast out of his world by a senior member of his family. For a formal evening party, a reunion of his graduating class, he dresses "his own way"—wearing an informal red shirt with a royal blue jacket. This unusual and colorful costume nearly causes a scandal when his uncle, a respected chairman of the board of trustees and benefactor of the school, arrives on the scene. The hero is driven out; he finds himself alone on a dark, snowy street outside the warm and brightly lit school building where his peers continue to enjoy the reunion. But soon after his public humiliation the hero is reminded of his "supernatural" powers. As he leaves the school building, the thought of setting it on fire flickers through his mind. In the morning the newspapers bring news of a fire that had broken out in the building that very night.

The episode of expulsion is narrated just before the beginning of his wanderings. Remizov prefers to see it as a symbol of his life in general: exile and

---

Nekljudov, E. S. Novik, D. M. Segal, "Problemy strukturnogo opisanija volshebnoj skazki," *Trudy po znakovym sistemam* 4 (Tartu, 1969).

[26] Remizov explained that his "clipped" eyes did not see less than the eyes of average people but more, for it was not the ability to see that was clipped but that which limited vision.

[27] He was the fifth child in the family, and after his birth his mother left his father.

[28] See E. M. Meletinskij, "Nizkij geroj volshebnoj skazki," *Geroj volshebnoj skazki* (Moscow: Nauka, 1958).

loneliness are the price he pays for his willfulnless, for going his own way. His arrest, which follows soon after, is described as a result of a misunderstanding, since at that time he apparently did not take part in any organized revolutionary activity. Once exiled to Penza, however, he throws himself into revolutionary propaganda with a vengeance, so his second arrest over a year later is not unexpected.

The "Nomad" chapter is first of all a story of his inability to manage his day-to-day existence, a theme familiar from his other works. In this case, it is inability to find a suitable dwelling; while in Penza he moves thirteen times. This is the first stage of his travels to the land of midnight sun—as Remizov calls Ust-Sysolsk, the northernmost point of his exile—which corresponds to the underworld of the fairy tale. The descent begins in Penza: his first dwelling is a room in a garret, and by the time of his arrest he lives in a basement.

The shortcomings and limitations of his numerous lodgings in Penza all point to prison: in one place he suffers from cold, in the next from a monotonous diet; in a boarding house he is starving; one lodging has severely limited space, its half-window located near the ceiling; in the next the window looks out onto a wall; and a room with entry through a window necessarily limits access to his quarters, which are devoid of all amenities. When he settles "behind the curtain" his friends stop visiting him, for there is no way of reaching him without disturbing another tenant. The lodging in which the narrator is arrested is hardly distinguishable from a prison cell: it is a half-empty basement room. At this point his revolutionary activity is at its peak, and as a precaution he does not have any visitors. "In the Basement" is the last stage before the final descent into the underworld—he will spend over a year in prison. His attempt at revolutionary activity, at working with people, has ended in disaster. This is not for him; his path is different and lonely.

Although it is mostly the shortcomings of his dwellings that force him to move, once in a new place he invariably regrets having abandoned the old. This underscores the consistent worsening of his circumstances. The chapter ends with the narrator's departure for an exile more distant and more severe, so his exclamation "And suddenly, for the first time in many years, I felt free" (153) comes as a surprise. This apparently paradoxical statement is justified, however, because the liberation he experiences is internal. It is a turning point and a new beginning: the revolutionary dies in the Penza prison, the writer is to be born in Ust-Sysolsk.

In the central chapter, "In the Damp Mists," the protagonist is the farthest removed from his world; he finds himself in the land of the midnight sun and polar night. In this underworld he comes face to face with spirits and sprites, the ability to discern whom he received at birth. The brief introduction to this chapter sets its tone. The narrator finds himself in the "enchanted land," but the beauty of the land only enhances his anguish. The author now manifests himself both as scribe and reciter of tales. The two fundamental aspects of his art are brought together naturally, for he narrates "in his own way" a largely forgotten story by the Russian romantic writer Orest Somov.[29] In this chapter there are many literary reminiscences: allusions to Russian romanticism pave the way for the fantastic story that follows. Just as in his versions of old legends, Remizov introduces the fantastic and magical into the contemporary and everyday.

The story, concerning the narrator's landlady and her family, begins with a fairy-tale formula. There are three daughters in the family: the eldest, a teacher, stands for the contemporary and the rational; the middle one represents the natural and possesses an animal-like innocence; and the youngest— to fit the fairy-tale scheme—is unlike the other two, a sleepwalker singled out by a sprite of Russian folkloric demonology, *kikimora*. Having unusual sensitivity, this daughter represents the otherworldly in man. In the end the chosen one dies smothered by the kisses of a *kikimora*.

Imprisonment in Penza and exile in Ust-Sysolsk correspond to the underworld of the fairy tale, whence the hero returns victorious, having passed the initiation. Released from prison, Remizov feels like "someone from another world" (141). The land of the damp mists is the point from which the protagonist's physical return begins. Now he moves from the northeast to the southwest. The next stage is Vologda.

Here Remizov, who started writing from prison, for the first time finds himself in the company of contemporaries who are also beginning writers. The history of the publication of his first work, the prose poem "A Lament of a Maiden Before her Marriage," is given in great detail. This is the point where he realizes that he is a writer and begins work on his first novel.

Although the early twenties of one's life are usually years of intensive development of personal and professional identity and so naturally fit into the scheme of wandering and initiation, Remizov's biography supplies ample material for the coincidence of the two: his search for self-identification and self-expression as a writer coincided with his exile and enforced travels in a faraway land. The narration is studded with fairy-tale details that are hardly accidental.

In a section titled "On Fowl's Legs," a usual attribute of the witch's hut in Russian fairy tales, the lady of the house has the role of the hero's generalized antagonist. This grandmother stands for all those characters in the story who persecute or simply do not appreciate the hero, from local authorities to established writers and fellow exiles. Her function is suggested in the description of her house; there are numerous references to her hut as that of Baba-Yaga: it stands by itself, hardly visible in the daytime, but under moonlight it rotates to welcome a visitor or keep him away, or it disappears altogether. She is suspicious of the hero from the start; he settles in her house during her ab-

---

[29] "Kikimora" in O. M. Somov, *Byli i nebylitsy* (Moscow: Sovetskaja Rossija, 1984).

sence, on the invitation of her grandson. On returning she accuses the hero of stealing the silver spoons and expels him from the house. The translation of the fairy-tale function of the villain into present-day terms is not without humor: it is not only a false but an obviously absurd, "classic" accusation.

Among the fairy-tale elements are the introduction of characters in twos and threes. Historical personages are introduced with fairy-tale formulas and mythological designations: "Once upon a time there lived in Vologda three titans," "two Herculeses," and "in Moscow two demons." Triple appearances continue: "During that year [1902] there appeared three new names in Russian literature and all three under a pseudonym" (211). Remizov's friends, assuming the role of intermediaries, approach *three* famous writers (Gorky, Korolenko, and Chekhov) with his first stories.

The intervention of helpers is not limited to this instance. In "Nomad" his fellow exiles find new lodgings for him and transport him from one room to the next by almost miraculous means. The narrator stresses his own passivity: "How could I have given notice, when, whether I like it or not, I have been taken like a kitten by the scruff of the neck and thrust into 'paradise at Mrs. Tjapkin's?' " (71). In Vologda the hero's helpers are historical personages: his fellow exiles Boris Savinkov and Pavel Shchegolev intercede with the authorities in order to prevent his return to Ust-Sysolsk. Like a fairy-tale hero, the protagonist does not make decisions, he is passive: exiled, transferred, moved, or saved either by his friends or by the police.

The unrecognized arrival of the protagonist, traditional for the fairy tale, is presented here as a joke. During his first unauthorized visit to Moscow, in order to disguise himself, Remizov is wearing a uniform of the Penza Surveying School. The effect is contrary to the desired one, for he attracts attention by the oversized uniform. On seeing him, his mother exclaims: "Why are you dressed like a scarecrow? One can pick you out easily even in disguise!" (92–93). In his letters of the early 1950s Remizov speaks of *Splinter* as a history of the contemporary with the mark of Cain, which is reminiscent of the fairy-tale branding that allows the princess to recognize the hero. It is his whimsical behavior and unconventionality as a writer that doom him to loneliness, which he chooses to interpret as the fate of an outcast.

In the fairy tale the hero, after passing the initiation, marries the princess and ascends the throne. In *Splinter* there are many female characters, but without exception they are minor. The eventual winning of the princess, his muse, is intimated in a dream long before his exile. It is a prophetic dream, the first since getting glasses at age fourteen caused him to lose the fantastic world of his myopic childhood and to discover the human world. In this dream a female figure—her green hair blown about her head without any wind—emerges from the woods and approaches the hero. She is silent, but he recognizes her as a forest sprite (lesavka) and hears her silent call. She offers him an apple of gold and honey; upon taking it into his hands he experiences an upsurge of words that roll like sea waves and leave him in a state of ecstasy (23). In this prophetic dream the forest sprite offers him a magical object that indicates the course he will pursue in reality.

On the train that takes the hero to his exile he meets a woman for the first time since his imprisonment. This encounter serves as a reminder of the forest sprite with the magic apple: the woman's water-sprite eyes reveal details of a misunderstanding that in his opinion helped get his first work published: the unknown author of "A Lament of a Maiden Before Her Marriage," concealed by a pseudonym, was taken for a woman.

Finally the hero, having passed the tests and received the reward, returns to the world from which he was expelled. He is not a passive character anymore; he now freely chooses his own way. Despite the misfortunes of his life that he liked to emphasize—not being accepted by the literary establishment, not having a wide audience, living as an emigré not being able to publish his books—at the end of his life he can say with conviction: "I have lived a full life that one can envy—consider only this: I write, and read, and draw only for my own pleasure, never on orders and nothing 'required'—but this also was difficult: all my life was like a steep staircase"(17).

. . .

Splinter is different in tone from *Music Teacher*, an autobiographical book about his life in emigration written mainly before World War II but finished only in 1949. It is a more sober book. Although one finds many misunderstandings and everyday mishaps, there are fewer complaints: the author accepts his fate as a free choice.

An unseemly informal costume worn on a formal occasion causes his expulsion from a ball of his graduating class just before his first arrest and exile. Remizov describes in great detail and with obvious relish his glowing "recognizes" him (53). Nor are his first steps in Penza devoid of the magical. Since he arrives there late on Christmas Eve, the connection with Nikolay Gogol's early story of that name is only logical. Remizov never failed to emphasize his debt to Gogol and, indeed, remained throughout his life under the spell of Gogol's verbal magic.[30]

His dream during his first night in Penza transforms the lady of the house where he is staying, the attractive and formidable mother of his fellow prisoner in Moscow, into a sad and ineffable witch. He snatches the willow stick that the witch leaves behind and flies after the sleigh in which she departed. He flies "faster than the wind and swifter than the moon." The witch and nocturnal flight are reminiscent of the Gogol story. The forest sprite, the fellow pas-

---

[30] Remizov devoted a large part of a book on dreams in Russian literature, *The Fire of Things* (*Ogon' veshchej*) (Paris: Opleshnik, 1954), to Gogol.

senger with the eyes of a water sprite, and the mysterious and sad witch in Penza all prefigure the young writer's muse. Remizov leaves Vologda not only with his first works in print but with a draft of his first novel in hand.[31]

During his exile the hero is persecuted not only by local police but by the literary establishment. His early stories are rejected by famous writers, but he does not give in and is not destroyed by a "hostile creature" from a fairy tale. At this stage he is aided by magic helpers—the demons, as he dubs the representatives of the new art (Leonid Andreyev and Valery Briusov)—and his works appear in print. His magical female helper has her hand in this also. Remizov narrates in a great red shirt and bright blue jacket. The episode becomes a symbol of his life: he pays for breaking with tradition by becoming an outcast. The vivid and under the circumstances unusual colors that signify his own unique path are reminiscent of Avvakum, who in his "Life" ("Zhitie") describes a vision of his own life as a multicolored ship that to him looked more attractive than pure gold.[32] In both instances this image is placed just prior to the peregrinations, literal and metaphorical, that are the subject of each book. Like Avvakum, whom Remizov admired not only for his native Russian language but for his steadfastness and faithfulness to his views, he follows his chosen path to the end. At the outset his unfitting attire causes his ouster from the society of his peers; later in his professional life it is his unfitting language and style that lead to his estrangement from the literary establishment.

Splinter can be seen as Remizov's professional credo not only because exploring his literary beginnings gives him a chance to reiterate the principles that guided him through his literary career but because thematically and stylistically the book is a microcosm of his art as a whole.

Literary problems in the narrow sense do not exhaust the book's significance. The protagonist is surrounded by his contemporaries, who were to play significant roles in the social and the intellectual upheavals of the twentieth century. Looking back at himself in that context, the old Remizov muses on human fate: "No wars or revolutions can change [human fate]" (278) and "historic precedent does not teach" (276). The clash of fatalism with the affirmation of free will forms a deep philosophical undercurrent in *Splinter*, so it is proper that the beginning and the end of the book invoke the names of the two twentieth-century philosophers, Lev Shestov and Vasily Rozanov, who were Remizov's personal friends.

[31] *The Pond* (*Prud*) (1908). See the history of the writing and a detailed analysis of the novel in the forthcoming book by Greta N. Slobin, *Remizov's Fictions: 1900–1925*.

[32] "A se potom vizhu tretej korabl', ne zlatom ukrashen, no raznymi krasotami ispeshchren—krasno, i belo, i sine, i cherno, i pepeleso,—ego zhe um chelovech' ne vmestit krasoty ego i dobroty. Junosha svetel, na korme sidja, pravit. . . . I ja vskrichal: 'Chej korabl'?' I sidjaj na nem otveshchal: 'Tvoj korabl'. Na, plavaj na nem'." *Pustozerskij sbornik. Avtografy sochinenij Avvakuma i Epifanija* (Leningrad: Nauka, 1975), 19.

Splinter can be seen as a book of memory. It tries to sum up, to make a last statement: in addition to the men whom he met while in exile, Remizov introduces those who were a part of his life as a man and a writer. This is why the unknown exiles with whom he shared lodgings in Penza appear side by side with Berdiaev, Savinkov, and Lunacharsky and Rozanov and Shestov alongside Avvakum, Gogol, and Dostoevsky.

CHAPTER 3

Andrey Bely's Memories of Fiction

Charlene Castellano

THE GENESIS OF BELY'S MEMOIRS IN HIS MEMORIES OF A PASSIONATE
  FRIENDSHIP

Andrey Bely (pseudonym of Boris N. Bugaev, 1880–1934) never enjoyed
fame as a popular writer. He did, however, achieve great notoriety during his
lifetime among the literati of Moscow and Petersburg. His wildly idiosyncratic
experiments in literary form and his strangely ebullient essays in esoteric literary criticism sometimes earned him respect, sometimes rage, but always an
audience of the finest literary minds of his nation. Novelist Evgeny Zamyatin,
for example, pronounced Bely "a writer's writer, a master" of the novel, "a
Russian Joyce."[1] But poet Osip Mandelstam diagnosed him "a sick and negative phenomenon in the life of the Russian language."[2] Applying all manner
of epithets, from "barbaric failure" to "unprecedented genius,"[3] the literary
community was intrigued by Bely's undissuaded efforts to forge—virtually
singlehandedly—both a theory and a praxis for Russian symbolists.

  The scope of Bely's goals, along with the cacophonous critical response to
his irrepressible strivings, have by now made Bely something of a literary
institution among scholars in the Soviet Union and the West. The motley efforts exerted by Bely's contemporaries to assess his contributions first to world
culture and then, after the Bolshevik Revolution, to Soviet culture, never
achieved consensus. Although the subject was strictured under Stalin's regime, which was suspicious of Bely's singular personality and eccentric

---

[1] Evgenij Zamjatin, "Andrey Bely," *Litsa* (New York: Inter-Language Literary Associates,
1967), 76 and 80. Available in translation by Mirra Ginsburg, *A Soviet Heretic: Essays by Ye-
vgeny Zamyatin* (Chicago: University of Chicago Press, 1970), 241–45.

[2] Osip Mandelstam, "O prirode slova," vol. 2 of *Sobranie sochinenij v trekh tomakh* (New
York: Inter-Language Literary Associates, 1971), 246–47.

[3] These conflicting judgments were both passed by Nikolaj Gumilev and are discussed by Gleb
Struve in "Andrey Bely Redivivus" in *Andrey Bely: A Critical Review*, ed. Gerald Janecek (Lexington: University Press of Kentucky, 1978), 32–33. As Struve points out, evidence of Gumilev's
mixed feelings about Bely appears in his "Review of Bely's *Urna*" in vol. 4 of *Sobranie sochinenij v chetyrekh tomakh* (Washington, D.C.: Victor Kamkin, 1968), 205–6. It is there that Gumilev writes that "Bely quickly mastered all the fine points of contemporary versification and
technique: this is how a barbarian learns at once that fish is not eaten with a knife." In citing this
review Struve adds that Gumilev's friend Nikolai Otsup once wrote that Gumilev used to say of
Bely: "This was a man endowed with genius, but he managed to ruin it."

works, the works continued to elicit commentary, some friendly and some disdainful, from writers and critics living in emigration in Europe. Curiosity about Bely seeped out of emigré enclaves when scattered translations and scholarly works by these same people began to appear in European presses in the 1940s and 1950s and in American presses in the 1960s. As Bely came to be better appreciated as prime mover in the development of Russian symbolism, Soviet scholars found in him an embarrassment of riches rewarding their own subsequent research and publications. Their studies have paralleled the continuing efforts among Western scholars to assess Bely's achievements.[4]

The achievements were many. Bely was a prodigious writer who experimented prolifically in many genres, and, as scholarship continues to reveal, he brought some noteworthy innovation to each of the forms in which he worked. In poetry it was his rhythmic inventiveness, sound orchestration, and unusual graphic layout that set Bely apart from his contemporaries.[5] In the criticism of poetry Bely was the first in Russia to elaborate a formal method for analyzing metrics.[6] In his novels Bely put the poetic technique of synesthesia to innovative use in organizing time and plot structure.[7] Finally, in his

[4] The best commentaries on research performed through the 1960s and early 1970s are found in John E. Malmstad, "The Poetry of Andrej Belyj: A Variorum Edition" (Ph.D. diss., Princeton University, 1968), i–xi (also published as *Stikhotvorenija*, ed. John E. Malmstad, 3 vols. [Munich, 1982–84]) and Struve, "Redivivus," 21–43. An international bibliography of Bely materials published since 1964 appeared in *The Andrej Belyj Society Newsletter*, no. 2 (1983) and is updated annually. This yearly newsletter also contains book reviews and abstracts of papers delivered at society meetings. For further information, contact Olga Muller Cooke, Department of Modern Languages, Texas A & M University, College Station, Texas 77843. A renewed momentum in Soviet studies of Bely was marked by the 1981 "Literaturnye pamjatniki" edition of Bely's novel *Petersburg* (Moscow: Nauka Press), which is supplemented with archival materials, histories, and commentaries edited by L. K. Dolgopolov and D. S. Likhachev. More recently a volume of Bely's critical essays entitled *Poezija slova: Sbornik statej* was published (Moscow: Sovremennik, 1987). Slated for publication in 1989 are a two-volume selection of Bely's poetry and prose edited by Vladimir M. Piskunov (Moscow: Khudozhestvennaja literatura) and a republication of Bely's Soviet trilogy of memoirs (see notes 17, 19, and 20 for references to the original volumes) by Aleksandr V. Lavrov. In addition, work on a volume of *Literaturnoe nasledstvo* to be devoted to Bely is now underway.

[5] For insightful commentary on these aspects of Bely's poetry, see Gerald Janecek's introduction to his translation of *The First Encounter* (Princeton: Princeton University Press, 1979); see also the chapter Janecek devotes to Bely in his monograph *The Look of Russian Literature: Avant-Garde Visual Experiments, 1900–1930* (Princeton: N. J. Princeton, University Press, 1984).

[6] See, for example, Bely's essays: "Ritm kak dialektika i 'Mednyj vsadnik' Pushkina" ("Rhythm as Dialectic and Pushkin's 'Bronze Horseman' ") (Moscow: Federatsija, 1929); "Lirika i eksperiment" ("Lyric and Experiment") and "Opyt kharakteristiki russkogo chetyrekhstopnogo jamba" ("Toward a Characterization of the Russian Iambic Tetrameter") in his *Simvolizm (Symbolism)* (Munich: Wilhelm Fink, 1969; reprint, Moscow, 1910). A comprehensive study of Bely's method and its significance to the development of Russian formalist criticism is found in Stephen Cassedy's introduction to his translations of *Selected Essays of Andrey Bely* (Berkeley: University of California Press, 1985).

[7] See my "Synesthesia: Imagination's Semiotic in Andrei Belyi's *Petersburg*" (Ph.D. diss.,

criticism of prose literature and other fine arts Bely elaborated what has proven to be a comprehensive aesthetic theory (it has been called a "consistent and distinctive . . . teleology of culture") upon which an entire school of Russian symbolism was based.[8]

The interest of the present study lies in outlining one of the original ways in which Bely developed the genre of memoir. My aim is to suggest one point of entry into what is a very versatile and complex autobiographical work. To date, the memoirs have not attracted the same efforts at exegesis as have Bely's novels, essays, and poetry. Neither have they been dismissed by Bely scholarship. On the contrary, they are often drawn upon for historical information, even though factual discrepancies and inconsistencies have been duly noted. With this precaution, the memoirs are generally termed "brilliant" and have even been said to have "no rivals."[9]

Yet critical argumentation in support of these accolades is lacking. This lacuna has been located by one scholar who, in describing "the changing historico-literary context that prompted Bely to set down his memoirs," sadly notes that other "scholars . . . have not . . . raised the question of the function of autobiography and memoirs both in Bely's own work and in the literary culture of his time." One wonders to what degree this apparent reluctance to confront the literary status of Bely's memoirs reflects an abiding ambivalence toward them and toward "the striking heterogeneity both in style and ideological intentions that over many years impelled the author to persist in the genre."[10]

When first published, intermittently over the last twelve years of Bely's life, the memoirs were considered audacious, bizarre, cranky, maddening, inexplicable, engaging, and important. As one commentator modestly but aptly put it, "It is extremely unpleasant and difficult to read them because of their annoying manner, but there is a great deal in them that is curious."[11] The general puzzlement is perhaps more vividly demonstrated by the contrast between the

---

Cornell University 1980). An abstract of its argument appears under the title of "The Synesthetics of Apocalypse," *The Andrej Belyj Society Newsletter*, no. 2 (1983): 4–5.

[8] The phrase belongs to J. D. Elsworth, *Andrey Bely: A Critical Study of the Novels* (Cambridge: Cambridge University Press, 1983). Elsworth's book contains a brief but excellent overview of the larger issues touched by "Bely's Theory of Symbolism." For a closer look at the theory, see Cassedy's thorough work on *Selected Essays*.

[9] Malmstad uses the first epithet in "The Poetry," lxvii; the second phrase is from Elsworth, *The Novels*, 1. Malmstad also refers to the memoirs as the "most criticized and least studied of Bely's works in *Andrey Bely: Spirit of Symbolism*, ed. John E. Malmstad (Ithaca, New York: Cornell University Press, 1987), 13.

[10] See Lazar Fleishman, "Bely's Memoirs," trans. Stephani Hoffman, in Malmstad, *Spirit of Symbolism*, 217. This essay is the most complete and enlightening history of the writing and publication of Bely's vast memoir oeuvre.

[11] The comment was made by Georgij Ivanov in his column "Pochtovyj jashchik," *Tsekh poetov* (Berlin, 1923) 4: 66. It is cited in English by Struve in "Redivivus," 34.

response made by Bely's friend Vladislav Khodasevich and his wife Nina Berberova when Bely read portions of his first published memoir to them. "Listening to these pages was for Berberova a "supreme, unforgettable joy,"[12] while for Khodasevich, the same pages "degenerated . . . into a sort of autobiographical diatribe."[13]

This was 1922, one year after the death of Alexander Blok, and the work in question was Bely's reminiscences of him. The much-loved and highly esteemed poet had been linked closely to Bely by an intimate but stormy friendship that left indelible marks on the lives and literatures of both men. The recollections were composed during what turned out to be a temporary stay among fellow emigrés in Berlin who looked to Bely for an expanded account of the testimonial to Blok's achievements that he had given in Petersburg upon Blok's death. It was their hope that Bely's reminiscences would provide the groundwork for a larger history of the efflorescence of Russian literary culture that so many attributed to Blok's leadership and to which so many of these expatriated writers had themselves contributed. Yet like Khodasevich many found in the reminiscences a sore disappointment.

Their disappointment was shared by Bely himself who, after returning to Russia in 1923, decided to refurbish and further expand his reminiscences of Blok.[14] The original work suffered, Bely later wrote, from an excess of

[12] Nina Berberova, *The Italics Are Mine* (New York: Harcourt, Brace & World, 1969), 159–60.

[13] Struve paraphrases Khodasevich in this way, "Redivivus," 23. His reference is to Khodasevich's essay "Andrey Bely" in *Nekropol': Vospominanija* (Paris: YMCA Press, 1976; Brussels: Petropolis, 1939), 94–99. For example, in lamenting the way Bely remembered his fellow writers who remained in emigration after Bely returned to Russia from Berlin, Khodasevich wrote, "And just as he demonized and caricatured everyone surrounding the hero in his novels, now he has caricatured and presented his former friends in a completely diabolical fashion" (translation mine, 98). Khodasevich also reviewed a volume of Bely's memoirs, *Nachalo veka*, in *Vozrozhdenie*, nos. 3312 and 3319 (28 June and 5 July 1934).

[14] According to Fleishman, Bely began writing his reminiscences of Blok on 11 August 1921, the day after Blok's funeral. Within a few months, he read them at two sessions of *Vol'fila* (the Free Philosophical Association) in Petersburg, and they were published in 1922 in the final issue of the journal *Zapiski mechtatelej* (*The Notes of Dreamers*), no. 6 (1922): 5–122, under the title, "Vospominanija o Aleksandre Aleksandroviche Bloke." Yet by the time that issue appeared, Bely was already in Berlin and was expanding the reminiscences for a journal he edited there, *Epopeja* (*Epopee*). Now variously entitled "Vospominanija o Bloke" and "Vospominanija o A. A. Bloke" they appeared in the three 1922 issues of *Epopeja* and in a fourth issue of the same appearing in April 1923. This latter version, published in *Epopeja*, is the one that was reprinted in Munich by Wilhelm Fink in 1969 as *Vospominanija o A. A. Bloke*. It is to be distinguished from the 1964 edition of the *Vospominanija ob Alexandre Alexandroviche Bloke*, which was published in Letchworth, England, with an introduction by Georgette Donchin. This is a reprint of the *Zapiski mechtatelej* (Petersburg) text.

Fleishman also reports that when Bely returned to Russia in 1923, he took with him only portions of the text that comprised only the third volume of the *Epopeja* reminiscences and that these are now preserved in Moscow (in *TsGALI*) and Leningrad (in the Saltykov-Shchedrin Library).

"youthful romanticism" and a desire, fueled by the immediacy of his grief over Blok's death, to make the mourned poet appear to be the better of the two men.[15] As a corrective for his misrepresentation of both Blok and himself, Bely undertook a series of memoirs describing his own "life and morals."[16] The projected work was never completed, but a trilogy of memoirs relating Bely's life from infancy through 1912 did emerge. The first volume, *On the Border of Two Centuries*, depicts Bely's early life as twenty years of continual trauma due to infant illness and ceaseless parental conflict. As its title suggests, the account is dominated by Bely's adumbration of the theme of "the border," a notion signifying not only his precarious position as the sole and sickly child of warring parents but also the fragile state in which human culture finds itself as the calendar turns from the nineteetnh to the twentieth century.[17] In volume 2, *The Beginning of the Century*, Bely traces out his share in the hopes for spiritual transformation that rose among the "decadent" generation of symbolists as cultural crisis deepened.[18] The volume's climax is the crushing of these hopes by the failed attempt at political revolution in 1905, an event

In another accounting of these events Struve reports that some of the archival holdings were published in 1974 in the Soviet journal *Voprosy literatury (Questions of Literature)*, no. 6: 214–44, under the title "Iz knigi 'Nachalo veka' (Berlinskaja redaktsija, 1923–25 gody)" ("From the book, 'The Beginning of the Century' [Berlin edition, 1923–25]"). Both Struve and Fleishman note that "The Beginning of the Century" was the title Bely had planned to use for a further revised and expanded multivolume publication in Berlin of reminiscences not only about Blok but more generally about "his time." These plans were frustrated, however, by his return to Russia, and the title "The Beginning of the Century" was applied instead to a different volume of memoirs appearing in the Soviet Union in 1933. See: Fleishman, "Memoirs," 218–24, and Struve, "Redivivus," 22–23.

For a report on the interplay of Bely's plans for an expanded version of *Epopeja* with the eventual emergence of his novels *Kotik Letaev, The Baptized Chinaman*, and *Notes of an Eccentric*, see Elsworth, *The Novels*, 118–19, 138–39, and 162.

[15] This comment is made briefly in *Nachalo veka*, 472, and in more detail in *Mezhdu dvukh revoliutsij*, 5–6 (see full references in notes 19 and 20). Fleishman expresses "serious reservations" about this interpretation, noting that the early portrait of Blok is not as idealized as Bely later claimed it was. Rather, the early work encompasses some of the more "shadowy moments" in Blok's life, according to Fleishman, and depicts them "at least as forcefully as the glowing ones, if not in such detail." See: Fleishman, "Memoirs," 224–25.

[16] Bely applies this phrase to his memoirs in the opening lines of *Mezhdu dvukh revoliutsij* (for full reference, see note 20), 1.

[17] This volume, *Na rubezhe dvukh stoletij (On the Border of Two Centuries)*, was written in 1929 and published in 1930 by the Moscow house Zemlja i fabrika. Further references to this work will be made in the text by noting the appropriate page number of volume 1. Page numbers correspond to the 1966 reprint by Russian Language Specialties (Chicago).

[18] It is thanks largely to Bely's memoirs that Russian symbolism is generally viewed as developing over two "generations." The first generation is said to consist of, among others, Valerij Brjusov, Konstantin Bal'mont, Dmitrij Merezhkovskij, Zinaida Gippius, and Fedor Sologub, who are grouped around their admiration for the French symbolists. Vjacheslav Ivanov joins rank with Bely and Blok as the second generation, inspired by the philosophies of German idealism and the theology of the Russian thinker Vladimir Solov'ev.

to which Bely's spiritual aims were pinned.[19] The third and last volume to be published, *Between Two Revolutions*, describes the personalities and issues shaping Bely's life in the literary circles of Moscow and Petersburg. Here Bely portrays a new generation of symbolist writers struggling to hasten through their words the realization of renewed and enlightened ideals of social, political, and cultural transformation.[20]

Since my aim is not to characterize the entire body of Bely's memoirs but rather to examine one particular manipulation of the genre, I will focus on one specific portion of the memoir trilogy: "A Petersburg Drama," the second chapter of the second volume. This chapter deals at length with two years in Bely's life that he considered critical, 1904 and 1905. Some twenty years before the memoir was written, the same experiences recounted in "A Petersburg Drama" had formed the basis of his novel *Petersburg*. In fact, parallels between the novel and his life are frequently drawn by Bely in "A Petersburg Drama." Since the "Drama" cites the novel as it presents the "real facts," the memoir gives rise to a number of questions, not only about the relationship between Bely's literature and his life but also about his use of the two different literary forms, memoir and novel, to render this relationship. Was the memoir intended to complement the novel—appending, correcting, or documenting it in some way?[21] Or did it aim to achieve an independent goal via an independent means? This is to say, did Bely consider one to be more factual than the other? More "artistic," fictional, fantastic? The answers to these questions should help to elucidate Bely's conception of the varying genres in which he worked and reworked the same materials.

The Changing Purposes of an Ever-Sharpening Focus upon the Self

The search for Bely's purposes in turning to memoir can begin in his own comments on the trilogy. His prefaces to the three volumes are worth examining, for they outline the evolution of Bely's autobiographical design. Espe-

---

[19] *Nachalo veka* (*The Beginning of the Century*) represents a 1930 reworking of the materials Bely left in Berlin in 1923 (see note 14). It was published in Moscow in 1933 by Khudozhestvennaja literatura. Further references to this work will be made in the text by noting the appropriate page numbers of volume 2.

[20] *Mezhdu dvukh revoliutsij* (*Between Two Revolutions*) was written in 1932–33 and published in 1934 in Leningrad by Pisateli v Leningrade. Further references to this work will be made in the text by noting the appropriate page number of volume 3. Page numbers correpond to the 1966 reprint by Russian Language Specialties (Chicago).

A fuller description of the contents of the memoir trilogy and an outline of some of the literary issues it raises are found in Ida Zeitchik, "Andrej Belyj's Memoirs" (Ph.D. diss., New York University, 1981).

[21] In his introduction to the 1934 publication of *Mezhdu dvukh revoliutsij* Cesare Volpe characterizes Bely's memoirs as "a special form of artistic literature based on precise documentation," xi. Volpe's thoughts provide a starting point for the present study.

cially telling are the variations that occur from volume to volume as he refor-
mulates his plan with each new phase of the work. Continuity is provided by
Bely's unwavering wish to capture "youthful perceptions" (2:7), yet with
each successive volume he seems to take a new approach toward its fulfillment.

We first encounter Bely's concern with youthful perception when, in introducing volume 1, *On The Border of Two Centuries*, he presents the decadent
generation to which he belonged as a group convinced that man stood on the
threshold of profound spiritual transformation and cultural transfiguration.
The name Bely used for this millenial event was "the dawn," while "the
border" referred specifically to the sensation of its imminence. Bely says that
during the period he calls the "epoch of the dawn," 1898 to 1901, the sensation of the border was perceived to be a "scent." "But the sense of smell,"
he goes on to explain, with a great deal of bravado and characteristic word-
play, "is an empirical, and not a mystical notion. . . . Otherwise known as
'instinct,' it is the acquisition of habits via a series of exercises in discerning
the real facts" (15–17).[22]

By equating sensory experience with instinct and redefining instinct as an
acquired skill in discerning what is real, Bely sets up an opposition between
reality and the knowledge of it, or between the actual facts and one's changing
ideas about what those facts might mean. He then points his book in the direction of pure facts when he declares, not without a touch of comic self-irony,
that "In this book I would like to eliminate ideology. I will take ideology into
account only insofar as it can be considered a symptomatology, an empirical
process of extracting certain of youth's 'scents' of the rains and the like, as a
result of which so many of us, having gotten wet, took on the shape of wet
chickens" (17). By improvising this epistemological framework and by coming down on the side of empiricism, Bely formulates his intention to supply
what he insists again and again are purely the "raw materials: the facts, facts,
facts" (2:7). His insistence upon serving up his data in a manner he considers
raw is a clear indication that he construes his memoir at this stage to be a
documentary enterprise. The raw quality upon which he insists of course suggests the absence of interpretation, that is, an abstinence from the imposition
of cause and effect and those principles earlier responsible for the youthful
ideology toward which Bely now takes such a cautious stance. In a more literary sense the sought-after raw quality of the narrative suggests the absence
of a shaping imagination, or that which the contemporary Soviet literary the-
orist Lydia Ginzburg discusses as the artist's act of enveloping his life experience in an aesthetic structure. This act, according to Ginzburg, is the process
of fictionalization, which in its fullest deployment makes the life experience

---

[22] Bely uses the word *njukh*, which can mean both "scent" and "sense of smell" and is also
used figuratively in expressions like "to have a nose for."

inside the envelope aesthetically irrelevant to and factually independent from the fictional work.[23]

What Bely seems to want to do in this first volume of his memoir is to remove any such envelope of fiction from his story and view the life experience enfolded in it for what it was—for whatever significance it might have had apart from any use Bely might elsewhere have made of it. In other words, he seems to be speaking directly to the expectations of the reader who is familiar with his fictions—and who might even consider them as high-water marks of the flood of self-absorption that saturated the literature of Bely's day with torrential cries of private pain induced by cultural crisis. To that reader Bely in effect says that his memoir is a different kind of work, one which, by virtue of its "empirical" outlook, will avoid meditating upon inner feeling and instead spotlight the outer reality upon which the crisis was visited.

By the time the third volume is written, all this changes. The gap between fact and idea narrows, and Bely comes to recount his life experience solely in terms of its significance to the artistic uses he makes of it. His memoir, in other words, presents that outer reality in its full and exclusive relevance to the aesthetics in which he (and like-minded writers) later enveloped it.

The seeds of change are to be found in the improvisatory epistemological framework present at the memoirs' outset. Bely's wish to exclude ideology from view raises questions about what remains when this is accomplished. What does he conceive as the underlying reality? Or, what does he wish to document? What constitutes a real life experience that only incidentally serves as fiction's source? We have already seen Bely suggest that reality resides in those "youthful scents" he now wants to "sniff out." We might suspect, then, that sensory impressions are the stuff of which Bely's world is really made; sensory perceptions are what remains when—and if—ideology is stripped away.

In the introductory comments to the second volume of memoirs the primacy of sensory perception in Bely's world view becomes more overt. Here he explains that the "raw materials: the facts, facts, facts" with which he works are things like the "jokes, conversations, gaffes" he saw and heard, that is, "all those little details" that add up to "the realities of the age" (12). There is a change, however, in the relationship of these "little" realities to ideas. In the first volume Bely was going to place some limit on the degree to which ideology could enter into his work—presumedly because ideology would somehow obscure the desired facts. Not so in volume 2, where ideas are inalienable from the impressions in which they are conceived: "Both people and facts were perceived in a haze of ideas, without which my memoirs are not memoirs. It defined friendships and arguments, and for that reason I cannot, with-

[23] Lydia Ginzburg, *O psikhologicheskoj proze* (*Psychological prose*) (Leningrad: Sovetskij pisatel', 1971; reprint, Khudozhestvennaja literatura, 1977), 5–33.

out distorting the past, confine myself to drawing noses, ears, warts, chance gestures, and words. My memoirs are not a collection of anecdotes. I am the memoirist, and I am not excluded from the memoirs'' (6). The switch in terminology from "ideology" to "haze of ideas" ("dymka idej") should not go unnoticed. It indicates an interest in minimizing the threat posed to the empiricism of the work by a point of view; it also indicates a disinterest on Bely's part in clarifying the relationship between those empirically all-meaningful sensory impressions and one's ideas about the reality that is sensed. It is not important to know whether one governs the other. It is important only to recognize that the memoirist's "I" emerges from the haze. The writer's mind, then, is not to be rooted out of the facts, facts, facts—rather, it is to take its rightful place among them:

> And so it must be that my task is to portray myself in this slice of time as an object and not only a subject: I am not summoned from my conscious maturity of the year 1932 to decorate or chastise, preen or flagellate myself. Rather, [my task is to] draw the image of a young man of the epoch, 1901–05, [to draw the image of] ideas in the process of arising in him—the ideas and the impressions of people whose relationship to him extended beyond those years and also people with whom he never actually made any acquaintance. Subsequent admissions, denials must not make their mark upon the impressions left by the first meetings. Many of the people portrayed here became something other than what I show them to be during this period of time . . . but . . . I portray them as they appeared to me, and even to themselves, more than a quarter of a century ago. (6–7)

By assuming personal responsibility for the facts he records, Bely moves away from his initial documentary presumptions and their supporting philosophical discourses on the nature of reality. As his "I" comes forward, his work begins to look more like an autobiography, a genre that conventionally accounts for the interaction of reality with the self—and a genre to which memoir is generally thought to belong.[24] By limiting his viewpoint to its makeup in the past, however, Bely makes it clear that his autobiography will not take its shape from the genre's conventional mold of retrospection and reevaluation. Rather, it will (at least, in terms of the principles Bely now lays down for it) authenticate its past purely by resurrecting it—by making it appear again now exactly as it appeared then, to the eye of the beholder.

---

[24] The difference is only a matter of degree. Memoir is considered to be directed more toward other people, while autobiography is directed toward the self. Which would be the more appropriate term for Bely's works is a matter open to question. Since, however, Bely referred to them as memoirs, or reminiscences (vospominanje), I will do the same. Perhaps it is exigent to note at this point that "autobiography" is a relatively new term, having been coined in England in 1809 and having made its way into Russia in 1817. Prior to that the terms "memoir" and "reminiscences" served the new term's purpose. See: "Autobiography" in *Handbook of Russian Literature*, ed. Victor Terras (New Haven, Conn.: Yale University Press, 1985), 27–29.

The means by which Bely will accomplish this feat is a subject that will be discussed shortly. It is important now to note that this severing of the past from the present represents a fundamental change in the conventional criteria for autobiographical authenticity. In its older forms autobiography, as a relative of medieval confessional narrative, achieved its penitent aim if it communicated an individual's acquisition of spiritual insight through his personal experience of the actual world. This kind of narrative derived its sense of reality, or empirical truth, from its scrupulous attention to historically accurate details that could be corroborated by other witnesses. At the same time a confessional narrative acquired a sense of spirituality or absolute truth insofar as it revealed in the particularities of the individual's life a pattern resembling those provided by traditional, Christian allegory. In short, an autobiography would ring true if the reader could recognize in the familiar world the formal attributes of what he believed to be the divine.

Once Rousseau got hold of the genre, confessional narrative made its appeal less to man's belief in divine truth than to his knowledge of human nature. As the writer's motives shifted from making amends for past wrongdoings to making past doings right, he came to substitute his own psychological patterns for religion's allegorical types. The motive still required that names, dates, and places be at least plausible if not fully verifiable—but what more importantly gave the reader the feeling that the autobiographer was telling the truth was his recognition that under the same circumstances he would behave the same way.[25]

The point to be made here is that the demand for authenticity in autobiography, whether of the old or new school, can be met only by assuming what Jane Gary Harris calls "some form of dual perspective" or "reperception."[26] The story requires, in other words, an exercise in self-scrutiny performed only when a latter-day self assumes a changed world view through which he revises his mental picture of his former being. The more consistently the revision is performed, the more integrated the autobiographer's character appears to be. His integrity earns for the autobiographer the reader's trust in the truthfulness of his account. It is thus the ability to maintain a prescribed and measured distance from the past that gives autobiography its historical dimension—with

[25] This crudely synoptic view of the development of autobiography is drawn from a variety of sophisticated sources. For changing notions of verisimilitude, see Lydia Ginzburg, *O literaturnom geroe* (*The Literary Hero*) (Leningrad: Sovetskij pisatel', 1979). For changing models in plot structure and character development, see Robert Scholes and Robert Kellogg, *The Nature of Narrative* (London: Oxford University Press, 1966). For the changing motives of confession, see Helena Goscilo-Kostin, "Guilded Guilt: Confession in Russian Romantic Prose," *Russian Literature* 14, no. 2 (15 August 1983): 149–82.

[26] Jane Gary Harris, "An Inquiry into the Function of the Autobiographical Mode: Joyce, Mandelstam, Schulz" in *American Contributions to the Ninth International Congress of Slavists* (Kiev, September 1983), ed. Paul Debreczeny (Columbia, Ohio: Slavica, 1983), 202.

all the empirical factuality and psychological candor that a history of the self implies.[27]

Yet Bely refuses to go the distance. He will not "write a book of sources . . . where . . . every deed is evaluated and weighed on modernity's scales" (2:1). He will apply only the weights and measures established in the past

[27] Current genre theory, in an effort to cope with the erosion of the distinction in modern literary culture between autobiography and other narrative forms, upholds retrospection as the one indispensable feature without which the story of a personal experience does not an autobiography make. A wide range of narratives comes to resemble autobiography when writers like Bely espouse views like the one he propounded when he said of his fictional works: "Subject, theme, plot are aberrations. There is only one theme, and that is to describe the panorama of consciousness; one task, and that is to focus on the 'I.' " A. Bely, "Dnevnik," *Zapiski mechtatelej*, no. 1 (1919), ch. 1:235. The equation of narrative with personal consciousness, extending far beyond Bely, leads contemporary critics like William Spengemann to say "Indeed, the modernist movement away from representational discourse toward self-enacting, self-reflexive verbal structures, and the critical theories that have been devised to explain this movement, conspire to make the very idea of literary modernism synonymous with that of autobiography." William Spengemann, *The Forms of Autobiography* (New Haven, Conn.: Yale University Press, 1980), xiii. The solution Spengemann proposes is to develop a theory of autobiography that integrates into the generic classification man's changing ideas about what the self is, how we know it, and how we should write about it: in short, his appeal is for a historical dimension. A number of critics have taken up Spengemann's call and have traced a variety of patterns in man's seemingly endless fascination with himself as a literary hero. Despite the variety, one feature is common to all patterns: the use of retrospection as a structural principle.

For example, when Elizabeth Bruss defines autobiography (and by the way, she diagnoses the problem in understanding autobiography to be a problem in understanding genre per se), she makes room for the changing social and literary institutions of which it is a part and includes room as well for the changes autobiography may in turn effect upon those very institutions to which it belongs. To define autobiography, then, is to mark out "a field within which the task of self-imaging and self-evaluation is understood to take place, making whatever *does* take place recognizable as a form of self-evaluation." Elizabeth Bruss, *Autobiographical Acts: The Changing situation of a Literary Genre* (Baltimore: Johns Hopkins University Press, 1976), 13. Her detailed explication of this assumption makes it clear that "recognizable self-evaluation" depends upon looking back at the self after a set of criteria has been advanced.

This same assumption was also made by Roy Pascal, one of the pioneers in this field: "Autobiography is a shaping of the past. . . . It establishes certain stages in an individual life, makes links between them, and defines, implicitly or explicitly, a certain consistency of relation between the self and the outside world. . . . The coherence implies that *the writer takes a particular standpoint, the standpoint of the moment at which he reviews his life, and interprets his life from it.* The standpoint may be the social position of the writer, his acknowledged achievement in any field, his present philosophy; in every case it is the present position which enables him to see his life as something of a unity, something that may be reduced to order" (Italics mine). Roy Pascal, *Design and Truth in Autobiography* (London: Routledge & Kegan Paul, 1960), 9.

In furthering Pascal's emphasis on time-consciousness while she explores Bruss's design for the "autobiographical act," Jane Gary Harris aptly notes that "If the 'autobiographical act' is initiated by the writer taking up his pen to confront his own experience of history, his consciousness of the moment of writing is complicated by the fact that he is simultaneously remembering his past and restructuring it according to both ideological and esthetic principles determined by his present experience. Nevertheless, the autobiographical mode, unlike any other mode of liter-

because now, as then, "my sensory organs are my measuring instruments" (1:17). Sensory perception provides Bely with the only knowledge of reality that he deems possible—like the "sense of smell" by which he learned to "discern the real facts." The "raw data" he refracts through his "prism of youthful perception" (2:7) is invested with the *status* of empirical reality, but its *substance* is another matter.

On what does Bely's pseudo-empirical world subsist? By his own admission, it is a world that "exists no longer" (2:12). How, then, will he invoke it? The following explanation of his world's passing is indicative of the recourse he takes to overcome the distance that time imposes:

> During the past thirty years we have undergone a profound change, the likes of which history has not known in previous centuries. The youth of today grows up under circumstances bearing no resemblance to those in which people of my generation grew up. Upbringing, education, the circle of readings, conditioning, psychology, personal interactions are all different. We did not read what they read today. Contemporary youth need not burden itself with the same things with which we burdened ourselves. Even deeds that seem savage and prejudiced today were considered heroic in my day. For that reason, one cannot translate my reminiscences of a distant past into the language of our time. (2:1)

The language of his time provides Bely the means by which to reenact his past for his reader. The equivalence he assumes between the past and its language is indicative of an assumed equation between language and perception. As we have seen, sensory perception is the constituency of Bely's world; now we see that this reality inheres forever in speech. The only way therefore to make his sensate experience of the past available to his reader is to reproduce its linguistic forms.

As a result, Bely devotes much effort to preparing the reader to accept the style of the work he is about to read. To cite one example:

> In this volume I have adopted the style of humorous puns, grotesques, stereotypes. But you see, I am describing a circle of real eccentrics who gathered around me (the "argonauts"). Much in our style of relating to one another and even in our style of perceiving one another can seem unnatural, stilted. But time is to blame for that, not me. Nowadays, they don't talk that way, they don't joke that way, and they don't apprehend one another in that way. But in 1902–04, in our circles, we construed each other exactly like that, and that is exactly how we joked. (2:11)

---

ary perception, allows the writer to assert himself simultaneously as a man in history and as a poet by confronting the immediacy of his present consciousness with his own past as a source of human value in history. It is this critical confrontation which is mediated through the autobiographer's consciousness and which provides the esthetic tension of the autobiographical text." Jane Gary Harris, "Inquiry," 203. Insofar as it derives from the imposition of a present point of view upon a differing view held in the past, the tension that for Harris describes autobiography eventuates in the author's distance from his material.

The efficacy of these explanations might be open to question. Their extent, however, makes one thing very clear: Bely means to be understood. His autobiography presumes a readership. It is not designed to be a private act.

The reader might at first be wary of the sanctity with which Bely treats his notion of his language. The emphasis on the peculiarities of his style does keep the reader at some remove from Bely's world. It is disturbing because it is a distance from which the reader has no way of knowing whether Bely will succumb to the temptations of the imagination that threaten the authenticity of any autobiography. Ironically, authenticity is the very quality that, through faithfulness to his language, Bely is trying to uphold.[28] It is problematic also in that an initiated reader, the one whom, as we have seen, Bely seems to address, might wonder whether his invocatory approach to a little-known past will lead him to create another one of his well-known fictions.[29] Yet the more Bely strives to explain the particularities of his style, the more he seems to implore the reader to trust that despite its lack of popularity, his language *will* be intelligible: "Many of our punning metaphors of that time would today seem like mysticism. For example, the mythological jargon of our jokes is now unintelligible. Well, who will venture into the fields of the 'galloping centaurs' as we did? . . . But 'centaur' and 'fawn' during those years were for us no mere 'elemental spirits'; they were, rather, our means of perception" (2:11). What Bely offers, then, to a reader willing to venture into those myth-

---

[28] Lydia Ginzburg argues that the "inauthenticity" resulting from an exercise of the imagination is a fundamental feature in autobiography, one that distinguishes it from a documentary text. By this exercise of the imagination she means the processes of selection, omission, organization, and evaluation that transform an unarticulated set of facts into a coherently articulated story. In her view imagination is therefore responsible for the aesthetic structure that is the basis of autobiography's appeal. This is roughly the same notion that I earlier referred to as the maintenance of "a prescribed and measured distance" from the facts, a formulation arising from the need to speak more directly to the issue of narrative point of view. When I refer here to imagination as a threat to autobiography, I have in mind, of course, the degree to which the imagination can fully undercut all attempts to establish factual precision. Ginzburg also maintains that such an attempt must be present to some degree in true autobiography. Its complete absence is, for Ginzburg, the sign of fiction. *O psikhologicheskoj proze*, 5–33.

[29] By "well-known fictions" I refer not only to Bely's published novels but also to his frequent efforts to entertain himself and his friends by reenacting past moments they shared. Nina Berberova mentions it in her memoirs, *Italics*, 161, and so does Bely's second wife, Klavdija N. Bugaeva. In her memoirs Bugaeva describes Bely's uncanny ability to conjure up in particular the atmosphere of the "dawn era" and to convince even her that he was somehow actually living in it. Bugaeva speaks also of her husband's arduous efforts to develop a poetic language that would continue to bring the dawn era to light, long after the anticipation of a millenial transfiguration had faded. The dawn era, as noted previously, is the period treated in the second volume of Bely's memoirs, and the poetry of which Bugaeva speaks, that contained in the book, *Zovy vremen* (*The Calls of the Times*), was written concomitantly with this volume. It would not be unexpected that efforts applied in one genre affect those in another. See K. N. Bugaeva, *Vospominanija o Belom* (*Reminiscences of Bely*), ed. and introd. John E. Malmstad (Berkeley, California: Berkeley Slavic Specialties, 1981), 223–44.

ological fields is a privileged glimpse into the private wealth of meaning of what is now considered to be a historical—and politically suspect—style. Initiated or otherwise, Bely admonishes his reader to "Remember, my account is of what was . . . even though it exists no longer" (2:12).

The reference made to the apparent mysticism of his style marks the political considerations that to a significant degree enter into Bely's autobiographical design. By excluding the viewpoint of the present as he purveys the sights and sounds of the past, Bely forces the reader to take on the role of reevaluation that normally belongs to the autobiographer. This is his way of confronting the two sources responsible for the accusations of excessive and impenetrable mysticism that were directed against his work. First came those fellow writers who held differing aesthetic values and inclined toward opposing literary schools.[30] Second, after the success of the Bolshevik Revolution, came the controlling literary institutions that aimed to make all literature bend to the demands of socialist realism and to serve the goals of the new Soviet state.[31] The latter did not look favorably upon Bely when he returned from Europe to the Soviet Union in 1923 and began to write his memoirs. His efforts in writing them were thus devoted to mitigating the hostility of this second group and to gaining from it a place for himself in the literary life of his newly socialized land. As the appropriate political jargon would have it, Bely was seeking rehabilitation.

Exactly what political rehabilitation would mean to Bely in practical terms is a matter of speculation, as he left no specific record of his thoughts on this subject. He was never known to be a practical thinker, and especially where politics were concerned, Bely was viewed to be at best fascinating in his naiveté.[32] However, the many aspersions cast on the quality of his political thinking should not belie the sincerity of his resultant convictions. His decision to return to the USSR, in contrast to his colleagues and at the expense of an ultimate but undesired separation from his by then estranged first wife, is certainly testimony to a considerably positive attitude toward the new regime—

[30] The acmeists provide one example. In contrast to symbolist endeavors to make new inroads into absolute knowledge, the acmeists strove to recover the equipose and acknowledged clarity of classical art.

[31] The doctrine of socialist realism was pronounced in 1934 at the Congress of the Union of Soviet Writers. The relevant statute requires that the artist supply "the truthful, historically concrete representation of reality in its revolutionary development. Moreover, the truthfulness and historical concreteness of the artistic representation of reality must be linked with the task of ideological transformation and education of works in the spirit of socialism." Many fascinating discussions of the consequences of this requirement could be cited, but perhaps the best starting point, and the one from which this summary is cited is Abram Tertz, *On Socialist Realism* (New York: Pantheon, 1960). A more recent account of the doctrine's history is found in Max Hayward, *Writers in Russia, 1917–1978* (San Diego: Harcourt Brace Jovanovich, 1983).

[32] Nikolaj Valentinov-Volsky, *Two Years with the Symbolists*, ed. Gleb Struve (Stanford, Calif.: Hoover Institution, 1969). Struve summarizes Valentinov's comments in "Redivivus," 26.

and toward himself as well. For Bely was not a political naif in his own view. He had studied political theory as a university student and had formulated opinions sympathetic to the Socialist Revolutionary party of 1902. He had also participated, he claims, in some labor protest activities in St. Petersburg and Moscow during the early years of the decade. After the October Revolution of 1917 he played a role in organizing various groups of young writers and had some of his own poetry published in the newspaper *Banner of Labor* and the journal *Our Path*, both organs of the Left Socialist Revolutionary party, which supported the Bolshevik seizure of power.[33] Thus, while others may have considered him a pitiful victim of his own idealistic refusal to grasp grim reality, Bely saw himself as an active member of a very real and emerging body politic.

In light of the political discord between Bely and the new government, the confessional strategy of his autobiographical method becomes apparent. By assimilating the story of his life to the style of its language, Bely casts himself in the role of something of a benefactor to his new nation, one who bestows assumedly desirable first-hand information about the past, which others withhold as they remain in self-imposed exile. In this way he secures for himself the opportunity to continue writing in the style he developed during his now disfavored past, without having to assume the present ideologies seeking to discredit it. By renewing that past for the edification of the present, Bely transforms himself into a historical type whose vision is worth seeing because it was at one time viable enough to attract a body politic (albeit one with literary interests) to itself. He is therefore free to suggest that the present has some continuity with the past, which he intends to unfold with the sincerest conviction in its importance to the historical knowledge of the present and future.

In the best possible performance of his own scenario, then, Bely would achieve rehabilitation without falsely recanting all that he contributed to the literary artworks, aesthetic theories, and cultural life of days gone by. The actual performance of the scenario was not the best however, and Bely's confessional strategy achieved a severely limited victory. His final years in the Soviet Union were marred by ceaseless struggle with the authorities. Although he managed somehow to get his memoirs published, they appeared only under the aegis of renewed accusations of both political and cultural naiveté. In the introduction to the 1933 edition of *The Beginning of the Century*,[34] for example, one L. Kamenev includes Bely among those intellectuals hopelessly crippled by their interest in ''problems of eternity,'' until:

---

[33] As reported by John Malmstad in ''The Poetry,'' xlix. The Russian titles are *Znamja Truda* and *Nash Put'*.

[34] This 1933 publication represents a revision Bely made of the reminiscences he wrote ten years earlier with the intention of publishing them in Europe. It is to be expected, then, that some of his revisions were determined by political exigency (see note 19).

The October Revolution saved some members of this [failed] generation of the bourgeois intelligentsia—the author of *The Beginning of the Century* is one example—and perhaps it will save a few more. But in order to save them, it would have to take them by the collar and tear them away from the direction in which they had been moving, for, by virtue of its own character, the group was condemned to perish. . . .

This book of Bely's reminiscences inevitably leads to this conclusion. That is its value. But the author does not reach this conclusion himself. We are obliged to do it for him. (2:14–15)

To be sure, under no circumstances would Bely have reached Kamenev's conclusion. Nonetheless, the Soviet critic's note that "we must do it for him" is significant. It tells us that in this second volume Bely's approach to his autobiography has changed again. He is no longer speaking, as he was in volume 1, as an outside observer, philosophically recording independently existing facts, but rather as a memoirist reporting the facts of his age as best he knew them. It is a short step from the viewpoint of this memoirist to that of the self-styled author who emerges in volume 3, explaining not merely the facts as best he knew them but, more pointedly, those facts that he knew best, those facts that only he knew—the facts of his own creativity.[35]

This is not the kind of writer or writing that the socialist-realist literary establishment would value, especially not in the early 1930s, when Stalin's grip on the nation's literary life was quite firm. Yet with the third volume of his memoirs Bely once again attacks the problems of writing a factual autobiography in a world hostile to those facts. He introduces the work with a disclaimer similar to the one he made in volume 2, when he first designated himself a memoirist. This time he says: "From this volume of memoirs, I, the *author*, am *not* excluded. A dispassionate tone is *not* maintained. I do *not* pretend to objectivity, even though in other portions of these memoirs, I approach myself as though separated from myself" (3:5) (my italics). Bely's new attitude toward himself as fully the performing subject rather than the passive object of study is explained by way of a playful simile in which he compares the prior, "objective" portion of his memoir to a "little hook" one might find among the pieces of a shattered bust. It is a find that he fantasizes would prompt one to say, " 'Here it is—Bely's nose, broken in 1906. What an unpleasant nose! And look—here is its bump' " (3:5). As Bely turns his simile into a generalization about the ceaseless efforts of self-consciousness to understand its failures, his message becomes clear: to divide his autobiography into slices of life viewed independently of one another is to fail to disclose the whole of one's identity. It is to allow any one randomly selected part to substitute for that whole, thus forever precluding it from view. Or, to recast

---

[35] Volume 3 was written immediately upon completion of volume 2 and published shortly thereafter (see note 20).

the argument in the terms set out in volume 1, Bely has lost his taste for serving up his data raw.

And so he forewarns us that in volume 3 he will review some of the materials covered in previous volumes, this time in order to disclose not apparent facts but essential principles governing his perceptions of those facts. He is, in other words, intensifying his scrutiny of what he termed a mere "haze of ideas" in volume 2. He is concerned in particular with the haze still surrounding Alexander Blok, and it is especially with respect to his differences with the other poet that Bely insists that he, Bely, "was right at least in principle" (3:5).

In this emphasis upon principle we see that Bely at last stands ready to engage in some form of interpretation. But what form will it take? Will he look back upon his life with one eye fixed on the present, so as to see it from a changed perspective? He says nothing of changing his style, the one we know to be based in the language of immediate perception, and indeed even the most cursory reading confirms that this style in fact has not changed. We might suspect, then, that Bely will render the "principles" of his life in the same way that he rendered the "facts," clothing them in the same forms in which he recognized them in the past—in the forms, in other words, of his immediate perceptions, the forms constituting his unique style. He will "interpret" by referencing the record left by that style—by reengaging himself with his own previous works.

The primacy of Bely's involvement with his prior works is evidenced early in volume 3 when he interrupts the tale of an emotional dilemma in which he was mired for over a year (1905–6), in order to point out that the events taking place in August 1906 became the basis of his novel *The Silver Dove*, while September's experiences became *Petersburg*.[36] He is also careful to point out that while these events transpired in 1906, the novels to which they correspond were written in 1909 and 1912, respectively (3:93). This sudden shift in focus from events to writings suggests that what is important to Bely is not what happened but how life's happenings were transformed through his agency into art. The transformation of life into art is the basis of Bely's appeal for the justification of both. The reader of the memoir who recognizes the continuity between Bely's life and art will agree that he was right—at least in principle.

Bely's extensive reliance upon his works to explain his life (the above-cited remark is only one small example) creates the suggestion that the autobiography has already been written—all across the face of Bely's uncollected works. What remains to be done in the memoir is to document the existence of that

---

[36] Bely's *Serebrjanyj golub'* (*The Silver Dove*) was first published in 1909, in serial form, in the Moscow journal *Vesy* and then in book form in 1910 by Moscow's Skorpion press. *Petersburg* (*Petersburg*) was serialized in 1913–14 in the Moscow journal *Sirin*; it appeared in book form in 1916 in Petersburg (Leningrad), which was then called Petrograd. A considerably revised version of the same novel was published in Berlin in 1922.

autobiography, so that the audience might judge its value—not in terms of historical accuracy or psychological verisimilitude but in terms of the truths it reveals about the essence of Bely's creativity.

THE AUTOBIOGRAPHICAL MOTIVES FOR SUBORDINATING FACT TO FICTION

Since, as noted above, so much of Bely's new-found approach to his autobiographical task takes its impetus from his problematic relationship with Blok, a few words about their friendship are in order. These will be followed by an examination of the way in which the application of unconventional autobiographical methods (namely, introspection rather than retrospection and documentation of texts rather than of past experience) to traditional motives (confession and, more especially, apologia) moves Bely's memoir out of the bounds of what has been understood as autobiography and into another literary arena.

Bely attributes the complexities surrounding his relationship with Blok to an unreasoned association formed in his mind between Blok and the idea of political revolution. "In my fantasies," he writes,

> Blok and revolution were reciprocally proportional [obratno proportsional'ny drug drugy]. In the degree to which I separated myself from Blok, I raised social protest. The epoch of our corresponding with one another coincided with my sympathy (and only that) toward radical manifestoes. In the moments when the sparks flew that led to my break with the poet, Pleve was killed and a bomb destroyed the crowned prince Sergei. The moment of the first clash with Blok [was the same moment in which] the uprising on the battleship Potemkin flared. I began to frequent meetings with the Social Democrats, building my own social rhythm upon them (my orientation toward Blok was an SR orientation). (3:6)

Bely is careful to note, however, that he did not "measure his relationship to revolution on the scale of the Bloks"; rather, the higher his feelings ran about revolution, the angrier he became at Blok (6). Today, we would tend to think of this tie between revolution and Blok in terms of psychological displacement. For Bely, however, their reciprocity emerges in a form resembling romantic inspiration: he compares his feelings toward Blok and revolution to Schiller's response to the smell of apples. Just as Schiller could not write poetry without a plate of apples before him, so too Bely could not be angry at Blok without needing to serve a political cause. By the same token, says Bely, his anger toward Blok fueled his attacks upon "the establishment" ("stroj"), while his real motives—as we will see—"outlived themselves" in his "awkward gestures" (6–7).

Later we will have occasion to see what these real motives might have been. For now, it is more useful to note how complex Blok's and Bely's delicate relationship was. Some of the issues upon which their arguments turned were political. (As indicated, Bely sympathized with the Social Revolutionaries, Blok, with the Social Democrats.) Other differences were more purely literary, emerging from the conflicting claims of Christian and decadent values in Symbolist art. Still other problems were of a personal nature, revolving as they did around Blok's wife Ljubov Mendeleeva (daughter of the famous chemist), with whom both Blok and Bely were in love—and she with both of them. The issue of the love triangle acquired tremendous proportions as it took on literary and religious manifestations. Both Blok and Bely saw Ljubov as the incarnation of the principle of Divine Femininity or "Sofia," a theological concept of creativity that they inherited from the philosopher Vladimir Soloviev.[37] As a result of this conflation of ideas, it was the better artist, not simply the better man, who had more right to Ljubov; she was, in the eyes of both writers, an emblem of a deeply spiritualized, aesthetic achievement.

Ljubov and Bely were closest during the years 1904 to 1906, during which time Ljubov considered leaving her husband and traveling to Italy with Bely. This move was of course encouraged by Bely; however, Ljubov's emotions underwent tremendous vacillations. Her frequent changes of heart left Bely physically and, by his own assessment, mentally ill and vacillating himself between conflicting desires to kill her, kill himself, fight a duel with Blok, or in lieu of either murder or suicide, perpetrate some politically terroristic act.

These violent and psychologically devastating fantasies of Bely's reached their peak in September 1906, when he and Ljubov made a mutual decision to sever their relationship. This emotional climax is the subject matter of "A Petersburg Drama," the second chapter of the third volume of Bely's memoirs. Since "A Petersburg Drama" provides an illustration of the way in which Bely relies upon his previous works in order to tell the story of his life, we now turn to that chapter. There we will see how the materials of Bely's life are handled in terms of his art, that is, how Bely, now speaking as author, subjects his life to the criteria of his aesthetic.

The tendency to interpret life as art appears in the chapter's title as well as in the indication Bely gives of the title's source: "Three times we [Ljubov and I] decided to go off to Italy. Each change of decision became a drama: 'Dramaturgy,' or, 'The Collected Works of Henrik Ibsen.' Nothing was decided, except for the gestures of illness in me" (3:93). With these proposed titles, Bely reveals that he sees life as imitating art—or at least, that transposing life into the terms of art is the only way he can understand life. A similar conclusion can be drawn from the opposite direction, by considering the title Bely gave to the novel that deals with the same events, *Petersburg*. In applying the name

---

[37] Vladimir Solov'ev's thinking provided the theological basis for aesthetic theories of the Christian tendency characterizing the second generation of Russian symbolists (see note 18). Solov'ev's relationship to the symbolists, as well as the differences between the two "generations," is clearly discussed in James West, *Russian Symbolism* (London: Methuen & Co., Ltd., 1970). Bely's memoirs, of course, explore the topic at many points.

of a real place (real in the empirical and historical sense) to a work belonging in the main to the genre of fiction, Bely again suggests that real life is actually an artistic creation. And indeed, the novel begins with a spoof of empirical epistemologies. Through a series of illogical associations it is "proven" that the empirical world is but an abstraction, that reality is merely man's fantasy.

By entitling a fiction with the name of a factual place and a memoir with the name of an aesthetic category, Bely creates an odd set of equations in which fact is fiction while art is reality. This curious disjuncture between fact and reality changes our perspective on Bely's insistence upon facts in the first two volumes of his memoir. As a result of this altered perspective we can perceive some continuity between those earlier efforts (those "little hooks," as Bely called them) and the third volume. It now seems as though the first two volumes were designed to establish Bely's reliability as an eyewitness observer of historical facts. Having thereby gained the reader's confidence, he is ready to broach his abiding concern with the aesthetic values exhibited by his life.

The similarity of the ploy by which the novel and memoir are entitled is but one of many points of contact by which the memoir forces upon a reader familiar with the novel a comparison of the two. Another such point, and one that we are well prepared for by now, is the similarity of the prose style. For example, while relating a disturbing visit to Dedovo, Vladimir Soloviev's country home (the philosopher's son Sergei was Bely's childhood friend), Bely notes: "I slushali shelest derev: narastajushchij; listovoroty raskrytye, vetvi, pavetvi, such'ja, suki trudno gnulis', kachalis', vse revmja revelo" ("And one heard the rustling of leaves: it is growing, leafgates are closed, branches, small branches, twigs, little twigs bent with difficulty, swayed; everything howled horribly" (3:84–85). The lexicon and the euphony of this description are reminiscent of the scenery in *Petersburg*, characterized as it is by alliterative, assonantal visions of autumn. In the novel this hypnotically shimmering scenery provides a locus for actions characterized by awkward gestures and quick, jerky movements conveyed by clipped, truncated syntax and metonymic imagery. The memoir conveys action in the same way, as for example when Bely describes how his attempt to escape the oppressiveness of Dedovo by going to his mother's country home was a failure that sent him running right back to Dedovo:

Ja—syznova v Dedove, gde nakhozhu pis'mo Shch. Perepiska—kak tren'e klinkov drug o druga; teper' ona—prosto reznja za moe vozvrashchenie v Piter, kotoroe— znachit: ot"ezd s nei v Italiju; vdrug—pis'mo Bloka (iz Shakhmatova), ob"jasnjajushchee, chto on budet v Moskve: imet' vstrechu so mnoj; ja—v pustuju kvartiru, v moskovskuju; kresla—v chekhlakh; naftaliny . . .

(I—[am] once again in Dedovo, where I find a letter from Shch [Ljubov is referred to in the memoir only by an initial, one that does not correspond to her name].

Correspondence—[is] like the rubbing of two blades against each other; now she—[is] simply carnage for my return to Peter[sburg], which—means: departure with her for Italy; suddenly—a letter from Blok (from Shakhmatovo) [Blok's country home] explaining that he will be in Moscow: to have a meeting with me; I—[go] into my empty room, Moscow room; armchairs—in slipcovers; mothballs . . .) (89)

The performers of similarly rhythmic actions in *Petersburg* often seem like caricatures, described as they are in terms of one or two dominant features. These features are usually the sensory organs.[38] In "A Petersburg Drama" we find Bely describing the important figures in his life in the same way. For example, Meyerhold the stage director:

Sperva mne kazalos': iz vsekh organov chuvstv—dominiroval "njukh" nosa, bro-sivshegosja vpered pred ushami, glazami, gubami i davshego velikolepnyj rel'ef profilju golovy s tochno prizhatymi k cherepu ushami . . . ; nos na tsypochkakh!

(At first it seemed to me [that]: out of all the sense organs—the "sniff" of his nose dominated, throwing itself forward in front of his ears, eyes, lips and throwing into terrific relief the profile of his head, with its ears seemingly pinned to the skull . . . : a nose on tiptoe!) (65)

Finally, the memoir and the novel share a rhetorical feature in their narrative style, a feature of a rather Socratic bent: "Iz dushi vstaval krik: bomboj ubit'—po komu popalo, chemu popalo: ubit'! A—kogo?" ("A cry was arising from the soul: Kill with a bomb—anyone, anything: Kill! But—whom?") (85). Every statement, every claim to an intention, every certainty is followed with a question. This technique makes both narratives, novel and memoir, mimic an inner monologue that, while riddled with doubt, imparts to each text a quality of immediacy. But this quality also creates dissonances in both texts, insofar as it conflicts with our expectations of both genres. From a memoir we generally expect a distanced past, but from this memoir we get a past turned present; from a novel claiming a third-person, eyewitness narrative point of view, we expect only those facts that an outsider might observe. But from Bely's novel we get strangely intimate repetitions of private thoughts belonging to characters other than the narrator.[39] This insistence upon inner monologue, no matter what the genre and narrative point of view, shows how deeply Bely believed that the "drama" of life, the stuff of reality, the substance shared by literature and life was essentially subjective and essentially in process. It could not be fixed long enough to be empirically studied or known; hence the fictionality of empirical fact and the untenability of the empirically factual memoir. If a memoir is to relate facts, then these can only be facts of

[38] Namely, Apollon Apollonovich's ears, Nikolaj Apollonovich's mouth, Dudkin's eyes.

[39] The structure of the narrative is somewhat more complicated than I have rendered it here. See my article "The Many Faces of Truth in Andrei Belyi's *Petersburg*," *West Virginia University Philological Papers* 30 (1984): 32–40.

a different order—not the facts of life as life is experienced, but rather, as it is embodied in art. Thus Bely's memoir now aims not to reminisce about the historical particulars but to study the facts of his creativity.

Aware of the similarities between ''A Petersburg Drama'' and *Petersburg*, and mindful also of Bely's stated intention to report in the memoir only the facts of his immediate perceptions, a reader must wonder how the style to which Bely is so committed, the style recognized as that of fiction, is going to convey these facts of creativity? Can it? Or, to approach the same question from another direction, how should this language, appearing here in a memoir, now be read? The question is not inappropriate, for a comparison of the two genres is part of Bely's autobiographical design. By frequently reminding the reader of his other works, he makes it clear that similarities are matters to be exploited. Sometimes the reminder consists of a footnote simply reading ''See *Petersburg*'' (94 and 95). At other times, whole sentences from the novel are cited while a footnote directs the reader to the appropriate chapter of that text (98). But most importantly, frequent mention is made of the novel's characters and symbols. These references sometimes explain how Bely resembled his characters and sometimes how he differed—but most of all how he lived with them. Thus we must accept familarity with Bely's novels as an assumption upon which the memoirs are predicated, and we must recognize Bely's conviction that without these and all his artistic works, the memoirist would have nothing to tell. Were it not for his fictions, Bely's memoirs would have no substance.

THE CRITICAL METHODS FOR CAPTURING THOSE ''YOUTHFUL PERCEPTIONS''

The portion of ''A Petersburg Drama'' entitled ''The Domino'' illustrates Bely's desire to document the source of the major images in his former works. The domino is familiar to the reader of *Petersburg* as the favorite costume of the novel's protagonist, Nikolay Apollonovich Ableukhov, son of the tsarist nation's most powerful senator. The plot of the novel is organized around Nikolay's involvement with a political underground movement that is attempting to overthrow the autocratic regime upheld by Nikolay's father. Simultaneously, Nikolay is suffering from rejection by the woman he loves.

With regard to Nikolay's costume, Bely recounts in the memoir how an image of himself in such a costume arose in his mind during the time he was trying to resolve the confusion of his relationship to Ljubov Blok. His friend and fellow writer Ellis happened to tell Bely about how he managed to frighten his housemaid with a black lace mask that he somehow stumbled upon. He offered the mask to Bely, who could see himself wearing it—and a red domino—standing before Ljubov with dagger in hand. This ''delirium,'' as Bely calls it, accompanied him everywhere during that difficult year. It appeared each time he spoke with Ellis about Ljubov. He saw it when he was out seeking refuge from his troubles in bars. And one night, upon returning home from one such failed attempt, he "sat with the mask on, raving about it, and seeing a symbol in it" (91–92).

This is one of two accounts Bely gives of his discovery of the symbolizing power of the red domino. Elsewhere in "A Petersburg Drama" he relates the image of the domino to the tight rein he kept on his feelings of pain. He claims that these feelings took their source in the sufferings of childhood and were only exacerbated by his feelings for Ljubov. Here, then, is where we catch a glimpse of what he referred to earlier as his "real motives" (3:7). To counter his pain, Bely developed a garrulous, flighty, and awkward persona that he maintained until:

> Ia rukhnyl; podnjalos'—"krasnoe domino," v chernoj maske, s kinzhalom v ruke, chtoby mstit' za sviatynju, v drugikh i v sebe. Obraz etogo domino sleduet za mnoj v bol'nykh godakh moej zhizni, prosovivajas' i v stikhakh, i v romane: senatorskij syn tak bezumstvuet v brede pereodevanija i v brede ubijstva, kak bezumstvoval ja . . .

> (I went crazy. The "red domino" rose up—in a black mask, with a dagger in hand, in order to take vengeance for the blessed thing: upon others and upon myself. The image of this domino followed me in the sick years of my life, obtruding into both my poetry and my novel: the senator's son is crazed with the delirium of disguise and murder, as I was crazed . . .) (74–75)

The first cited of these two accounts presents the domino as arising from a coincidental intersection of Bely's feelings with the fact of Ellis's proffering him the anecdote and the mask. The second account cited elaborates upon the nature of the feelings Bely attached to the mask—those of utter disorientation and desire for revenge. The latter account highlights the obsessive quality of the image: Bely's choice of the word "obtruding" ("prosovyvajas' ") suggests that the domino's appearance in his novel and poetry was a matter of its own will rather than his. In making this suggestion, Bely seems to be excusing his works for whatever arbitrary quality their symbolism might possess. Insofar as his world was actually populated by such peculiar symbols, he implies, his fiction must be considered realistic. This is Bely's answer to the accusatory labels of mysticism that, when the memoir was written, were applied to his works. By documenting the sources of the style developed in those works, that is, by recounting his experiences in terms of the sensory impressions they made upon him, Bely serves the apologetic purposes of his text.

Bely's apologia, then, is tantamount to teaching his audience how to read his works. Here, for example, we have learned that the red domino represents a disorienting obsession with revenge. We have also learned that the relationship between the domino and this desire is purely coincidental. These lessons assist us in making sense of *Petersburg*. First, they allow us to understand the novel's substance as psychic reality, and second, they explain how the language of that reality functions. However, the point at which Bely's apologetic motive meets with his pedagogical method is also the point at which the genre of his autobiography begins to unravel. In attempting to make the memoir provide the raw data that should encourage the reader to formulate for himself the tautology between Bely's life and his works, Bely necessarily creates a tautological relationship between this work and his others. It is a relationship that erodes traditional distinctions between autobiography and fiction and demands that new means for organizing Bely's prose works be found.

As I see it, the selectivity Bely exercises in his memoir makes it subordinate to his earlier prose works. His memoir aims neither to tell a comprehensive story of his life nor to indulge in the nostalgia of reminiscence, but rather to document primarily those memories that came to life in those earlier works (which I will continue for convenience's sake to call fictions). To illustrate the subordination of fact to fictionalization, I turn to the point in "A Petersburg Drama" where Bely describes a chance meeting with Blok. He cites the exact intersection in Petersburg ("at the little square where Caravan Street intersects . . . Italian Street") where one night he saw running toward him "a man in a Panama hat, carrying a cane, bearing himself as straight as a stick, deathly pale, with an unpleasant curve to his offensive lips." It was Blok, and he ran right past Bely, not seeing him. Bely felt "this gesture like the crack of a whip" across his face:

> "Kak on smeet?"
>
> Chto?
>
> L'gat'! Potomu chto—uvidelos': zdes' na uglu Karavanoj, ego obrashchenie s "Borja"—slashchavaja maska, sletevshaja pod nogi v mig, kogda on pologal, chto ego ne razgljadyvajut; eto "goloe," zloe litso krepko vljapalos' v pamjat'; i—stalo litsom Ableukhova-syna, kogda on idet, zapakhnuvshis' v svoju nikolaevku, vidjas' bezrukim s otpljasyvajushchim po vetru shinel'nym krylom; stsena—reministsentsija vstrechi.

> ("How could he?"
>
> What?
>
> Lie! Because—we saw one another: here on the corner of Caravan Street, his greeting of "Little Boris" [Bely]—sugary mask, slipping under his feet the instant he supposed that no one was looking at him any longer; this "naked," evil face stuck firmly in my memory; and—it became the face of Ableukhov Jr., as he walks, wrapping himself more tightly into his coat, looking armless as the cape of his coat flaps in the wind; that scene—is a reminiscence of this meeting.) (94–95)

The narrative here is clearly intended not simply to report that this meeting with Blok took place but rather to explain that a scene in the novel took shape at that meeting. The memories from which Bely created his earlier prose works are the ones that remain present to him. This is evidenced in his use of verb tense in the above-cited passage. The meeting with Blok is described in the historical past tense, while the description of Nikolay Ableukhov is narrated in the present. It is the present-tense narration that Bely calls his "reminiscence."

Similarly, on the day following this unfortunate meeting, Bely sits at his desk writing an essay, "On Mystical Anarchism." As he writes, he notices a strange book lying on his desk:

Zaglavie—"Sutta-Nipata;" ja siljus' buddijskoj Nirvanoj prervat' svoju bol'; snova: eto sluchajnoe peresechen'e fantazii o "domino" s mysl'ju Buddy vsplyvaet v romane moem, kogda staryj turanets javljaetsja pered senatorskim synom, zasnuvshim nad bomboj.

(The title is "Sutta-Nipata." I try to stop my pain by means of Buddhistic nirvana. Once again, this chance intersection of a fantasy about "the domino" with the thought of Buddha erupts in my novel, when the old Turanian appears before the senator's son, who has fallen asleep atop the bomb.) (95)

Here again Bely reminisces less about the act of writing the essay or seeing the book than he does about the fact that what he imagined in this moment made its way into the novel. In addition, this passage bears a footnote, "See *Petersburg*." The message conveyed by the note is clear. The experience of this moment has been memorialized in the novel: it can be referred to, but not repeated, here.

So caught up is Bely in his former creations that they continue to have a psychic reality for him, which in turn continues to orient his perceptions and organize his world. For example, in describing the torture of waiting for an answer to his letter to Ljubov (he calls it torture "to the domino" ["do domino"], 92), he refers to a particular sunset he saw over the Neva River in Petersburg. This sunset attached itself in his mind to "a race through life in reverse order." He imagines the race would allow him to throw himself at the knees of his childhood governess, who would stroke his head and whisper soothing words while his mother sang an old romance in the background:

Pod purpurnym zakatom stojal na Gagarinskoj naberezhnoj, pod ornamentnoj lepkoj ugrjumogo zheltogo doma; chrez mnogo let ja uvidavshi ego s ostrovov,—soznaju: eto—dom, iz kotorogo Nikolaj Apollonovich, k r a s n o e   d o m i n o, videl— e t o t   z a k a t; videl—shpits Petropavlovskoj kreposti;[1] no eto ja tut pod zheltoj stenoju stojal vspominaja o detstve: s toskoju gljadel na zakat.

   [1] Sm. "Peterburg."

(Under a purple sunset, I stood on the Gagarin bank, under an ornamental seal on a gloomy, yellow house. Many years later, upon seeing it from the island—I recognize [sic] it; this is the house from which Nikolaj Apollonovich, the r e d   d o m i n o, saw—t h i s   s u n s e t; saw—the spire of the Peter-Paul fortress;[1] but it is I [who] stood beneath the yellow wall, remembering my childhood: I watched the sunset in anguish.) (94)

[1] See *Petersburg*.

The curious feature about this passage is the reversal in the order of events by which Bely comes to interact with the scene. It is much like the reversal of the imagined race through time. Bely recognizes the house not primarily for the meaning it had in his life but for the use he made of it in his novel. It is the novel that mediates the experience of his childhood pain. This is the experience he ascribed to Nikolay in the novel, but once that transposition had taken place, the house and the sunset could no longer communicate that experience without the novel's presence. Bely's reminiscence is thus focused not on the sunset but on the "fact" that Nikolay saw it too. What is important is not Bely's life but how he apportioned it to his art.

The passage continues:

Kogda padala noch', ja sidel v restoranchike, na uglu Millionnoj, s kakim-to pote-jushchim borodachom, okazavshimsja kucherom; my s nim kogo-to svergali; on so stranits "Peterburga," vnushaet Neulovimomu[2] podozren'e; gazetoju kroet Neulo-vimyj svoj uzelochek, v kotorom—"sardinitsa"—bomba; takoj uzelochek, nevidi-myj, tochno javilsja v ruke moej; ja ego vsjudu taskal za soboj; i tochno kto vshe-ptyval v ukho—"pora tebe;" pal'tsy szhimali lish' vozdukh pustoj.

[2] Sm. roman "Peterburg."

(When night fell, I sat in a little restaurant, on the corner of Millionaya Street, with some sort of sweating, bearded old man who turned out to be a coachman. Together we overthrew somebody. He is from the pages of *Petersburg*. He fills the Elusive One[2] with suspicion; the Elusive One covers his little bundle with a newspaper, a bundle containing the "sardine tin"–bomb. Just such a little bundle, an invisible one, seemed to appear in my hand; I carried it with me everywhere; and it was just as if someone whispered in my ear—"It's time for you"; my fingers squeezed but empty air.) (94)

[2] See the novel, *Petersburg*.

Here again, as both text and footnote confirm, the reference is to events in *Petersburg*. And here again, in recalling the actual events providing the background for the novel, Bely relies upon that novel to mediate the experience. The language he created for the novel is still the language of his life. His memoirs cannot be related in any other terms.

There is, however, one essential difference between the language of the novel and that of the memoir. Although the memoir relies upon the terms of the novel (its characters, situations, images) to bring the memory to light, an important distinction is made between the experience that created the fiction and the memory of that creative experience now. In the memoir, as cited above, Bely speaks of feeling *as if* the bundle appeared in his hand, *as if* someone whispered in his ear, but his fingers squeezed empty air. By comparing the feeling to its figuration, he communicates the awareness of a difference between fact and fiction, experience and imagination, life and art. It is a difference that Bely more frequently chooses not to acknowledge, yet its appearance here opens a gap between the writing of a memoir and the writing of a novel. The gap consists of an inner distance whereby the memoir becomes aware of itself as a reenactment rather than an original, creative sensation. It is a distance that separates fiction from memoir, making one an artistic work and the other meta-artistic.

What the memoir has to say about the novel is that the novel aims to make its delirious fancies as real for the reader as they were and still are for the author himself. In the above-cited passage Bely acts out the appropriate reader response to his work: to feel *as if*. The equivocal nature of the feeling experienced is fundamental to the novel's design: all of its characters, situations, images, and events reside on some undesignated border between imagination and fact. Some characters suffer "deliriums" like Bely's while other characters produced by those deliriums somehow exist outside the delirious mentality, becoming independent of it to the point where they interact with still other characters and *their* deliriums—and so on. The substance of the novel ultimately remains a mystery: its source, that is, its creating or conceiving consciousness, is never defined; its status as wholly dream, wholly reality, or some admixture of the two is never determined. Once we read Bely's account in his memoir of the confusion reigning in his mind during this period of his life, we realize that the confusion which the novel visits upon its reader resembles the confusion that the author once experienced—and continues to experience in his memories not of his life but of his artistic work. The act that transforms experience into art is more real, more immediate, more readily available than is the event that inspired the transformation. To aestheticize the past, then (that is, to formulate it in terms proffered by the imagination), is the only way to reclaim it.

The relationship of Bely's memoir to fiction, and of reminiscence to fact, is prefigured in the role memoir plays in *Petersburg*. In the epilogue to the novel it is noted that the senator, Apollon Apollonovich Ableukhov, retires to the countryside to write his memoirs, which soon become famous all over Russia. As noted earlier, one of the peculiarities of the novel's narrative technique consists of the prevalence of inner monologue ostensibly reported by an outside observer. By noting the existence of Apollon's memoirs, the author plants the suggestion that a written record could make such intimate thoughts known. (This is only the final one of several suggestions made within the text that the whole tale takes place largely within Apollon's mind.) While this narrative ruse does not answer the question whether any of the narrative material is to be taken as really happening or as purely imaginary, it does forecast the relationship between Bely's memoirs and his artworks as a whole. The reader's sudden discovery at the end of the novel that Apollon wrote memoirs suggests that the author projected the present-tense action of the novel into the future to a point from which Apollon could remember it as something past. It is *as if* Bely contemplated, when he was writing the novel, that someday he "too" would write his memoirs"—to "prove" the factuality of the *Petersburg* tale.

But the suggestivity of the role memoir plays in the novel does not end there. Just as the existence of Apollon's memoirs can prove nothing about the facts save that Apollon remembers them in the way they appear in the novel, so too Bely's memoirs might prove nothing about his life save his commitment to the aesthetic that assimilates life to art—a commitment that demands an innovative approach to artistic form. What the memoirs explain, then, is the reason why Bely's works simply cannot be contained by the classical measures upon which generic criticism is conventionally based. For classical criticism is predicated on the assumption that art imitates life, while Bely's aesthetic reverses these terms, asserting art as the prime mover.

Memory's Role in Recreating Life and Reliving Its Fictions

The role memory plays in the assimilation of life to art is explored in an essay Bely wrote in 1930 for inclusion in a volume of works by writers about their writing.[40] The date of its writing places this essay between volumes 2 and 3 of his memoirs, and the ideas Bely elaborated in the essay aid in understanding the evolution of Bely's thinking about this work.

In the essay, "How We Write," Bely introduces himself as a "writer, formalist critic, and a man long interested in the problems of the psychology of creativity" (9). He isolates the problem as residing in the need to pinpoint the source of creative writing. Using himself to mark the parameters of the problem's definition, he says that the source of creative writing is unidentifiable because it is a part of "living life in general" ("Vot ja ne pishu; zhivu obshchej zhizn'ju," 9). More specifically, he explains that creative writing is an unconscious process, hence his interest in its psychology.

In order to describe the creative process more fully, Bely juxtaposes creative writing, that is, that which produces "artistic literature" ("khudozhestvennaja literatura"), to that which he calls simply "writing" ("pisanie"), that is, the tasks a writer performs in order to earn a living. The fundamental difference resides in the degree to which they engage conscious and unconscious efforts. Whereas artistic literature is the result largely of unconscious

[40] Bely's essay "Kak my pishem" ("How We Write") appeared in a volume by the same name published in Leningrad in 1930 by Pisateli v Leningrade. Further references to this essay will be made by noting the appropriate page numbers in the text. The pagination corresponds to that of the 1983 reprint published by Chalidze (Benson, Vt.). This essay is reprinted also as an appendix to K. N. Bugaeva, *Vospominanija*.

activity directed from within, writing is the result of a conscious response to a demand imposed from without. (He cites the request to write the present essay as an example of such a demand.) To write is to "move a pen across the page" ("strochit'," 10). To create artistic literature is, in contrast, to submit to a way of life. It is to search constantly and uncontrollably for artistic form in life and in particular to search for those forms that will communicate the specific impression, acquired unconsciously, that the writer wishes the reader to experience as Bely does, "in his soul" (11). Creativity, then, for Bely, subsists in an exchange between the conscious and unconscious minds, where the latter is the crucible of those communicable impressions of which the writer is barely aware until he himself recognizes their forms.

To this category of artistic literature Bely assigns all his poetry and his novels *The Silver Dove, Petersburg*, and *Moscow*. In the category of writing he places his memoirs, criticism, philosophy, essays, and journalism. He calls the latter group "trifling," devaluing them because they can be so precisely measured: the time it takes to write them is exactly equivalent to the time spent sitting at the desk. Although Bely says he often applies to these trifling works "a light, literary polish" that makes use of "the former achievements of 'Bely,' "[41] he claims that they represent a kind of writing different from that of artistic literature, which "can never be measured in hours or adequately paid" (10).

In his explanation of the coextension of the act of creative writing and the art of living "a general life"[42] we find Bely's views of the role played by memory in creativity. Bely perceives memory as that medium which records the writer's impressions and synthesizes them over time. The uncontrollable searching that precedes the moment of sitting down at one's desk to write artistic literature is a search for some one or thing (words, phrases, gestures, situations, characters) bearing that same trait which impressed the writer in the past. The feverish application of effort required to find such a form (effort so great as to be called "delirium") is fueled by the writer's desire to retrieve that trait from memory and contemplate it to his fill ("dorazgljadet' ee," 12). The moment when present form and past impression cohere is the moment when Bely will put pen to paper. And the actual writing will seem to take only a moment because it is merely the end point of a long process.

Although much of Bely's analysis of the writing process is romantic, even mystical, it is nonetheless instructive with regard to his memoirs in a number of ways. Of primary importance is the integration of memory and creativity described by the essay, making it abundantly clear that memory is a crucial

[41] As noted previously, Andrey Bely is a pen name; hence Bely encloses it in quotation marks here. A similar emphasis upon the status of the name is made in volume 3 of the memoirs, when he writes, " 'Andrey Bely' is a fiction" ("fiktsija"), 8.

[42] The same equivalency between art and life finds expression in volume 2 of the memoirs, when Bely says, "Art is the art of living" ("Iskusstvo est' iskusstvo zhit' "), 114.

component of the creative faculty. What the artist seeks, according to Bely, is a correspondence between his immediate perception of the present and his unconscious memories of the past. An "artistic" form, for Bely, is one that closes the gap between past and present by assimilating all to presently available forms. This is precisely why a retrospective attitude is untenable in Bely's artistic literature and impractical in his writing about that literature. For, while memory occupies a major place in his aesthetic, the past occupies no place at all. It obtains no accessible form save that which changes its very nature into immediate experience. To put it in other words, Bely simply will not acknowledge a past that remains past. Therefore he cannot reconsider his past; he can only continue to live it, as he does in artistic literature, or contemplate the human faculty that makes reliving possible, as he does in writing.

It is curious that in Bely's view of memory the past impressions that memory transforms are those residing in the unconscious. Bely sees memory as a road into this vast record, where the springs of creativity lie hidden. Within this framework the exercise of memory is tantamount to the acquisition of self-knowledge. As such, the creative exercise of memory acquires the status of universal principle, and it is its universality that justifies creativity and all it produces.

What is even more curious about Bely's view of memory is its allowance for the possibility that the only impression remembered is the one made by the very effort (the "delirious," "feverish" effort) to find a present correspondence to what is remembered. This possibility comes about by virtue of the dual role played by the unconscious: it is both the record of the impression and the energizer of the effort to make the record. In light of the dual service the unconscious performs as both cause and effect, the whole creative process is revealed to be thoroughly tautological, where what is written about is the process of writing what is written. If there indeed be an initial impression that comes from somewhere outside the act of writing, it is completely obscured by writing's focus on its own efforts to capture that impression. The written record can ultimately be valued only as testimony to the fact—the only fact—that the effort was made. In this view of writing, the act of reliving that which writing facilitates is more intense than living. Hence, it is the reliving that memory remembers.

What emerges from this understanding of Bely's view of memory is the reciprocal nature of the relationship between Bely's written forms. Just as memory and creativity are dependent upon one another, so are memoir and artistic literature, the latter category including those novels that we generally call fiction. And just as Bely's memoirs serve to explain something about the novels, the novels explain something about the memoir. Within the terms of the narrative fiction of *Petersburg* Apollon had to write his memoirs in order for the novel to exist. By the same token *Petersburg* had to be written in order for the memoir to exist. What we find in Bely's fiction, then, is a rehearsal of that which he believes to happen in life. By rehearsing his life, he collapses the distinction between fiction and reality. It is this collapse that requires the development of new generic terms for describing Bely's works and new criteria for evaluating them.

Bely's essay "How We Write" provides an initial distinction upon which to base a description of the many forms of his art. The essay suggests first what the criteria might be for judging his memoirs and second how we might locate his autobiography within the vast realm of his works. As to the first concern, the memoirs might be judged on the basis of their ability to illustrate the tautological workings of memory. As to the second, the autobiography *must* be located in the novels, for they represent what Bely takes to be primary experience. Whether *we* see it as the experience of life or the experience of art is inconsequential; it *alone* is the experience the memoir remembers. In this tautological ordering of living, writing, and remembering the memoirs emerge as a supplement to the "fiction," as a work describing the aesthetic that governs the evocation of life *as* writing. As supplement, the memoirs serve not to undermine the complexity of the novels but to elucidate their autobiographical nature and thereby to enrich them.

In "A Petersburg Drama" we discover the value of the autobiographical aesthetic to be the acquisition it facilitates of self-knowledge—the kind of knowledge without which, in Bely's view, life is not possible. This explanation of the dependency of life upon the knowledge of one's own unconscious experience, afforded by writing, is made in the memoir in the form of Bely's affirmation that through his domino delirium he came to see "a strangely joyous light." Under its auspices he abandoned both his claim to Ljubov and his desires for murder and suicide. Through his engagement with the images of his conflict, he was able to come to a mutual decision with Ljubov to part. This decision, made possible only by artistic activity was, in Bely's words, his "cure" ("vyzdorovlenie," 3:100).

More importantly, this cure is the event to which the whole story points. Once it is pronounced, Bely says, "I will not describe how we decided to part." The actual parting, which we might have expected to provide the climax, becomes a mere detail, having only secondary importance. Bely's primary concern is with the catharsis provided by art; accordingly, he demonstrates how memory seeks to retrieve not the particulars of the experience but the universal acts of self-consciousness in which the experience is based.

What is innovative about Bely's memoirs is the use he makes of them. They serve less as a form of autobiography than as a form of what we might call "auto-criticism" ("samokritika"). The stance of the memoirs is critical insofar as they address directly the processes fundamental to Bely's art. The purpose they serve is explanatory and to some degree ancillary to his fictional prose—which, within the terms of Bely's own aesthetic, must be redefined as autobiographical. For the fiction contains what Bely would consider to be the "more real" story of his life.

The fiction represents fully and solely Bely's creative process, while the memoir provides that process with a background in journalistic facts. It is precisely the additional dimension of a background that separates the memoir from the fiction, making one the analytical fact and the other the autobiographical fact. The "story" of Bely's life, that is, the one contained in the memoir, approaches the realm of critical discourse in that it presents a set of principles which move from the particular to the general and the individual to the typical by baring the workings of that highly specified language whose tautological structure allows for maximal assimilation of meaning.

By providing the background that makes the principles of Bely's art accessible, the memoir moves out of the domain of artistic literature and into the arena of criticism. What is interesting about the application of the memoir form to the ends of criticism is the severing it brings about of the tie that conventionally binds memoir to autobiography. By severing this tie Bely sets memoir on a course to becoming an independent genre. As such, Bely's memoirs constitute a unique kind of criticism, one written not in an analytical but in an artistic language, allowing criticism to be enacted exclusively on the artwork's own terms. This self-critical form preserves the accuracy and authenticity appropriately belonging to the genre of memoir while at the same time seeking out those very qualities in the work toward which it is directed. Thus, Bely's handling of the memoir ascertains the truth and the value of both his art and the study of it.

But this appraisal of Bely's memoirs as literary criticism is just a beginning for a reconsideration of genre that would need to proceed through an evaluation of memoirs by other writers who came into contact with his work. Did Bely demonstrate the potential memoir has as critical vehicle in a way that was beneficial outside of his personal domain? Only by answering this question can we assess the significance of this particular innovation.

We might be motivated to pursue this question by isolating the advantages gained in approaching Bely's memoirs on these terms. To be sure, one could use all the materials of my argument to arrive at an opposing conclusion, to demonstrate that Bely's memoirs are another one of the diverse forms of autobiography that this volume is designed to celebrate. It seems to me, however, that when viewing the memoirs as literary criticism we find they have more to offer than just a pale version of that which the novels so brilliantly achieve: the elaboration of an artistic language capable of elevating the materials of self-awareness to universal experience. By approaching the memoir as criticism we free it from the aesthetic demand of evoking a comprehensive experience, allowing it to speak to us instead *about* that aesthetic demand and how it is fulfilled. From this freedom we gain new insights into the goals and values of the author, and we learn how those brilliant novels worked for him.

Finally, I must concede that Andrey Bely would most likely disagree with this approach. Because of the identity of life and art that he maintains, he would admit of no difference between understanding the novels and understanding the artist. However, in our postmodern day of deconstructive and reader-response criticism I feel we can look beyond symbolist tautologies and theories of knowledge to ever more descriptive epistemologies and ever more expansive appreciations of artistic genius.

CHAPTER 4

Autobiography and History: Osip Mandelstam's *Noise of Time*

Jane Gary Harris

READERS OF *Noise of Time* (*Shum vremeni*, 1923–25) have long admired Mandelstam's lyric autobiography as one of the finest literary portrayals of prerevolutionary Russia. However, those who expected a more conventional nineteenth-century autobiographical form have been disappointed, even though Mandelstam's programmatic statement clearly rejected a traditional approach; others who have tried too hard to distinguish between the poet's prose and verse have also concluded that the prose is wanting. The most pertinent criticism of *Noise of Time* has focused on locating either a semantic or a chronological pattern as the source of its aesthetic unity.[1] In this essay, I suggest that the principle of aesthetic coherence in *Noise of Time* may lie in Mandelstam's choice of a new genre and narrative strategy—the creation of an autobiography based on a complex set of parallel structures that examine, define, and interpret his intellectual and aesthetic relations with history and time.

Noise of Time, the poet's first creative endeavor in the autobiographical mode, initiates a new phase in his work. It follows the publication of his two earlier verse collections, *Stone* (*Kamen'*, 1913 and 1916) and *Tristia* (1922) and coincides with the writing of numerous critical essays as well as a new poetic cycle, *1921–1925*, published in 1928. Not only does Mandelstam introduce his own life for the first time in *Noise of Time* as basic poetic material,

---

[1] For other discussions of this work, see: N. Berkovskij, "O proze Mandelstama," *Tekushchaja literatura* (Moscow: Federatsija, 1930); C. Brown, "The Prose of Mandelstam" in *The Noise of Time: The Prose of Osip Mandelstam*, ed. and trans. C. Brown (San Francisco: North Point Press, 1986); B. Filipoff, "Proza Mandel'shtama" in *Sobranie sochinenij (SS)*, ed. G. Struve and B. Filipoff (New York: Inter-Language Literary Associates, 1967–81): 2:i–xviii; Grigory Freidin, "The Whisper of History and The Noise of Time," *Russian Review* 37, no. 4 (1978): 421–37; an earlier version of this essay in Jane G. Harris, *Osip Mandelstam* (Boston: Twayne Publishers, 1988) ch. 4; Charles Isenberg, *Substantial Proofs of Being: Osip Mandelstam's Literary Prose* (Columbus: Slavica Publishers, 1987, ch. 2); Dmitry Segal, "Voprosy poeticheskoj organizatsii semantiki v proze Mandel'shtama," *Russian Poetics: Proceedings of the International Colloquium at UCLA, Sept. 22–26, 1975*, ed. T. Eekman and D. Worth, UCLA Slavic Series 4 (Los Angeles: University of California Press, 1983); N. Struve, "Le Bruit du Temps' dans l'oeuvre de Mandelstam" in *Le Bruit du Temps*, trans. E. Scherrer (Paris, 1972), i–xviii.

but he chooses to shape his autobiographical myth in terms of Russia's cultural history, linking his "literary genesis" with the history of his age.

In "End of the Novel," an essay conceived within a few years of the autobiography, Mandelstam notes that the "pivot" of the nineteenth-century novel was "human biography"—the "sense of time man possesses to act, to conquer, to perish and to love" (*CPL*, 200; *SS*, 2:269).[2] Simultaneously, however, he indicates his fear that twentieth-century man is "devoid of biography." He therefore had no choice but to dismiss the novel as a viable genre if he were to seek an appropriate form in which to examine his own sense of time as a man *and* as a poet. What is more, *Noise of Time* also rejects the nineteenth-century genres of self-reflexive prose because, as Mandelstam claims in his programmatic statement to his autobiography, there was nothing but a "hiatus" in his biography where a traditional family history "ought to have been." It should also be noted that in the poems of *1921–1925* Mandelstam expresses similar anxiety over problems of the poet and the age, of memory and time, and for the first time introduces into his lyrics poignant personal references.[3]

In the programmatic statement with which Mandelstam opens the penultimate chapter of *Noise of Time* the primacy of memoir is established and emphasized—the presentation of the self with reference to historical context. In addition, it is here that Mandelstam establishes his concern for his literary genesis as opposed to his family heritage. He does so first by continuing the thematic impulse of his most recent collection of verse, *Tristia*, in which he reveals the negative impulses of his memory as significant sources of inspiration, and second by rejecting outright a conventional self-image based on the "personal" or familial.

The object of Mandelstam's autobiography, then, becomes the recovery of a sense of time through an examination of analogies or parallels between his individual destiny and Russia's cultural history. As a man "devoid of biography," he has first to comprehend the epoch that influenced his formative years and only subsequently to define his self-image in the context of that history. And as a poet, he has to acquire a language to articulate that history, for his is to be an act of cultural memory, a biography created out of history and literature, not the conventional story of the evolution of an individual's inner psyche. As presented in *Noise of Time*, consciousness of personal identity came to Mandelstam only after the Revolution—as a result of its sudden illumina-

---

[2] Page citations to Mandelstam's essays refer first to J. G. Harris, ed. and trans. (with C. Link), *The Complete Critical Prose and Letters* (*CPL*) (Ann Arbor: Ardis Publishers, 1979), and second to G. Struve and B. Filipoff, eds., *Sobranie Sochinenij*. In the text these works are cited as *CPL* and *SS*, respectively.

[3] See Omry Ronen, *An Approach to Mandel'shtam* (Jerusalem: The Magnes Press, 1983). This book provides exceptionally fine readings of the poems of this period, providing detailed analyses of "Slate Ode" and "January 1, 1924."

tion of Russia's historical and cultural traditions—and with the poet's consequent identification of the stages of his own personal, aesthetic, and intellectual growth with developments in Russia's cultural heritage. His
programmatic statement follows:

> My desire is to speak *not about myself* but to *track down the age, the noise, and the*
> *germination of time*. My memory is inimical to all that is personal. If it depended on
> me, I should only make a wry face in remembering the past. I was never able to
> understand the Tolstoys and Aksakovs . . . enamoured of family archives. . . . I
> repeat—my labor is not to reproduce but *to distance the past*. A *raznochinets* needs
> no memory—it is enough for him to tell of the books he has read, and his biography
> is done. Where for happy generations the epic speaks in hexameters and chronicles,
> I have merely the sign of the *hiatus*, and *between me and the age there lies an abyss*,
> a moat filled with clamorous time, the place where a family and reminiscences of
> *family ought to have been*. What was it my family wished to say? I do not know. It
> was tongue-tied from birth—*but* it had, nevertheless, *something it might have said*.
> Over my head and that of many of my contemporaries hangs congenital tongue-tie.
> We were not taught to speak but to babble—and *only by listening to the swelling*
> *noise of the age* and the bleached foam on the crest of its wave *did we acquire a*
> *language*. (109–10; 2:99)[4]

Since Mandelstam sought and found the source of his consciousness neither
in his inner psyche nor in his family but rather in history and in the books he
had read, he came to define his adult self-image as that of a "*raznochinets-*
writer," a critical intellectual with leanings toward the "fourth estate" seeking his roots in Russia's cultural history. Indeed, he sought his literary genesis
in "the *bookcase* of early childhood":

> The *bookcase* of early childhood is a *man's companion* for life. . . . There was
> nothing haphazard in the way that strange little library had been deposited, like a
> *geological bed*, over decades. The paternal and maternal elements were not mixed,
> but existed separately, and a cross-section of the strata showed the *history of the*
> *spiritual efforts of the entire family*, as well as the innoculation of it with *alien blood*.
> (78; 2:57)

He eventually substituted Russian writers and literature for his own family
by imagining his teacher and mentor Gippius (VVG) as the source of literature
and his home as "literature's own house." Everything familial was displaced
onto literature or "the word."

> I would come to him (VVG) to wake up the beast of literature. . . . *I would come to*
> *my teacher of Russian at home*. The whole savor of the thing lay in that coming to
> him "at home." *Even now* it is difficult for me to free myself from *the notion that I*

---

[4] Page citations to *Noise of Time* refer first to C. Brown, *The Noise of Time*, 69–117, and second
to *Shum vremeni* in Struve and Filipoff, *SS*, 2:45–108. Italics are mine unless otherwise indicated.

was then at literature's own house. . . . . Beginning as early as Radishchev and No-
vikov, V.V. had established *personal relations with Russian writers*, splenetic and
loving liaisons filled with noble enviousness, jealousy, with jocular disrespect,
grievous unfairness—as is *customary between the members of a family.* . . . V.V.'s
judgments continue to hold me today. (115–16; 2:106)

To more fully understand Mandelstam's autobiography, it is essential to
examine its structural elements and the means by which his ideas—philosophical, historical, and aesthetic—are incorporated into the text. First of all, the
opening phrase "I well remember" immediately initiates the reader into the
poet's autobiographical task by affirming the power of memory and relating it
to historical consciousness. The personal experience is directly established as
part of a given historical context.

Second, the reader is alerted that a significant element of aesthetic coherence in this text derives from the juxtaposition of visualized historical details
pictured "in scenes" and aural images, the "noises of time," depicting the
historical undercurrents associated with music and performances.

I well remember the godforsaken years of Russia, the deaf years, the decade of the
nineties. . . . At morning tea there would be talk about Dreyfus, there were *the
names* of Colonels Esterhazy and Picquart, vague disputes about some "Kreutzer
Sonata" and, *behind the high podium* of the glass railroad station in Pavlovsk, *the
change of conductors* which seemed to me a *change of dynasties* . . . and, all in all,
I picture the nineties . . . *in scenes* scattered apart but *inwardly bound* together by
the quiet misery and the painful, doomed provincialism of the life that was dying.
(69; 2:45)

Third, the autobiographical narrator introduces the reader to his faith in the
word as the vehicle of cultural memory, emphasizing that his experience is of
memory and history, for his autobiographical imagination restructures experience by subjecting it to aesthetic interpretation. For example, the immediacy
of the child-hero's first memories—a precise historical occasion—are mediated through the adult narrator's retrospective transformation of those "perceptions" into "spectacle."

My first conscious sharp perceptions were of gloomy crowds of people in the streets.
I was exactly three years old. It was 1894 and I had been brought from Pavlovsk to
Petersburg for the purpose of seeing the funeral of Alexander III. Having crawled
up on the windowsill and seen the crowd-darkened street, I asked, "When will they
start?" and was told "tomorrow." (75; 2:53)

Indeed, Mandelstam's concluding chapter proposes the art of retrospection
as the *only* path for comprehending the "modern age," contemporaneity:

To remember not living people but plaster casts struck from their voices. To go
blind. *To feel and recognize by hearing.* Sad fate! *Thus does one penetrate into the
present*, into the *modern age*, as via the bed of a dried up river.

As you know, those were not friends, nor near ones, but alien, distant people!
Still, it is only with the masks of other men's voices that the bare walls of my house
are decorated. *To remember*—to make one's way alone back up the dried riverbed!
The first literary encounter is irremediable. (113; 2:104)

Noise of Time is thus unique in that historical data and aesthetically conceived events are lyrically transformed to create rather than recreate the life of
the hero out of Russia's cultural history. The proliferation of historical nomen-
clature—accurate historical names, places, and events—is used to create a
self-image in which a vivid historical context enriches the personal as a concrete physiological reality engenders the spiritual. Mandelstam's attempt to
gradually identify the destiny of his autobiographical hero with Russia's cultural destiny, with Russian history, derives from his philological and philosophical conviction that the Russian language *is* Russian history, an idea associated with his interpretation of Bergson, first ennunciated in his essay "On
the Nature of the Word."

As Mandelstam understood it, Bergson's theory of time as duration (*la durée*) was concerned not merely with the operation of the individual psyche but
with the enduring self "in its flowing through time," that is, with the self in
history. In his *Introduction to Metaphysics* of 1903 Bergson states: "There is
one reality, at least, which we all seize from within, by intuition and not by
simple analysis. It is our personality in its flowing through time—our self
which endures."[5]

Mandelstam's theoretical reformulation of this idea, his conceptualization
and literary expression of the "awareness of experience as continuous process," was not fully realized until *Conversation about Dante*, written ten years
after *Noise of Time*, wherein he declares: "Poetic material . . . exists only in
performance . . . [the] finished poem is no more than . . . the inevitable result
of the impulse to perform." However, *Noise of Time* may perhaps be read as
an early effort to create that same sense of "performance" or continuous process by using the open prose genre of autobiography rather than the closed
forms of lyric poetry that dominated his creative work until 1923. The hero's
aesthetic consciousness is thus revealed *in process*, in performance, as the
memorable events and moments of the poet's life and of Russia's history are
filtered through the hero's growing awareness and poetic imagination.

In his essay "On the Nature of the Word," which preceded *Noise of Time*
by one year, Mandelstam cited Bergson in his endeavor to comprehend the
nature and source of the word, in particular, the "Russian literary language,"
which he goes so far as to equate with Russian history: "So highly organized,
so organic a language is not merely a door into history, but *is history itself*."
He even tells the reader why he perceives the Russian language as "historical": "The Russian language is historical by its very nature, since in its total-

---

[5] Henri Bergson, *Introduction to Metaphysics*, trans. T. E. Hulme (New York, 1949; original,
Paris, 1903), 8.

ity it is a turbulent sea of events, a continuous incarnation and activation of rational and breathing flesh" (CPL 121; SS, 2:246).

The poet's role then, as Mandelstam perceives it here, is the articulation of Russian history. He takes this notion one step further in his autobiography, wherein he depicts his own "personality in its flowing through time," thus expressing Russian history through his autobiographical myth. In this way *Noise of Time* may be said to articulate Mandelstam's philological and philosophical conception of the poet's intuitive grasp of time, specifically, the fluid quality of reality, the awareness of experience as continuous process, in keeping with his reading of Bergson and his reformulation of his acmeist poetics in "On the Nature of the Word."

Mandelstam's strategy of parallelism is introduced to the reader gradually as the chronological phases of the autobiography unfold, each one concretizing the poet's intuitive sense of self in a given period by portraying its integral relationship to the flow of time—Russian cultural history. The autobiographer's intense interest in the historical theme elevates it to a structural level in his text parallel to the psychophysiological theme anticipated in the development of traditional nineteenth-century autobiography. That is, in traditional autobiography psychological detail and physiological description are expected to denote changes in the developing hero's state of mind and physical characteristics. In addition, Mandelstam's declaration of his aesthetic doctrine "not to reproduce but to distance the past" superimposes an aesthetic dimension on his treatment of temporality and time consciousness. The theme of aesthetic consciousness is thereby elevated to a structural level parallel to the themes of historical and psychophysiological consciousness.

The parallels drawn in Mandelstam's autobiography, then, include: (1) the periods of historical consciousness: 1890s, 1900s, and postrevolutionary Russia, which are marked by dates and events; (2) the stages of psychophysiological growth of the hero, which are marked by the imagery of music: childhood (Tchaikovsky's *1812 Overture*), adolescence (Tchaikovsky's *Symphonie Pathetique* and the concerts of Hoffman and Kubelik), and maturity (poetry or the word marked by the refrain "Sing, Mary" in his subtextual allusion to Pushkin's *Feast During the Plague*); (3) the phases of aesthetic consciousness presented in the text as "police aesthetics," "the aesthetic of the intellect," and the aesthetic of conscience, "literary savagery"; and (4) the types of literature associated with each aesthetic-historical epoch, which are expressed through the symbolics of literary performance: the literature of reflection (Nadsonism and the Literary Fund), the literature of disengagement (symbolism), and "genuine Russian literature" or the literature of conscience (Pushkin's *Feast during the Plague*).

How does this parallelism function as narrative strategy in the text? The narrative structure of *Noise of Time* emerges from the gradual identification of the hero's consciousness with the historical periods under discussion. These periods correspond to the stages of the hero's psychophysiological growth, which in turn correspond to the phases of aesthetic consciousness first experienced by the narrator-hero and then recalled and reimagined by the poet-autobiographer. The literary reminiscences that metaphorically reiterate the process of aesthetic-historical change are singled out by the autobiographical narrator as links between the personal, historical, and aesthetic layers of this work, for they reflect the stages in the poet-hero's literary genesis. Moreover, the literary references are all to performances and hence suggest the as yet unformulated concept expressed later in *Conversation about Dante* that "poetry exists only in performance." In the autobiography, aesthetic consciousness is represented as in process. *Noise of Time*, then, may be read perhaps as poetry in the process of formation or as a prose poem in performance.

Some examples can be offered here. As the reader is carefully guided into the first period, the decade of the 1890s, by the autobiographical narrator, he initially perceives the epoch through the mind of the narrator-protagonist or child-hero. The reader is gradually led to realize that the child's subjective perspective on this period in Russian history is synonymous with the mature autobiographical narrator's distant retrospective evaluation. In a word, the epoch itself is judged as "childhood" to the "adolescence" of Russia's 1900s and to the "maturity" of postrevolutionary Russia. To illustrate this point, while the aesthetic consciousness of the period is defined as "police aesthetics" from the narrator's retrospective vision, the vitality of the age is illuminated by the child's subjective views on growing up in Russia's cultural capital.

> All this mass of militarism and even a kind of *police aesthetics* may very well have been *proper* to some son of a corps commander with *appropriate* family traditions, *but* . . . the Petersburg street *awakened in me a craving for spectacle*, and the very architecture of the city *inspired me* with a kind of *childish imperialism*.
>
> Even *death first appeared to me* in a totally *unnatural, elegant and festive* guise. (74; 2:52)

Furthermore, the police aesthetics of the 1890s that so enthrall the child are offered to the reader as the dominant aesthetic value of the period, just as the most popular reading matter, the fantastic "miscellanies," indicate that the interests and values of the child—his favorite reading matter—are identical with the spirit of the age, with the interests and values of the adults:

> I loved the "miscellany" about ostrich eggs, two-headed calves, and festivals in Bombay and Calcutta, and especially the huge, full-page pictures: Malayan swimmers . . . the mysterious experiment of a M. Fouque. . . . *I have a feeling that the grownups read the same thing as I*, that is, mainly the immense, burgeoning supplements to *The Field* and the rest. *Our interests were, in general, identical.* . . . At seven or eight I was *fully abreast* of the age. (70; 2:47)

Consequently, the portrayal of the historical and aesthetic consciousness of the 1890s emerges through the eyes and mind of the child-hero who, in turn, reflects the childishness of Russia's own childhood from the autobiographical narrator's postrevolutionary perspective.

It is not surprising, then, that this entire epoch is characterized by childishness, frivolity, naiveté, and tranquil pleasures, on the one hand, and by its "deafness" to the serious—to the undercurrents of ideological, economic, and social change, on the other. The predominantly visual imagery of the period establishes its superficiality and artificiality, while alluding to its external harmony, visual beauty, and architecture as "childish imperialism." All this is opposed to the undercurrents of dissonance, discord, and confusion that characterize the coming age of adolescence, marked by heightened aural and musical imagery. The intellectuals of the 1890s emerge as visually acute but deaf, for these are the "deaf years of Russia, the decade of the nineties."

Hence, the perception of the 1890s as the childhood of contemporary Russian history derives from autobiographical retrospection, engendered by Mandelstam's recognition and acceptance of the Revolution as the catastrophic event that, paradoxically perhaps, made comprehension of prerevolutionary Russia possible and consequently inspired him to write his autobiography, thus preserving its memory. On the very last page of the text, the autobiographer—now the mature "*raznochinets*-writer" living in the new, intensely historically conscious, postrevolutionary age—clarifies this aesthetic revelation:

> Looking back at the entire nineteenth century of Russian culture—shattered, finished, unrepeatable, which no one should repeat, which no one dares repeat—I wish to hail the century, as one would hail settled weather. I see in it the unity lent it by the measureless cold which welded decades together into one day, one night, one profound winter, within which the terrible State, glowed, like a stove, in ice. (117; 2:108)

In this way the reader is introduced simultaneously to the first period of the autobiographer's life experience, childhood, and to the earliest sources of his awakening historical and aesthetic consciousness. In addition, the subjective childhood experience is both objectified through the "*raznochinets*-writer's" memory of nineteenth-century Russia and aestheticized through his new poetics of conscience and challenge—"literary savagery."

The hero's and the author's personal experience are identified with Russia's cultural history as the "*raznochinets*"-autobiographer speaks as its bard interpreting the "noise of time."

A similar case can be made for the correlation of the second phase of the narrator's life experience, the period of adolescence, with Russia's 1900s and for the correlation of maturity or adulthood with the postrevolutionary years, the time of the composition of the autobiography.

From the retrospective vision of the autobiographical narrator, adolescence intensified and further defined his aesthetic and historical consciousness, paving the way for their eventual and, in Mandelstam's postrevolutionary view, inevitable synthesis. In contrast to the 1890s, marked by police aesthetics, the 1900s are characterized by the aesthetic of the intellect, conveyed through the adolescent hero's friendship with Boris Sinani and his family: "The central feature of the Sinani household was what I should call *an esthetic of the intellect*. Positivism is usually hostile to esthetic contemplation, the disinterested pride and joy of the movements of the mind. But for these people the intellect was joy, health, sport and almost religion, all at once" (105; 2:93).

Adolescence is marked by the intensity of the young hero's responses to music in conjunction with his psychophysiological identification with the power of art. Psychological response is clearly identified here with expressions of physical/sexual emotions and pain. Ideologically, the intensity of his response to music also indicates that neither he nor the 1900s in general is deaf any longer to the anxiety and agitation of the age.

> At this time I conceived for Tchaikovsky a painfully nervous and intense love that recalled the desire of Dostoevsky's Netochka Nezvanovna to hear the violin concert behind the red flame of the silk curtains. . . . I heard from behind a barbed-wire fence [in Jewish Dubbeln the orchestra strained at Tchaikovsky's *Symphonie Pathetique* . . .] and more than once I tore my clothes and covered my hands with scratches as I made my way gratis to the orchestra shell. . . . What a thread it is that runs from these first wretched concerts to the silk flame of Nobility Hall. (87–88; 2:70)

The intensity of the adolescent perspective, then, reflects the heightened historical and ideological consciousness of the immediate prerevolutionary years, found everywhere but marked especially in this work in the concert halls, where art alone seems to be charged with the power to control imminent catastrophe.

> In the season of 1903–04 Petersburg witnessed concerts in the grand manner. . . . The concerts of Hofmann and Kubelik in the Nobility Hall during Lent . . . would reach a kind of rage, a fury. This was no musical dilettantism: there was something threatening and even dangerous that rose up out of enormous depths, a kind of craving for movement; a mute prehistorical malaise was exuded by . . . the almost flagellant zeal of the guards in Mikhailovsky Square, and it whetted the Petersburg of that day (the year 1905 had not yet struck) like a knife. . . .
>
> Hofmann and Kubelik . . . [held] sway over the stunned musical mob. . . . [They] would try with all the means of their art . . . to chain and cool the unbridled Dionysian element. . . . But what in their performance was clear and sober served only to enrage and incite the crowd. . . . Such was the power in the rational and pure playing of those two virtuosos. (88–90; 2:71–73)

The value of art is subtly charged with increasingly more power as the turmoil and excitement of the intellectual commitment and ideological and emotional confusion experienced by the adolescent hero seeking to comprehend the age in its entirety is portrayed through both psychological responses to his environment and intellectual efforts to interpret history through aesthetic models.

> I was troubled and anxious. All the agitation of the times communicated itself to me—from the longing for suicide to the expectation of the end of the world. The literature of problems and ignorant universal questions had just taken its gloomy malodorous leave, and the grimy, hairy hands of the traffickers in life and death were rendering the very words life and death repugnant. . . . The dull polka from [Andreyev's] *Life of Man* . . . the symbol of vulgar tawdry symbolism, was picked out . . . on the piano . . . in every house. . . . That was all the vilest scum when compared to the world of the Erfurt Program, the Communist Manifesto, and agrarian debates. (108–9; 2:98)

Contemporary literature, reflected in the dominant tenets of symbolism, is represented both in the false values and vulgarity attributed to Andreyev and in the magnificent but ultimately alien productions of Komissarzhevskaya's Dramatic Theater. If on the one hand the problems of life and death were perceived as vulgarized, on the other the refined beauty of *Hedda Gabler* was appreciated. Nevertheless, in Mandelstam's view, the aesthetics of symbolism could not be altered even by the artistic devotion of Komissarzhevskaya.

> Unlike the Russian actors of that day—and also, perhaps, of the present day—Komissarzhevskaya possessed an inner sense of music; she raised and lowered her voice just as the breathing of the verbal sequence required. Her acting was three-quarters verbal and was accompanied by only the most essential, spare gestures. . . .
> I do not think that any perspectives for the future of the threatre were opened up here. That chamber drama came to us from Little Norway. . . . The apothecary from Christiania [Ibsen] was able to lure terror into a professor's henhouse and to raise to the heights of tragedy the maliciously polite squabbling of Hedda and Brack. (111; 2:100–101)

Although the objective consciousness of the autobiographical narrator intrudes in this passage through his drama review, it merges with the hero's subjective vision. The sensitive adolescent is represented as having fully experienced the prerevolutionary age; his search for new values is reinforced. Hence, the critical review of Komissarzhevskaya and her theater actually provides a necessary dialogue with Andreyev's "vulgar, tawdry" symbolism. But while Komissarzhevskaya's acting, due to her emphasis on the word, is received in a most positive manner, her repertory is considered inappropriate to the complexity of Russia's future needs.

The tribute to Komissarzhevskaya concludes the penultimate chapter of

Noise of Time. Mandelstam's programmatic statement, which opens the chapter, is followed first by a strangely lyrical passage on revolution and then by the drama review. Revolution is perceived here as natural, organic, inevitable, genuine, and serious, hence as the antithesis of symbolism with its "idle chatter about life and death": "A revolution is itself life and death and cannot endure idle chatter about life and death in its presence. . . . Nature—revolution is an eternal thirst, an inflamation (perhaps it envies those ages when thirst was quenched in a quiet homelike way by simply going off to the place where the sheep were watered)" (110; 2:99).

The period of adolescence is thereby directly associated with the ideological and sociopolitical undercurrents of the day as well as with the search for a new and genuine aesthetic truth, values that could support an attitude toward life. It rejects contemporary literature, however, both the refined and the vulgar tenets of symbolism.

Indeed, the young hero's efforts during this period to invoke aesthetic models to understand history and life lead him to ponder the paradoxical equation of Marxism (Kautsky) and Tiutchev:

> Everything that represented an attitude toward life was greedily devoured. . . . Early, O Erfurt Program, Marxist Propylaea . . . you gave a sense of life in those prehistoric years when thought hungered after unity and harmoniousness. . . . Is Kautsky Tiutchev? . . . But just imagine—for a person of a certain age and at a certain time Kautsky . . . is Tiutchev, that is, the source of cosmic joy, the bearer of a strong and harmonious attitude toward life, the thinking reed, a cover thrown over the abyss. (100–101; 2:87)

Nevertheless, it is only in the concluding chapter of *Noise of Time*, when the poet-hero achieves maturity and merges with the adult autobiographical narrator, that he is finally mature enough to comprehend his literary genesis and write his autobiography. It is only in this phase of adulthood, set in the postrevolutionary period, when his aesthetic and historical consciousness have merged, that he can identify himself as a *raznochinets*-writer and evaluate and assimilate his past—the Judaic chaos amidst the tranquil harmony of his childhood, the abyss of adolescence, and the Revolution of his adulthood—by confronting the challenge of the new age—the "wintry period of Russian history." In this phase, by identifying with the "*raznochinets*-writer," Mandelstam gains an awareness of a new bond between art and history, between aesthetic and intellectual values, taking his aesthetic of "literary savagery" (literaturnaja zlost) as his own autobiographical challenge. He thus confirms the power of art or the word to challenge history and time, for the mature writer is portrayed as someone who must judge the past by confronting it with the challenge of his own temporality and potentiality.

Literary savagery! Were it not for you, what should I have to eat the salt of the earth with?

You are the seasoning for the unleavened bread of understanding, you are the joyful consciousness of injustice, you are the conspiratorial salt which is transmitted with a malicious bow from decade to decade, in a cut-glass salt cellar, with a serving cloth! That is why I so love to extinguish the heat of literature with frost and barbed stars. Will it crunch like the crust of snow? Will it brighten up in the frosty weather of the Nekrasovian street? If it is genuine, the answer is yes. (113; 2:103)

How is this phase of adulthood actually conveyed in *Noise of Time*? First of all, it is established only in the final chapter, or indeed, the epilogue, written in 1925, a year and a half after the completion of the major portion of the text. Here Mandelstam seems to have recognized the autobiographer's dilemma and to have attempted to overcome it by creating both an autonomous image of his narrator-hero as having achieved maturity as a "*raznochinets*-writer," and a synthetic portrait of his hero as having recovered his literary genesis through authoring his autobiography.

To represent this synthesis Mandelstam first goes back to the figure of V. V. Gippius, his teacher and mentor, presenting him as a kind of alter ego to complement the image of the mature "*raznochinets*-writer"; his image is that of the "*raznochinets-literateur*." By way of explanation, the reader is told that Gippius had taught young Mandelstam "not literature, but the far more interesting science of literary savagery." He is symbolically recalled here as the "beast of literature" whose "lair of an apartment" originally inspired young Mandelstam to imagine it as "literature's own house." In this final chapter of *Noise of Time* Gippius emerges as Mandelstam's equal, as his "companion."

The portrait of Gippius, therefore, is presented both subjectively and objectively in order to express and explicate the source and genesis of the autobiographer's self-image and his aesthetic of conscience: "literary savagery." Thus the doctrine of "literary savagery," acquired unwittingly by the adolescent schoolboy from his "teacher of literature," is here recognized by the mature poet-autobiographer and adopted as the aesthetic bond uniting protagonist and autobiographer.

The epilogue opens with the coming together of the two companions—the *raznochinets*-writer and the *raznochinets-literateur*—against the emblematic background of Petersburg's postrevolutionary, wintry night atmosphere. A series of oxymoronic images blend and juxtapose cold and night, heat and flame, burning, glowing, or light in the "winter of Russian history": "Towards *midnight* the waves of a *snowstorm* were *raging* along the streetcar tracks of Vasilievsky Island. . . . *Now*, the raspberry *globes* of pharmacies *burn there in the winter*. My *companion* emerging from his *literateur's lair* of an apartment . . . my *companion* became downright cheerful. . . . He bellowed for a cabby'' (112; 2:102). Further descriptions include the paradoxical association of ''literary savagery''—the instinctual ''feral relationship to literature''—and familial ''warmth,'' that of ''the house [and] family'':

> The person who bellowed for a cabby was V. V. Gippius. . . . *He differed* from other *witnesses* of literature. . . . He had a kind of *feral relationship* to literature as if it were the *only source of animal warmth*. . . . *I would come* to him to wake up *the beast of literature*. . . . Never again was *literature to be a house, an apartment, a family.* (114–16; 2:104–6)

Finally, to support the complex of values presented in this concluding chapter, subsumed under the unique and paradoxical aesthetic doctrine of literary savagery, Mandelstam summons up Pushkin's ''little tragedy,'' *Feast during the Plague*, as an authoritative literary model—a subtext exemplifying ''genuine literature''—and an example of his aesthetic of conscience.

While expressing the poet's anxiety before the challenge of the future, this subtext simultaneously encourages the idea that the word provides the ''only source of warmth'' in ''this wintry period of Russian history'' and is therefore essential to human existence.

Moreover, besides echoing Pushkin's dramatic formulation of the theme of individual destiny and affirming poetry's role in the survival of human values, this subtext reinforces Mandelstam's theme of the power of poetry and, more specifically, of the power of poetry to avert catastrophe, first expressed in his 1921 tribute to Blok entitled ''Badger Hole.'' In that essay he states the principle: ''*Poetic culture arises from the attempt to avert catastrophe*, to make it dependent on the central sun of the system as a whole, be it love, of which Dante spoke, or music, at which Blok ultimately arrived'' (*CPL*, 137; *SS*, 2:275).

Although there is no direct reference in *Noise of Time* to the ''Hymn to the Plague'' recited by Pushkin's hero Walsingham, Mandelstam's final chapter is bathed in images that seem to mime its imagery, just as the poet's theme of faith in the survival of the word is seemingly inspired by the challenge of the hymn's thematic statement. The applicable stanzas (1, 3, and 6) of the ''Hymn'' read as follows:

> When fearlessly King Winter swoops
> Upon us with his hoary troops
> And brings against us in his ire
> A mighty host of frost and snow,
> Then we will gather at the fire
> And feast with cups of wine aglow.
>
> The way we meet the Winter's tide
> So let us meet the Plague outside—
> With light, with lights ablaze, and wine!

And so with laughter and with jest
Come dance and drink, with praise divine
To hail her majesty Queen Pest!

And so, O Plague, we hail thy reign!
We laugh at graves, at death and pain.
We die no cowards in the night!
We drink, carefree! The baneful breath
Of dying beauty's our delight,—
Our daring in the face of Death![6]

This subtext, then, is far more complex than it appears initially. Like Pushkin before him, Mandelstam seems to acknowledge aesthetic challenge in adversity, in historical destiny. Thus, as the plague was to compel Pushkin's heroes to rise to its challenge, for Mandelstam the Revolution emerges as but one more catastrophe, one more challenge in the series of challenges he has to confront as he grows up: Judaic chaos amidst the tranquility of the 1890s, which ultimately stimulated his child's imagination; the abyss of adolescence and dissatisfaction with symbolism amidst the turmoil of the early 1900s, which he imaginatively assimilated through his synthesis of Kautsky and Tiutchev, and now the Revolution and the immediate postrevolutionary years—the wintry period of Russian history. Backed up by Pushkin's themes of individual destiny and the power of the word, Mandelstam's doctrine of literary savagery, his aesthetic of conscience, the moral force behind his acmeist aesthetic as redefined in "On the Nature of the Word," thus evokes a response as intellectually vital and challenging as it is aesthetically novel.

Mandelstam's postrevolutionary aesthetic, then, both affirms the need for the word and confirms its survival as an organic process as natural and as necessary as animal instinct, the weather, and the alternation of night and day, winter and spring. As Pushkin realized that his heroes had to create new songs to avert the imminent catastrophe of the plague outside, so in his final chapter Mandelstam recognizes that at this historical moment a new literature must be formed by "winter and night." Hence, the autobiography concludes with the passage:

And *in this wintry period of Russian history*, literature, taken at large, strikes me as something patrician, which puts me out of countenance. . . . No one is to blame in this and there is nothing to be ashamed of. A beast must not be ashamed of its furry hide. Night furred him. Winter clothed him. *Literature is a beast.* Its furriers are *night and winter.* (117; 2:108)

---

[6] E. M. Kayden, ed. and trans., *Little Tragedies: Four Short Verse Dramas by Alexander Pushkin* (Antioch, 1965), 91–93.

In the last period that Mandelstam treats in his autobiography, his new aesthetic of conscience—''literary savagery''—is proffered as the inevitable successor both to the childishly naive ''police aesthetics'' of the 1890s and to the adolescent ''aesthetic of the intellect'' marking the 1900s. Just as Nadson's poetry reading before the Literary Fund expressed the Russian intelligentsia's cultural zenith in the 1890s and Komissarzhevskaya's *Hedda Gabler* reflected the culmination of cultural values in the 1900s, Pushkin's *Feast during the Plague* conveys the postrevolutionary *raznochinets*-writer's new aesthetic challenge.

In this way Mandelstam's autobiographical reflections on time and history are reinforced by literary symbolics, refracted from references to three key performances, each of which culminates a phase in the poet's literary genesis and marks the juncture of the three parallel periods in Russia's cultural history treated in *Noise of Time*.

The symbolics of Mandelstam's autobiographical discourse reinforce and develop the thematics of his text, in particular, the theme of the poet's destiny as the bard of Russia's cultural history, preserver of cultural continuity—indeed, as the bard of transition from the tranquility of the nineteenth-century heritage to the new and harsher challenges of the twentieth century. Through the art of his autobiographical act Mandelstam articulates for the first time the tension and interplay between his life experience and its aesthetic interpretation.

CHAPTER 5

Boris Pasternak's *Safe Conduct*

Krystyna Pomorska

PASTERNAK'S AUTOBIOGRAPHY is in many respects comparable to all his prose pieces that deal with his life story.[1] The reason for this is revealed in the autobiographical text of *Safe Conduct* (*Okhrannaja gramota*),[2] written between 1929 and 1931 and first published in 1931. Here the author confesses that one of the ideas inherited by him from the symbolists was "an understanding of life in general as the life of a poet."[3] And even though he rejects this concept, declaring that "outside of romantic legends this plan is artificial,"[4] he follows this "plan," particularly in one basic respect: in treating a poet as a chosen man. For this reason we can draw a parallel between his understanding of a poet's life and that of Pushkin and Mayakovsky.

Mayakovsky in his "anti-biography" declared that he would speak only about "what defended itself *in a word*" ("chto otstojalas' *slovom*"). Pasternak chose for his autobiography a title that refers to the tradition of the biblical prophet whom God gave the *word* for his "safe conduct" as he went "into the people." The same idea was developed by Pushkin in his poem "The Prophet" ("Prorok"), after Lamartine had declared that a real poet—a visionary and a powerful orator—is but a variation of a biblical prophet.[5] Such are the literary connections of the title of this peculiar biography. The poet's life, thus, is interesting only by virtue of those moments that can "defend themselves" with the poetic word. Hence its primary feature: a fragmentary character. What in fiction can be taken as a purely compositional device acquires here a new, deeper dimension. The lack of a systematic, sequential narration

[1] This piece has been slightly adapted for this collection from Krystyna Pomorska, *Themes and Variations in Pasternak's Poetics* (Lisse: Peter de Ridder Press, 1975), 64–73. Due to Krystyna Pomorska's untimely death, I am much obliged to Professor Stanislaw Pomorski for permission to reprint it in this volume.

[2] All citations from *Safe Conduct* refer to the Russian text published as "Okhrannaja gramota" in *Proza 1915–1958* (Ann Arbor: University of Michigan Press, 1961). An English translation by Beatrice Scott is available in Pasternak, *Safe Conduct, An Autobiography and Other Writings* (New York: New Directions Publishing, 1958.

[3] "Ponimanie zhizni kak zhizni poeta." "Okhrannaja gramota," 281.

[4] "Vne legendy romanticheskoj etot plan fal'shiv," Ibid., 282.

[5] See for example W. Weintraub, *Literature as Prophecy* (S' Gravenhage: Mouton & Co., 1959).

has its source in the profound conviction of the author that "only a hero deserves a real biography, but the story of a poet in this aspect is quite unpresentable. . . . The poet gives his whole life such a voluntarily steep incline that it is not possible for it to exist in the vertical line of biography."[6]

The question now arises: what is it that the poet has chosen to speak about? In the light of the text the question seems useless: Pasternak stipulates that it is insignificant *what* he has chosen, for he could have *exchanged* these fragments with others equally important.[7] This declaration, however, together with the metaphor of the "steep incline" of the poet's life, requires further interpretation. Obviously they both refer to the idea of the particular richness of the poet's life—a thought well-known in poetic mythology. In modern times Oscar Wilde canonized it saying that a person of profound feelings (that is a poet) dies not once but several times.[8] Such a person therefore lives not one but several lives, and his life story can therefore not fit "the vertical" of the biographic scheme. Not by chance Pasternak referred several times to the well-known poetic personality who strove for more than one life, Faust. In *Safe Conduct* itself Faust is mentioned as having lived his young years twice;[9] a much more eloquent example is found in the poetic cycle *My Sister—Life*, where the poet is directly compared to Faust: "How could he let/A star surpass his reach,/ When he is Faust, when he's a dreamer?" ("So they begin.")[10] All this is by no means incidental but underscores the idea that the poet's life possesses that unusual shape that cannot be presented as a straight line of events, with its finite and sequential order. The only solution is to make a "random" choice and discard an infinite number of events that took place at the same time.

Yet the question *what* was chosen as a sample of the poet's life remains valid. Because for the literary fact it represents the obligatory totality of the composition.

The meeting with Rilke, the contact with Scriabin, studying with Cohen, love for one of the V. sisters, and Mayakovsky—these are the five main complexes of the protagonist's experience in *Safe Conduct*. The names themselves show that these are not ordinary meetings but contacts with people who are creative and who at the same time create the hero of the biography himself. This casts light on the author's statement: "I do not offer my reminiscences to

[6] "Nastojashchego zhizneopisanija zasluzhivaet tol'ko geroj, no istorija poeta v etom vide vovse nepredstavima. . . . Vsej svojej zhizni poet pridaet takoj dobrovol'no krutoj naklon, chto ee ne mozhet byt' v biograficheskoj vertikali." "Okhrannaja gramota," 213.

[7] Ibid., 214.

[8] Oscar Wilde, "The Ballad of Reading Goal."

[9] "Okhrannaja gramota," 207.

[10] "Kak on dast/Zvezde prevysit' dosjagan'e,/ Kogda on—Faust, kogda—fantast" ("Tak nachinajut").

the memory of Rilke. On the contrary, I myself received them from him as a gift.''[11]

The common denominator of all these encounters is that thanks to them the poet begins his life in a different dimension. The opening episode works here as an initiation: the little boy meets Rilke, whom he immediately recognizes as being different from other people, as a physically striking contrast against the ordinary crowd: ''[He was] a silhouette in the midst of bodies, an imaginary figure in the density of the unimaginary.''[12] The image of the Austrian poet disclosed to him for the first time the possibility of living in a dimension different from the ordinary.

The next four meetings shape another interesting invariant. Each of them implies some sort of new life career for the hero. Everything, however, ends up as a defeat: the hero has to give up his chosen path, together with friendship or love for the second person involved. The four situations can be presented in the following tabular sketch:

Scriabin = involvement in music → defeat
Cohen = involvement in philosophy → defeat
Miss V. = involvement in love (marriage) → defeat
Mayakovsky = involvement in poetry of a certain type → defeat

The last episode has a particularly tragic denouement. The partner not only disappears from the protagonist's horizon but disappears from life altogether. This event can be better presented by another relation between all five episodes. With each of the persons that the author meets he first equates, or rather co-measures, his own world, his own essence. After having done this, he finally withdraws the relation, which has resulted in a lack of equality. Each episode from this point of view can be represented by the following formula:

$$X = \text{``I''}$$
$$X \neq \text{``I''}$$

Rilke appeared before the young boy as a different measurement of things. The boy himself did not yet represent this measurement and so did not equal him.

The second relationship, with Scriabin, is more complicated and is analyzed by the author in depth. As was the case with each person involved in the five meetings, Pasternak deified Scriabin. This tension grew in years filled with music as ''the only acceptable life.'' But at the end of adolescence a moment

---

[11] ''Ja ne darju svoikh vospominanij pamjati Ril'ke. Naoborot, ja sam poluchil ikh ot nego v podarok.'' ''Okhrannaja gramota,'' 213.

[12] ''[On byl] siluetom sredi tel, vymyslom v gushche nevymyshlennosti.'' ''Okhrannaja gramota,'' 203.

comes when the hero challenges his deity. His "bargain with fate" ("sdelka s sud'boj"), which takes the form of challenging Scriabin to the confession that he does not have perfect pitch, is precisely the kind of equation mentioned before: does the X equal the "I?" Does he have (or does he lack) the same properties? It occurs in the purest form since we have no information about Scriabin's perfect pitch; the question is asked about X just because the "I" does not possess this property himself. The result is X $\neq$ "I" (because the composer does not answer in the expected way and therefore proves to lack another expected property), and thus X disappears from the life of the hero. Scriabin, just as any other X, not only represents a certain personality but the whole world connected with him and stimulated by him. This world is dominated by music. That very same night the protagonist "broke with music" and, simultaneously, as he characteristically declares, "Completely without my knowledge, the world which only the night before had seemed forever innate, was melting and breaking up inside me."[13]

There is another important dimension to the Scriabin episode. As a result of this encounter Pasternak learns to differentiate between "the reverses of fortune" and "eloquence of fact,"[14] two sides of one occurrence. The former side is his, the latter is for ordinary people. The fact itself may be positive: Scriabin's opinion about the young musician is very high. But this counts as victory only for Boris's parents. They alone take it as "happy events. In such a guise, they did not belong to me,"[15] comments the hero. It is the antithesis of a naked fact and its special lyrical, emotional, individual dimension that belongs to the hero. The "adults" would certainly classify this as a childish trifle, as they did with the little heroine in the story "The Childhood of Ljuvers."

But this dialectical opposition also has its synthesis. Scriabin proved not to equal the hero, but this did not debase him in the eyes of his young admirer: "Did this accident dethrone my god? No, never—it lifted him from his former height to yet another."[16] On the other hand, it is clear that Scriabin showed himself as a rather petty man: the manner in which he handled the burning question of perfect pitch was a sheer cliché, his behavior as an edifying teacher was pompous and patronizing. Which Scriabin is the true one: the one represented by the facts of his conduct, or the one surrounded by the mystery of his unconfessed secrets that lifted him to new heights in the heart of the young

---

[13] "Sovershenno bez moego vedoma vo mne tajal i nadlamyvalsja mir, eshche nakanune kazavshijsja navsegda prirozhdennym." "Okhrannaja gramota," 211.

[14] "Prevratnosti gadanija" and "krasnorechie fakta." Ibid.

[15] "Schastlivye sobytija. Mne oni v takom vide ne prinadlezhali." Ibid.

[16] "Razvenchivala li eta sluchajnost' moego boga? Net, nikogda,—s prezhnej vysoty ona podymala ego na novuju." Ibid.

poet? What is victory and what is defeat: Scriabin's high opinion of Pasternak's talent, or the proof that his world does not equal the world of the poet? The only answer is that the result of this episode was poetry. Having broken with music at this point, Pasternak became a poet. This is the only thing that matters. And *this* is the basis for the choice of episodes from his biography: "Having thrown them out as though for an estimate to indicate what my reality was at that time, I shall ask myself at this point where and through what agency at work in it poetry was born."[17] This is victory. Otherwise, "you yourself should not discern defeat from victory."[18]

The three other relationships have still different turns but the same result: withdrawal from the world of the X. In the love episode with Miss V., the heroine is obviously afraid of the impetus and of the excessively charged feelings of the hero. As if oppressed by it, she "retreats" before him who "attacks": "She rose from her chair, *retreating* before the obvious fact of my anxiety, which seemed to be *attacking* her. Suddenly by the wall she remembered that a means existed to put an end to all this once and for all, and—she refused me."[19] The idea of a retreat also precedes the main scene: the younger sister, meets the hero in the corridor of the hotel before he speaks to the elder: "Having glanced back . . . and realizing that something was afoot, she *retreated* without a greeting and locked herself in her room."[20] This time X ≠ "I" because "I" is bigger than X.

The poet tears himself away from Cohen because the latter represents "the causal mind" ("prichinnyj um"), whereas the poet's own mentality was full of puzzles "that artificially shortened life," and for the philosopher it meant "falseness and incoherence" ("fal'sh i bestoloch' ").[21] Each measured the world with a different yardstick, and therefore they did not equal each other.

Love and occupation with philosophy coincide, simply because it all happens in Marburg, in Germany. But contiguity turns to similarity: as love is finished, any further interest in philosophy also vanishes. The hero comes to his room, packs all his books, and pushes them with his foot under the bed. "The end, the end! The end of philosophy, that is, the end of whatever thoughts I had entertained about it."[22] It happens as suddenly as the break with

---

[17] "Oboznachiv imi vprikidku, kak na raschetnom chertezhe, moju togdashnjuju dejstvitel'-nost', ja tut zhe i sproshu sebja, gde i v silu chego iz nee rozhdalas' poezija." "Okhrannaja gramota," 214–15.

[18] "Porazhenija ot pobedy ty sam ne dolzhen otlichat'."

[19] "Ona podnjalas' so stula, *pjatjas' nazad* pered javnost'ju moego volnenija, kotoroe kak by *nastupalo* na nee. Vdrug u steny ona vspomnila, chto est' na svete sposob prekratit' vse eto razom, i—otkazala mne." "Okhrannaja gramota," 236.

[20] "Vzgljanuv . . . i chto-to soobraziv . . . ne zdorovjas', *otstupila* nazad i zaperlas' u sebja v nomere." "Okhrannaja gramota," 235–36.

[21] Ibid., 249.

[22] "Konets, konets! Konets filosofii, to est' kakoj by to ne bylo mysli o nej." Ibid., 241.

music: in one night, after the crucial talk with Scriabin. And again, it happens as something impossible for other people to conceive; this act is interpreted by them from its purely factual side: the landlady, seeing the room emptied of books, congratulates her tenant on the occasion of "having finished the hard work."[23] Again the question arises: is it defeat or victory? The only thing that is born from it is poetry. This is significantly confirmed in the volume *My Sister—Life* by the cycle entitled "Occupation with Philosophy" ("Zanjatie filosofiej"): according to the principle of contiguity it contains, instead of philosophy, "definitions" of love: a definition of poetry, of the soul, and of creation.[24]

The last encounter follows the same pattern. The hero sees Mayakovsky as his alter ego, he deifies him: "When I was invited to say something about myself, I would start talking about Mayakovsky. There was no mistake about it. I was deifying him: I personified in him my spiritual horizons."[25] But this time the object of his love turns out to be too large for him. Mayakovsky is constantly referred to as something huge in every way. He can be only "a sort of mounting or frame to any landscape."[26] As such, he threatens to engulf his companion. The hero apparently is afraid of becoming dissolved in Mayakovsky's hugeness. "I considered myself to be completely devoid of talent. . . . Had I been younger, I would have given up literature. But . . . after all my metamorphoses I couldn't bring myself to reshape myself for the fourth time."[27]

This episode has a different denouement from that with Scriabin: poetry, like music earlier, is not discarded: only the close friendship is finished and gradually turns to even greater differentiation (as shown in the later "Essay in Autobiography"). Besides, Pasternak apparently rid himself of the poetic influence of Mayakovsky, which he considered as endangering his originality: "There were similarities in our works. I noticed him. I understood that unless I did something with myself, they would become more frequent in the future. . . . I decided to renounce that which caused them. I renounced the romantic manner."[28]

[23] "Ibid.

[24] "Opredelenie poezii," "Opredelenie dushi," "Opredelenie tvorchestva."

[25] "Kogda zhe mne predlagali rasskazat' chto-nibud' o sebe, ja zagovarival o Majakovskom. V etom ne bylo oshibki. Ja ego bogotvoril. Ja olitsetvorjal v nem svoj dukhovnyj gorizont." "Okhrannaja gramota," 275.

[26] "Chem-to bortovym i obramljajushchim k ljubomu pejzazhu."

[27] "Ja soznaval sebja polnoj bezdarnost'ju. . . . Esli by ja byl pomolozhe, ja brosil by literaturu. No . . . posle vsekh metamorfoz ja ne reshilsja pereopredeljat'sia v chetvertyj raz." "Okhrannaja gramota," 218.

[28] "U nas imelis' sovpadenija. Ja ikh zametil. Ja ponimal, chto esli ne sdelat' chego-to s soboju, oni v budushem uchashchatsia. . . . Ja reshil otkazat'sja ot togo, chto k nim privodilo. Ja otkazalsja ot romanticheskoj manery." Ibid.

But the most important part of this denouement is the death of Mayakovsky, with which Pasternak characteristically ends his autobiography. It is suggested by the text that the reason for the death is the gigantic dimension of the victim. Symbolism of hugeness dominates in the final scene, the mourning for the dead poet. The dimension of Mayakovsky is too vast for "our time," and for that he pays with his life. His hugeness qualifies him to fit only the future by which he is "spoiled" and toward which he aimed too fast: "From childhood he had been spoiled by the future, which he had achieved rather early and apparently without great effort."[29] By his gigantic standard he is equal to nothing but "our state," the only measure for which he is cut:

Suddenly, down under the window, I saw his life, which was now definitely past. It sidled away from the window in the form of some sort of . . . street. And the first person on it, by the very wall, was our state, our state which was bursting into the centuries and which had been accepted in them forever, our unheard-of impossible state. . . . In its plausible usualness it somehow reminded one of the deceased. The bond between them was so striking that they might have been twins.

And then it occurred to me that this man was actually the only citizen fitted for that state.[30]

And so the hugeness that threatens the main hero engulfs its bearer himself. The relation is not only X ≠ "I" but simply ceases to exist because the X disappears.

The fact of so many types of similarities between episodes poses the question of their specific character. Equivalence seems to be the leading axis in the entire structure. Indeed, the principle of equivalence not only ties all the episodes together but also permeates each episode to its very heart. The hero tends to identify with each person he meets and thus with each situation brought about by the given person. But on the other hand this identification is only temporary or intentional, and what was supposed to be the element of similarity of the main hero remains only his metonymy. In this sense he leaves his own biography "under the names of others." Thus the dynamism of the episode lies in the fact of their oscillation between the metaphoric and metonymic poles.

The character of the episodes plays a decisive role in the principle of their

---

[29] "On s detstva byl izbalovan budushchim, kotoroe dalos' emu dovol'no rano i, vidimo, bez bol'shogo truda."

[30] "Vdrug vnizu pod oknom mne voobrazilas' ego zhizn', teper' uzhe nachisto proshlaja. Ona poshla vbok ot okna v vide kakoj-to . . . ulitsy. I pervym na nej u samoj steny stalo nashe gosudarstvo, nashe lomjashcheesja v veka i navsegda prinjatoe v nikh, nebyvaloe, nevozmozhnoe gosudarstvo. . . . V osjazatel'noj neobychajnosti ono chem-to napominalo pokojnogo. Svjaz' mezhdu oboimi byla tak razitel'na, cho oni mogli pokazat'sja bliznetsami.

I togda . . . ia podumal, chto etot chelovek byl sobstvenno etomu grazhdanstvu edinstvennym grazhdaninom."

combination. The strong axis of equivalence makes the syntagmatic axis weaker. For example, the causal relation between episodes is completely abandoned. The fact that the hero goes over from music to philosophy does not create the implication "because—therefore." Those events model individual *transubstantiations* of the hero, independent of one another. Each episode indicates not so much the *continuation* of the poet's life but his *starting from the very beginning*.[31] This factor, in turn, is connected with the diminished sense of chronology and of time in general. The text represents not the chronological life line but rather a kind of *series of personalities*. Here we find yet another sense of the author's comment that "The poet gives to his whole life such a voluntarily steep incline that it is not possible for it to exist in the vertical line of biography."[32]

The difference between a biography of the poet and a biography of the hero rests precisely on the fact that in the latter case the kinship between events is built on a chain of cause and effect. The latter case is evident in the classical novel, where one event generates a chain of further events. Let us take, for example, *War and Peace*: because Andrey meets Natasha at the ball, he falls in love with her and decides to marry; because he decides to marry, he gets into a conflict with his father; because he does not wish to break with his father, he delays his marriage and parts with Natasha for a year; because of the parting, Natasha attempts to escape with Kuragin; etc. This is *story-stuff* and it is charged with an element of *sensation*. Pasternak rejects the very principle of story-stuff and along with it excludes the sensational element that accompanies classical plots. While speaking about the selection of the material for his autobiography, the author informs the reader that what he discarded is not worth describing: "*I will not describe* for you . . . how, in the spring . . . a company of Amazons was exhibited at the zoo. . . . How, in the summer of 1903, at Obolenskoe . . . the ward of some acquaintances of ours fell into the river. . . . How the student who jumped in to save her was drowned, and how afterwards she went insane. . . . How I broke my leg . . . and how . . . the house of our acquaintances . . . burned. . . . How, galloping with the doctor that night . . . my father went grey. . . ."[33]

All the enumerated motifs are, as we see, distinctly *sensational*, and as such are appropriate for the traditional plot that the reader likes so well. But for the

[31] Cf. here the formulation of the author after the defeat of his love for Mayakovsky: "Ja ne reshalsja *pereopredeljat'sja* v chetvertyj raz." Cf. also in his verses: "Ljubimaja, zhut'!/ Kogda ljubit poet . . . / . . . khaos opjat' vypolzaet na svet, / Kak vo vremena iskopaemykh."

[32] "Vsej svoej zhizni poet pridaet takoj dobrovol'no krutoj naklon, chto ee ne mozhet byt' v biograficheskoj vertikali, gde my zhdem ee vstretit'." "Okhrannaja gramota," 213.

[33] "*Ja ne budu opisyvat'* . . . kak vesnoj . . . v Zoologicheskom sadu, pokazyvali otrjad dagomejskikh amazonok. . . . Kak letom devjat'sot tret'ego goda v Obolenskom . . . tonula vospitannitsa znakomykh. . . . Kak pogib student, brosivshijsja k nej na pomoshch', i ona za tem soshla s uma. . . . Kak ja slomal sebe nogu . . . [i kak] . . . goreli . . . znakomye. . . . Kak skacha v tu noch' s vrachem . . . posedel moj otets."

CHAPTER 6

The Imagination of Failure: Fiction and Autobiography in the Work of Yury Olesha

Elizabeth Klosty Beaujour

> Man always constitutes himself as what he is in order not to be it.
> —Jean-Paul Sartre

> What might have been and what has been point to one end, which
> is always present.
> —T. S. Eliot

YURY OLESHA[1] always said that his talent was essentially autobiographical.[2] In his speech to the First Congress of Soviet Writers in 1934 he stated: "People told me[3] that Kavalerov [the hero of his novel *Envy* (*Zavist'*)] had many of my traits, that it was an autobiographical portrait; that, indeed, Kavalerov was me. Yes, Kavalerov did look through my eyes. Kavalerov's colors, light, comparisons, metaphors and thoughts about things were mine."[4] To this admission that Kavalerov's sensibility, though not his activity, were Olesha's own, one may add the apparently autobiographical material of the childhood stories "The Chain" ("Tsep'," 1929), "A Writer's Notes" ("Zametki pisatelja," 1934), and "Human Material" ("Chelovecheskij material," 1928)

---

[1] This essay appeared in a slightly different form as "Proust-Envy: Fiction and Autobiography in the Works of Iurii Olesha," *Studies in 20th Century Literature* 1, no. 2 (Spring, 1977): 123–34.

[2] For example, writing in the manuscript almanac *Chukkola* in February 1930, Olesha affirmed: "Fiction is condemned to death. It is shameful to compose. We thirty-year-old intellectuals should write only about ourselves. We must write confessions, not novels." Quoted in M. O. Chudakova, *Masterstvo Jurija Oleshi* (Moscow: Nauka, 1972), 79 (my translation).

[3] The formulation "people told me" recurs constantly, as though self-definition must be prompted from outside. Olesha accepts what "they" say about Kavalerov as, in *No Day without a Line*, he accepts "people's" desire that he write an "autobiographical novel." See *Ni dnja bez strochki* (Moscow: Sovetskaja Rossija, 1965), 10. There is an English translation by J. Rosengrant, *No Day without a Line* (Ann Arbor: Ardis Publishers, 1979), but the translations in this article are mine.

[4] "Rech' na pervom vsesoiuznom s'ezde sovetskikh pisatelej," in Jurij Olesha, *Povesti i rasskazy* (Moscow: Khudozhestvennaja literatura, 1965), 426. Translated as "Speech to the First Congress of Soviet Writers" by Andrew R. MacAndrew in Yuri Olesha, *Envy and Other Works* (New York: Doubleday Anchor, 1967), 214.

and the special pleading of "Something from the Secret Notebooks of Fellow Traveller Zand" ("Koe-chto iz sekretnykh zapisej poputchika Zanda," 1932). Taken together, these and other avowedly autobiographical works form a coherent image that we are asked to contemplate: the self-portrait of the artist as failure. Olesha's picture shows us that his childhood, his bourgeois family values, and his relationship to his father inevitably led to a socially and psychologically determined doom in the postrevolutionary world. The Revolution, which no individual could control, deprived Olesha of his birthright, his past; it declared his childhood impressions irrelevant, crippling his talent by depriving it of sustenance.

This is a radically self-censored self-portrait. Not only does Olesha omit the successes that were in fact his, but even among the failures he writes only about those, personal and artistic, of which he could say, paraphrasing Kavalerov, "It's not my fault; it's their fault."[5] Olesha's works therefore present us less with a set of autobiographical fictions than with a series of episodes for a fictional autobiography: the autobiography of the artist as victim.

This is, of course, Olesha's perfect right. It is not the place of the reader to make a value judgment about the manner in which the artist sees himself and wishes to have himself seen. As John Cooper Powys says, a man's life illusion should be as sacred as his skin.[6] Furthermore, it is axiomatic that no one's autobiographical writing can be taken at face value as an ingenuous rendering of his psychic life.[7] Nevertheless, whatever we may write, on whatever subject, comprises a constantly revised self-portrait that denounces us, and whatever the immediate truth of the matter, it must be said that the prediction of failure at the heart of Olesha's fictional autobiography was catastrophically self-fulfilling.[8]

Let us begin with *Envy*. To the extent that Kavalerov was indeed endowed with Olesha's sensibility, colors, and verbal imagination, *Envy* contains a self-portrait. But it differs from the norm of early, partially autobiographical fiction in that the young novel writer usually interprets himself and invents a situation to reveal what he feels to be his *potential* reality.[9] He can, and very often does, allow his character the fulfillment of which he feels he is intrinsically capable, but of which real life has deprived him because of his personal appearance or historical circumstances. The author can overcome what is fortuitous in his

---

[5] "It's not my fault; it's his fault" ("Eto ne ja vinovat . . . Eto on vinovat"), *Zavist'* in *Povesti i rasskazy*, 49. Translations from *Envy* are essentially MacAndrew's.

[6] Quoted in Roy Pascal, *Design and Truth in Autobiography* (London: Routledge and Kegan Paul, 1960), 71.

[7] See Boris Eikhenbaum, *The Young Tolstoy* (Ann Arbor: Ardis Publishers, 1972), 7.

[8] Other opinions as to the relationship of Olesha's life to his works can be found in Chudakova, *Masterstvo Jurija Oleshi*; Arkady Belinkov, *Sdacha i gibel' sovetskogo intelligenta: Jurij Olesha* (Madrid: private publisher, 1976); William Harkins, "The Theme of Sterility in Olesha's *Envy*," *Slavic Review* 3 (September 1966): 444–57.

[9] Pascal, *Design and Truth in Autobiography*, 178.

own existence and obey the "sense of life."[10] Olesha rejects this option and does not allow Kavalerov to fulfill a single dream, positive or negative. Kavalerov achieves neither notoriety nor romantic destruction. His descent into indifference is in fact an abnormally early achievement of the final equilibrium characteristic not of early autobiographical fiction but of mature autobiography: the coming to terms with what has been rather than with what might have been. *Envy*, written by a twenty-seven-year-old author at a time when he was well-introduced in and moving up rapidly in Soviet literary life, already defines the terms of Olesha's own memoirs written thirty years later.[11]

Soviet reality of the NEP period did not *oblige* Olesha to make Kavalerov a failure, and at least one of his works of the period proves this point. Shuvalov, the hero of "Love" ("Ljubov' "), is a healthy and functioning but love-smitten Marxist. He is certainly uneasy about the "unscientific distortions" of natural laws caused by his infatuation, but he boldly and resolutely defends his proletarian right to life and love in his final refusal to "eat blue pears."[12] So once or twice Olesha did use his colors positively and gave them to characters who did not resemble his preferred image of himself. But the narrative tone in the other stories is already an almost exclusive identification of the authorial sensibility with failure and a concomitant resolve to achieve artistic success only by creating and manipulating images of that failure.

Given both this early commitment to the depiction of failure and the subsequent difficulties of Olesha's "complicated path" ("slozhnyj put' ") for which he was not in fact responsible, it is not surprising to find the same images of failure in Olesha's last work, the retrospective, fragmentary *No Day without a Line* (*Ni dnja bez strochki*, 1965).[13] Olesha announced *No Day* as an autobiographical novel of a new, modern kind,[14] but it remains only a preparatory exercise for such a novel, the flexing of long atrophied artistic muscles. In it he relives events of his own life and retells passages from the books

---

[10] At its most elaborate, as in *A la recherche du temps perdu*, it can show the multiple modifications possible to the author.

[11] The sixty-year-old Olesha bore a striking resemblance to Ivan, extemporizing in bars and spinning tales. In the beginning of the second part of *Envy* Ivan creates the fictional autobiography of a failed magician.

[12] "Liubov' " in *Povesti i rasskazy*, 278.

[13] Large parts of *Ni dnja bez strochki* had appeared under the title "Iz literaturnykh dnevnikov" in *Literaturnaja Moskva* (1956), 2:721–51. Another selection containing some of the same texts appeared under the title "Ni dnja bez stroki [sic]" in *Oktjabr'* 7 and 8 (1961): 135–56. Selections from *Ni dnja bez strochki* were also included in Olesha's *Izbrannye sochinenija* (Moscow: Khudozhestvennaja literatura, 1956) and in the 1965 publication *Povesti i rasskazy* under the heading "Iz zapisej 'Ni dnja bez strochki.' " The book *Ni dnja bez strochki* contains some fragments that had not, to my knowledge, been printed before and leaves out certain others, notably a paean to Khrushchev on the occasion of seeing a newsreel covering his enthusiastic reception in Paris (*Oktjabr'* 8:155–56).

[14] *Ni dnja bez strochki*, 10–11, 69.

of others that have become an integral part of his own consciousness.[15] The dominant modes are recall and recapitulation, but the book cannot be defined simply as autobiography. It is a strange hybrid. Of course, *No Day* is flawed and unfinished, composed of fragments that Olesha himself did not have the chance to arrange in a final montage. Yet this unresolved form is so appropriate to Olesha's life illusion of failure that it might as well be deliberate—as perhaps it in fact was.

Any literary self-portrait is a metaphor of the self at the moment of composition,[16] and the broken, unfilfilled structure of the book is analogous to the metaphors of artistic destruction of which it is composed. Given the workings of symbolic memory,[17] imagination is necessarily an element of recollection, and the imagination that recapitulates Olesha's life in *No Day* is consistently an imagination of fragmentation, deprivation, and failure.

In *No Day* Olesha asserts that the circus was the foundation of his imaginative life. He says that his childhood dream of liberation and glory was to be able to perform a complex somersault and speculates that perhaps this dream of acrobatic competence was the first stirring of the artist within him. (As we shall see shortly, the athletic metaphor is no accident.) Although he is never actually able to perform a *salto mortale*, he tells people that he can, and they believe him.[18] Olesha mentions this to us so that we should *not* believe it, so that we should convict him of false boastfulness and know that his first "artistic" aspiration was crowned with failure.

The theme of nonrealization of early aspirations is carried further and becomes more complicated in his discussion of the female acrobat with whom he fell in love: "As she cartwheeled, the girl was transformed into a vision which stunned me, although nothing really happened except that her hair flew around her head as she cartwheeled."[19] Thus far, the memory follows a relatively standard pattern of reminiscence: the memory of an early love for an untouchable embodiment of almost superhuman grace or beauty. But following the ever-present principle of deprivation, the vision is not only presented as unattainable, it is destroyed as such. One day Olesha recognizes the girl's two male partners walking toward him, accompanied by a pimply, unattractive youth who spits through his teeth. He realizes that the sickly looking, disagreeable youth is in fact the "girl acrobat" and that the lovely waves of flying hair were a wig. Although Olesha loyally declares that he is in love with the girl to this day, he also admits to a sudden surge of shame each time he sees such flowing hair. Thus even the image of absolute feminine perfection,

---

[15] On the importance of "retelling" ("pereskazanie"), see Chudakova, *Masterstvo Jurija Oleshi*, 88.

[16] James Olney, *Metaphors of the Self* (Princeton: Princeton University Press, 1972), 32.

[17] E. Cassirer, *Essay on Man*, quoted in Pascal, *Design and Truth in Autobiography*, 35.

[18] *Ni dnja bez strochki*, 104.

[19] Ibid., 105–6.

of first love, comes to us defiled, transformed into a recollection of deprivation, early disillusionment, and shame.

Many of the recollections of childhood in *No Day* carry the same stamp of shame as do the stories of the late twenties.[20] Contrary to expectation, one of the few memories of bliss in *No Day* is not a childhood memory at all but belongs to old age. Moreover, it is an imaginary memory, the memory of an event that Olesha says did not and could not have occurred in real life:

> Sometimes, through the real circumstances of my life, through its furnishings, through the objects and walls of my home, the images of a somehow different life show through. It is my life, too, but it is not always perceptible to me; it goes on somehow out of my range of vision. Suddenly a room appears, bluish because of the twilight and because of the glossy, painted walls. It is a clean room, with toys in the middle, with beds along the walls and on the painted walls a frieze, which also depicts toys. A children's room? Whose? I never had any children. Suddenly, for an instant, I feel that these are the children of my daughter. I never had a daughter. I know that, but I have nonetheless come to visit my daughter. I am a father and grandfather. I am a guest at my daughter's and grandsons' house on Sunday. They had been expecting me for dinner. Maybe I did come for dinner. More probably I didn't make it for some reason . . . that's why I brought along a cake. God, how I remember that square cake. How awkward it was to carry![21]

The main point of the passage would seem to be to make the reader feel the material weight and bulkiness, the solidity, of an imagined object. Yet the relationship of the two lives merits closer scrutiny. Even in the second, imaginary life Olesha has for some reason been prevented from coming to share the dinner. He has disappointed himself and somehow failed his family: that is why he has brought the cake—to make amends. Still, the second life *is* more attractive. There he is not a lonely, isolated old man; he has the children and grandchildren of whom his real life has deprived him. The net effect of the passage is to make us pity the deprivation of his real life.

Here I must pause for a moment to consider certain facts. Olesha was married twice and had a stepson who committed suicide by jumping out of a window in his and his wife's presence.[22] Olesha never mentions either the existence or the death of Igor. Instead he declares categorically: "I never had any

---

[20] Consider in this connection the discussion of the "bad habit" of which the boy was wrongfully suspected in "I look into the Past" ("Ja smotrju v proshloe" in *Povesti i rasskazy*, 276–77), the shame and vengeance in "The Chain" ("Tsep' ") and the following passage from "Notes of a Writer": "Even mother, even that beautiful figure mother was distorted in that terrible world of lies" ("Notes of a Writer," *International Literature* 3 [July 1934]: 151).

[21] *Ni dnja bez strochki*, 171.

[22] Igor's suicide is discussed by his cousin Vsevolod Bagritsky in *Dnevniki, pis'ma, stikhi* (Moscow, 1964), 48. I am indebted to Professor Richard Sheldon for calling my attention to this text.

children.'' Nor does Olesha ever mention his wife.[23] Why does he avoid speaking of these and other complexities of his adult personal life? It is a delicate question and one which I need not pursue very far, as I am interested here in the fictional autobiography rather than the real events. But at least part of the answer would seem to be that much of what Olesha omits is rather strong stuff.[24] It does not fit the carefully elaborated picture of sadness, loneliness, and wistful deprivation by life for which he is not responsible. I do not wish to press this point but merely to note the flattened and isolated quality of the life that Olesha shows in *No Day*. There is no mention of tragedy and very little of joy or even of high spirits.

One reason for this curious principle of selection is that *No Day* is more a *journal intime*[25] than a real autobiography. As Alain Girard notes, it is rare to encounter moments of peace, serenity or simple happiness in a *journal intime*.[26] Nor does it usually record the most difficult moments of life. Many of Girard's general conclusions about *intimistes* apply perfectly to Olesha. For example, the *journal intime* usually comes into being at those moments when the writer feels that there is a spring broken within him. The habit of looking at himself combined with the practice of frequent notations aggravates his sensation of the fragmentation of time and of the decomposition of duration into a series of successive moments. His retrospective attention cannot embrace the whole past but only those instants that detach themselves in relief. These are usually moments at which the personality could have appeared in all its force but has not succeeded in meeting its own standards. The "I" of the *intimiste* remains in the past conditional. It seems to him that he is always looking backward: that something might have been but wasn't. He is weighed down by the consciousness of his body and its fragility. The foretaste of death is within him at every instant. Girard states further that the writer's perception of his persona changes in the process of such writing. The "I" that is in the body, and is consequently linked in affectivity to the body, exists in time as

---

[23] Olesha was married successively to two of the sisters Suok. He does use the family name as the given name of the charming heroine of his first work, *Three Fat Men* (*Tri tolstjaka*), but neither of the women is mentioned in *Ni dnja bez strochki*. While there are laudatory memoirs of Bagritsky, Olesha does not say that he and Bagritsky were brothers-in-law.

[24] Perhaps Kavalerov's comment to himself about his resemblance to his father is of some relevance here. Seeing this resemblance in his reflection in the mirror, Kavalerov remembers that as a boy he had felt sorry for his father, who was "cooked, finished, not famous for anything," able to be only what he already was. The sudden perception of this "sexual resemblance" to his father is for Kavalerov like being told "You're cooked, finished, nothing more will happen: produce a son" (*Zavist'*, 34). Even this fulfillment is denied.

[25] I retain the French term as more accurate than "diary" because the genre is characterized less by the daily recording of physical events than by a somewhat less regular collection and compilation of meditations, introspections, and comments on reading.

[26] Alain Girard, *Le journal intime* (Paris: PUF, 1963): 529, 517–19, 528.

well as space. Instead of being one, resistant and like unto itself, the "I" feels itself as multiple, crumbling, and successive.

Girard's formulations apply point by point to the image of Olesha's talent on which *No Day* insists: the image of the broken statue, the ruined athlete.

> I know that a certain powerful athlete is alive within me, or rather the fragment of an athlete. A torso without arms and legs, stirring within my body, tormenting himself and me. Sometimes I manage to hear what he is saying; I repeat it and people think I am clever. . . . But it is the genie, the broken statue, stirring within me, in its chance envelope, expressing together with it the effects of some strange and terrible enchantment, some detail of a myth from which I can understand only one thing: my own death.[27]

The mutilated and fragmented talent appears as an alien being within Olesha's body. Nowhere is there wholeness.

Almost all the fragments of *No Day* dealing with Olesha's life echo this vision of a disconnected and fragmented being. In his mirror Olesha sees an old man whom he will not and cannot recognize as himself, since his consciousness of himself is the same as it was when he was young. "Now there are two of us, I and he."[28] The old man cannot be accommodated in a continuous vision of himself as the locus of a succession of previous selves: Olesha refuses to admit time, just as his earlier characters have rejected the law of gravity.

Yet Olesha aspires to be like Proust, and several times he places his efforts to overcome time under Proust's aegis. Olesha even begins the second section of *No Day* with the explicit statement: "I would like to go backwards through life the way Marcel Proust succeeded in doing in his time."[29] To compare Olesha and Proust would at first seem unfair, but Olesha brings it up himself, thereby proposing one more contest that he is certain to lose. In fact, a comparison with Proust is helpful in better understanding Olesha's aspirations and limitations. There are some interesting initial similarities between the two writers, particularly the fact that *A la recherche du temps perdu* is also based in the imagination of failure.

As Roger Shattuck and others have noted,[30] Proust insists on the critical importance for the development of Marcel's character of an early victory that is also a defeat and a failure of the will: the night his mother spends in his room, the night, "perhaps the saddest of my life, when I had obtained a first

---

[27] *Ni dnja bez strochki*, 170.

[28] Ibid., 172. "*Teper' nas dvoe—ja i tot.*" The use of *tot* here is reminiscent of Andreyev's "*Tot, kto poluchaet poshchechinu*" in "He Who Gets Slapped."

[29] *Ni dnja bez strochki*, 59.

[30] See Shattuck's article in *The New York Review of Books* (19 September, 1974): 34. See also Serge Doubrovsky's *La Place de la Madeleine* (Paris: Mercure, 1974), particularly for the scatological interpretation and an extraordinary elaboration of the theme "I eat mama."

abdication from my parents, the night from which I could date both the decline of my health and of my will, my increasingly unhealthy renunciation of a difficult task.''[31] The book *François le champi* is present both at this first failure and at the gathering at the Germantes when Marcel realizes his own aging while he ponders the spectacle of the infinitely variegated ways in which the *other* guests and the hosts have both changed and remained the same.[32] For Proust, the realization of one's own aging is brought not by self-contemplation in a mirror but by the contemplation of others.

It is at this same moment that Marcel also discovers that he is ''the bearer of a work of art.'' Like Sarah, he has received the annunciation of an almost impossibly late parturition: he must bear and bring to term the work that is he himself reborn. But for Olesha, old age brings no rejuvenation, only degeneration. Duration has no value save that it has allowed a ruin of his former self to survive. Even when Olesha does write, composition is experienced as the painful repossession of something already written sometime in the past and then destroyed:

> I have completely lost the ability to write. To write one line after another in unbroken succession is becoming impossible for me, I compose separate lines. . . . I don't compose, striding forward; I write as if I were looking backward. I don't create, shading, structuring, pondering; I remember. It is as though what I was intending to write had already been written. Written, and had then somehow fallen apart, and I want to gather the fragments again into a whole.[33]

This is not creation but a joyless salvage operation. Proust can tranquilly admit the existence of successive ''I''s because the ''real I'' is not the boy or the adolescent or the old man but the one who experiences the joy that is the first crucial sign of the reemergence of time past, the ''I'' whose activity links and integrates a series of successive ''I''s.

For Proust, an interminable snake of memory links the current sensation, the past event, its recall, and its contemplation anew. Olesha, deprived of the sensation of new creativity, must insist that he is still the *same* as the boy that he was because of his anguished consciousness of otherwise unbridgeable gaps and irreducible fragmentation.

This tendency to fragment perception, a persistent characteristic of Olesha's talent from the beginning, also determines Olesha's vision of what Proust was trying to do.[34] He misunderstands Proust's procedure. Proust does not really

---

[31] *Le temps retrouvé* (Paris: Bibliothèque de la Pléiade, 1956): 886–87, repeated and elaborated upon, 1044.

[32] Ibid., 921–22.

[33] *Ni dnja bez strochki*, 51.

[34] See my discussion of the Golo episode in *The Invisible Land* (New York: Columbia University Press, 1970), 181–82. Although Olesha does not remember it as such, the episode of Golo and the magic lantern is in fact an image of the deprivation of the comfort of habit, rather than an

go backward through life, as Olesha says he does.[35] Proust brings past time *forward* to the present. All of Combray bursts out of that soggy madeleine, and the scene in which the father leads the family to an unknown place that suddenly reveals itself to be the totality of a familiar world is an analogue of the whole work. Furthermore, while for Olesha the original sensation is primary, for Proust the value lies in the *remembered* sensation: the first time around, Aunt Léonie's madeleine or the feel of the paving stones of Venice did not make a particularly strong impression.

Not only does Olesha misplace Proust's locus of value, in doing so, he also misconstrues the working of involuntary memory in accordance with his own practice. Olesha deliberately closes his eyes and says, "Now I am going to remember something from my childhood," and then an unexpected fragment, a moment, a scene swims up to the surface of memory.[36] What is involuntary in Proust is the joy caused by the chance coincidence of a present sensation with a lost one. Beyond that moment of grace which provides a temporary sensation of immortality, the writer must concentrate and work to liberate lost time, to find the guiding string thinner than a hair that passes through it all, to discover through the glass of memory a meaning in his experience that was not there before and exists now only as a present creation.[37]

With the exception of one fragment,[38] Olesha persistently refused the revaluation of experience in *No Day* as he refused the transformation fundamental to Proust's project as defined in *Le temps retrouvé*:

Wasn't the creation through memory of impressions that one then must deepen, illuminate and transform into their intellectual equivalents one of the conditions, indeed, almost the very essence, of the work of art as I had conceived of it just now in the library?

. . . .

I suddenly thought that if I still did have the strength to complete my work, then this "matinée" (as formerly, certain days in Combray had an immense influence on me), this matinée, which had on this very day given me both the idea of my work and the fear that I would never be able to complete it, would certainly bear in that work the

---

illustration of the fullness of childhood sensation and wonder. The two experiences seem inextricably linked in Olesha's memory.

[35] *Ni dnja bez strochki*, 59.

[36] Ibid., 4.

[37] Interesting here is Proust's description of the "glass" used. Olesha makes the common error: "Même ceux qui furent favorables à ma perception des vérités que je voulais ensuite graver dans le temple, me félicitèrent de les avoir découvertes au 'microscope,' quand je m'étais au contraire servi d'un téléscope pour apercevoir des choses, très petites en effet, mais parce qu'elles étaient situées à une grande distance, et qui étaient chacune un monde. Là où je cherchais les grandes lois, on m'appelait fouilleur de détails." *Le temps retrouvé*, 1041.

[38] *Ni dnja bez strochki*, 115.

form that I had glimpsed long ago in the church at Combray, a form which usually remains hidden from us; the form of Time.[39]

Because he felt his talent broken within him, Olesha bore only fragments; because he rejected the old man in the mirror as an alien clown, Olesha could never accept the accretions of time as they affected his own individual life. He never made his peace with time, continuing to present us with the portrait of the artist as a talented young man betrayed by circumstance. That, I think, is the source of the irreparable sadness that overcomes the reader upon completion of *No Day without a Line*, a sadness that Proust never provokes.

Both Proust and Olesha could join T. S. Eliot in saying: "In my beginning is my end. . . . In my end is my beginning."[40] Proust, like Eliot, might also have said of his work: "Here the impossible union / Of spheres of existence is actual, / Here the past and future / Are conquered, and reconciled."[41] But for Olesha, fishing in his memory for privileged moments, the most appropriate concluding lines would seem to be:

> Sudden in a shaft of sunlight
> Even while the dust moves
> There rises the hidden laughter
> Of children in the foliage.
> Quick now, here, now, always—
> Ridiculous the waste sad time
> Stretching before and after.[42]

---

[39] *Le temps retrouvé*, 1044–45. It is interesting that there is no spatial image of time anywhere in Olesha comparable to that of the church at Combray in Proust.

[40] T. S. Eliot, *Four Quartets*: "East Coker," I, l. 1; v, l. 38.

[41] T. S. Eliot, *Four Quartets*: "The Dry Salvages," v, ll. 33–36.

[42] T. S. Eliot, *Four Quartets*: "Burnt Norton," v, ll. 33–39.

CHAPTER 7

Autobiography and Conversion: Zoshchenko's *Before Sunrise*

Krista Hanson

THE PUBLICATION in November 1943 of Mikhail Zoshchenko's autobiographical novella *Before Sunrise* (*Pered voskhodom solntsa*) must have taken his readers very much by surprise. Unlike many American readers of Russian literature, they were aware that in the previous decade Zoshchenko had been moving away from the ironic tone and clowning persona that defined his humorous works of the 1920s. He had produced documentary novellas about the fall of Kerensky and about a heroine of the Revolution and even wrote an infamous story about the reform of a swindler in a Soviet labor camp. Nevertheless, the serious tone and the intensely personal and revealing subject matter of *Before Sunrise* must have been at the very least unexpected amidst the numerous contemporary works dedicated to the wartime struggle against Nazism.

Because Zoshchenko's book was suppressed midway through its serialization in the magazine *October* (*Oktjabr'*) and its author severely criticized, there is little information available on its reception by its original readers. According to a letter by Zoshchenko, the book made quite a sensation. The magazine disappeared from the shelves immediately and Zoshchenko was barely given an extra copy.[1] However, many of the book's readers may well have been shocked by Zoshchenko's discussion of his sexual exploits with married women and other less than heroic deeds, by his occasional lack of enthusiasm for the icons of Soviet culture (Gorky, Blok, and Mayakovsky are presented in nonheroic guises), and, above all, by his concern, during a time of national calamity, with his own emotional pain, mental illness, and fear of death. The Soviet press depicted Zoshchenko in its negative reviews as a hooligan occupied with himself alone. Three years later Party spokesman Andrey Zhdanov returned to these charges in his proclamation expelling Zoshchenko from Soviet literature.

[1] Quoted in Dmitrij Moldavskij, *Mikhail Zoshchenko* (Leningrad: Sovetskij pisatel', 1977), 255. At least one reader, the literary critic Emma Gershtejn, hoped that it heralded a new direction in Soviet prose. She wrote in her diary, "But these glimmerings of dawn, how can you know?—maybe they are a pledge for the future." Quoted in Marietta Chudakova, *Poetika Mikhaila Zoshchenko* (Moscow: Nauka, 1979), 182.

In the West *Before Sunrise* long remained in the shadow of this political debacle, partly because the remainder of the book did not appear in the Soviet Union until 1972 under the title *Novella About Reason* (*Povest' o razume*).[2] What is more, no mention was made of its connection with the first part, which consists mainly of very short autobiographical vignettes depicting the genesis and progression of Zoshchenko's chronic mental illness. Lacking this second part, which is largely devoted to an analysis of the illness, commentators were unsure how to interpret *Before Sunrise*. Like Gleb Struve, many may have suspected that this apparently serious document was but the preface to an elaborate hoax, given Zoshchenko's history of pulling the reader's leg.[3] It was difficult to believe that a writer best known for two decades of humorous and ironic writing could possibly mean this as a serious autobiographical statement.

If, however, we examine *Before Sunrise* in the context of Zoshchenko's work as a whole, we can avoid two major misconceptions. First of all, this autobiographical narrative does not stand as an unprecedented example of autobiographical prose in Zoshchenko's work. Although suppressed for many years, his latent autobiographical impulse had been present since the beginning of his career. Secondly, *Before Sunrise* is closely linked to his earlier works. Zoshchenko had treated and parodied the book's central theme—the psychological and emotional rebirth of an individual—on more than one occasion, but it is only here that he uses it to structure his own story.

This essay will explore the growth and maturation of Zoshchenko's autobiographical impulse and the literary predecessors to *Before Sunrise*. The main emphasis, however, will be on Zoshchenko's approach to autobiography and the effect of his concept of the self on the ultimate form of *Before Sunrise*. Finally, this essay will examine why the work was so controversial and why, then, Zoshchenko may have chosen to write and publish it.

As early as 1921 Zoshchenko told his friend and fellow writer Mikhail Slonimsky that he was working on a novella about his war experiences to be entitled *Notes of an Officer* (*Zapiski ofitsera*). In it he would describe a moral crisis he underwent during the war that fundamentally altered his views on the relations between the upper and lower classes. In 1928 he told Slonimsky that he was still hoping to write it but that to do so he needed to be healthy. It was to be "a completely healthy work with a happy ending. . . . [In it] there will be a certain line from [my] point of departure. I'll return to it. I went through a certain period of bravado, when I was ashamed to write lyrical things. I'm

---

[2] The book has since appeared in its entirety both in the United States and in the Soviet Union: Mikhail Zoshchenko, *Pered voskhodom solntsa* (New York: Izdatel'stvo imeni Chekhova, 1973) and M. Zoshchenko, *Pered voskhodom solntsa, Sobranie sochinenij* (Leningrad: Khudozhestvennaja literatura, 1987), 3: 447–693.

[3] Gleb Struve, *Russian Literature Under Lenin and Stalin* (Norman: University of Oklahoma Press, 1971), 342.

slowly coming back to them."[4] Slonimsky believes that Zoshchenko was unable to complete the book because he could not convey the significance of his experience in words and did not want to sully the recollection. Moreover, the result would have been yet another treatment of the overworked theme of "the intelligentsia and the Revolution."

Zoshchenko suppressed his autobiographical impulse for many years partly because he so excelled at humor and irony. His humorous stories and feuilletons, narrated in *skaz* by a linguistically confused philistine who is himself the object of irony made him by far the most popular prose writer in the 1920s.[5] Although he often endowed his narrators with some of his own characteristics, the alien language and ubiquitous irony effectively distanced him from them. Not only the narrative technique but also the subject matter combined to render his work of this period radically nonautobiographical, at least on the surface. He rarely wrote about the subject that was gaining ever more prominence in his own life—illness and healing.

Mental illness was a very real and at times devastating fact for Zoshchenko. Varying in intensity and form, it was expressed in protracted episodes of depression, phobias, hypochondria, apparent psychosomatic illness, and obsessive-compulsive behavior. The onset of his depressive episodes and first suicide attempt date from adolescence. During World War I he was wounded and gassed, sustaining permanent heart damage, which subsequently contributed to his hypochondria. He began seeking treatment in the 1920s—hydrotherapy, post-hypnotic suggestive therapy, and rest at health spas—but this apparently only worsened his condition. In 1926 he experienced an acute crisis at the end of a vacation in Yalta. Unable to eat or move, he spent several days confined to his hotel room. During this period he was subject to severe phobias and hallucinations and would sometimes lock himself in a room for a week at a time. In 1934 a certain Freudian psychiatrist named Morgulis introduced Zoshchenko to psychoanalysis.[6] Subsequently, Zoshchenko embarked on a course of autotherapy that is mentioned in the memoirs of his contemporaries and that forms the subject of *Before Sunrise*.

Despite the importance of illness in Zoshchenko's own life, medical themes appear only occasionally in his work of the 1920s and are generally treated ironically. "Matrenishcha" (1923) concerns a very sick, hen-pecked man whose wife refuses to let him die until he has provided more money for her

---

[4] Mikhail Slonimskij, "Mikhail Zoshchenko," *Kniga vospominanij* (Moscow: Sovetskij pisatel', 1966), 161–62. See also 157–58.

[5] I. V. Vladislavlev (Gul'binskij), *Literatura velikogo desjatiletija (1917–1927)* (Moscow, 1928), 25. Cited in Rebecca Domar, "The Tragedy of a Soviet Satirist: The Case of Zoshchenko," *Through the Glass of Soviet Literature*, ed. Ernest J. Simmons (New York: Columbia University Press, 1953), 208.

[6] Vera Zoshchenko, "Tvorcheskij put' Zoshchenko," in *Neizdannyj Zoshchenko*, ed. Vera von Wiren (Ann Arbor: Ardis, 1977), 150.

welfare. He goes out to beg and after a few days recovers. The activity cures him. In "Four Days" ("Chetyre dnja," 1926) autosuggestion has the opposite effect. A man, frightened by the gray tinge he sees in his face reflected in the mirror, becomes progressively sicker as others express concern. When a doctor claims he is feigning illness, he arises, washes his face, and immediately feels better upon realizing that the gray tinge was simply dirt. In "A Homeopathic Remedy" ("Gomeopaticheskoe sredstvo," 1928) and "A Medical Case" ("Meditsinskij sluchaj," 1929) healers apply a version of the Freudian technique of abreaction—coming to terms with a traumatic experience by reliving it. The patients react, however, not in words but in deeds, and the reader cannot agree with the naive narrator that the cures are satisfactory.

In 1928 Zoshchenko approached an autobiographical theme to which he later returned in *Youth Restored* (*Vozvrashchennaja molodost'*, 1933) and *Before Sunrise*. "Not All Is Lost" ("Ne vse poterjano") tells how an ill, exhausted, melancholic intellectual named Barinov regains the will to live by struggling against misfortune. During a campaign to prevent the settling of strangers in his apartment, the apartment is burglarized and he dislocates an arm, and this increased activity drives away his depression. His rather petty trials and responses, such as calling an ambulance, are depicted on a heroic scale. Both the narrator and his hero are equally the target of irony, which pervades the entire story. The concluding statement, for example, is deflated by the addition of the emphatic particle -*to*: "Not for nothing did comrade Budenny exclaim in his time, 'And all, indeed all, of our life is a struggle' " ("Nedarom v svoe vremja tovarishch Budennyj voskliknul: 'I vsja-to nasha zhizn' est' bor'ba' ").

By the end of the 1920s Zoshchenko was becoming weary of masquerading behind a series of comic masks. He was disturbed by the fact that many critics identified him with his philistine hero. Even worse, the vast majority of his readers saw him as nothing more than a humorist and ignored the serious moral intent underlying his works. He was concerned that his ironic stance was becoming a prison, that he could write in no other vein, and that irony was dictated to him by his chronic mental illness. The critic Korney Chukovsky, who had known Zoshchenko since 1919, writes that in 1931 Zoshchenko told him "that he hated the complexity in himself and would give up several years of his life to become naive, simple. . . . He would say that his ironic tone that literary epicures like so much was detestable to him, that in general he considered irony a vice, a serious illness for which he, a writer, must receive treatment."[7] By overcoming his illness, he hoped to develop an optimistic world view that would eradicate irony in his writing.

The 1930s saw a great evolution in Zoshchenko's work, primarily, I be-

[7] Kornej Chukovskij, "Zoshchenko," *Sobranie sochinenij v desjati tomakh* (Moscow: Khudozhestvennaja literatura, 1965), 3: 538–39.

lieve, motivated by his deep-seated hatred of his illness. He began to limit his use of irony and attempted to develop a new literary genre that incorporated documentary material into the literary text. This move was in part a response to calls made by critics of LEF (the Left Front of the Arts) for a new "literature of fact" ("literatura fakta"). Such works, it was said, would satisfy the intellectual needs of a new class of readers, drawing material from scientific, historical, medical, and biographical sources.[8] Zoshchenko produced three examples of this genre, *Youth Restored*, *The Blue Book* (*Golubaja kniga*, 1935), and *Before Sunrise*, which he referred to as his "trilogy." Although superficially quite diverse, these texts actually have much in common. Most notably they share a theme of great personal significance to Zoshchenko, that of regeneration or moral transformation. Where previous treatments of this theme had been totally ironic, here Zoshchenko begins to experiment with a serious tone.

Youth Restored, the first novella in this sequence, focuses entirely on the theme of illness and autotherapy. It tells how an aging professor supposedly restored his health and vitality through a strict physical fitness regimen and, incidentally, by having an affair with the pretty and fickle nineteen-year-old next-door neighbor. When she betrays him, he has a stroke and returns to his wife and family, there to achieve his aims in a slower, more temperate manner. Although the story is permeated with irony, it illustrates the general outline of Zoshchenko's own experience of illness, research, and autotherapy. The second half of the book consists of footnotes and commentaries of a serious nature on various medical issues raised by the text. Throughout the text the narrator uses the editorial "we" or "the author" and indulges in a great deal of irony at his protagonist's expense. In the commentaries, however, his tone is considerably more sober and the distant formulaic narration yields increasingly to the personal pronoun "I." It would seem that "the author" really does refer to Zoshchenko.[9]

Any doubt that Zoshchenko shares his "author's" concerns should be dispelled by the concluding commentary, wherein he presents the reader with a fairly detailed autobiographical sketch. There he discusses his literary credo, reviews his career, and promises to return to his former manner after this "temporary respite." He wrote *Youth Restored*, he says, to help people who work hard to understand the rules for regulating their bodies. The book is based on personal experience: "These medical discourses of mine are not copied from books. I was the dog on which I performed all the experiments."[10]

---

[8] See Victor Erlich, *Russian Formalism*, 3rd. ed. (The Hague: Mouton, 1969), 120–21, and Jurij Tynjanov, "Literaturnoe segodnja," *Russkij sovremennik* 1 (1924): 291–306.

[9] He uses this pronoun in a passage relating a personal conversation with Mayakovsky. M. Zoshchenko, *Vozvrashchennja molodost'*, *Sobranie sochinenij*, 85.

[10] Ibid., 159.

The problem, of course, is that Zoshchenko's ironic treatment of his theme in the text overshadows and invalidates the serious nature of his commentaries. If, as he claimed, Zoshchenko was in fact trying to present useful information on matters of health, why did he choose to illustrate it with a deflationary story that threatens to undermine the whole project? He allowed such dissonance, I think, because *Youth Restored* concerns highly personal, and therefore highly volatile, autobiographical material, an individual's struggle to conquer his illness by the exercise of conscious control. Zoshchenko was not yet ready to treat such personal material seriously. His habit of and success at writing in an ironic vein were too well established to be overcome by his nascent autobiographical impulse.[11]

As opposed to *Youth Restored*, the next novella in the trilogy, *The Blue Book*, is a retreat from autobiography. Zoshchenko revives the simple, semi-educated "author" of his earlier writings, with his disharmonic language and ironic tone, to present a "history of human morals." In this work reprinted short stories and often inaccurate historical anecdotes combine to illustrate the basic theme of the trilogy, that "not all is lost." *Youth Restored* is meant to show that there is hope of altering one's reactions to events in order to achieve and maintain conscious control over one's health. *The Blue Book* is intended to accomplish the same on a social and moral level. It explores the causes of human failings and claims that they are being eliminated in the Soviet Union, where people are rewarded according to their merit and work, not their privilege and wealth.

Here, as in many other works by Zoshchenko, the pervasive irony calls into question his overall seriousness. Zoshchenko certainly did enjoy provoking the official political-literary establishment but always considered himself a loyal Soviet citizen. He welcomed the elemental strength of the Revolution, which he hoped would sweep away society's preoccupation with weakness, illness, and death. Identifying his own illness with that of society, he initially hoped that a basic reorganization of society would cure them both. He viewed his own literary role, in his trilogy and elsewhere, as that of a moralist and enlightener.

Nadezhda Mandelstam writes of him:

A pure and wonderful man, he had sought points of contact with the times he lived in. He believed in all the high-sounding programs promising universal happiness and believed that everything would settle down, since all the cruelty and savagery were only incidental, only a ripple on the water, not the essence, as he was told at

[11] The impression of dissonance in tone between the text and commentaries is greater when each section is read in sequence. Zoshchenko, however, probably intended them to be read in parallel. Despite his facetious suggestion that the reader of little patience or refinement simply skip ahead to the story about the aging professor, neither the story, the text as a whole, nor the commentaries can stand alone. For a more detailed discussion, see Krista Hanson, "Writing a Path to Health: Autobiography and Autotherapy in Zoshchenko's Work" (Ph.D. diss., University of California, Berkeley, 1985), 84–112 and 128–29.

political lectures. . . . Many people failed to notice the transition from the popular upheaval of the Revolution, cruel and savage, to the systematic work of a machine. Those who had been inclined to justify the first phase transferred their attitude to the second. Such a one was Zoshchenko, one of the subalterns of the Revolution (in 1917 his actual rank was higher, but psychologically he belonged precisely to this category).

Zoshchenko, a moralist by nature, tried by means of his stories to bring his contemporaries to their senses, to help them become people, but his readers took it all as humor and neighed like horses when they read him. Zoshchenko kept his illusions and was completely without cynicism. . . . With his artist's eye he sometimes got to the heart of things, but he could not make sense of them because he believed piously in progress and all its wonderful consequences.[12]

If one considers the serious dedication of *The Blue Book* to his mentor Maxim Gorky, the published correspondence between them about this text, and the testimony of Nadezhda Mandelstam to Zoshchenko's sometimes blind belief in the Soviet system, it is likely that his irony once again masks a serious effort of enlightenment.[13] He seems to have been hoping to convince himself as much as his readers that human behavior can be modified and improved.

The message of hope that informs much of Zoshchenko's writing in the 1930s does not, of course, spring exclusively from his own imperatives. Optimism is a principal component of the doctrine of socialist realism imposed upon all writers in 1932. Zoshchenko was not immune to the Stalinist directives regarding literature, and he produced "positive" works in response to the "social command." His most infamous piece is "Story of One Life" ("Istorija odnoj zhizni," 1934), the result of a government-sponsored excursion to observe the construction of the White Sea-Baltic Canal by convicts and political prisoners. A group of twenty-six writers, including Zoshchenko, was to meet with prisoners and then show in a collective work how the latter were becoming socially useful citizens under the benign but firm hand of the NKVD penal system. Zoshchenko's contribution concerns the reformation of a swindler, a certain R., who is persuaded to work by the camp authorities. Plying him with tea and cookies, they explain that everyone in the Soviet Union, by striving to create a better life, is really working for himself. Soon he is overfulfilling his work quota and even convincing other recalcitrants that "the crash has come for our criminal world."[14]

This work has justifiably been cited as Zoshchenko's most obvious conces-

[12] Nadezhda Mandelstam, *Hope Abandoned*, trans. Max Hayward (New York: Atheneum Press, 1974), 358. The original text appears in Mandel'shtam, *Vtoraja kniga* (New York: Association Press, 1972), 403.

[13] M. Zoshchenko, *Golubaja kniga, Sobranie sochinenij*, 162; "Gor'kij-Zoshchenko: Perepiska," *Literaturnoe nasledstvo: Gor'kij i sovetskie pisateli: Neizdannaja perepiska* 70 (Moscow: Akademija Nauk SSSR, 1963): 163–68.

[14] M. Zoshchenko, *Istorija odnoj zhizni, Izbrannye povesti* (Leningrad: Khudozhestvennaja literatura, 1936), 288.

sion to governmental pressure.[15] To anyone familiar with Soviet prison camp literature, R.'s claim that the guards were forbidden even to threaten the prisoners, much less strike them, is patently absurd. Even so, it would be ill-advised to dismiss this and other ventures into socialist realism as nothing but time-serving or as thoroughly foreign to Zoshchenko's true interests. He wanted badly to eradicate his own illness and to believe that it is possible to repudiate one's past and "reforge" oneself into a useful, healthy member of society. It is because his own stylistic and thematic imperatives happened to coincide with those sanctioned by the authorities that Zoshchenko was able to keep evolving as a writer during this arid period. He moved closer to the orthodox Soviet literary position not only for reasons of survival but because its proclaimed ideals of health, comprehensibility, and positive thinking corresponded in part to his own aspirations.

Moreover, in "Story of One Life" and later in *Retribution* (*Vozmezdie*, 1937) Zoshchenko experiments with the autobiographical voice, although it is not his own "I." "Story of One Life" is told in the first person by R. himself, whose semiliterate manuscript Zoshchenko claims merely to have revised for publication. It is possible, of course, that Zoshchenko wrote the entire piece himself. In either case, however, it is an experiment with a serious autobiographical style, a creative identification with a person telling his own life story.

At the end of the 1930s Zoshchenko wrote a cycle of stories entitled *The Most Important Thing: Lelya and Min'ka* (*Samoe glavnoe: Lelja i Min'ka*, 1938–40). Based on events from Zoshchenko's childhood, these stories may well have been part of an early draft of *Before Sunrise*. As they stand, however, they differ greatly from the introspective, problem-oriented novella. Each one is self-contained and ends with a clearly stated moral.[16]

Before proceeding to *Before Sunrise* itself, it is appropriate to ask whether the book is, indeed, an autobiography. The traditional definition of autobiography is an account or history of one's own life, written by oneself. It generally views the life as a whole, reviewing it from a particular moment in time.[17] An autobiography follows the author's development through different stages and concentrates on more than just one aspect of the life experience. Modern autobiographies usually cover the period of childhood and focus more on the

---

[15] See, for example, Alexander Solzhenitsyn's devastatingly ironic account of this "outing" to the labor camp in *The Gulag Archipelago: 1918–1956*, vols. 3–4, trans. Thomas P. Whitney (New York: Harper and Row, 1975), 81. The original text is in Aleksandr Solzhenitsyn, *Arkhipelag GULag: 1918–1956* (Paris: YMCA Press, 1974), 3–4: 78.

[16] For a comparison of one aspect of these stories with *Before Sunrise*, see Krista Hanson, "Kto vinovat? Guilt and Rebellion in Zoshchenko's Accounts of Childhood" in *Russian Literature and Psychoanalysis*, ed. Daniel Rancour-Laferriere (Philadelphia: John Benjamins Publishing Co., forthcoming).

[17] Roy Pascal, *Design and Truth in Autobiography* (Cambridge, Mass.: Harvard University Press, 1960), 1–20.

self than on the autobiographer's contemporaries. According to Roy Pascal, an autobiography may contain the subcategories of reminiscence, which concerns private relationships, and memoir, which gives more weight to public events. If closer to a memoir, an autobiography may verge on becoming an apologia, an account of one's life written to justify one's chosen path to others.

Before Sunrise fits this traditional definition only approximately. A major emphasis in the first part is Zoshchenko's childhood and its effect on his later life. The author omits discussion, however, of his most recent years, claiming that they have no bearing on the subject of his book, the search for the genesis of his mental illness and his final victory over it. After this victory there is nothing left to tell. Chronologically the work is fairly complete, although the time segments are purposely jumbled for artistic effect. However, it focuses so narrowly on one aspect of the author's experience that it does not provide a well-integrated view of his personality. Although not all the stories concern his depression per se, the majority of them illustrate contributing causes. The subject matter pertains so directly to the narrator that we are a bit surprised when it expands, in his young adulthood, to include reminiscences of his contemporaries. The second part of the book stretches the autobiographical genre to include discussion of psychological and physiological theories. On the whole, *Before Sunrise* fits the definition of autobiography in more ways than it does not.

Zoshchenko himself referred to this book only as a "literary work," half of which would concern his early years. The first part, especially, impresses the reader as being highly literary. The very short, compressed stories are arranged in blocks in reverse chronological order, following the narrator's progression further and further into his childhood. Their emotional immediacy, frequent lack of denouement, and minimal authorial commentary are reminiscent of the technique of film montage. Perhaps most important is the system of interrelated symbols that pervades the stories and provides the author with data to analyze in his search for the genesis of his illness. These symbols, especially those relating to water and animals, have a long history in Russian literature, going back via Bely and Dostoevsky to the Petersburg theme of Pushkin's *Bronze Horseman*.[18]

Although Zoshchenko makes no claim for absolute veracity, the major events of the book and the fact of his chronic illness are corroborated by the memoirs of his contemporaries.[19] His widow writes that the book is not com-

---

[18] For a more detailed discussion of these symbols, see Irene Masing-Delic, "Biology, Reason, and Literature in Zoshchenko's *Pered voschodom solnca*," *Russian Literature* 8, no. 1 (1980): 77–101.

[19] See especially Kornej Chukovskij, Mikhail Slonimskij, and Konstantin Fedin, "Mikhail Zoshchenko," *Sobranie sochinenij v desjati tomakh* (Moscow: Khudozhestvennaja literatura, 1973), 9: 169–78; and Elizaveta Polonskaja, "Iz literaturnykh vospominanij: Moe znakomstvo s

pletely autobiographical, that "many facts of the autobiography were either thought up by him or distorted to unrecognizability in comparison with reality."[20] Regardless of his or Vera Vladimirovna's terminology, however, Zoshchenko does present the story of his illness and recovery as his own.

Of all the forms Zoshchenko could have selected to embody his major autobiographical statement, the one he chose bears the closest resemblance to a conversion narrative. This is not surprising, given his interest in stories of personal transformation. The cure, which separates the old from the new man, is presented in *Before Sunrise* as a true conversion experience. It takes the form not of an engaging narrative like that of the stories or even a dry but precise explication. Instead, the reader is offered a scene depicting an allegorical battle between Zoshchenko and his barbaric adversary from the unconscious:

> These forces did not retreat when I came face to face with them. They took up the battle. . . . But now, as the sun lit up the duelling place, I spied the miserable, barbarian snout of my enemy. I spied his naive ruses. I heard his bellicose cries which previously had so frightened me. . . .
>
> But now my consciousness controlled his actions.
>
> The enemy fled.
>
> But what this struggle had cost me!
>
> I rolled around in my bed. My weaponry—paper and pencil—lay beside me. And sometimes I even lacked the strength to pick them up again.
>
> It seemed that life was leaving me. (626/K242)[21]

This military imagery, reminiscent of World War II Soviet antifascist posters, reports only the author's perception of the struggle. We can only surmise that his "weaponry" was used to record either dreams or the very stories we have been reading, along with the explication of their symbols. Indeed, many of the stories bear a certain resemblance to recorded dreams.

At this crucial moment, the military imagery yields to language usually employed in a religious or mythological context:

> I was slain, torn apart, cut to pieces, so that I might rise again from the dust.
>
> I lay almost without breathing. . . .
>
> Life began to return to me. And it returned with such speed and force that I was startled and even perplexed.

Mikhailom Zoshchenko,'' *Trudy po russkoj i slavjanskoj filologii*, 6, *Uchenye zapiski Tartuskogo Gosudarstvennogo Universiteta*, 139 (1963), 379–89.

[20] Vera Zoshchenko, "Tvorcheskij put' Zoshchenko," 151.

[21] The first number refers to the page in M. Zoshchenko, *Pered voskhodom solntsa* in *Sobranie sochinenij* and the second to that in the English translation, *Before Sunrise*, trans. Gary Kern (Ann Arbor: Ardis, 1974). Quotations from the novella will be cited in the text in the following manner: (448/K1).

> I got up from the bed a completely new man. Unusually healthy, strong, with a great joy in my heart, I arose from my bed. (626/K243)

The solemnity of this moment is emphasized by the repetition "I got up from the bed," "I arose from my bed"—and the placement of the latter clause in the syntactically dominant position of the sentence. It also harks back to Christ's words, when healing a person suffering from palsy, "Arise, and take up thy bed, and walk" (Mark 2:9). What Zoshchenko gives the reader desirous of learning his techniques of autotherapy, then, is an account of a dramatic recovery with overtones of the miraculous.

A comparison with St. Augustine's *Confessions*, often called the first autobiography of Western literature, yields a surprising degree of similarity. Augustine's narrative is addressed to God, to whom and before whom the writer confesses both the sins of his past and his love for the Deity. It is intended, however, to be read by others as an exemplary tale of his long and labored journey from sin to salvation. Augustine, whose mother was a Christian, was aware of Christianity from childhood but resisted it for many years as intellectually unsatisfactory. Even after Augustine became disillusioned with Manichaeanism and began exposing himself increasingly to Christian doctrine, he could not resolve to abandon the pleasures of the flesh. He depicts his spiritual state as one of sickness, and in the first stages of conversion realizes how far his malady has progressed: "You [God] were setting me before my own eyes so that I could see how sordid I was, how deformed and squalid, how tainted with ulcers and sores. I saw it all and stood aghast, but there was no place where I could escape from myself."[22] In a state of spiritual turmoil, he believes he hears a child's voice instructing him to read the Bible, thus accomplishing the conversion. Afterward he is a new man with little more to relate. As the sinful events of the past have yielded to a present state of spiritual calm and rejoicing, so the past-tense narration is replaced by present-tense discussions of doctrine and the praise of God.

Zoshchenko's work is also the story of a radical change in the writer's world view, a progression from depression, obsessions, and phobias to mental health. It is addressed to, and intended for, the edification of other potential sufferers. Like Augustine, Zoshchenko voluntarily exposes himself to the teachings of those who, he thinks, might help him, including Sigmund Freud, Ivan Pavlov, and the lesser-known Swiss popularizer of psychological theories Paul Dubois. Despite their differences, they are all emissaries of Reason, which for Zoshchenko occupies the place of God.

In the first stages of his cure, Zoshchenko also realizes the severity of his illness:

---

[22] St. Augustine, *Confessions*, trans. R. S. Pine-Coffin (Baltimore: Penguin Books, 1961), 169.

In an instant I saw myself as I really was—a dark little savage frightened of every shadow. Holding my breath, looking around, listening to the bellowing of tigers, I walked and ran through the undergrowth of the jungle. And what could there be in my heart besides despair and exhaustion!

No, I was not simply upset by what I had seen, understood. I was horrified, jolted, driven to desperation. (616/K229)

His "conversion," like Augustine's, seems to take place within a short time period. Following the crisis, he too has become a new man. Writing about his younger years, Zoshchenko says in the prologue, "is the same thing as speaking of the dead." He will extend his story only up to the age of thirty because "after thirty, I became an entirely different man—no longer an appropriate subject for my composition. . . . You can't even call [what happened] a change. An entirely different life began, completely unlike what had been before" (452/K6).

Zoshchenko's narrative essentially breaks off following the conversion passage. He writes that the first burst of health so freed him from inner restraint that he moved through the fields of his life "like a tank," inflicting suffering on people with his "barbarian forces" (627/K243). The elated, energetic state of mind that Zoshchenko takes for a cure would probably be interpreted today by a psychologist as hypomania, a mild form of mania that can alternate with depression in a bipolar affective disorder.[23] Indeed, the return of the military-barbarian imagery suggests that all his "cure" accomplished was to free the powers of the unconscious, which had then to be restrained again by channeling them into his art. The remaining pages of his narration concern not himself but others who have suffered similar phobia-induced psychosomatic ailments (630–38/K247–58). In most cases his insight helps them to realize the true source of their troubles, facilitating a cure. One young woman suffering from water on the knee even abandons her crutch in his room. These cures are grouped together immediately following his own, reminding the reader by their placement of stories of healing by a saint generally located near the end of a saint's life. Analogous to Augustine's *Confessions*, the end of *Before Sunrise* is devoted to praise of the power that saved its writer, in this case, Reason, acting through the human brain.

The goal of psychoanalysis, which Zoshchenko employed in his autotherapy, is to help the patient develop more effective defenses against his fears than those he has had previously. Zoshchenko agrees that we must learn to deal with "the brain's mechanisms," which are capable of causing such suffering, since they cannot be eliminated. His overall goal, however, is far more ambitious. Criticizing a neurasthenic who claims to have stabilized his illness by resigning himself to it, Zoshchenko fumes:

[23] "Affective Disorders: Bipolar Disorder, Mixed," *Diagnostic and Statistical Manual of Mental Disorders*, 3rd ed. (Washington, D.C.: American Psychiatric Association, 1980), 216.

Do you understand what this man said? He said that you must get used to depression. Not drive it away, not destroy it . . . but get used to it, learn to love it.

What servile feelings! . . .

Such examples of protesting "sufferers" convince me all the more that the control of reason is necessary. (691/K328)

Zoshchenko desires not merely to come to terms with or ameliorate his illness but to become a new person, to be reborn or "restructure himself" ("perestroit'sja"). This is essentially a religious goal. He asserts a total discontinuity between his former and present self.

This orientation toward self-transformation accounts for the novella's similarity both to a conversion narrative and to a work of socialist realism. Although socialist realism has been interpreted in a variety of different ways,[24] its main objective is to depict events in their "revolutionary development," not necessarily as they are but as they "should be." In such works an optimistic attitude toward life in the collectivized society must prevail. The doctrine's novelistic standard bearer, the "positive hero," points the way to the future and embodies the qualities that will speed its approach. These include unquestioning loyalty to the Communist Party, self-discipline, and voluntary acceptance of personal privation.

Although the positive hero has subordinated all aspects of his life to the collective, represented by the Party, he supposedly interacts with his environment as an autonomous, determining force. Having voluntarily chosen to aspire toward the Party's goal, he is "free," according to contemporary Soviet psychologists, for " 'Freedom,' they echo, 'is the recognition of necessity.' "[25] It is the Party, of course, that defines the necessary. The positive hero influences his environment as well as himself through self-training or self-discipline. In the service of his goal, the positive hero disregards all obstacles, especially his own suffering.

In his book *The Positive Hero in Russian Literature* Rufus Mathewson points out that in socialist realist works tragedy is impossible. The hero, who is "master of his fate," fuses his will with that of the collective and thus can never be defeated. Even if he dies, the cause he serves triumphs, and the reader is inspired to follow the example of his dedication. "This is not to be taken seriously as a tragic formula since there is no real torment, doubt, or 'stretching,' only physical extinction, which the hero confronts unflinchingly."[26] Isolated by his dedication to the cause, he often endures great phys-

[24] Struve, *Russian Literature under Stalin and Lenin*, 255–63, and Edward J. Brown, *Russian Literature Since the Revolution*, rev. ed. (Cambridge, Mass.: Harvard University Press, 1982), 168.

[25] Raymond Bauer, *The New Man in Soviet Psychology* (Cambridge, Mass.: Harvard University Press, 1952), 133.

[26] Rufus W. Mathewson, Jr., *The Positive Hero in Russian Literature*, 2nd ed. (Stanford: Stanford University Press, 1975), 236.

ical suffering and emotional aridity, sacrificing himself for the happiness of future generations. Mathewson characterizes him as "an *alienated* man, as that concept has been communicated by the great writers of the Russian past. There is a pathos in the fact that a tradition which since its inception called for wholehearted engagement in history should play itself out with heroes who are disengaged from life, cut off even from a recognition of their own suffering."[27]

Thus, suffering has no value for the model of the individual personality upheld by socialist realism. Suffering brings neither maturity, wisdom, nor self-knowledge and therefore should not be celebrated in literature, since the future victory of socialism will eliminate its causes. Mathewson quotes a negative review of Leonid Leonov's *Road to the Ocean* (*Doroga na okean*, 1935) that acknowledged the magnitude of suffering endured by its hero: "All the harm the 'soothers' and 'glorifiers' of suffering bring is clearly seen . . . It is necessary not to sing the sufferings, but to hate them, to destroy them, to struggle with them, it is necessary to show that the popular mass can deliver itself from them—and is delivering itself from them."[28]

This statement is remarkably similar to one Gorky included in a 1936 letter to Zoshchenko: "Suffering is the shame of the earth, and we must hate it in order to eradicate it."[29] Zoshchenko quotes this at least twice in *Before Sunrise*, which he regards as a fulfillment of Gorky's suggestion that he write a book ridiculing the nobility of suffering. He goes further, however, in investigating the causes of suffering as a means to its elimination.

The model of the self toward which Zoshchenko aspires and which he claims to have attained in *Before Sunrise* adheres closely to the ideal of the "new man." The old, complex self, riddled with contradictions, is discarded in favor of a radically new self free from the constraints and groundless fears of the past. The old self was a victim of circumstance, tortured by "false conditioned connections" or associations formed according to mechanisms discovered by Pavlov.[30] The new self conforms to a more organic, internally motivated model. It is healthy and optimistic and completely controls its reactions to the environment. Moreover, Zoshchenko even claims to have forgotten the color of melancholy and despair (627/K244). Although he has not forgotten the fact of his suffering, he intends the book, in part, as an expose of people who regard suffering with awe, submit to it, or even consider it at all valuable. Like works of socialist realism, *Before Sunrise* ends on a note of affirmation: the sun is rising, the fascist enemy is in flight, and the speaker has left tragedy and complexity behind him. In this autobiographical narrative

---

[27] Ibid., 25.

[28] Quoted in Mathewson, *The Positive Hero in Russian Literature*, 241.

[29] *Literaturnoe nasledstvo*, 166.

[30] Zoshchenko's understanding of the role of "false conditioned connections" in his illness is discussed most thoroughly in *Pered voskhodom solntsa*, 619–40/K234–60.

Zoshchenko finally attempts to realize the goal that he had mentioned as far back as 1928 of representing a "positive type," of writing a "completely healthy work with a happy ending."[31]

His adoption of this autonomous model of the self presents certain problems, however, both for the autobiographical enterprise itself and for the book's internal coherence. The model functions in the service of a totalitarian ideology that emphasizes above all blind loyalty to the Party's programs, whatever they may be at any given time. All human loyalties and personal idiosyncracies are viewed with disfavor if they do not further these programs, which supposedly represent the will of the collective. Paradoxically, this autonomous model of the self essentially extinguishes the private self by dissolving it in the public one. It denies any value to suffering, for that is a purely private affair that has nothing to contribute to the collective's goals.

Writing an autobiography to deny the value of the private self is, perhaps, a strange proposition, but one with a long history. Augustine wrote his *Confessions* not because he felt the story of his past was important in itself but because it marks out the path he traveled to God. Even the gravity of his sins honors God, who helped him to overcome them. For Augustine, anything appreciated or existing in itself alone, without reference to God, was sinful. Thus he could justify telling the story of his private self only because it was useful to others and because by doing so, he praised God and his providence. Benjamin Franklin similarly denigrated the private self in writing an autobiography in which, although he played a central part, the narrative of his private life yields to a survey of the civic affairs of Philadelphia. He drew no distinction between the private self and the one displayed to the world, believing that one's actions and the habits that underlie them are the true indications of the personality. Franklin's autobiography, like Augustine's, was written not just to entertain but to provide his readers with a useful model which they could follow to achieve the goal he valued—in this case, worldly success. Franklin's belief in self-improvement by the practice of virtue has much in common with the Soviet doctrine of self-training adopted by Zoshchenko. The latter's autobiography shares Franklin's didactic purpose, functioning almost as a self-help book.

Unfortunately, however, Zoshchenko's denigration of the private self results in a certain lack of internal coherence in his narrative. Although the book discusses suffering and death, the fear of which lies at the root of many of Zoshchenko's phobias, he seems to have intended the work to conform to the canons of socialist realism. In the chapter on death he states "It seems to me that a discussion of this subject does not contradict the principles of socialist realism. With all its great optimism, socialist realism certainly does not close its eyes to everything that goes on in the world" (664/K292).

---

[31] Slonimskij, "Mikhail Zoshchenko," 161.

This attempt to extend the legal boundaries of socialist realist subject matter contradicts its fundamental premise that "suffering is irrelevant, uninteresting, and obstructive, whenever it is brought to public attention. . . . The too frank recognition of suffering, quite apart from its celebration, might contradict the certain assurances that the removal of all known causes of human suffering was next on the Party agenda."[32] Zoshchenko, however, clearly sees enough value and interest in his past suffering to devote half a book to an engaging narrative depicting his suffering self. The first part of the narrative is thus by far the most attractive part of the book. It is true literature and, as such, engages not only the reader's logical powers but also his emotions and aesthetic sense. As readers we sympathize and identify with the narrator, who is victimized by the powers of the unconscious. This fundamental contradiction in Zoshchenko's evaluation of his past goes unresolved and is the main reason, I submit, that the book has been criticized as lacking unity.[33]

Before Sunrise documents not Zoshchenko's actual repudiation of his past but his passionate desire to do so in order to approximate better the model of the self held out by the "new man." In *The Blue Book* the narrator purposely presents historical events in distorted or incomplete form. He repeatedly cites his poor memory or claims that accuracy does not matter, since the past is a dead letter. He stresses instead the moral that can be drawn from these simplified stories, for the book offers moral guidance to an age that has rejected many traditional values of Western civilization.

In *Before Sunrise*, on the other hand, Zoshchenko places great emphasis on the accuracy of his memories. Speaking of a section in which he reviews the beloved poetry of his youth to test the validity of his nostalgia for the old world, Marietta Chudakova writes:

> What was erased from memory so persistently on the pages of *The Blue Book* is here evoked in memory again, [this time] with great accuracy and without obfuscating reservations. . . . It turned out that it was necessary to recall [quoted poetry] precisely word for word; there are many exact quotes in the novella from a poetic heritage which, it would seem, had been forced out of memory forever.[34]

In this passage, as in *Before Sunrise* as a whole, Zoshchenko presents a body of data from which he draws a conclusion, in this case, that the poetry reflected prerevolutionary society's preoccupation with death and disease. He omits at the outset a discussion of Blok's poetry, which was equally marked by a feeling of melancholy and catastrophe, since "he was a genius. He ennobled with his genius everything that he thought, wrote" (600/K207). He quotes instead a bit of ecstatic prose and a few verses by lesser symbolist and

---

[32] Mathewson, *The Positive Hero in Russian Literature*, 242, 241.

[33] Chukovskij, for one, felt that the stories should be separated from the commentaries, which detract from the whole, "Zoshchenko," 549–50.

[34] Chudakova, *Poetika Mikhaila Zoshchenko*, 181.

decadent poets, which hardly do justice to the period of poetic flowering at the turn of the century. Zoshchenko ends his review thus: "The tears have long since dried in my eyes. No, I no longer regret anything. I don't regret the loss of that world" (601/K209).

The passage is an attempt to analyze emotions that Zoshchenko thinks are misplaced and may provide an example of self-training. Unlike the allegorical military passage, it does not follow the process of a conversion but is intended to consolidate its result, to guard against emotional backsliding into the pre-conversion state. Reading this passage, however, one gets the uncomfortable impression of witnessing a show trial in which the evidence is rigged and the verdict foregone. If Zoshchenko really is able to change his emotional reaction to his past solely by considering such grossly slanted evidence, the prospect for other sufferers is dim. This technique invites comparison with the Soviet penchant for rewriting history; one considers only what conveniently suits present ideological needs. His attempt here to sever the emotional ties to his past meets with failure and calls into question his success in repudiating his past and former self.

Given the narrator's preoccupation with guilt and punishment explored in the stories of the first part of *Before Sunrise*, the attraction of this model of the self is obvious. If the past totally lacks continuity with the present, then the present self bears no responsibility or guilt for past actions. It also frees the autobiographer to discuss his unworthy actions without undue discomfort. Unfortunately for the book's internal coherence, however, Zoshchenko is unable to rid himself of all remorse for past deeds. He claims in one story, for example, that abandoning his beloved Nadya was the most foolish thing he has ever done, for he still loves her (482/K49).

Before Sunrise suffers from yet another basic flaw. Its ostensible raison d'etre is to demonstrate, by personal example, the possiblity of overcoming mental illness. The cure is intimately linked with conversion to a view of the self as discontinuous, that is, capable of being divided and reconstituted by a conversion experience, and as autonomous but freely choosing to subordinate that autonomy to a higher power. A true conversion, like Augustine's, justifies the writing of an autobiography designed to subordinate the private self to something larger, such as the glory of God or that of serving the public.

The problem in Zoshchenko's case is that neither the conversion discussed above nor the cure can be given much credence. We are told very little about the actual mechanics of the cure, only that Zoshchenko overcame his fears by severing the false conditioned connections that gave rise to them. "The cure consisted in this. The absence of logic was cured by logic" (628/K244). Such a laconic generalization makes the cure considerably less persuasive than the dramatic narrative presentation of the genesis of his illness. In fact, his failure to discuss the stages of his cure or the specifics of his technique makes it difficult to believe that a cure took place at all. If his condition did improve temporarily, as Chukovsky claims and Vera Vladimirovna denies, this may well have happened spontaneously and not as a result of his efforts.[35]

The main reason to doubt the efficacy of his therapeutic technique, however, is methodological. Zoshchenko makes an equally strong claim for his autobiographical narrative as literature and as scientific document. His theory about the etiology of his illness rests on data introduced in the stories for the veracity of which, though they may reveal a deeper truth, the narrator makes no categorical claims (451–52/K5). Indeed, Zoshchenko goes out of his way to stress their literary quality. Although autobiography is always more or less a literary construct that cannot be expected to convey absolute truth, Zoshchenko's insistence on the scientific validity of his theory invites the reader to analyze its supporting data with a critical eye. It is this that makes his enterprise seem suspect.

As Chudakova has pointed out, *Before Sunrise* is a belated answer to questions Zoshchenko had posed more than twenty years earlier in his planned book of literary criticism. The need to decide questions of power and love and, above all, the attitude he should take toward his chronic depression[36] evidently became more intense with the years. It accompanied a growing autobiographical impulse that did not find expression easily. Chudakova accurately notes:

> Having begun, like many of his contemporaries, by repudiating a biographically oriented style and material, and having turned toward various forms of *skaz*, alien words about alien world views, Zoshchenko engaged for a longer time and more consistently than others in settling accounts with the psychological theme connected with the "experiences of the intellectual."[37]

Even to begin writing he had to overcome a deep-seated distaste for this theme, and traces of his distaste are quite evident in the finished product.

Chudakova holds that it was only in the 1940s that Zoshchenko evolved a directly self-expressive "authorial style" (*avtorskoe slovo*), one adequate to convey his true attitudes without irony. Although it is surely true that Zoshchenko would not have attempted an autobiography at this point unless he had developed a direct means of expression, this reason does not stand alone.

We must not forget that Zoshchenko had made a career out of taking risks and breaking taboos. Although he consciously supported the ideals of the socialist society, he repeatedly acted to provoke the wrath of authority. This provocation may have been unconsciously motivated. By writing *Before Sunrise* Zoshchenko took a bigger risk and shattered more significant taboos in one blow than he had in any other work.

---

[35] Chukovskij, "Zoshchenko," 546; Vera Zoshchenko, "Tvorcheskij put'," 151.

[36] Chudakova, *Poetika Mikhaila Zoshchenko*, 181.

[37] Ibid., 178.

The basic taboo Zoshchenko broke was that of speaking so candidly about his personal life. Contemporary and later apologists for the government's suppression of the book consider his decision to speak of his private suffering at a time of war to be tactless or worse.[38] This opinion, though it masks other, more political considerations, nevertheless has a certain basis. The picture Zoshchenko paints of himself is one of a man victimized by hypersensitivity, illness, upbringing, and the corrupt prerevolutionary world. This picture, however, also has a shadow less well defined and perhaps not intentional, one of egocentrism, gratuitous hostility, and emotional exhibitionism.

An example is the account given in the novella of his courtship and marriage, an account diametrically opposed to the rosy picture painted of the same events in his widow's memoirs.[39] In *Before Sunrise* the narrator's marriage to an unnamed woman is described in about eight sentences. It occurs consequent to his mother's death and at the woman's initiative:

> In my life there is a change.
>
> I could not stay in an apartment where death had been.
>
> A certain woman who loved me said to me, "Your mother has died. Move in with me."
>
> I went to the marriage bureau with that woman. And we registered. Now she is my wife. (501/K74)

In this pointedly deromanticized account of a marriage of convenience, the woman's identity is immaterial; she is but a mother substitute and the mistress of an apartment. There is a total, striking absence of emotional coloration. The narrator's role is purely passive.

The wife appears again later, this time with their small son. Since the baby's crying interferes with his work, the narrator does not live with them. When he goes to them during a flood, they are happy to see him, but he once again mentions them without emotion. This episode is followed by an emotionally charged account of a quarrel with his nineteen-year-old mistress. When she storms out, the narrator writes, "God, how I would have cried now! But then I was pleased" (513/K90). Such a juxtaposition only underscores his indifference toward his marriage.

These accounts, which reveal devastating hostility toward the wife in the book may, of course, have no bearing on Zoshchenko's real-life relationships. Possibly the hostility is actually directed toward the mother, whom the wife seems merely to replace. Within the book, however, it is completely unmotivated and causes the reader to question its origin and intended effect.

If Zoshchenko was trying to enlist the reader's sympathy by emphasizing how sick he was, he succeeds only partially. Depression does cause passivity

---

[38] See, for example, Moldavskij, *Mikhail Zoshchenko*, 256.

[39] Vera Zoshchenko, "Kusochki avtobiografii" in *Neizdannyj Zoshchenko*, 89–92.

and can cause its victim to mistreat others. But the fact that Zoshchenko lives apart from his family because his infant's cries disturb him hints at egocentrism. He seems to be punishing either his son for interfering with his career or his wife for placing the care of an infant before that of her husband. If Zoshchenko had given more information, this seeming desertion might be more understandable.[40] As it is, we must condone it as a necessary sacrifice in the service of literature or suspect him of other reasons for desiring a separation. His numerous affairs and his willingness to document them in his book and elsewhere with no concern for the feelings of his wife lead one to conclude that he was indeed capable of egocentrism and perhaps exhibitionism. Korney Chukovsky writes in his diary (21 March 1958) of Zoshchenko's "tactless" recounting of his various affairs while at a gathering at Chukovsky's house.[41] These oral anecdotes drew on the same material as the novella and some may have been simply retellings. Chukovsky, however, took them as genuine and was dismayed at Zoshchenko's behavior.

Nevertheless, *Before Sunrise* was unacceptable not only because Zoshchenko spoke in it of his extramarital affairs or even of his own suffering. It was unacceptable because he chose illness and recovery as the central theme of his autobiography, which could, after all, have been organized around some other significant strand in his life. He may have chosen this image to contain his life because it presents him as a secular savior of those afflicted with similar ailments. By passing on his supposed experience of conversion, he hopes to convince himself as well as others of its finality. One difficulty here is that he attributes his illness largely to his childhood experience, to his upbringing in the corrupt, diseased society that deeply scarred his psyche. In a sense, he suffers for the sins of that society. The fact that his illness reaches a crisis considerably after the Revolution and is "overcome" only by the patient suffering in isolation could also be construed as a subtle indictment of the new world, since he never specifically withdraws the equation between personal and social illness.

In 1943 Zoshchenko was a successful writer whose immediate family and career had not been endangered by the widespread purges and terror of the late 1930s. Speaking from the opposite experience, Nadezhda Mandelstam writes that it is a feat to retain a feeling of personal identity, a true "I," in an era of mass destruction and death. Most people, she says, experienced a shrinkage of their egos expressed either in extreme individualism and egocentrism or in prolonged torpors of self-disregard. She herself belonged to the latter category. Both were pathological. At such a time, she says, "the word 'I' disap-

---

[40] This seemingly harsh assessment of Zoshchenko's role as father and husband is given not for extraliterary condemnatory reasons but because it is the task of the critic to probe beneath the surface of an autobiographer's account of his or her life. This is particularly true in an area highlighted by the autobiographer himself.

[41] Cited in Chudakova, *Poetika Mikhaila Zoshchenko*, 177.

peared. It became almost shameful—a forbidden theme. Who dares to speak of his fate when it is the fate of everyone?''[42] Like many others of her generation, she disapproves of excessive self-involvement, which she implies is a Western trait. Given this attitude, it is possible that, leaving the official reaction aside, *Before Sunrise* was greeted by both appreciation among some people for its literary value and by disapproval among others because of its author's perceived egotism.

It is difficult to say whether Zoshchenko experienced a liberating effect from his autobiographical writings, considering the book's immediate ill fate. He certainly considered it his most important book, perhaps because it culminates the gradual development in his work of an interest in writing on autobiographical themes. Despite all of Zoshchenko's attempts to weave the disparate threads of his life into a unified tapestry, some escape, revealing the tension underlying his project. The contradictions that cleave *Before Sunrise*—the conflicting views of the self and of the value of past experience—are those which Zoshchenko himself had failed to overcome. In this regard the book accurately reflects its author's image, precisely as an autobiography should.

Zoshchenko's autobiographical impulse and the struggle with illness that underlies it are worthy of respect, regardless of their outcome. For in a society that purports to furnish its citizens with a single set of answers to all existential questions, the attempt to make sense out of one's own life and experience, to create one's private meaning, is admirable. Even in the West, where ''under the tutelage of Freud, we have come to accept [neurosis] as the condition of man,''[43] we must recognize the heroism in one man's refusal to submit. By writing of this struggle, Zoshchenko struck a blow at his illness and, he hoped, at the power of unreason and suffering all too frequently unleashed in the twentieth century.

[42] Mandel'shtam, *Vtoraja kniga*, 8. Her attitude toward the ''I'' is more complex than space allows me to present here. Please see the entire passage in her book, 7–13, or my summary in Hanson, ''Writing a Path to Health,'' 259–60.

[43] John M. Morris, *Versions of the Self* (New York: Basic Books–Harper and Row, 1966), 92.

CHAPTER 8

A Tremulous Prism: Nabokov's *Speak, Memory*

John Pilling

ALMOST ALL "mature" Nabokov has provoked widespread discussion as to his merits and demerits as a writer, generating something like a critical consensus, but not *Speak, Memory*. A decade after its author's death, some twenty years after his "authorized" version, and more than fifty years from its inception, Nabokov's autobiography continues to be considered ancillary to his other achievements, *of* but not in the fullest sense *in* the canon of work that constitutes his principal claim on our attention.[1] This may very possibly tell us as much about our nervous reaction when we come face to face with any author as it does about the special case of Nabokov, whom even his most fervent admirers have found occasionally given to excessive self-love. But it is the special case that concerns me here, or rather—given the aptness of the analogy with *matrioshkas*—the special case within the special case. No one in the least familiar with Nabokov criticism can have failed to register that *Speak, Memory* has for the most part been viewed (and especially by interpreters intent upon providing "keys" to particular novels) as a book to be quoted from rather than lived with. From such a perspective it is bound to seem an awkward anomaly within a career largely devoted to the manufacture of fiction. But to see *Speak, Memory* piecemeal, as it were, is to fail to engage adequately with a work no more anomalous—and a good deal less forbidding—than Nabokov's notorious "translation" of Pushkin's *Eugene Onegin*. What no one, or next to no one,[2] seems to have stressed by contrast is the quite extraordinary amount of time, energy, and finesse Nabokov devoted to the composition, translation, and recomposition of *Speak, Memory*, not always perhaps in the

---

[1] An earlier version of this essay appeared in John Pilling, *Autobiography and Imagination: Studies in Self-Scrutiny* (London: Routledge and Kegan Paul, 1981), 103–15. This is obliquely reflected, but at the same time compounded, by Norman Page's omission of *Speak, Memory* from his *Critical Heritage* volume (London: Routledge and Kegan Paul, 1982).

[2] The principal exceptions are: Elizabeth Bruss, *Autobiographical Acts* (Baltimore: Johns Hopkins Press, 1976); Jane Grayson, *Nabokov Translated* (Oxford: Oxford University Press, 1977); G. M. Hyde, *Vladimir Nabokov: America's Russian Novelist* (London: Marion Boyars, 1977); D. Barton Johnson, "The Alphabetic Rainbows of *Speak, Memory*" in *Worlds of Regression: Some Novels of Vladimir Nabokov* (Ann Arbor: Ardis, 1985); Dabney Stuart, "The Novelist's Composure: *Speak, Memory* as Fiction," *Modern Language Quarterly* 36 (June 1975): 177–92, reprinted in *Nabokov: The Dimensions of Parody* (Baton Rouge: Louisiana State University Press, 1978). *SO* designates *Strong Opinions* (London: Weidenfeld and Nicolson, 1974).

focused way that usually obtained when there was a novel to be written, but invariably with an eye to creating a work no less personally "monogrammed"[3] than those that gained him fame and prestige on two continents, in two languages, through the fabrication of a dazzling series of personae.

The first publication in England of Nabokov's *Speak, Memory* (1951) carried the subtitle "A Memoir" and a brief "author's note"—the first and least characteristic of all the "forewords" that Nabokov later developed into almost a minigenre of his own invention—to the effect that the book was "as truthful as he could possibly make it" and that any lapses from the truth were "due to the frailty of memory, not to the trickery of art."[4] Even the title of the original American edition, *Conclusive Evidence* (later glossed by Nabokov as meaning "conclusive evidence of my having existed"[5]) suggests that Nabokov's concern was with offering as veridical an account of his life as he was capable of.[6] But even a cursory reader of the book in those pre-*Lolita* days who knew nothing of Nabokov's two English and nine Russian novels (only two of which had then been translated) could not fail to have been struck by how artful Nabokov had been in reconstructing his European past. Certainly it would be impossible now, with the Nabokov oeuvre in front of us, to swallow Nabokov's disclaimer regarding the trickery of art, and it is not surprising that Nabokov omitted the phrase in the very much longer foreword to the 1966 edition of *Speak, Memory* now subtitled "An Autobiography Revisited." In the interim Nabokov had translated his 1951 text into Russian as *Drugie Berega* (*Other Shores, 1954*) and had "tried to do something about the amnesic defects of the original" (12).[7] In retranslating his Russian version he created what is, in detail if not in overall shape, a different work and as definitive a version as we can now hope for—a "final edition" (12), in fact.

Nabokov's 1966 foreword is both informative and elusive, clear and yet out

---

[3] Nabokov obliquely alludes to this notion at the end of the second section of chapter 1 of *Speak, Memory* where he speaks of "a certain intricate watermark." In *The Real Life of Sebastian Knight* "V" suggests that "the intricate pattern of human life turns out to be monogrammatic"; in *Look at the Harlequins!* "VV" suggests that in his "oblique autobiography" his wives and his books are "interlaced monogrammatically like some sort of watermark."

[4] *Speak, Memory* (London: Gollancz, 1951), 7.

[5] *Speak, Memory: An Autobiography Revisited* (London: Weidenfeld and Nicolson, 1967), 11. All subsequent references to this edition are, where practicable, incorporated into the text in parentheses.

[6] Cf. "facts are never really quite bare," (*Nikolai Gogol* [London: Weidenfeld and Nicolson, 1971], 119,) and *SO*, 10ff., for what Nabokov understands by "reality."

[7] *Drugie Berega* would remind a Russian reader of Aleksandr Herzen's *From the Other Shores*, written in exile in England. "I am an ardent memoirist with a rotten memory," Nabokov told an interviewer at about the time of completing *Ada* (*SO*, 140). Grayson, *Nabokov Translated*, 141ff., deals fully with the way Nabokov has attempted to remedy amnesiac defects in earlier versions in the 1967 *Speak, Memory*, but there are inevitably still some trifling errors (cf. *The Nabokov-Wilson Letters*, ed. Simon Karlinsky [New York: Harper and Row, 1979], 333 n. 2).

of focus, like *Speak, Memory* itself. The almost manic scholarly accuracy of the bibliographic information is both disorientating and seductive, much like the thousand-page commentary that Nabokov appended to his translation of *Eugene Onegin*. It is not, however, mere window dressing, any more than the *Onegin* commentary is; it is fun, certainly, but serious fun. If it seems at first glance to court disaster, this is only in order to, in the author's own words, "annoy the vulgar" and "please the discerning" (16). In this respect, indeed, it is precisely designed to educate the reader and to prepare him for what the author has in store for him. In the third section of chapter 14 of *Speak, Memory* proper Nabokov reminds us that "competition in chess problems is not really between White and Black but between the composer and the hypothetical solver (just as in a first-rate work of fiction the real clash is not between the characters but between the author and the world)" (290). This may not be an adequate account of a "first-rate work of fiction," but it is a more than adequate account of a first-rate work of autobiography like *Speak, Memory*. For the reader (and hence the critic) of this work finds himself, from beginning to end, in the role of problem solver, and the first problem he has to solve is Nabokov's foreword.[8]

The first thing in the foreword that might annoy the vulgar is Nabokov's claim that the book is "a systematically correlated assemblage of personal recollections" (9). It irritates, first, because "assemblage" sounds precious; second, because it sounds alien to "systematically" and "correlated"; and third, because the subsequent details suggest a genesis more heterogeneous than systematic. The seemingly irrelevant details of the photograph in which Nabokov is "wrongly identified" (9) are important here, a reminder that printed matter is inherently less accurate than it appears to be. This is a subject to which Nabokov returns at the end of the foreword when he speaks of "those blessed libraries where old newspapers are microfilmed, as all our memories should be" (15). The sheer diversity of publication dates, titles, and magazines, followed by Nabokov's implicit admission that the book could have been called by any one of five different titles, is intended to make us marvel that the book actually exists as a book at all rather than as a lot of fragments immured in French and American magazines. And it is precisely at this point that Nabokov chooses to tell us that he "had no trouble . . . in assembling a volume" because since 1936 the chapters had "been neatly filling numbered gaps in my mind which followed the present order of chapters" (10).[9] It hardly

---

[8] The *last* problem, in spatial terms at least, is the book's index, to which the last words of Nabokov's foreword point. Stuart, "The Novelist's Composure," 189–92, and Johnson, *Worlds in Regression*, 20–21 and 44, n. 22, make useful comments on the index, which obviously invites comparison with the indices of *Pale Fire* and the *Onegin* translation. Andrew Field (*Nabokov: His Life in Art* [London: Hodder and Stoughton, 1967], 371) roundly condemns the index to *Drugie Berega* as "useless."

[9] Nabokov makes a similar claim, with more obvious justification, regarding *Pnin* (serialized

seems to matter to Nabokov that even the discerning reader will be tempted to dismiss this as a patent fabrication with a liberal sprinkling of hindsight, because he has bombarded the reader with so many facts of a provable kind and sees no reason why the reader should not grant him the one unprovable fact. Nabokov intends us to marvel at the sheer labor of hammering these fragments into a unity, just as he later intends us to marvel at the "diabolical task" of " 're-Englishing' . . . a Russian re-version of what had been an English retelling of Russian memories in the first place" (12). He also intends us to share his wonderment at the difficulty of establishing, through the medium of memory, "conclusive evidence" of any kind; hence the excursus that corrects the chronological blunders of the 1951 version and describes Mnemosyne as "a very careless girl" (13).

The foreword is only uncharacteristic of the book that follows in that it elects to confine itself primarily to facts that have not been filtered through the distorting (and yet focusing) prism of the imagination. But even here there are moments when Nabokov cannot forbear from coloring the facts in an imaginative and distinctive way. Speaking of the "cornerstone" of his edifice—the fifth chapter that began the "erratic sequence"—Nabokov suggests that it "already held in its hidden hollow various maps, timetables, a collection of matchboxes, a chip of ruby glass, and even—as I now realize—the view from my balcony of Geneva lake, of its ripples and glades of light, black-dotted today, at teatime, with coots and tufted ducks" (11). This is not so much self-regarding applause at his own prophetic powers as an illustration of how time, at privileged moments, effectively ceases as a stable entity. It links a real 1966 Montreaux to a piece of writing originally published as a short story. Later in the foreword Nabokov relates how prolonged attention to a single object "which had been a mere dummy" elicited that the object was an "oystershell-shaped cigarette case, gleaming in the wet grass at the foot of an aspen . . . where I found on that June day in 1917 a hawkmoth rarely met with so far west, and where a quarter of a century earlier, my father had netted a Peacock butterfly" (12). Both these instances, the one linking the past with the present, the other relating the past to the remote past, are illustrations of a principle most memorably expressed in Nabokov's introduction to his Pushkin translation: "In art as in science there is no delight without the detail, and it is on details that I have tried to fix the reader's attention."[10] The foreword to

---

in *The New Yorker*) in *SO*, 84; cf. *SO*, 16, 31–32, 69, 99–100. Andrew Field (*VN: The Life and Art of Vladimir Nabokov* [London: Macdonald, 1987], 257) considers *Speak, Memory* as composed of "autonomous pendants."

[10] *Eugene Onegin* (London: Routledge and Kegan Paul, 1964), 8. Nabokov habitually correlates art and science (see *SO*, 16, 44, and 79, and the 1951 *Speak, Memory*, 159) like the good monist he claimed to be (*SO*, 85, 124). In *Vladimir Nabokov: A Critical Study of the Novels* (Cambridge: Cambridge University Press, 1984) David Rampton describes him as "an operative dualist" (44). Writing to Edmund Wilson on 7 April 1947 (Karlinsky edition, 188) Nabokov

Speak, Memory is full of details designed to "fix the reader's attention" in the preparation for what will follow, details so physically present that the reader stumbles over them and has to reorient himself. Later, in section 6 of chapter 6, Nabokov unveils the suppressed principle of his devious foreword: "I confess I do not believe in time. I like to fold my magic carpet, after use, in such a way as to superimpose one part of the pattern upon another. Let visitors trip" (139). This may smack of arrogance, but it is not quite so devil-may-care as it sounds. For it is only at the beginning of *Speak, Memory* that the reader is a mere visitor; by the end of chapter 6 the reader has become aware of the folds in the magic carpet and effectively become, under the spell of the artist, "one of those creatures that [are] not oneself that [are] joined to one by time's common flow" (20). *Speak, Memory* is not so much a Proustian quest, a *recherche du temps perdu*, as a "recovery" of lost time,[11] a monument designed to withstand time and to bring time to a halt.[12] The atomized time of the foreword prefigures the disregard for chronology in the body of the book. But despite this disregard the book begins with a cradle rocking above an abyss and ends with the Nabokovs' departure for America. However much of a "chronophobiac" (20)—Nabokov's own coinage for himself as a small boy[13] but equally applicable to the adult who does not want to believe in time—the author is, he also knows that "the prison of time is spherical and without exits" (20). From his "present ridge of remote, isolated, almost uninhabited time" (22) Nabokov looks back to "a radiant and mobile medium that was none other than the pure element of time" (21)[14] and aims, in this connection, to make his book *Speak, Memory* as radiant and mobile a medium as possible.

The foreword, then, is only apparently confined to the "multiple metamor-

---

spoke of *Speak, Memory* as "a new type of autobiography . . . *a scientific attempt*," and it is now, since the publication of his *Lecutres on Literature*, abundantly clear how often he encouraged students to draw maps and how insistent he was on details (cf. *SO*, 22, 55, 90—where he brings these two emphases together in relation to *Speak, Memory*—168, and 186, the latter in the context of being a memoirist). *Speak, Memory*, 92–93 suggests that his teacher Dobuzhinskj was very influential in this respect.

[11] *SO*, 197: "My sense of places is Nabokovian rather than Proustian"; Hyde, *Vladimir Nabokov: America's Russian Novelist*, 148 n. 56, 192, demurs.

[12] Nabokov hints that he has inevitably failed by adding to the 1951 version an account of how he tried "in vain to reach the sub-base of Pushkin's 'Exegi monumentum' " (cf. *SO* 76; Nabokov's translation of the poem in *Pushkin, Lermontov, Tyutchev* [London: Lindsay Drummond, 1947]; the notes to lines 75–76 of the poem "Fame" in *Poems and Problems* [London: Weidenfeld and Nicolson, 1972], 113; and 97–98 and 196 n. 67 in David Rampton's study of the novels). The remark provides Nabokov with a link to the Horatian "Eheu, fugaces" paraphrase that opens the final chapter of *Speak, Memory*.

[13] In the 1951 edition (9) Nabokov is much vaguer: "a sensitive youth." For the changes in Nabokov's perspective on time between editions of *Speak, Memory* see Grayson, *Nabokov Translated*, 150–51.

[14] Cf. Stuart, "The Novelist's Composure," 192 and Bruss, *Autobiographical Acts*, 130 (on the general problem of time for any biographer) and 147 (on *Speak, Memory* specifically).

phosis'' (13) of a book; what it is really alerting us to is the multiple meta-morphosis of a life now being relived and narrated in its own space-time. Nabokov's nostalgia is, by his own admission, ''a hypertrophied sense of lost childhood'' (73), and the writing of *Speak, Memory* obviously exacerbated the nostalgia to a point that was barely endurable. It is no surprise to learn that several of the chapters were written ''at a time of great mental and physical stress'' (10). But the confident arrogance of the foreword is predicated upon a hypertrophied sense of recovered childhood, of time relived rather than simply regained, a memorialization rather than a mere memoir.

There are beauties enough in *Speak, Memory* proper not to dwell unduly on the book's foreword,[15] and I have done so only because it enables us more easily to unravel the threads of the magic carpet Nabokov is weaving. But even after taking cognizance of its foreword, *Speak, Memory* is by no means a straightforward book. Although the title suggests that the author has only to command his mnemonic apparatus, or Muse, for recollection to come flooding back, the process is inevitably attended with ''blank spots, blurry areas, domains of dimness'' that only ''come into beautiful focus'' for a reader prepared to emulate, however vainly, the ''intense concentration'' Nabokov himself has tried to achieve when confronted by a ''neutral smudge'' (12). *Speak, Memory* is full of the ''elaborate interlacements and expanding clusters'' that made Nabokov want to call the book ''The Anthemion'' (11).[16] This is because, as in a chess problem, it is the themes that matter most to the author. ''The following of . . . thematic designs, through one's life,'' Nabokov states in the third section of the first chapter, ''should be, I think, the true purpose of autobiography'' (27). But Nabokov does not intend these thematic designs to be immediately apprehensible, being skeptical in any case as to the possibility of life surviving ''captivity in the zoo of words'' (233).[17] In the very last paragraph of the book, where the fall (autumn) of 1939 is linked to the fall (collapse) of Paris in 1940 (and thus linked further to the suggestion that ''everything has fallen through''[18] in section 3 of chapter 1), Nabokov describes a

---

[15] Cf. Grayson, *Nabokov Translated*, 139, for what Nabokov does *not* mention in his foreword and Johnson, *Worlds in Regressions*, 11, for the two topics—his marriage and his literary career—''conspicuously absent'' from the book as a whole.

[16] Alluding to the concentric rings or nimbuses seen (chiefly in alpine or polar regions) surrounding the shadows of an observer's head projected on a cloud or fog bank opposite to the sun; but Nabokov also wished to call the book *The Person In Question* and *Rainbow Edge* (*The Nabokov-Wilson Letters*, 188, 259). Johnson, *Worlds in Regression*, 11, identifies the rainbow as the ''master motif'' of *Speak, Memory*.

[17] Cf. *SO*, 14: ''I don't think in any language, I think in images.'' In the foreword to *The Gift* and elsewhere Nabokov bemoans his loss of Russian as a creative medium. The photographs in the final version of *Speak, Memory* are doubtless designed to recall things more vividly than mere words can. But the young Nabokov also had a fondness for illustrated books (*Speak, Memory*, 195, 244).

[18] *Speak, Memory*, 27. Stuart, ''The Novelist's Composure,'' 179, sees this as ''one of the basic perspectives from which the autobiography is constructed.''

garden that he and his wife and child are walking through on their way to catch the boat to America: "Laid out on the last limit of the past and on the verge of the present, it remains in my memory merely as a geometrical design which no doubt I could easily fill in with the colors of plausible flowers, if I were careless enough to break the hush of pure memory that (except, perhaps, for some chance tinnitus due to the pressure of my own tired blood) I have left undisturbed, and humbly listened to, from the beginning" (309). This is Nabokov at his most elegantly deceptive and ironic. For the tinnitus, the ringing in the ears, that has colored his memories throughout is by no means random and haphazard, and the construction of the book has been much more than simply listening to a memory that has been ordered to speak.[19] The clue to the construction of the book is, in a sense, embedded in the final sentence of all,[20] where Nabokov contrives to describe not only the reactions of himself and his family at a particular point in time but also, and more importantly, the ideal attitude to be taken by anyone who has read his book this far: "There, in front of us . . . where the eye encountered all sorts of stratagems . . . it was most satisfying to make out among the jumbled angles . . . something in a scrambled picture—Find What The Sailor Has Hidden—that the finder cannot unsee once it has been seen" (309–10).

This serpentine concluding sentence, from which I have extracted the essential utterance, makes a satisfying conclusion to the book precisely because it does not identify what the finder (or reader) should be looking for. And the allusion to a child's game is not quite as innocent as it looks, for the sailor in this case in none other than Nabokov himself, who appears in one of the photographs[21] in the sailor suit to which he often refers in the narrative and who has, of course, deceived and dazzled our eyes throughout with "all sorts of stratagems" designed to send us up blind alleys. In this respect, the end of the fifteenth and final chapter is very like the end of the penultimate chapter, which describes Nabokov's composition of a particularly cunning chess problem. (This is itself a gloss on the beginning of chapter 14, where Nabokov indulges in a prolonged speculation about spirals and circles and how they may be subsumed under Hegel's triad of thesis, antithesis, and synthesis).[22] The

[19] Nabokov seems, however, to have been fascinated by the imperative mood. Andrew Field reports that possible titles for the never completed second volume of memoirs were *Laugh, Memory*, *Smile, Memory*, and *Speak, America* (*Nabokov: His Life in Part* [New York: Viking Press, 1977], 293) and in *VN* (256) adds *Speak On, Memory* to the list. Cf. *SO*, 294, and *Speak, Memory*, 14.

[20] Bruss, *Autobiographical Acts*, 152, stresses that "the final words of the autobiography catch consciousness in the act." Brian Boyd, in *Nabokov's Ada: The Place of Consciousness* (Ann Arbor: Ardis, 1985), has written very well on this aspect as revealed in the works of Nabokov generally.

[21] The photograph is found facing page 129.

[22] Bruss, *Autobiographical Acts*, pp. 150ff., interprets the fifteen chapters of *Speak, Memory*

chess problem is too long to quote but involves a typically Nabokovian exploitation of a "false scent."[23] The passage concludes with an account of a document stamped with a violet imprint and lettering, together with an ostensibly helpful comment from Nabokov himself: "It is only now, many years later, that the information concealed in my chess symbols, which that [passport] control permitted to pass, may be, and in fact is, divulged" (293). Now in terms of *Speak, Memory* itself it is clear that only Nabokov himself is in control of the information; in this respect, it is never a fair contest between author and reader, for the author cannot fail to win, either by disclosing irrelevancies or by covering up relevancies, or even (as to some extent happens here) changing the game altogether—in this instance, from chess to ciphers. It is easy to imagine even a sophisticated reader getting irritated with Nabokov here and accusing him (as indeed many critics have done) of being absurdly ivory tower and mystagogic. But Nabokov has, in a way, divulged information here, and the actual solution of the chess problem is embedded in a passage three paragraphs back (291). What Nabokov is doing here is pretending to observe the golden rule that a magician never explains how a trick is done[24] and at the same time offering, to those who can find what the sailor has hidden, a key to unlock the mystery. There is another passage, from the end of the second section of section 1, that seems relevant here: "The individual mystery remains to tantalize the memoirist. Neither in environment nor in beauty nor in heredity can I find the exact instrument that fashioned me, the anonymous roller that pressed upon my life a certain intricate watermark whose unique design becomes visible when the lamp of art is made to shine through life's foolscap" (25). If the individual mystery (which is also the mystery of being an individual) cannot be solved by the memoirist, what chance does the reader or critic have of unlocking it? The solution to the chess problem can be found if one looks hard enough (either at the board or at the book). But the key that will unlock life has very obviously yet to be invented, so that even if "the following of . . . thematic designs" is, as Nabokov claims "the true purpose of autobiography," it is not supposed that the critic's articulation of those designs will reveal the whole mystery of a personality. It is ironically appropriate that Nabokov should tell us, in the foreword, that he was disappointed at the way the title *Conclusive Evidence* "suggested a mystery story" (11),

---

as a triad of five chapters each; Johnson, *Worlds in Regression*, (79–80), emphasizes that the triadic mode of resolution of the chess problem is emblematic.

[23] W. W. Rowe (*Nabokov's Deceptive World* [New York: New York University Press, 1971], 153) says of these pages that they "contain a sustained potential sexual analogy"; Bruss, *Autobiographical Acts*, 136, explores this further. Nabokov vigorously pooh-poohed the idea (*SO*, 304–7). On combinations and deceptions see *SO*, 12; on *Lolita* as at once composition and solution see *SO*, 20. The chess problem and its solution are in *Poems and Problems*, 182, 201.

[24] "A good writer is first of all an enchanter" (Nabokov, in a letter of 27 Noember 1946 to Edmund Wilson, on 177 of the Karlinsky edition of the correspondence).

for in a sense *Speak, Memory* is nothing less than a mystery story in which the puzzle is never solved.[25]

This does not, of course, absolve us from entering the mystery and attempting to demystify those parts of it that are open to interpretation; it is, indeed, clear that Nabokov expects the discerning reader to do so and to derive delight from the activity. Strangely, it is only when we stand too far back from the book that is seems shapeless and indecipherable. When we look at it close up, each facet seems to possess a logic and charm of its own. There is a moment in chapter 4 when Nabokov obliquely indicates that this is the only way to read it: "In an English fairy tale my mother had once read to me, a small boy stepped out of his bed into a picture and rode his hobbyhorse along a painted path between silent trees. While I knelt on my pillow in a mist of drowsiness and talc-powdered well-being, half-sitting on my calves and rapidly going through my prayers, I imagined the motion of climbing into the picture above my bed and plunging into that enchanted beechwood—which I did visit in due time" (86).[26]

Charming as this is as a description on a realistic level of the magical transformations of childhood, it seems to me that it also describes what Nabokov is doing in *Speak, Memory*, stepping as he is into a picture of prerevolutionary Russia and plunging into a time that the power of art has filled with fairy-tale enchantment. But above and beyond that, it invites the reader to climb into the picture and ride his own hobbyhorse, under the personal supervision (Nabokov, in a sense, as mother) of an artist who can, seemingly, carry out metamorphoses at will. Nabokov claims in chapter 1 that the harmonious world of a perfect childhood possesses "a naturally plastic form in one's memory, which can be set down with hardly any effort" (24–25), whereas the recollections of adolescence make Mnemosyne "choosy and crabbed." But it must be clear to any reader—as Nabokov half admits in the foreword—that a very considerable amount of imaginative effort is required on the part of both author and reader, if the full effect of this harmony is to be perceived.

The great attraction of *Speak, Memory* is that while Nabokov is always pointing out how this connects with that, there are any amount of important connections that the author leaves the reader to work out for himself. At the end of chapter 1, for instance, Nabokov recounts "a marvellous case of levitation" involving his father being rewarded by grateful peasants tossing him in the air (31). The explicit comparison is with an angel, although (like the map at the beginning of the work) it inevitably reminds one of the butterflies

---

[25] See *SO*, 129, for Nabokov's dislike of mystery fiction. In *VN*, 257, Field stresses that "the life described cannot be confidently 'possessed' by any person other than Nabokov himself."

[26] Cf. Stuart, "The Novelist's Composure," 180, for a different interpretation of the last words of this quotation.

that the young (and the old) Nabokov relentlessly pursued.[27] The passage ends by referring to "funeral lilies conceal[ing] the face of whoever lies there . . . in the open coffin" (32), which prefigures his father's death described later in the book and confirms the wisdom of an old governess who has predicted that one day he will fall. (Chapter 2 ends similarly, with an account of how Nabokov sees the dead in dreams; chapter 3 ends with a dream world in which "nothing will ever change, nobody will ever die";[28] thereafter each chapter ends more optimistically, although chapter 9 concludes with a duel that does not take place and a real death—once again his father's assassination—several years later.[29])

Again in chapter 7, after describing in the previous chapter his first expedition into "the vast marshland beyond the Oredezh" (137), an expedition that makes him think of America and leads up, by a process of inner logic, to the passage in which he declares his disbelief in time—Nabokov recounts his first experience of puppy love, with a girl called Colette with whom he used to play by the sea at Biarritz. Three chapters later he describes his fruitless affection for a servant girl called Polenka, past whom he used to ride on his bicycle.[30] Later still, in chapter 12, with his bicycle again much in evidence, he devotes most of a chapter to his passionate affair with a girl he calls Tamara, during which he is reminded of Biarritz and the now inappositely named Rocher de la Vierge (236). Between these two chapters, in chapter 11, Nabokov describes the composition of his first poem. This helps to explain two apparently casual references to the poet Blok in the twelfth chapter[31] but relates more centrally to the failure of the affair, as Nabokov explains: the "banal hollow note, and glib suggestion that our love was doomed since it could never recapture the miracle of its initial moments" (238). The love and liter-

[27] For a full analysis of chapter 6 of *Speak, Memory* (originally entitled "Butterflies") see Stuart, "The Novelist's Composure," 184ff; cf. Grayson, *Nabokov Translated* 146. Field, *VN*, 255, sees it as one of only two "emotionally fervent" chapters, the other being chapter 2, whereas my whole essay is designed to show that every chapter is, in its own way, emotionally fervent.

[28] *Speak, Memory*, 77. Bruss, *Autobiographical Acts*, 149, relates the beginnings and ends of chapters (most noticeable in the journey from "cradle" to "coffin" in chapter 1) and stresses the importance of the present-tense aspect. She further suggests that the first five chapters all end "on a note of childish defenselessness and trust" (150).

[29] *Speak, Memory*, 193. Cf. Stuart, "The Novelist's Composure," 183–84 for another approach to the issue of Nabokov senior's death. Field, *VN*, 255, finds the pages on Nabokov *père* "wooden and constrained" and records that Nabokov had to force himself to write them (231).

[30] *Speak, Memory*, 208ff. "Pretty" Polenka first appears in section 3 of chapter 2.

[31] *Speak, Memory*, 229, 241. On Nabokov's fondness for Blok, see Field, *VN*, 44. *Drugie Berega* stresses that Tamara's taste is more indiscriminate. In real life "Tamara" (cf. the Tamara Gardens in *Invitation to a Beheading*) was Valentina Shulgina, and Nabokov's affair with her is described in detail in Field's *VN*. Johnson, *Worlds in Regression*, 162ff. and 181 n.9, indicates the importance of the *tam* element; *tam* means "there" in Russian. In *Deceptive World*, 68, Rowe mentions the pun Tamara/tomorrow (*Speak, Memory*, 213) without explaining the point of it.

ature motifs[32] have been circling round one another previous to this, for example in chapter 10, where the account of Polenka grows out of a discussion of the effect on the young Nabokov of the Wild West fiction of Mayne Reid (itself developing naturally out of the previous chapter's description of Nabokov's love for his father before an abortive duel and a reference to the famous love duel in which Pushkin died). But it is only in chapter 12 that Nabokov combines the themes openly or, to use his own terminology, "blends" the "lines" of a "difficult composition" (193).

These are only two, albeit the most important, of the combinations that Nabokov has left for the discerning reader to discover for himself.[33] Chapters 10, 11, and 12 of *Speak, Memory* are indeed particularly rich in "elaborate interlacements and expanding clusters" (11), and Nabokov seems actively to be encouraging the reader to collaborate with him in making his memories coherent.[34] There is so much detail in the foreground that it becomes exceptionally difficult to find what the sailor has hidden. But the sailor is always implicitly prompting us, as for instance at the end of chapter 11, when Nabokov's mother is deeply moved by his recitation of his first poem: "She passed me a mirror so that I might see the smear of blood on my cheekbone where at some indeterminable time I had crushed a gorged mosquito by the unconscious act of propping my cheek on my fist" (227). We are not encouraged to make anything overly symbolic out of this, although it is difficult not to feel the indicent has something to do with the death of Nabokov senior that dominates the end of several of the preceding chapters.[35] If, however, like Nabokov himself, we concentrate simply on the details, this squashed mosquito begins to connect with other dead lepidoptera mentioned in the text. In chapter 7, for example, describing the girl who preceded Colette in his youthful affections,

[32] On the love and literature question see also Stuart, "The Novelist's Composure," 189 and Grayson, *Nabokov Translated*, 157–58. In *Blue Evenings in Berlin* (New York: New York University Press, 1978) Marina Naumann has an interesting discussion of the relationship between the real-life Tamara and the story "A Letter that Never Reached Russia" (42). One could be forgiven for being reminded, at the beginning of chapter 12, of Proust's *jeunes filles* at Balbec as Tamara "catches up with two other, less pretty girls who were calling to her" (*Speak, Memory*, 230).

[33] For other patterns, see Stuart, "The Novelist's Composure," 178–79, and Hyde *Vladimir Nabokov*, 195–96. In *Nabokov's Ada* Boyd points out very usefully that it is precisely the independence of items that makes possible the attempt to relate them (23).

[34] Cf. Bruss, *Autobiographical Acts*, 160–62. *SO*, 40, shows that Nabokov tends to think of writer and reader as cooperative; but in more arrogant moods he thinks otherwise (114, 117).

[35] Nabokov dwells on other deaths in *Speak, Memory*, however. One important network of relationships implies connections between the Hanged One (63, 156; cf. *Eugene Onegin*, 2: 434) and the headless horseman (195, 200; cf. Pushkin's "The Bronze Horseman," referred to on 166). Analogous instances occur on 278 and 303. On "headlessness" and decapitation see Johnson, *Worlds in Regression*, 182 n. 12, and Boyd, *Nabokov's Ada*, 208–9. It is difficult to feel, in spite of the attention given to *Invitation to a Beheading*, that critics of Nabokov have fully explored the significance of this motif.

Nabokov recalls how he arrived one morning to be given "a dead humming-bird moth found by the cat" (149). In the following chapter, before the affair gets under way, Tamara kills a horsefly, which is clearly intended to relate to the "dead horsefly . . . on its back near the brown remains of a birch ament" that Nabokov sees at the beginning of chapter 11, when he is sitting in a pavilion composing poetry. Each of these details seems quite innocent on first reading, but on rereading[36] they become ominously charged with meaning. The effort of the first poem runs aground on a squashed mosquito; the great hopes of the first love affair come to nothing.[37] "Etymologically," Nabokov casually notes, " 'pavilion' and 'papilio' [butterfly] are closely related" (216), but they are also very closely related emotionally.[38] Life has a nasty habit of upstaging art; the butterfly is even more elusive than the poem. At the end of chapter 4 Nabokov speaks of "a queer shock . . . as if life had impinged upon my creative rights by wriggling on beyond the subjective limits so elegantly and economically set by childhood memories that I thought I had signed and sealed" (93), and *Speak, Memory* is shot through with the realization that, however much Nabokov may "picket nature," nature will have the last word. This is why, to return to the end of chapter 11, there is such drama[39] in the perfectly ordinary act of a mother handing a mirror to her child: "I saw more than [the smear of blood]. Looking into my own eyes, I had the shocking sensation of finding the mere dregs of my usual self, odds and ends of an evaporated idenity which it took my reason quite an effort to gather again in the glass" (227). The drama here is more subtle than it seems, because Nabokov is also trying to tell us about his difficulties with the autobiographical genre. The book has begun by stressing how unusual the young Nabokov is; now, on the brink of first love, a conventional enough subject, he is confronting his "usual" self. The raw material of *Speak, Memory* is, in a sense, little more than "odds and ends of an evaporated identity" and the considered composition of the book obviously cost Nabokov a considerable effort of reason before the glass was recomposed.

Nabokov is attempting in *Speak, Memory* to recompose (to *re*-compose also) a lost identity by means of an effort of reason. But it cannot be achieved by reason only; the forces of the imagination, described by Nabokov in the foreword to the novella *The Eye* as "ultimately the forces for good," must have some part in it.[40] And not just the author's imagination but the reader's

---

[36] Nabokov himself is a great rereader, as his forewords indicate; see also *Eugene Onegin*, 1: 17. He is even more obviously (cf. *SO*, 4), at least as far as *Speak, Memory* is concerned, an obsessive rewriter.

[37] Cf. in this respect the dead leaves of *Speak, Memory*, 152 (Nabokov and Colette) and also 162 (Lenski and his fiancée).

[38] Cf. Bruss, *Autobiographical Acts*, 153ff., and Stuart, "The Novelist's Composure," 189ff.

[39] Stuart, "The Novelist's Composure," 182, also stresses how dramatic *Speak, Memory* is.

[40] Cf. "Imagination is a form of memory" (*SO*, 78).

also. The figure of Nabokov looking into the glass at the end of chapter 11 links up with the hypothesized image of the reader looking into the puzzle at the end of chapter 15. *Speak, Memory* is an attempt to merge the real estate of Nabokov's youth with "the beauty of intangible property, unreal estate" (40), the estate of the imagination. It is a book of great sadness, and yet it ends on an optimistic note,[41] as Nabokov realizes that the fragments have at last added up to something:

> I do not doubt that among these slightly convex chips of majolica ware found by our child there was one whose border of scroll-work fitted exactly, and continued, the pattern of a fragment I had found in 1903 on the same shore, and that the two tallied with a third my mother had found on that Mentone beach in 1882, and with a fourth piece of the same pottery that had been found by *her* mother a hundred years ago—and so on, until this assortment of parts, if all had been preserved, might have been put together to make the complete, the absolutely complete, bowl. (308–9)

Like James, of whose golden bowl this may remind us, Nabokov has reached the conclusion that "it is art which makes life." But he has not so much set the two in opposition as tried to see how they relate reciprocally. It is no accident that in describing the birth of his son in the last chapter[42] Nabokov discusses theoretically the "stab of wonder" that he has all along been dramatically recording: "It occurs to me that the closest reproduction of the mind's birth obtainable is the stab of wonder that accompanies the precise moment when, gazing at a tangle of twigs and leaves, one suddenly realizes that what had seemed a natural component of that tangle is a marvellously disguised insect or bird" (298). This not only prefigures the last words of the book, the "find what the sailor has hidden" puzzle but also sends us back to the beginning where "the mind's birth" of the four-year-old Vladimir Nabokov is rendered with great economy and power. It is easy to forget what Nabokov has planted there and thus to overemphasize the sadder aspects of the book: "To a joke, then, I owe my first gleam of complete consciousness—which again has recapitulatory implications, since the first creatures on earth to become aware of time were also the first creatures to smile" (22).

It is rare for Nabokov to make us laugh out loud, because his humor is almost always tinged with melancholy (as in the splendidly circular account

---

[41] Cf. Grayson, *Nabokov Translated*, 155, on Nabokov's "increase in humor" between editions of *Speak, Memory*; Hyde describes the final version as his "most mellow" book (*Vladimir Nabokov*, 196), and there is a general tendency, which I do not share, to treat the memoir as "happier" than other Nabokov books. Nabokov did, of course, speak many times of America as a second home and called a "happy expatriation" in *SO*, 218. But he suffered several expatriations before he left the continent of Europe, and the intimate evidence of his poems confirms the feeling generated by *Speak, Memory* that Russia was a terrible loss.

[42] Cf. Bruss, *Autobiographical Acts*, 152, for a different interpretation of the implications of this event; Hyde, *Vladimir Nabokov*, 75 n. 35, emphasizes the "crucial" moral part played unwittingly by Dmitri.

of his two visits to his Cambridge tutor, both of which end with him trampling on the teacups[43] or the equally circular account of "Mademoiselle O" that begins the ostensibly "erratic sequence" in 1936.[44] But his melancholy is almost never cloying, because the stab of wonder heals as well as wounds. Nabokov obliges his reader to become fascinated, as he is, by puzzles, because life discloses itself to him as a puzzle to which human beings can only find a temporary solution. This is why he describes his life (and implicitly his book) as "a colored spiral in a small ball of glass" (275), for it is both fragile and strong, simple and complex, precious and yet as ordinary as a marble.

There is a moment in chapter 2 of *Speak, Memory* where Nabokov speaks of inheriting from his mother "an exquisite simulacrum, the beauty of intangible property, unreal estate" that "proved a splendid training for the endurance of later losses" (40). This is an important remark because it helps explain why Nabokov is finally not, despite his passion for puzzles and ciphers, an exponent of "art for art's sake." He is ultimately, like any great writer, a moralist, which is why the remark in the foreword to the novella *The Eye* needs to be stressed: "The forces of the imagination are in the long run the forces for good." This is why he tells the absurd story of "the giant polygonal Faber pencil" that his mother bought for him, "far too big for use and, indeed . . . not meant to be used" (39). The pencil is extraordinary and wonderful but unreal.[45] Nabokov concludes the story by saying: "All one could do was to glimpse, amid the haze and the chimeras, something real ahead . . . somewhere beyond the throes of an entangled and inept nightmare, the ordered reality of the waking hour."

In order to see clearly, it is imperative for Nabokov to lift himself about the haze and the chimeras. Otherwise he will become like the waxwing slain by the false azure of the windowpane in the first line of John Shade's poem *Pale Fire*. There is an implicit gloss on the conclusion to the story of the pencil at the end of chapter 2: "It is certainly not then—not in dreams—but when one is wide awake, at moments of robust joy and achievement, on the highest terrace of consciousness, that mortality has a chance to peer beyond its own limits, from the mast, from the past and from its castle tower.[46] And although

---

[43] *Speak, Memory*, 259, 273.

[44] Cf. Grayson, *Nabokov Translated*, 147ff. Field (*VN*, 254) identifies "Mademoiselle O" as Mademoiselle Miauton. Johnson, *Worlds in Regression*, 28–29, discusses the "alphabetic chromesthesia" (which he finds much increased in the successive versions, 43 n. 13) involved in using the letter "O." Nabokov mentions in the foreword that this section was first published by Jean Paulhan, who has been mentioned as the possible author of *Story of O* behind the pseudonym Pauline Réage; but *Story of O* was first published in book form in July 1957, so any connections here are at best ex post facto.

[45] Cf. Stuart, "The Novelist's Composure," 179, for a different approach to this pencil.

[46] Chess players will note the absence of "rook" here. Analogous images may also be found on 25, 146, 240, 244. Stuart, "The Novelist's Composure," 186–88, writes well on the importance of high perspectives in *Speak, Memory*.

nothing much can be seen through the mist, there is somehow the blissful feeling that one is looking in the right direction'' (50). The mixed metaphors here, of land and sea (and inevitably, if only implicitly, chess), are very clearly not the products of an inept writer but rather the product of a mind trying to bring experience together. Nabokov repeatedly images himself as a sailor[47] adrift on a sea of phenomena or as a balloonist drifting vaguely through the air (90). But he also sees himself on terra firma, as the goalkeeper, ''the lone eagle, the man of mystery, the last defender'' (267). Much of the poignancy of the love affair with Tamara—and indeed the composition of his first poem—stems directly from the fact that he has been flying and has been brought down to earth with a bump. In the end Tamara, or her letters, become, like almost all Nabokov's memories, butterflies beating their wings in vain: ''Letters from Tamara would be still coming, miraculously and needlessly, to southern Crimea, and would search there for a fugitive addressee, and weakly flap about like bewildered butterflies set loose in an alien zone, at the wrong altitude, among an unfamiliar flora'' (251).[48]

If there is a fear here on Nabokov's part, as I think there is, that we who read his book will be bewildered—for all readers of autobiography are by definition in an alien zone, among an unfamiliar flora—it is a needless fear. For though we can only respond to his book vicariously and must always to some extent be fugitive addressees, it is precisely what Nabokov calls the ''almost pathological keenness of the retrospective faculty'' (75) that keeps us in touch with the author. The robust reality of Nabokov's obsessively detailed evocations do indeed make ''a ghost of the present'' (77). For, however much trickery of art is employed in *Speak, Memory*, Nabokov's orientation is indeed, as he claimed in the 1951 foreword, toward the truth. ''The man in me,'' he writes, ''revolts against the fictionist'' (95),[49] and it cannot be accidental that whereas he entitled an early novel *Camera Obscura* (later *Laughter in the Dark*), we find him talking in *Speak, Memory* of ''certain camera-lucida needs of literary composition'' (92). There is a great moment in chapter 5 where Nabokov catches himself idling in a ''stereoscopic dreamland'' where ''All is still, spellbound, enthralled by the moon, fancy's rear-vision mirror,'' and then suddenly awakens: ''The snow is real, though, and as I bend it and scoop up a handful, sixty years crumble to glittering frost-dust between my fingers'' (99–100).[50] Something similar occurs at the end of chapter 8, which Nabokov has begun with the apparently casual and gratuitous aim to ''show a few slides'' (153) and which ends with a reality that is enduring and permanent:

---

[47] For example, 73: ''the sense of receding endlessly, as if this was the stern of time itself'' (cf. *SO*, 72); and 85.

[48] Cf. Grayson, *Nabokov Translated*, 161: ''Nabokov's treatment of the correspondence with Tamara can also be read as a retrospective commentary on [*Mary*].''

[49] Cf. Bruss, *Autobiographical Acts*, 135.

[50] Stuart, ''The Novelist's Composure,'' 183, relates to the child's fairy tale.

"I witness with pleasure the supreme achievement of memory, which is the masterly use it makes of innate harmonies when gathering to its fold [cf. the fold of the magic carpet][51] the suspended and wandering tonalities of the past. . . . Through a tremulous prism, I distinguish the features of relatives and familiars, mute lips serenely moving in forgotten speech" (170–71). The prism here is not so much the glass of the cinema projector upon which Nabokov's slides are to be run as the prism of *Speak, Memory* itself.[52] The cinematic image is habitual to Nabokov (as Alfred Appel has very ably shown),[53] but the natural image (the sunset at the end of chapter 10, for instance, or the waterlilies he touches when coming out of a poetic trance)[54] is even more powerful in *Speak, Memory*. It is not only with Tamara that Nabokov parts "the fabric of fancy" and tastes "reality" (232);[55] the whole book is committed to doing precisely that.

Notwithstanding his devotion to imaginative processes, then, Nabokov very obviously sees his task in *Speak, Memory* as decisively different from, and in some ways more complex than, his enterprises in fiction.[56] Nabokov hints as much in chapter 12: "That twisted quest for Sebastian Knight [1940] with its gloriettes and self-mate combinations, is really nothing in comparison to the task I balked in the first version of this memoir and am faced with now" (256).

The task is also more complex than biography, a genre to which Nabokov has also contributed with his "rather frivolous little book" (167) *Nikolai Gogol* (1944). Nabokov believes that the temptation to blend biography and fiction must be resisted at all costs because it gives rise to those "*biographies romancées* which are by far the worst kind of literature yet invented" and requires instead "a delicate meeting place between imagination and knowl-

[51] The image is common in Nabokov; for two typical instances see section 8 of "The Paris Poem" of 1943 (*Poems and Problems*, 123) and *Invitation to a Beheading* (New York: McGraw-Hill, 1965), 94.

[52] Cf. *Speak, Memory*, 186: "I viewed his activities through a prism of my own." The camera lucida (113) operates by means of a peculiarly shaped prism. Some indentification with Sebastian Knight's book *The Prismatic Bezel* would seem in order in view of what Nabokov wrote in a letter of 24 March 1951 to Edmund Wilson (*The Nabokov-Wilson Letters*, 259).

[53] See his *Nabokov's Dark Cinema* (New York: Oxford University Press, 1974), passim. Appel's only important comment on the memoir, however, is that in its first form (*Conclusive Evidence*) it was the last work he asked his friend and Wellesley College colleague Sylvia Berkman to read with a view to correcting his English (85).

[54] *Speak, Memory*, 213, 222.

[55] Johnson, *Worlds in Regression*, 139, shows the close association between "you" and "reality" in *Look at the Harlequins!* (cf. footnotes 6 and 64 to this essay).

[56] Cf. Stuart, "The Novelist's Composure," 181; Grayson, *Nabokov Translated*, 156–59, 227–31, who also relates *Ada* specifically to chapter 12 of *Speak, Memory* (120ff.); Rowe, *Deceptive World*, 139n, adds parallels with *Mary*. In his preface to *The Annotated Lolita*, (New York: McGraw-Hill, 1970) Appel sees *Lolita* as in part a parody of the 1951 *Speak, Memory*. Hyde, *Vladimir Nabokov*, 192, sees *Speak, Memory* as a work of fiction.

edge.''[57] The only analogy he can find is the composition of chess problems,[58] which is precisely why he deals with the subject in so much detail. In *Speak, Memory*, as in the chess problem, he has been prepared to "sacrifice purity of form to the exigencies of fantastic content, causing form to bulge and burst like a sponge-bag containing a small furious devil" (290). But he has gone further, for although "beautiful" and "complex,"[59] *Speak, Memory* is at no time "sterile" (288) like a chess problem.[60] It is more like an actual game of chess, full of "simple and elegant" moves (245). The "circle . . . has ceased to be vicious" (275) and has become a "spiritualized" circle, a spiral.[61] If "defocalization" (240) periodically occurs, unlike in the crystalline world of the chess problem, this is because it is endemic to the genre, however "carefully wiped" the "lenses of time" (230) may be. The moments when Nabokov feels, as he did in childhood, "a sense of drowsy well-being" when he has "everything neatly arranged" (145) are counterbalanced by those in which he is left holding a "wisp of iridescence, not knowing exactly where to fit it" (152). In this respect the book, like most autobiographies, seems to require the reader's "collaboration" and "corroboration" (308).[62] Just as there must be "perfect cooperation between headsman and victim" (278),[63] so there must also be cooperation between the artist and the world. Even the dedication, as usual to his wife, Véra, has a part to play in this minutely considered book, for it is of course Véra who is the "you" that Nabokov refers to with increasing frequency.[64] This device, which is so surprising on its first

---

[57] *Eugene Onegin* 2: 314.

[58] Cf. "V" 's discussion, *The Real Life of Sebastian Knight* (Harmondsworth: Penguin, 1964), 79, of Knight's "method of composition," often extrapolated to apply to Nabokov's works.

[59] Quite unlike Sebastian Knight's "autobiography," *Lost Property*, which "V" considers his "easiest book" (*Real Life*, 95). Nabokov interestingly disavows any "sorrow for lost banknotes" in the often-quoted fifth section of chapter 3 of *Speak, Memory*.

[60] The potential sterility of chess is advertised in the novel *The Defense*, where Luzhin (as Nabokov describes him in the 1951 *Speak, Memory*, 216) goes insane "when chess combinations pervade the actual pattern of his existence."

[61] Cf. *SO*, 52, 127.

[62] Rowe, *Deceptive World*, 63ff., offers several instances from *Speak, Memory* in which "reader participation" is essential if the full force of Nabokov's subtlety is to be felt.

[63] Cf. *Speak, Memory*, 166, 195, 200, 278, 303 and footnote 35 *supra*. In the 1951 version Nabokov describes *Invitation to a Beheading* as "the most haunting of Sirin's works" (215).

[64] In the 1951 version (183) Nabokov again combines the themes of love and literature by suggesting that his writing was "talentless and derivative" until 1925, "the year I met my present wife." Nabokov actually *met* Véra in 1923, as Brian Boyd reveals in his *TLS* review of Field's *VN* ("Getting Nabokov Wrong," 24 April 1987; 432); they *married* in 1925. Bruss, *Autobiographical Acts*, 160, discusses the role of Véra, the dedicatee of almost all Nabokov's books but never, perhaps, more aptly so (if one considers that *vera* in Latin means "real things") than in the case of *Speak, Memory*. Nabokov tells us in chapter 12 of the final version that "until the writing of a novel [*Mary*] relieved me of the fertile emotion, the loss of my country was equated for me with the loss of my love" (245). This implicitly underpins my inference that the writing of an autobiography, however protracted, does not relieve "all the pangs of exile" (244).

occurrence that it seems not only to buttonhole the reader but also to bundle him into the book (just as the child in the fairy tale stepped into the picture), indicates that the book is by no means a self-contained artifact but rather a retroactive gift,[65] from art to life. In the end our experience of *Speak, Memory* is qualitatively different from the ''best novels'' of V. Sirin (Nabokov, of course)[66] in which Sirin ''condemns his people to the solitary confinement of their souls''[67] and more complex than the ideas of the philosopher Vivian Bloodmark (Nabokov again, as the incident of the squashed mosquito and the index remind us). For if the poet ''feels everything that happens in one point of time'' (218), the memoirist,[68] however chronophobiac, cannot defeat time definitively. *Speak, Memory* has the ''yielding diaphanous texture of time''[69] that Nabokov experienced in Cambridge, so that ultimately ''Nothing one look[s] at [is] shut off in terms of time, everything [is] a natural opening into it'' (269).

[65] The retroactivity involved is in some ways comparable with that operative in the partially autobiographical novel *The Gift*, which contains a brilliant (initially suppressed) ''biography'' of Chernyshevsky to which Nabokov alludes obliquely in *Speak, Memory*.

[66] Cf. Stuart, ''The Novelist's Composure,'' 182, on the artistic effect of ''disguising'' oneself as ''Sirin''; and Bruss, *Autobiographical Acts*, 156, on the artistic effect of ''disguising'' oneself as ''Bloodmark.''

[67] *Speak, Memory* (1951 edition), 189.

[68] Bruss, *Autobiographical Acts*, 157, would restrict the term ''memoirist'' in a pejorative sense to Humbert Humbert in *Lolita*.

[69] Cf. *SO*, 184, and above all part 4 of *Ada*, most fully analyzed in part 4 of Boyd's study of the novel.

CHAPTER 9

Yury Trifonov's *The House on the Embankment*: Fiction or Autobiography?

Fiona Björling

THE QUESTION of fiction or autobiography concerns the discursive aspect of literature rather than its content.[1] Whether events related in literature are taken from the imagination of from history is less relevant than the significance of the historical writer as the ultimate authority behind the work. We find ourselves at the slippery junction between the writer's original intention and the authorial position as emanating from within the text itself. My investigation is concerned with the problem of authorial position as manifest in a work where autobiographical sections intrude in an overtly fictional text. Yury Trifonov's novels, in particular *The House on the Embankment (Dom na naberezhnoj)*, manifest extreme complexity on that level of discourse. In analyzing the problems incurred in establishing the authorial position manifested in this novel, I hope to provide an interpretation of the text and a motivation for its narrative peculiarities, as well as to elaborate the unique status of the voice "behind" narrative fiction in general.

Crucial to the consideration of narrative fiction is the concept of the implied author (IA), in the Slavic field alluded to variously as: the image of the author (obraz avtora, V. V. Vinogradov); the author, the author's voice, the authorial position, or the final position of meaning (avtor, avtorskij golos, avtorskaja pozitisija, poslednjaja smyslovaja instantsija, M. M. Bakhtin); the abstract subject (abstraktni subjekt, Jan Mukařovský), etc.[2] By the term IA we allude to the ultimate authoritative standpoint to which a reader refers when proffering an interpretation of a work of narrative fiction. Understanding a literary work is tantamount to understanding its purpose, not the meaning of the words themselves but their import in the given structure. The concept of IA allows us to posit an abstract authority, a sender position with a communicative purpose who directs the fictional narrative but is emancipated from the historical

---

[1] This article originally appeared in *Biografi og Vaerk* (special issue of *Svantevit* 9–1) (Aarhus, Denmark: Forlaget Arkona, 1983): 9–30. Slight amendations have been made in the present edition.

[2] Slobodanka B. Vladiv gives a useful survey of the development of the concept in Slavic literary theory. See the introduction in her book *Narrative Principles in Doestoevskij's Besy: A Structural Analysis* (Berne: European University Papers: series 16, Slavonic Languages and Literatures 10, 1979), 17–33.

writer of the text. For we know that while the real-life writer of the text may be converted to a new faith, dead and buried, a directing force remains an inherent part of the text itself. Interpreting a work of fiction is tantamount to identifying its IA.

With the structural approach to literature in general, and to fiction in particular, the distinction between the creator of a text (the historical writer) and the authorial position inherent to the work itself (IA) has been established.[3] Notwithstanding the general acceptability of the term, however, several seminal theories of narrative as well as studies specifically devoted to "point of view" fail to take adequate account of this all-important position of meaning in fictional narrative.[4] Furthermore, few analyses help us to chart how the reader— intuitively—actually negotiates meaning in fiction toward the IA. Point-of-view studies tend to revolve around two axes of disparity: the disparity between the teller and the tale, that is between the narrator's and the narrated character's point of view, and the disparity between the author's and the narrator's point of view. In the latter case the distinction between the historical writer and the implied author is left vague; furthermore, the distinction between author and narrator is drawn only in those cases where the narrator is obviously unreliable. Given a reliable narrator, the concepts "author" and "narrator" tend to be used indiscriminately.[5] In actual fact, of course, the

[3] Ibid. For a non-Slavic reference see Seymour Chapman, *Story and Discourse: Narrative Structure in Fiction and Film* (Ithaca: Cornell University Press, 1978), 147–51. An equivalent distinction between the living artist and the sender position inherent to the work of art holds true for all art forms, but only in fiction can we talk of the implied author; lyrical poetry and drama, to speak of the verbal arts, each require a specific set of terms.

[4] See for example Gérard Genette, *Narrative Discourse: An Essay in Method*, trans. Jane E. Lewin (Oxford: Oxford University Press, 1980), and in particular chapter 5, "Voice." Genette is concerned here with what he calls the "narrating instance," and he is careful to distinguish the narrating from the writing instance. He does not, however, consider a position from which the narrating instance itself may be judged (212–15). Likewise Lubomir Doležel in his article "The Typology of the Narrator: Point of View in Fiction" in *To Honor Roman Jakobson* (The Hague: Mouton, 1967), 1:541–52, dismisses the relationship between the narrator and the author as being "irrelevant for structural theory" (542). By "author" both Genette and Doležel allude to the living writer but it seems strange that in a theory of fiction, especially of point of view in fiction, these eminent theorists do not need to introduce the category of the implied author. Similarly Norman Friedman's much-cited survey of point of view ("Point of View in Fiction," *PMLA* [1955]: 1160–84) discusses how the author is gradually eliminated from fiction, depending on the status of the narrator (from "editorial omniscience" to "the camera"). The author is considered as a private individual who can be more or less present, more in and out of "his" work at will. Friedman does not consider the authorial position as a structurally necessary part of the work, according to which the absence of the author is as significant as his presence.

[5] Thus Robert Scholes and Robert Kellogg, *The Nature of Narrative* (Oxford: Oxford University Press, 1966) posit three levels of point of view in narrative attributed to characters, narrator, and audience. Only in a particularly sophisticated form of fiction does there arise a fourth point of view, namely that of the author as distinct from the narrator (240). Even Wayne Booth, father of the term "implied author," who is meticulous in distinguishing the real author from his "sec-

reader can only judge the narrator to be reliable or unreliable according to the position of authority "above" the narrator himself: the concept of IA is no less crucial in works of apparent neutral narration (say, Tolstoy) than in works of obviously eccentric narration (say, Gogol).

Thus, for example, Gary Rosenschield's intricate analysis of narration in Dostoevsky's *Crime and Punishment* is marred by the fact that he too quickly concludes that "the narrator is, throughout, a spokesman for the implied author."[6] The subtitle of the book reads *The Technique of the Omniscient Author*, but the purpose is to show that the narrator's (the author's) evaluative position provides a "higher point of view" that makes of the story of Raskolnikov's crime and punishment a morality play, a story with a metaphysical message.[7] Having at the beginning of the book identified the narrator as the spokesman of the implied author, Rosenshield proceeds to treat the narrator as the ultimate authority of the novel and to interpret his words as implicitly valid. The narrator of *Crime and Punishment* may indeed be totally trustworthy, but there must be a higher point of view that signals that this is so, and it is this higher point of view, the position of ultimate meaning, the director of the narrator as well as of the "story," that credits interpretation of the novel as a work with a metaphysical truth to proclaim.

To reduce this three-tiered hierarchy characteristic of all fictional narrative to two tiers is to ignore a distinguishing feature of fictional as opposed to communicative narrative. Disparity of point of view between the teller and the

---

ond self," the implied author (71–76) allows that the reliable narrator is a dramatized spokesman for the latter. Thus Booth claims: "In Hemingway's 'The Killers,' for example, there is no narrator other than the implicit second self that Hemingway creates as he writes" (151). He speaks of those cases "when the second self is given an overt speaking role in the story (71) and of the author Cid Hamete's role in *Don Quixote* says: "Our admiration or affection or sympathy or fascination or awe . . . is more intense just because it has been made personal; the telling is itself a dramatic rendering of a relationship with the author's 'second self' which in strictly impersonal fiction is often less lively because only implicit" (213). Wayne C. Booth, *The Rhetoric of Fiction* (Chicago, 1961).

[6] Gary Rosenshield, *Crime and Punishment: The Techniques of the Omniscient Author* (Lisse: Peter de Ridder, 1978), 13. Robin Feuer Miller's *Dostoevsky and The Idiot; Author, Narrator and Reader* (Cambridge, Mass.: Harvard University Press, 1981) is an admirable study of the intricacies incurred by the fact that the narrator is clearly not the spokesman for the implied author. Unfortunately, I did not have her book available during the writing of this article.

[7] Of the narrator in *Crime and Punishment* Rosenshield says: "Only a certain amount of critical probing reveals that he indeed carries out all the traditional functions of the omniscient author. The narrator of *Crime and Punishment* does not merely comment on the action and characters; he provides the novel with a unity of vision" (125). I would contend the meaningful application of the term "omniscient" to the concept of author. It is of course the narrator who assumes omniscience, who presumes to relate as fact that which, as a single human being, he can never know (for the narrator himself never admits the fictionality of what he narrates). The implied author on the other hand merely sets the stage for the omniscient narrator; the author does not assume omniscience or argue for the truth of the story related, he simply urges the story and its narration as meaningful.

tale is a feature of all narrative, be it communicative or fictional. That which distinguishes fictional from communicative narrative is in fact the added level of disparity that arises when we have to interpolate an abstract, implied position of authority over and above the narrator himself. This difficulty of positing or proving the existence of an IA consists in the fact that it is, by definition, only implicit. As Bakhtin expresses it: "The author of a literary work is present only in the whole work, and he is not to be found in any one isolated part of that whole" ("Avtor literaturnogo proizvedenija prisutstvuet tol'ko v tselom proizvedenii, i ego net ni v odnom vydelennom momente etogo tselogo").[8] The existence of the IA in fictional narrative assures, therefore, not only an added level of disparity but that this disparity will be in itself elusive, difficult to pin down. Built into the notion of fictional narrative is a dimension of uncertainty on the level of discourse;[9] ambiguity or dual-voicedness is the mark of fictional narrative and no doubt accounts for the particular pleasure afforded in reading a short story or novel: in order to understand the work, the reader has to cast off in search of the IA, he has to actively locate a position according to which interpretation becomes valid.

The existence of an IA in fictional narration is easier to posit in theory than in practice. The concept is necessitated by the fact that in fiction the identity between the writer (the creator) of the text and the narrator (the speaker) of the text is severed. We know that the voice of the underground man is not to be confused with the voice of Dostoevsky, his maker. Furthermore, we know that the writer can never refer directly to himself in fictional narrative by means of the first-person pronoun. But the fact that the writer instigates a speaker other than himself does not mean that the speaker now assumes a position of ultimate authority within the text. Between the writer as creator and the narrator as speaker arises a gap; this gap must be filled by an authoritative sender position according to which the text may be interpreted as constituting meaningful communication. Notwithstanding the fact that during his act of creation the writer feeds his intention into the texture of the work, hoping for its realization in the IA position, with the completion of the text he loses all direct control. From the moment when the text begins to function as such, the IA or sender position may only be inferred from the words of the narrator. For in fictional narrative the actual words of the narrator bear always within themselves an unwritten signal to the reader as to how they should be interpreted. Now we can formulate the distinguishing feature of fictional narrative in terms of the traditional communication model according to which a *sender* sends a message to a *receiver*. Setting aside for now the question of the receiver, we can say that fictional as opposed to communicative narrative is distinguished ac-

---

[8] M. M. Bakhtin, "K metodologii literaturovedenija," *Kontekst* (1974): 203. Translations are mine unless otherwise indicated.

[9] See Scholes and Kellogg, *The Nature of Narrative*, 240.

cording to a peculiarity in the status and identity of the sender. In communicative narrative the sender is by definition also the speaker (that is, the narrator) and the concept of a "creator" is superfluous. In fictional narrative, on the other hand, the sender emerges as an integral part of the message itself, forcing the added concept of a creator. Creator, speaker, and sender each have distinctive status as regards the communication situation. The creator creates a speaker who in turn implies a sender not to be identified with the original creator. Both speaker and sender are accordingly to be classified as part of the text itself; so that while a communicative narrative presupposes a sender whose identity is independent of the communication act itself, a fictional narrative creates its own sender position as it goes along. It is not the sender who creates the message but the message that creates the sender, to put the matter paradoxically.

Difficult as it may be to negotiate in practice, this distinction, based on a peculiarity of the sender position in fictional narrative, provides us with a theoretically adequate means of distinguishing fiction from autobiography. Instead of asking "fact or fiction?" we now ask "whose voice—the writer's personal voice or the IA's inherently textual voice?"

We have shifted the dichotomy from the level of content to the level of discourse. It is, of course, on the discursive level that fiction differs from autobiography. As Roman Jakobson has pointed out in his comparison between Macha's poetry and his diaries, all writing, both fictional and factual, is furnished with facts. Furthermore those facts are transposed, organized, and arranged as soon as they become articulated in language, whether the language in question is proferred as fiction or autobiography.[10] In order to decide between autobiography and fiction, we have to establish whether or not a given narrative implies an authoritative sender position other than the narrator. This is no easy matter, but it is nevertheless crucial to interpretation: for if we understand a writer to be speaking in his own personal voice, we shall allow all manner of extraneous biographical evidence to influence our interpretation; on the other hand, if we track down an authoritative position emanating from within the text, we shall confine our attention to the disparities of viewpoint (IA, narrator, and characters) parried within the text itself.

The problem is of course far more complex than I have so far suggested, for if structuralists have posited in theory a distinction between the writer as individual and the authorial position inherent to a literary text itself, the fact remains that readers of literature in general, and of fiction in particular, do try to feel their way through the text to the individual who created it. As readers

---

[10] Roman Jakobson, "What is poetry?", *Semiotics of Art: Prague School Contributions*, ed. Ladislav Matejka and Irwin R. Titunik (Cambridge, Mass.: Harvard University Press, 1976), 164–75.

we are quite frankly curious about the person who wrote the book. And once we know that Dostoevsky lived in exile for a decade and that he suffered from epilepsy, a passion for gambling, and a chronic state of financial pressure, we absorb that knowledge and allow it to influence our interpretation of his literary works. Such curiosity on the part of the reader is in part due to the concept of the artist as bequeathed to us from the Romantic era onward, according to which art is the creation of a particular and special individual. On a different level, and perhaps more legitimately, we build up a conception of a writer's collective authorship: we understand Dostoevsky's novels better when we have tuned into his ''code,'' his way of writing; reading one novel helps the reading of a second notwithstanding that each novel has its own specific IA.[11]

Given the intricacy of a distinction that seems to be at the heart of the fictional genre, indeed of art altogether, it is necessary to proceed with concrete analysis. We have to learn to tabulate intuition, to screen fictional texts for those points of disparity that alert us to the fact that the narrator is not the ultimate authority of the text but merely a puppet whose gestures not only communicate their own meaning but reveal a mind behind, a mind that communicates more by communicating indirectly. In tracking down the IA, we have to look at the ''gaps'' of meaning as created by disparate points of view within the text; we have to trace how meaning is parried backward and forward, to examine the signals that allow us to conclude whether or not a given narrator is reliable. The greater the disparities of meaning, the easier they are to chart. For this reason Trifonov's novel *The House on the Embankment* gives ample scope for analysis, rooted as it is in an apparent confusion between the writer's personal voice and an elusive implied author.

Trifonov's novels or longer short stories, such as *Another Life (Drugaja zhizn')*, *The House on the Embankment*, *The Old Man (Starik)*, and *Time and Place (Vremja i mesto)*, rely for their effect and meaning on what may be called narrative confusion, an extreme disparity of viewpoint as described above.[12] Narrative confusion results from a combination of the following features: uncertainty as to the identity, that is, narrative position, of the narrator; outright inconsistency in the narrative position expressed in inconsistency of grammatical person and verbal tense; extensive use of quoted documents and

---

[11] See Taranovsky's notion of ''closed'' vs. ''open'' analysis in Kiril Taranovsky, *Essays on Mandelstam* (Cambridge, Mass.: Harvard University Press, 1976), 21–47. In Soviet semiotics the idea of the self-sufficient text is rejected altogether. Here a text is experienced against the background of a body of texts, and Zholkovsky coins the term ''poetic world'' to denote a specific writer's code. See, for example, A. K. Zholkovskij and Ju. K. Shcheglov, ''K ponjatijam 'tema' i poeticeskij mir,'' *Trudy po znakovym sisteman* 7 (Tartu): 143–67.

[12] The Russian texts for *Drugaja zhizn'* and *Dom na nabereznoj* are taken from Yuri Trifonov, *Povesti* (Moscow, 1978); *Starik* from the edition published in Moscow, 1979; *Vremja i mesto* was published posthumously in *Druzhba narodov* 9–10 (1981). All translations of Trifonov given here are mine unless otherwise noted.

letters that may or may not be taken from historical archives and that distract from the basic narrative situation (*The Old Man*); the interweaving of different time levels both in discourse and in story; extended use of free indirect speech that shifts point of view from that of the narrator to that of the narrated characters.[13] Since the signals pointing to the IA are emitted (unwittingly) through the words of the narrator, instability and inconsistency in the narrative position obscure the position of the IA. The reader, so to speak, cannot find his interpretative bearings.

Confused narrative as technique is an essential element of Trifonov's prose. From *Another Life* to *The Old Man* a steady development may be noted toward increased complexity of the narrative situation.[14] This technique is motivated on the thematic level by the works' apparent concern with the necessity—but also the impossibility—for human beings to face the truth of their own lives. A crucial simile in *The Old Man* elaborates the dilemma expressed in Trifonov's works as a whole: just as one who moves in a stream of lava cannot know how hot it is, he who moves in time is caught without perspective on his past and future life.[15] The heroes in Trifonov's novels have all for one reason or another been thrown onto the banks of their regular, unreflecting lives to be faced by their past. The intrigues of the novels revolve around the characters' attempts to recapitulate that past and their failure therein. Some characters, like Glebov and Kandaurov, who have made their way in life through moral compromise, are bound to fail: no jolt of personal crisis could set them back into original innocence. But other characters, specifically the old man in *The Old Man*, appears passionately bent on finding the truth. Like Serezha in *Another Life*, the old man is a historian, he has devoted several years to uncovering the truth about Migulin. The book ends with the quoted thoughts of the research scholar who takes up the task after the old man's death:

The truth is that dear, kind Pavel Evgrafovich in 1921, asked by the interrogator whether he conceded the possibility that Migulin participated in the counter-revolutionary uprising, answered sincerely: "I concede the possibility," but of course he forgot about that, not surprising, everybody thought that way then, everybody or

---

[13] The Russian term is *nesobstvenno-prjamaja rech'*. I have adopted here the term usually used in Anglo-Saxon contexts. See Roy Pascal, *The Dual Voice* (Manchester: Manchester University Press, 1977), for a survey of the concepts and terms.

[14] These ideas are further developed in my article "Morality as History: An Analysis of Yuri Trifonov's novel *Starik (The Old Man)*" in *Text and Context: Essays to Honor Nils Åke Nilsson*, ed. Peter Alberg Jensen and Barbara Lönqvist et al., Stockholm Studies in Russian Literature, no. 23 (Stockholm: Almqvist and Wiksell, 1987).

[15] "When you move on the stream of lava you don't notice the heat. And how can you perceive time if you are within it? The years have passed, life has passed, you start to take a look: how and when, why was this and that that. . . . Seldom has anyone seen and understood all that from a distance, with the mind and the eyes of another age" (81–82).

nearly everybody; there are times when truth and belief fuse indissolubly, like a bar of metal; it's difficult working out what happened when, but we'll work it out. (240)

The words are devastating. The old man's painstaking efforts to find out the truth about Migulin are waived aside as a total failure. And the confident assertion, "we'll work it out" ("my razberemsja") sounds hollow and naive against the background of the story now coming to a close. Why should the new student be any less biased than the old? What is his motive for studying the history of Migulin? Perhaps in his biography too lies a personal reason, a reason for the quest and at the same time the reason why the quest is bound to fail.

The idea emerging from these books is not that truth is relative but that human beings have no access to the truth. On the one hand there is neither perception of truth nor authority beyond the confines of the individual human mind; but on the other hand no human being is able to lift himself out of his own perspective, a perspective that, being individual, is bound to be biased. Now multiple or confused narrative gives iconic expression to the fundamental human dilemma that the novels articulate. For just as one narrative pose discredits another, so one human truth discredits another. The old man can pinpoint exactly the point that Asya forgets in telling her story (190–92); but in bewailing the selective quality of Asya's memory, he proceeds to fall into exactly the same trap. Thus one truth seeker discredits another. Furthermore confusion on the level of narrative perspective makes it difficult for the reader to identify the arbitrating position of the implied author. There seems to be a lack of clear directives as to which side the reader should take; and no final truth position is revealed.

.   .   .

The purpose of this analysis is to examine the "confused narrative" in *The House on the Embankment* and to motivate it in terms of the work's total meaning. In this work the basic, impersonal narration, in itself ambiguous, is disturbed by a mysterious first-person narrator. This "disturbance" occurs five times in all and comprises 21.5 of the total of 132.5 pages. The identity of the first-person narrator cannot be determined from within the novel itself, and my thesis is that it is best understood as an autobiographical insert whereby the first-person singular pronoun refers to Trifonov the writer, that is, the historical individual. This interpretation gives us a strange hybrid in which fiction and autobiography are juxtaposed, forming a kind of montage. The problem occurs as we try to identify the implied author inherent in the fictional genre: do the autobiographical sections too submit to the design of the implied author? Or do they remain aloof, exempt from any authority other than their real-life communicative sender?[16]

I shall begin by examining the thickening of narrative confusion as it is built up along the linear axis of the novel. The text begins with a paragraph separated from the following text by typographical spacing. This paragraph sets for the narrator an omniscient, all but cosmic tone. An impersonal narrator situated in an unspecified present initiates the text by disposing of the existence of a group of boys: "None of these boys is now to be found on the face of the earth."[17] While the demonstrative pronoun "these" indicates that the existence of the boys is assumed, clearly the narrator does not count himself among them (the narrator lives to tell the tale). The narrator observes and defines the (negated) lives of the boys from without. Not only does the narrator dismiss the physical existence of the boys, he also speaks disparagingly of the metaphysical quality of their lives. In a cosmic image he describes them as swimming helplessly in the stream of life, rushing ahead senselessly and without the strength to contemplate the life that they have left behind. Clearly the narrator and his subjects are of two different species. The effect of distance expressed in the meaning of the words is strengthened by the rhetorical quality of the passage: note for example the repetitions ("One's been killed in the war, another's died from illness; . . . they rush, they drift, they are borne by the current; . . . quicker and quicker, day after day, year after year; . . . we must hurry, hurry"[18]) and the contrast between the complex and repetitive syntax and the exclamation in the middle of the paragraph ("But why bother about them and their slow wits!"[19] The first-person reference in "I fear" ("bojus") I understand to allude to the omniscient narrator himself. It might appear feasible to make a case for this first paragraph as constituting one of the first-person, autobiographical sections, accordingly attributing it to Trifonov the writer. This cannot be done, however, on the grounds that Trifonov (the "I" of the first-person sections) was himself one of "those boys" and as such without the omniscience that characterizes this paragraph. In the five first-person sections the narrative perspective is limited to what the "I" himself has experienced, and nowhere does he pose as being omniscient. The first paragraph is extremely important in that it gives expression to an evaluative position that in spite of the fact that it is directly expressed on very few occasions, is potentially present throughout the novel.

In the second paragraph, after the topological spacing, the narrative position shifts abruptly. A third-person narrator now takes up the position of neutral

---

[16] We must not forget the reading public's avid respect for the writer himself.

[17] "Nikogo iz etikh mal'chikov net teper' na belom svete," 373.

[18] "Kto pogib . . . kto umer . . . letjat, plyvut, nesutsja v potoke . . . vse shorej i shorej, den' za dnem, god za godom . . . nado speshit, speshit'."

[19] "Nu i bog s nimi, s nedogadlivymi!"

mediator between the internal musings of the main character, Glebov, and the reader. The narrator apparently adds little of his own either physical description or evaluative comment; he merely relays. In other words, the narrator does not narrate anything not experienced by Glebov himself. This narration relies heavily, almost oppressively, on the use of free indirect speech. The first sentence of this paragraph is a subtle mixture of exposition from scratch and assumed knowledge. We learn that the scene is set in Moscow in August 1972. But we learn this as it were, by the way; it was "one of those unbearably hot August days" (which we all remember, it is understood). Likewise the place designation, Moscow, is interpolated indirectly and not stated as main-clause information. This lengthy interpolation reflects the syntax of Glebov's unwinding inner thoughts. In the same way the paragraph is saturated with expressions reflecting his emotionally charged experience: "As ill luck would have it, at the back of beyond, a strange thing, from ancient times, well actually."[20] What do we learn from this paragraph? We learn in fact two things, or rather we focus on one set of circumstances from two disparate points of view. On the one hand we focus on Glebov as on a spoiled Soviet citizen who by means of private contacts is able to make privileged purchases (cooperative apartment, antique table). On the other hand, we focus on a man who is hardly done by, forced to run errands in the enervating heat while everyone else relaxes in the country. The use of free indirect speech assures that the reader identifies with Glebov: whether or not we approve of him, the words and thoughts expressed are Glebov's and we the reader see the events largely through his point of view. At the same time, because the narration is not formally conducted as first-person narration and Glebov is still referred to in the third person, there remains a kind of gap—a "no comment" comment—on the part of the impersonal, strictly neutral narrator. Into this deadpan "no comment" we are at liberty to read all sorts of unspoken evaluations. Free indirect speech thereby opens the ground for more than one evaluative standpoint. For this reason it can be disquieting, particularly in the present case, when the character in question does not arouse spontaneous sympathy. At the same time the technique is productive in that it demands active participation from the reader. It does not spell out the answer but provokes the reader to seek out the elusive IA.

Since this technique and its effect is so important for the novel, I shall elaborate one more example. Shulepa has arrived in the embankment house in his creaking leather trousers and with sandwiches smelling of cheese and ham. Glebov feels his position in the class threatened. There is a plan to deprive Shulepa of his leather trousers and Glebov is one of the initiators of the operation. The preparations are described in free indirect speech that conveys Gle-

---

[20] "Kak nazlo, u cherta na rogakh, strannaja istorija, dopotopnykh vremen, voobshche-to."

bov's pleasure of anticipation. "That would be a treat, to pull down those fantastic, creaking trousers, just let him squirm and whimper with the girls looking on through the window, we'd let them know beforehand. Glebov ardently instigated a showdown with Shulepa whom he disliked.[21] Glebov's anticipation is expressed in free indirect speech, but intriguingly, in the denouement and within the confines of a single sentence, the narration suddenly switches to a neutral style dramatically lacking Glebov's own thoughts: "But at the last moment he decided not to take part. Perhaps he suddenly felt a bit ashamed. He looked on from the door which gave on to the back stairway."[22] Whose is the "perhaps" ("mozhet")? Is this Glebov's subsequent account to himself of his past, one of those moments of cowardice that he cannot face? Or does this mark a shift to a neutral narrator who sees only from the outside and who has no means of detecting the cowardice within Glebov's soul? In either case this switch from elaborate free indirect speech to a sudden ultra-neutral style constitutes the "no comment," the gap through which the IA must be sought, all the more effective for not providing a straightforward answer.

By far the greater part of the novel relies on this narrative situation, on a narrator who shuttles in and out of Glebov's psyche by using free indirect speech extensively and interspersing it with neutral "no comments." Only occasionally does the initial, all-knowing narrator enter the scene: for example, after six pages of narrative the omniscient narrator returns to give a formal introduction of Glebov: "Almost a quarter of a century ago before Vadim Aleksandrovich Glebov has become a baldish, fattish man with breasts like a woman's."[23] The authority normally assumed by the omniscient narrator is challenged by the sheer amount of narration turned to Glebov's own point of view. This means that at least three lines of interpretation concerning Glebov's behavior are open, each one presented with considerable force notwithstanding their mutual incompatibility: (1) the omniscient narrator sees Glebov together with the other boys from "above," from a superior point of view, whence they appear to him as helpless creatures not responsible for their own lives; (2) the considerable attention paid to Glebov's own inner experiences opens the way for another interpretation: accordingly Glebov is seen to have had a bad start in life; he was a victim of spoiled types like Shulepa who began life with an unfair advantage. As a child Glebov developed a leaden lump of envy in his heart, and it was this lump that poisoned his life and deeds. The

---

[21] "Eto bylo by sladost'ju: stashchit' s nego udivitel'nye skripuchie shtany, pust' by on poplja-sal, ponyl, a devchonki smotreli by na eto iz okna, ikh predupredili. Glebov gorjacho podgova-rival raspravit'sja Shulepoj, kotoryj emu ne nravilsja."

[22] "No v poslednij mig reshil ne uchastvovat.' Mozhet, emu stalo nemnogo stydno. On smotrel iz dveri, vykhodivshij na zadnjuju lestnitsu," 383–84.

[23] "Pochti chetvert' veka nazad, kogda Vadim Aleksandrovich Glebov eshche ne byl lysova-tym, polnym, s grudjami kak u zenshchiny," 379.

psychological, "forgiving" interpretation is not quite persuasive, not only owing to the narrative compulsion to the reader to identify with Glebov's point of view but because the crucial psychological event in Glebov's history occurred when he was still a child, not yet a full-fledged, responsible human being. The pages devoted to Glebov's early childhood years express genuine pathos. They cannot be entirely dismissed as the kernel and cause of all that was to come; (3) finally, we sense in this novel an interpretation that nevertheless accounts Glebov responsible for his life of carefulness and betrayal. No utterance on the part of the narrator actually condemns Glebov, but as was mentioned above the switch from extensive free indirect speech to bland neutrality is in itself provocative; it seems to be indicating something between the lines, and this something could amount to the conclusion that Glebov is morally responsible from start to finish, that he is weak and dangerous, that his primitive envy and self-survival instinct are at odds with all that is meant by moral courage and human dignity.

After twenty-seven pages of third-person narrative, heavily dominated by the use of free indirect speech, comes the first "intrusion" of a first-person narrative:

I remember all that childhood nonsense, the losses and the finds, how I suffered because of him, when he didn't want to wait for me and went to school with someone else, and how the building with the chemist's was moved, and I remember there was always a dampness in the backyards, it smelt of the river, and the smell of the river was inside the rooms, especially in my father's big room, and when a tram went over the bridge, a metallic jingle and the clank of wheels could be heard far away. I remember running in one breath up the huge staircase at the side of the bridge; stumbling in the evening under the archway upon the flying Derjugin gang as they came running out of the cinema like a pack of coyotes; walking toward them with clenched fists, wooden with fear.[24]

I allow myself to call this narrative switch an "intrusion" on the following grounds: firstly, the break in narrative position has not been anticipated in the preceding text. The third-person narrative has not reached a point of natural closure but is, so to speak, broken off in full swing; secondly, the narrative break is not marked by any formal indicator other than the use of the first-person singular form. There is no typological spacing otherwise used as a

[24] "Ja pomnju vsju etu chepukhu detstva, poteri, nakhodki, to, kak ja stradal iz-za nego, kogda on ne khotel menja zhdat' i shel v shkolu s drugim, i to kak peredvigali dom s aptekoj, i eshshe to, chto vo dvorakh vsegda byl syroj vozdukh, pakhlo rekoj, i zapakh reki byl v komnatakh, osobenno v bol'shoj ottsovskoj, i, kogda shel tramvaj po mostu, metallicheskoe brenchanie i ljazg koles byli slyshny daleko. Pomnju: vzbezhat' odnim dukhom po gromadnoj bokovoj lestnitse mosta; natknut'sja vecherom pod arkoj na letuchuju mosta; natknut'sja vecherom pod arkoj na letuchuju derjuginskuju bratvu, begushchuju iz kino, kak staja kojotov; idti navstrechu, szhav kulaki, dereveneja ot strakha," 400.

means of segmentation in this text; thirdly, the text itself does not explain the identity of the mysterious first person narrator who, it appears, directly witnessed the childhood events to which the narrative has so far been devoted.

The identity of the first-person narrator cannot be unambiguously determined from within the text. As such its function seems partly to arouse confusion and speculation. Striking for the first time, the first-person narration follows a passage of third-person narrative that focused on Glebov's inner experience of disappointment over the cowardice of the ferocious dog Abdul. It would seem plausible then that extensive use of free indirect speech has modulated to Glebov's directly quoted inner monologue. But it soon emerges that "I" lived in the embankment house itself (cf. Glebov, who lived in the humble house behind), and furthermore Glebov is referred to by "I" in the third person. Critics have alluded to the first person voice as "the author" ("avtor," Kozhinov), "the reminiscences of the narrator" ("vospominanija rasskazchihika") and "the author's voice" ("avtorskij golos," Bocharov).[25] Disa Håstad calls the first-person sections "autobiographical chapters," at the same time attributing them to the narrator, thereby failing to distinguish between the writer and the narrator.[26] While it is feasible that "I" is identical to Trifonov himself, the idea of an identity between this "I" and the third-person narrator must be rejected. The third-person narrator has assumed two roles: an omniscient role and the role of mediator, formulator of the world as seen by Glebov. The first-person narrator on the other hand is in no sense "omniscient": he reports only what was available to him as a child and later adult; neither does he claim insight into the private workings of his classmate Glebov's experience. In other words, the experiences of both "I" and Glebov are equally and naturally limited by the experience of a single individual. As fictional subjects "I" and Glebov are on the same level, acting as foils to one another. A difference lies in the fact that "I" is his own narrator; on the level of discourse he acts a foil to the third-person narrator. To equate the "I" with the narrator is to ignore a crucial aspect of narrative perspective.[27]

The first-person narrator has to be identified with one of the children who

---

[25] V. V. Kozhinov, "Problema avtora i put' pisatelja," *Kontekst* (1977): 40, passim; A. Bocharov, "Energija trifonovskoj prozy" in Trifonov, *Povesti*, 522.

[26] Disa Håstad, *Samtal med sovjetiska författare* (Stockholm 1979), 32, 44–45.

[27] We are not dealing with the phenomenon found in, for example, Dostoevsky's *Besy*, where the narrational pose is inconsistent: sometimes the narrator limits himself to what he personally witnessed, and sometimes he behaves as an omniscient narrator; accordingly, the narrative seems to be inconsistent on the level of person, first as opposed to third. In actual fact, the distinction is artificial: whether or not a narrator chooses to refer to himself as "I," he is at liberty to do so since he is the speaker. In Trifonov's *Dom* the "I" cannot be identified with the narrator, which places the inconsistency on the level of the sender not the narrational pose. Similarly, Trifonov's text is to be distinguished from those—often modernist—texts where narration is conducted from different characters' points of view, as for example in Lawrence Durrell's *The Alexandria Quartet*. In such works only the narrative position is inconsistent while the narrative mode (that is, fiction) remains consistent.

lived in the embankment house and who featured in Glebov's childhood. It would have been textually consistent had the first-person voice belonged to Shulepa, for it is against Shulepa's early fortune and subsequent misfortune that Glebov's life drama is played out. But the voice is not Shulepa's. And the disturbing fact is that all the boys who feature with any significance must be eliminated since the details do not fit. It is possible to identify ''I'' with the character known as Medved', although the details given about Medved' in the third-person narrative do not tally exactly. But even if we give ''I'' a name and locate him in the main body of the story, we do not solve the dilemma. The point remains that there is no reason from within the story itself for the narration suddenly to be handed to a character whose role has so far been without significance. The first-person narrative does not grow organically from within the text itself but appears to be artificially tacked on.

The first-person narrative occurs five times in all, on each occasion continuing unbroken for a few pages. Sometimes these sections are marked by typological spacing and sometimes they are not. The first-person narrative does not dispute directly the facts given in the third-person narrative, nor does it cover precisely the same ground. It is as though the same body of events are touched upon from different points in time, place and personal involvement. This confrontation remains on the level of story. At no time do the two narrators acknowledge one another's existence; each one narrates as though he alone possessed the story to be told. The two narrators are alternated without respect to natural break-off points. A certain asymmetry arises owing to the fact that while Glebov features in both third- and first-person narratives, ''I'' remains incognito in the third-person narrative sections. Accordingly, we have two contrasting impressions of Glebov but only one for the first person narrator, only his own word for it, so to speak.

As readers we are not obliged to accept mystification in fiction. On the contrary our business is to try and work out how pieces of the fictional jigsaw puzzle fit together. When, as in *The House on the Embankment*, the text itself thwarts coherence, we have to seek out other, fictionally less ''legitimate'' solutions. If we allow that the anonymous first-person voice in fact belongs to Trifonov himself, to the writer of the novel but not to its narrator, the pieces fit together and the text becomes coherent; although as a hybrid of fiction and autobiography, it constitutes an original kind of text. The autobiographical interpretation accounts for the fact that the two narratives never become properly integrated with one another; fiction and autobiography constituting as they do two distinct narrative modes cannot mix. Likewise the absence of ''I'' in the main bulk of the narrative is explained on the grounds that the ''real'' writer simply does not belong in the fictional work that he has created in the story centering on Glebov.[28]

[28] On the other hand we have to allow that the names in the autobiographical sections are

Earlier on I argued that the distinguishing feature of fictional as opposed to communicative narrative is located on the level of discourse and not on the level of story: we are concerned with voice and not facts. Accordingly the style of the autobiographical sections is more pertinent to my thesis than is their content. In fact, though, Trifonov's biographical data do support the interpretation of the ''I'' sections as constituting autobiography: we know that Trifonov lived in the house on the embankment and that his parents were arrested in 1937, after which he moved from the embankment house with his grandmother to live in a room in a collective apartment on the outskirts of Moscow.[29]

Turning on the question of voice we must ask: What features of the ''I'' narrative allows us to conclude that it constitutes the personal voice of the writer Trifonov, that the speaker or narrator is identical to the sender of the message? We have seen that instability of narrative positioning is a dominant feature of the main narrative of *The House on the Embankment* and that this pivoting between narrator and fictional characters with the implicit presence of an abstract authorial position is in itself a signal of the fictional mode. By contrast, the ''I'' sections of the novel are characterized by a marked absence of multiple viewpoint, ambiguity, and what I have called ''gaps'' of meaning. In these sections there is no disparity between the narrator on the one hand and an implied sender on the other.

The first two ''I'' sections are introduced by the proposition ''I remember'' (''ja pomnju''), the third by the proposition ''I still remember'' (''i eshche pomnju''). Thus the first-person narrator makes a bid for inherent authority: he alone possesses the details that he is about to relate. In this way the axis of the text shifts from a concern with ''what happened'' to a concern with ''what I remember.'' In accordance with this shift the narration leads into an enumeration of details the mutual relevance of which is guaranteed only because they are part of one and the same memory collection. The details related are intimate, details which for the autobiographer have captured the essence of childhood: smells, sounds, and feelings etched into his mind in the intensity of childhood. These are not the kinds of details open to dispute and accordingly there ''I'' sections manifest a single-voicedness in stark contrast to the fictional narrative of the text so far; they would appear compatible with genuine autobiographical narration. The passage quoted above conveys the lyrical tenor of the first-person narration: the emotion with which the childhood memories are charged is expressed in metaphors, in pathetic intonation: ''My whole childhood was shrouded in a crimson cloud of vanity. Oh those exer-

---

fictionalized. Since our criticism is not fact or fiction but personal or implied author, this discrepancy is not disturbing.

[29] My authority is Håstad, *Samtal med sovjetiska författare*, 32–33.

tions, the thirst for a moment of glory!''[30] Anecdote replaces straight narration, and accordingly the symbolic value of each detail is raised as the pure
narrative element is weakened. These features of the first-person narrative assure its natural authority and are the mark of a message where speaker and
sender are one and the same person.

I have suggested that in fictional narrative the narrator always emits an unwitting signal as to the degree of his own reliability. In first-person narrative
concerned precisely with what the ''I'' remembers there is less room for a
point of view other than the ''I'' 's own. I am not claiming that overtly fictional autobiography is an impossibility, merely that the given ''I'' sections in
no way signal their own fictionality. A glance at the opening lines of Anthony
Burgess's *Earthly Powers* reveals artifice and multiple positioning in pseudo-
autobiographical narration:

> It was the afternoon of my eighty-first birthday and I was in bed with my catamite
> when Ali announced that the archbishop had come to see me.
> ''Very good, Ali,'' I quavered in Spanish through the closed door of the master
> bedroom. ''Take him into the bar. Give him a drink.''
> *''Hay dos. Su cappellan también.''*
> ''Very good, Ali. Give the chaplain a drink also.''[31]

Here the combination of ''eighty-first birthday,'' ''in bed with my catamite,''
the archbishop, his chaplain, and the bar, not to mention Ali's untranslated
words, assures that the single-minded evaluative and emotional tenor normally
associated with autobiography is thwarted from the beginning. Not so with the
''I'' sections in *The House on the Embankment*. Here we are hard put to find
an angle on the first-person narrative according to which it reveals a higher
perspective, the wiser position of an implied author. This can be tested by
reading aloud: I believe these sections would be read with a ''sincere'' intonation whereas the main body of the third-person narrative in the novel would
be read with a fair amount of intonational irony, in direct correlation to the
multiple viewpoint denoted in the text.

My conclusion so far is that the first-person sections *in themselves* emit no
''wiser than the narrator'' signals and that stylistically they are compatible
with nonfictional, autobiographical texts.[32] But these sections occur within a

[30] ''Vse detstvo okutyvalo bagrjanoe oblako tshcheslavija. O eti staranija zhazhda sekundnoj
slavy!'', 400.

[31] Anthony Burgess, *Earthly Powers* (London: Hutchinson, 1980), 7.

[32] The distinction between communicative and artistic texts is in the last resort functional. There
is nothing to prevent an author presenting fiction as autobiography and vice versa. The wave of
so-called ''confessional literature'' from the past decade provides examples of autobiography
presented as fiction: Sylvia Plath's *The Bell Jar* and Lisa Alther's *Kinflicks* are presented as novels, while they manifest the kind of consistency and lack of artifice (lack of dual-voicedness) that
I associate with autobiography. On the other hand, Anthony Burgess's *Earthly Powers* and Iris

textual context that is clearly fictional, and they are therefore distinguished as fiction. It is to be expected that in the fictional narration of the novel so far there will have emerged an implied-author position according to which the reader is able to deal with the abrupt switch to first-person narration. In other words the reader should by now be implicitly equipped with an interpretive standpoint. I suggest, however, that this is not the case, that the first-person sections create such a radical break with the implied-author position so far established that the reader becomes disoriented and is forced to begin again, readjusting his understanding of the sender position. He knows that the text in hand is a single text and that he has to find a sender position that accounts for all narrative poses, first as well as third person. Twenty-seven pages into the narrative the reader is abruptly left to his own detective devices. Given this rather drastic narrative situation, it is not far-fetched to consider whether the first-person sections might not be autobiographical inserts on the part of the writer Trifonov. I emphasize once again that it is not a question of establishing whether the first-person narrator reports facts or fiction, whether or not the content of these sections is untrammeled truth. The crucial question is which sender position must we understand the narrative to have in order for it to make sense? Does the text presume a sender independent of itself, or does it, on the contrary, create its own sender?

Obviously we cannot pretend to discern two different senders of one and the same text. We have to decide which of the two authorities takes precedence, the implied author or the writer himself. For the reader adhering to the biographical approach to literature this question will be superfluous; from his position the implied author leads directly to the writer himself, and the voice of the text is tantamount to the voice of the writer. Identifying the "direct" voice of the writer, this reader would automatically assume it to express the "truth" of the text. But from a structural point of view, I contend precisely the opposite: by entering his own voice directly, as "writer," Trifonov here undermines his own right to make definitive statements, to assume the position of ultimate authority with regard to his text. He submits his voice to the arbitrating viewpoint of the IA, admitting his voice to be "less' than the voice of the fictional implied author.

Interpretation of *The House on the Embankment* will depend on whether or not we consider the first-person narrator to constitute the ultimate authority. For if we do, then we shall have to settle for an attitude toward Glebov rooted in dislike, and accordingly the point of the story will be to discredit Glebov according to "I's" dislike of him. We shall read the main third-person narrative with a view to unmasking Glebov. But such an approach does not tally with the narrative structure as a whole: for the fact remains that the IA has had

---

Murdoch's *The Sea* are clearly works of fiction, notwithstanding their blatantly autobiographical pose.

time to establish quite a different evaluative position before the first appearance of ''I.'' In these first pages—and indeed in the third person narrative altogether—the authorial position seems to be concerned not with intimating the degree of Glebov's moral innocence or culpability but rather with exposing so many conflicting aspects of Glebov's case as to create in the reader an ambiguous response of both sympathy and moral reproach. The introduction of a first-person narrator does not solve the dilemma; it merely increases the same. For to the impersonal narration inspiring impersonal understanding or condemnation of Glebov is added the first-person narrator's personal witness based in strong dislike. The first-person narrator does not raise the narration to a level of greater perspective: on the contrary, he settles into a private memory niche that, to all intents and purposes, matches Glebov's own memory niche. Since ''I'' 's narration is limited to his personal and emotionally charged memories, he is no more reliable than Glebov himself, whose memories are relayed to us through the narrative technique of free indirect speech. Only of the first-person narrator had taken direct issue with the fictional third-person narrative, superseding it and revealing it in a new light, could he have been understood to have usurped the position of the IA and redirected the text from its initial fictional mode to straightforward autobiography. But in fact the autobiographical sections remain just that, sections, which are inserted into the narrative, causing confusion and disorientation but never actually becoming an integrated part of a whole. The impression that one has in reading this novel is that the different narrative poses have to be dealt with in succession: the text remains a montage structure where the fictional and the autobiographical narratives never conjoin in coherent narrative synthesis.

How then is this dislocation in narrative position to be explained and motivated? On one level the first-person narrative may be seen to correct or balance the story as presented from Glebov's point of view. On the level of story, ''I's'' childhood and youth witness challenges Glebov's, on identically personal terms. Like Glebov, ''I'' is trapped in a dominant emotion that prejudices him against objective assessment: Glebov suffers from retrospective envy and ''I'' suffers from dislike of people like Glebov. But this kind of balance could have been achieved more conventionally by resorting to sections that present the past from Shulepa's point of view. Obviously simple Polemic for and against Glebov is not what is intended. I submit that the technique is used to achieve something far more radical than mere multiple viewpoint, a trial-by-jury effect. Inconsistency in the narrative position, in this as in other works by Trifonov, gives iconic expression tot he pessimistic idea that impartial assessment of the world is beyond the reach of each and every single individual: every individual is in the last resort trapped in the perspective of his own prejudices. But if this is the theme directly expressed in the narrative technique of such works as *The Old Man* and *Time and Place*, it is carried one step further in *The House on the Embankment*. For in this work the writer, by entering his fiction directly in the form of autobiographical inserts, contends even his own claim to vouchsafe impartiality. The writer, submitting his personal voice to that of the implied author, discredits his personal witness.

. . .

We have come to the crux of the matter: what narrative confusion in Trifonov's works, in particular the montage of fiction and autobiography in *The House on the Embankment*, has to do with the role of the writer in present-day Soviet society.[33] In the last resort this narrative anomaly may be understood as a disavowal of the myth of the writer who speaks directly to the people: the myth that lies at the heart of the biographical approach to literature and the myth that has characterized the literary situation in Russia from the middle of the nineteenth century. Belinsky looked to literature as to a source of enlightenment: the writer bore a social and national mission; his business was to present a true picture of society in such a way as to inspire change for the better. From this time onwards the role of the writer in Russia was defined according to his status as a reliable witness: he was to assure the clean conscience of a society beset by social ills, to guarantee the voice of truth and justice. But as this tradition of cynical realism is reworked, in the Soviet Russia of the 1930s, to become "positive," so-called socialist, realism, the position of the writer becomes untenable. The writer's status as social truth teller remains sacrosanct—witness the importance attributed to writers and literature in Soviet society. But now the writer is expected to defend the ideal of socialism rather than to criticize temporary shortcomings actually manifest in reality. The definition of "realism" remains, while the epithet "critical" is no longer adequate. A confusion of modality—what is ideal replaces what is real—gives expression in literature to the ethical dilemma that underlies So-

---

[33] In *The Modes of Modern Writing* (London: E. Arnold, 1977) David Lodge develops his idea of the "short circuit," the attempt to erase the distinction, to close the gap, between life and literature, and considers this a feature of the postmodern novel. One way of achieving this short circuit is to combine "in one work violently contrasting modes—the obviously fictive and the apparently factual: [to introduce] the author and the question of authorship into the text," 239–40. The question then arises: How far is the fiction/autobiography dichotomy manifest in *The House on the Embankment* part of a general Western literary tendency? Lodge's short-circuit model is certainly pertinent to Trifonov's novel as well as to novels such as Vonnegut's *Slaughterhouse Five*; on a deeper level, however, there are significant differences. While Trifonov's work articulates an ethical dilemma, the American equivalent articulates an existential dilemma. For the American writer reality itself has become illusory; unable to orient himself within the world at large, he retreats into his personal world (see John Hallowell, *Fact and Fiction: The New Journalism and the Nonfiction Novel* [Chapel Hill: University of North Carolina, 1977). The Soviet writer, however, is not yet free of a superimposed dogmatic outlook: he does not question the reality of reality but rather the ability of the individual to contemplate the same objectively.

viet society: the criteria for distinguishing what should be and what should not be are dissolved, proclaimed superfluous. Characters like Glebov are the natural product of a society that cannot afford to question what is right and wrong. Even the writer—in this case Trifonov—is a product of the same society, and the import of the novel *The House on the Embankment* is that the writer's role of social conscience has become an impossibility. When the concepts of right and wrong in society at large become taboo, the role of the writer too is thwarted. Only if the writer is able to admit freely of his own prejudice, submitting his personal truth to the greater perspective of an implied author, can we hope, in literature, to transcend the limits of each and every individual consciousness. But, as we have seen, the IA in this novel, as in Trifonov's works on the whole, offers little clear moral guidance. Rather the IA refrains from proclaiming a higher truth, from judging and taking sides. And herein lies precisely a position of greater perspective, of truth about the nature of literature and truth about the position of the individual and the writer in Soviet society.

Finally, I should like to submit that Trifonov's narrative technique, in particular the autobiographical insertions in *The House on the Embankment*, have an interesting effect on the position of the reader. In literature with a clearly defined authorial position the reader is able to take shelter, conveniently knowing himself to be in colusion with the IA and therefore automatically on the "right" side. But in Trifonov's works the IA position is deliberately played down. The reader stands as it were face to face with the unmediated characters and events. Hereby moral onus is transferred directly onto the reader: he must actively engage in sorting out the good and the bad of the story, choose sides, and draw moral conclusions. Historical writer and historical reader are drawn into the web of the text and inculpated by it. The problem effected by the characters—how to overcome personal bias and reconstruct history truthfully—rubs off on writer and reader alike. Through his own autobiographical inserts in *The House on the Embankment* Trifonov "admits" his own personal bias. Similarly the reader must ask himself whether or not he too is guilty of betraying the truth of the past in one way or another.[34]

Implicit in Trifonov's work is the idea of the writer as bearing the responsibility of a historian, whose business is to transcend his personal bias of the moment in order to guarantee his country a truthful picture of its past. At the same time Trifonov shows that even serious investigators of the past suffer from human prejudices that obstruct a truly objective vision. Further, the narrative technique used in these stories has the effect of widening the circle of those who play a historical role to include the reader. Each and every human

[34] Another autobiographical insert, indicated by the narrative technique, is to be found in *The Old Man* in the section concerned with San'ja Izvarin. See note 14.

CHAPTER 10

The Rhetoric of Nadezhda Mandelstam's
Hope Against Hope

Charles Isenberg

DESPITE the critical and popular acclaim accorded Nadezhda Mandelstam's two volumes of memoirs, *Hope Against Hope* (in the original Russian, simply *Vospominanija* or "Memoirs") and *Hope Abandoned* (*Vtoraja kniga* or "Second Book")[1] not much attention has been paid to her qualities as a writer.[2] Owing to the combined effect of these qualities and a congeries of historical accidents, her writings have tended to merge with those of her husband. A contrast may clarify this point: If we are arguing about the meaning of some passage in Dostoevsky, most of us are unlikely to appeal to the authority of Anna Snitkina-Dostoevskaya. Nadezhda Mandelstam's work, on the other hand, has become the enabling condition, the virtual horizon, of Osip Mandelstam's. Her commentaries align her husband's writings in a lyrical biography or a history of consciousness. She becomes his coauthor first by restructuring his texts, establishing connections between one piece and another and between text and world, and second, by rethinking Mandelstam, partly as a representative figure and partly as the exemplar of his own philosophy. Thus, her volumes aim not just at preservation but at canon formation, and she constructs a canonical image of the poet to match the canonical ordering of his work. In all this she has been so spectacularly successful that we do not even need to read her. Take up any edition of Mandelstam's work, beginning with the four-volume *Collected Works*,[3] and you will be sure to find at least a digest of Nadezhda Mandelstam's glosses.

[1] An earlier version of this piece appeared in *New Studies in Russian Language and Literature* (Festschrift for Bayara Aroutounova), ed. Anna Lisa Crone and Catherine Chvany (Columbus, Ohio: Slavica Publishers, 1986), 168–82. See Nadezhda Jakovlevna Mandelstam, *Hope Against Hope*, trans. Max Hayward (New York: Atheneum, 1970) from *Vospominanija* (New York: Chekhov Publishing House, 1970); *Hope Abandoned*, trans. Max Hayward (New York: Atheneum, 1974) from *Vtoraja kniga* (Paris: YMCA Press, 1972). Page references are to the original Russian and are given in the text. The translations are my own.

[2] Richard Pevear's "On the Memoirs of Nadezhda Mandelstam," *Hudson Review* 24, no. 3 (1971), which begins with a brilliant appreciation of Nadezhda Jakovlevna's qualities as a literary artist, is a notable exception.

[3] See Gleb Struve and Boris Filipoff, eds. *Osip Mandel'shtam: Sobranie sochinenij*, vols. 1–3 (Washington: Inter-Language Literary Associates; Second revised edition, 1967–71) and vol. 4 (supplementary) (Paris: YMCA Press, 1981).

But Nadezhda Mandelstam is a writer worthy of consideration for her own achievement and not simply in her capacity as the most privileged interpreter of Osip Mandelstam. Jonathan Culler has argued that every reading of a text entails the story of a reading.[4] Briefly, the story of my reading of her memoirs comprises an initial reading in search of information about Osip Mandelstam's life and work, a second reading in which I saw them as primarily a meditation upon the fate of the Russian intelligentsia, and subsequent rereadings in which my attention has been increasingly drawn to the rhetorical strategies that subserve—and occasionally subvert—her themes. This essay will attempt to situate Nadezhda Mandelstam as a writer by focusing on two qualities in her first volume of memoirs: her representation of her marriage and her rhetoric—and by rhetoric I intend both the traditional meaning, that is, those uses of language that seek to persuade us as to the authority of a writer's point of view, and also the more recent definition proposed by the Liege rhetoricians in the *General Rhetoric*, that is, all the uses of language proper to literature.[5] As far as possible then, this study will be concerned with the intersection of power (that is, of textualized authority) and poetics, and it will use feminist theory and rhetorical criticism as sources of questions to put to the text.

Phyllis Rose's *Parallel Lives*, a study of five Victorian marriages in which at least one member of each couple was a writer, can clarify what is at stake in Nadezhda Mandelstam's representation of her marriage. The main lesson I draw from Rose's work is the usefulness of considering a marriage as a narrative construct; as she puts it, "a subjectivist fiction with two points of view often deeply in conflict, sometimes fortuitously congruent."[6] Two further considerations follow: first, the story of a marriage will turn on the clash of assumptions about power and authority. This we find in great detail in *Hope Abandoned*, which is more openly concerned with the story of the Mandelstams' marriage. In *Hope Against Hope*, on the other hand, the thematic of the martial power struggle are present but submerged. Here the Russian title is instructive: *Vtoraja kniga*, literally the *Second Book*, a title that suggests the secondary or supplementary value placed by Nadezhda Mandelstam on the story of her marriage.

A second consideration that follows from the treatment of a marriage as a narrative is simply the exceptional narrative interest that attaches to an unusual marriage. Rose argues that "the 'plots' of our loves and marriages tend to banality and sterility."[7] Thus it is remarkable when an exception appears. The

---

[4] Jonathan Culler, *On Deconstruction: Theory and Criticism After Structuralism* (Ithaca: Cornell University Press, 1982), 64–83.

[5] Group μ, *A General Rhetoric*, trans. Paul B. Burell and Edgar M. Slotkin (Baltimore: Johns Hopkins University Press, 1981), 19: "Rhetoric is the knowledge of the techniques of language characteristic of literature."

[6] Phyllis Rose, *Parallel Lives* (New York: Alfred A. Knopf, 1983), 7.

[7] Ibid., 8.

Mandelstams were not only extraordinary writers but had an exceptionally interesting relationship. There is the casually undertaken commitment, the testing through extramarital affair, the refusal of children, the long separation with their letters and telegrams, the perpetual homelessness, the wrenching poverty and constant, grinding scutwork,[8] the utter subservience of Nadezhda to Osip's gift—and then decades later the revelation of her own gift, and finally, the will evident in Nadezhda Mandelstam's prose to make the marriage, in retrospect, both a counter society and a laboratory for understanding the spouses' own social formation.

There is something exemplary or emblematic in the Mandelstams' relationship that calls to mind another famous couple, Jean-Paul Sartre and Simone de Beauvoir. Of course this is an uncomfortable comparison in many ways. Sartre's and Beauvoir's writings scarcely intertwine to the same extent as do the Mandelstams'; Nadezhda Mandelstam was contemptuous of Sartre's Marxism, and I suspect that Beauvoir's feminism would have been equally alien to her. Nevertheless, these partnerships do share some common ground. In each case it is the writings of the female partner that create the relationship as a literary phenomenon, and both the Russian and the Frenchwoman represent their primary relationships as a critique of, and counter example to, the ideology of marriage in its Stalinist-bourgeois and French-bourgeois forms. And both women portray couples morally exemplary in their determination to live their values.

Other concerns of feminist criticism can be brought to bear upon the memoirs. On the most general level, it hardly needs to be argued by now that it pays to attend to an artist's sense of "gender arrangements," the engendering of social roles and functions as masculine or feminine, as a key to his or her poetic universe. In Osip Mandelstam's verse from the *Tristia* period on, gender, in this sense, plays a totalizing role. For our purposes one famous example should suffice:

> So be it: the transparent shape
> Is lying on the clean clay dish,
> Like a splayed-out squirrel hide;
> A maiden peers, bent over the wax.
> It's not for us to guess about the Geek Erebus:
> Wax is for women what bronze is for a man.
> Our lot is cast only in battles
> While for them it is given to die telling fortunes.[9]

---

[8] In "O. Mandel'shtam—Materialy k biografii," *Russian Literature* 15, no. 1 (January 1984): 1–27. A Grigor'ev and N. Petrova give a bibliography of the Mandelstams' translations that substantiates the sheer mass of work they undertook and accomplished as translators.

[9] Da budet tak: prozrachnaja figurka / Na chistom bljude glinjanom lezhit, / Kak belich'ja rasplastannaja shkurka, / Sklonjas' nad voskom, devushka gljadit. / Ne nam gadat' o grecheskom

If we read Osip Mandelstam's fate as a metaphorical death in battle, and if we read the verb *gadat'* (translated here as "to guess" but also meaning "to prophecy" or "to tell fortunes") metaphorically as "to interpret," this final stanza of "Tristia" sounds uncannily like the poet allocating his own fate and that of his wife/widow. It is of no import that Osip and Nadezhda Mandelstam had not even met when "Tristia" was written, since the roles are universalized: men perish in struggle, and women interpret their struggle, commemorate them—and, as other lyrics of this and later periods suggest—resurrect them.

Hence the first inference to be drawn from a gender-based criticism is that Nadezhda Mandelstam shares her husband's view concerning the division of the work of the world between men and women. She represents her writing as a posthumous continuation of her marriage role: unable to save Osip Mandelstam's life, she is determined to save his writings, and her own prose becomes part of that magnificent effort.

A more radical feminism would raise different questions. It would acknowledge that the role Nadezhda Mandelstam represents is what Barbara Dane Clement calls "the suffering servant" of the Russian patriarchal tradition and that this role sets the criterion according to which the many daughters, wives, and mothers portrayed in the memoirs are to be praised or blamed.[10] It would also acknowledge that gaps and silences about the authorial self are built into the project; after all, the memoirs are not primarily autobiography or even biography. But it would still seek to discover tensions arising from the situation of the female writer, along with attendant strategies of indirection that would serve to authenticate her claims to speak. The canonical, classic Russian literature is, after all, largely a male preserve. And in view of this last circumstance, the kind of inquiry for which Elaine Showalter has proposed the term "gynocritics" would also look for connections to a tradition of female writing.

To take the last point first, in addition to her unflagging sense of her own mission, Nadezhda Mandelstam does seem to be empowered by several strands of a Russian woman's culture. First of all, there are the heroines-in-adversity of the suffering servant tradition, and Nadezhda Mandelstam is aware of predecessors in the wife of Archpriest Avvakum and in the Decembrists' wives following their husbands to prison and exile. Second, from the time of Princess Dashkova's memorializing (in French) the history of her friendship with Catherine the Great, the memoir had been *the* central genre of

---

Erebe, / Dlja zhenshchin vosk, chto dlja muzhchiny med'. / Nam tol'ko v bitvakh vypadaet zhrebij, / A im dano gadaja umeret'." ("Tristia," *Sobr. soch*, vol. 1, 73–74.)

[10] Anna Akhmatova, the most problematic female character in *Hope Against Hope*, is the partial exception.

female writing in Russia.[11] In the twentieth century one thinks not only of Nadezhda Mandelstam but of writers like Evgenya Ginzburg and Lydia Chukovskaya. Third, beginning with the generation preceding Nadezhda Mandelstam's women were claiming a place in Russian poetry. In the age of Gippius, Akhmatova, Tsvetaeva, and Petrovykh a serious literary artist would not necessarily find being female such an isolating circumstance.

Yet the tensions inherent in the situation of the female writer do figure in the memoirs, albeit in a slightly transposed form. Nadezhda Mandelstam's writing addresses an anxiety that comes not so much from her status as a woman writing as from her status as a nonpoet—more specifically, her status as a poet's *wife*. This anxiety is very close to the surface in the portrayal of her relations with Anna Akhmatova. There is, in my view, a kind of shadow narrative here, one that proceeds by indirection, its unfolding suggested by scattered hints. And one of the thematic centers of this shadow narrative is the implicit triangle with Osip at its apex and Nadezhda and Anna Akhmatova at its corners.

Whatever the scenes portraying Akhmatova may evoke (for instance, admiration for her poetic gift, gratitude for her moral solidarity with Osip and with his memory), they do not suggest an affection for Akhmatova independent of Osip. In fact, for all the tributes to Akhmatova, there is nothing remotely approaching Nadezhda's words about Vasilisa Shklovskaya: "and Vasilisa greeted us joyfully and tearfully. Even then I understood that the only real thing in the world was this woman's blue eyes. And that is what I think even now" (369).

When she writes about Akhmatova, Nadezhda often implies a certain discomfort, giving the reader to understand that she is not writing about a friendship between two women but about the somewhat edgy relations between the poet's wife and the poet's friend. In an oddly self-effacing passage Nadezhda speaks of the friendship linking the two poets as their "sole reward for all the bitter labor and the bitter path each of them traveled" (196). She also claims that Akhmatova could not stand poets' wives but made an exception for her (247). Hence, along with her insistence on the role played by Anna Akhmatova in Osip's life and in her own, there is also at least the suggestion of a threat to the writer's wifely status, an anxiety about being the odd one out, there on sufferance an awareness of being the exception.

I would go further, connecting these hints with a larger but more diffuse pattern, one that emphasizes the exemplary quality of Nadezhda Mandelstam's marriage by alluding to another story, which she represents as far more typical: the story of the writer's wife whose lot it is to be rejected and abandoned by her husband. This nightmare surfaces early in *Hope Against Hope*,

---

[11] See Barbara Heldt, *Terrible Perfection: Women and Russian Literature* (Bloomington: Indiana University Press, 1987), chs. 5–7, for a discussion of this tradition.

when Nadezhda Mandelstam comments on the irony of her having been the would-be rescuer of the poems of Vladimir Pjast, which Osip admired, "perhaps because lawful wives were cursed in them" (22). This leads to a reflection on what will become a leitmotif of the book, the idea of "broken hearts, scandals, and divorces" as the essence of the "normal" life barred to the Mandelstams; a fate to be envied, like Pjast's good fortune in dying from cancer before his second arrest. Nadezhda Mandelstam is unrelentingly ironic about the stuff of the bourgeois family romance, claiming that Freud's interpretative categories are only relevant to the "genial atrocities" ("dobrodushnye zverstva," 142) of those with a settled address. Within the context of Stalin's Russia, normal life would have meant joining the privileged caste of the Writers' Union. The normal denouement to that kind of marital history can be gathered from Nadezhda's jibe at her friend Sonya Vishnevskaya for failing to recognize how lucky she was that her playwright husband "died a timely death, without having managed to transfer his earthly goods to some rival of Sonya's" (280). Valentin Kataev is another exemplar of normal life, with his "new wife, new baby, new money, and new furniture" (296).

The upshot of all this is that the rhetoric of the memoirs has to manage two varieties of terror. The Stalinist terror is of such magnitude that it reduces the everyday terror of marital abandonment to an object of irony. But the danger from without does not entirely eliminate the danger from within. The situation is paradoxical: the writer arraigns Stalinism for its destruction of the possibility of an ordinary life, yet her text risks implying that the special pressure exerted by the state upon the Mandelstams has the effect of saving their marriage from the usual fate of such marriages.

Both the feminist and the rhetorical orientations lead to a concern with what the former would term strategies of empowerment, and the latter strategies of authentication, that is, with the writer's claims to authority. And, since I propose to treat Nadezhda Mandelstam as a literary artist, this concern must allow for an emphasis upon the fictionality of her work. With the appearance of other accounts treating Mandelstam and his circle, Nadezhda Mandelstam's version of particular events is being called into question in large and small ways. Consider, for example, the alternative interpretations to be found in the memoirs of Olga Vaksel', Boris Kuzin, Lydia Chukovskaya, Emma Gershtein, and in Gregory Freidin's study of the Stalin ode, not to mention the mass of archival materials that will eventually be unearthed.[12] How could it be otherwise? Nadezhda Mandelstam wrote her books decades after the death of their central

---

[12] Ol'ga Vaksel', "O Mandel'shtame (iz dnevnika)," *Chast' rechi: Almanakh literatury i iskusstva* (New York: Serebrjannij vek, 1980): 251–62; Boris S. Kuzin, "Ob O. E. Mandel'shtame," *Vestnik Russkogo Khristianskogo Dvizhenija* (VRKhD, Paris) 140 (1983): 99–129; Lidija Chukovskaja, *Zapiski ob Anne Akhmatovoj*, 2 vols. (Paris: YMCA, 1976 and 1980); Emma Gershtein, *Novoe o Mandel'shtame* (Paris, Atheneum, 1986); Gregory Freidin, "Mandel'shtam's Ode to Stalin: History and Myth," *Russian Review* 41, no. 4 (1982): 400–26.

figure, she did not witness every episode she describes, and under these conditions there is bound to be considerable amplification of a dynamic observed by Freud, namely, that our beliefs tend to follow our desires. We put an impossible burden on the memoirist if we demand an objective record of what happened rather than her version of events. Of course Nadezhda Mandelstam's writings are not fictions in the sense of some ideal imaginative fiction, appealing chiefly to a semantic coherence. But if she does not want her work to be read as belles lettres ("literatura," 44), neither should we read her as a chronicler of facts.

I suppose that it must be true of memoirs in general that they display a tension between the heuristic and the reportorial, that is, between an authority based on rhetoric and an authority based on accuracy. Thus in Nadezhda Mandelstam's *Hope Against Hope* many passages seek to set the record straight, to refute the testimony of others—of Georgy Ivanov, for example; not the least of Ivanov's services to Russian literature is his role in stimulating memoirs of Mandelstam, including not only Nadezhda Mandelstam's but also Akhmatova's and Tsvetaeva's. But Nadezhda Mandelstam is also obsessed throughout her narrative by the unreliability of *all* witnesses—not only those who, like Ivanov, are writing from the emigration but also the survivors of Stalinism. She wonders how historians will ever be able to reconstruct the truth about an age in which deliberate lying on a massive scale is the central mode of discourse (26), and she does not exempt herself from the symptoms of the crisis of humanism and the Stalinist terror: "All of us become psychologically unhinged. . . . Can such as we serve as witnesses?" (94). No one, she concludes, escaped the Terror without psychic damage (317).

Reflecting on Viktor Shklovsky's determination to survive as an eyewitness, she observes that "by the time the Stalinist era came to an end, we had already managed to grow old and to lose that which makes a person a 'witness,'" that is, an understanding of things and a point of view. That's what happened with Shklovsky" (319). If Shklovsky is the target, still, that "we" must also include the writer, Nadezhda Mandelstam. In such passages she both undercuts and authenticates her own account, inviting us to believe her because she admits the inevitability of error, while strongly implying that we should also disbelieve her. In an attack on her contemporaries who want to remember the 1920s as the Golden Age of Soviet culture, she seems to offer a way of reading the past that undermines her general stance in a similar manner. Memory, she says, is not a direct reflection of events but a representation of the legends that form around events. In order to get at the truth, you must first demolish the legend, and to do that you must first establish what social circles gave rise to the legend (176). This strikes me as a sophisticated formulation of the inseparability of fact and interpretation but also as an invitation to read Nadezhda Mandelstam in this way.

What is at stake, then, is not so much truth as whose version shall prevail.

Nadezhda Mandelstam believes, at least in her first volume of memoirs, that the poet's friends will always have the final say as to how he will be remembered, because theirs is the only body of opinion that does not shift with every new ideological current. However, this hardly privileges the poet's circle with respect to some objective truth. It is striking that such a moral absolutist as Nadezhda Mandelstam should, in effect, so complicate her own claims to be setting the record straight, but then no honest writer tells the truth; unilinear truths are incompatible with the polyvalence of literary discourse. Besides, the habit of conflating fact and interpretation in the concept of an ostensibly value-free truth is weaker in Russian culture; *pravda* and *istina* (the Russian words for "truth") are always produced by some moral vision. And—fortunately for those of us who teach fiction—what is not true is not necessarily a lie. When a writer interprets her experience, she narrativizes it, turning it into a "fiction" ("legenda") or, less pejoratively, a "story."

The quality of *Hope Against Hope* as sheer narrativity is underlined by the absence of documentation. Except for the final two chapters, in which Nadezhda Mandelstam attempts to reconstruct the story of Osip Mandelstam's last days in the camps, she functions more as an omniscient narrator than as memoirist of the type of, say, Lydia Chukovskaya, who takes great pains to inform us as the circumstances that condition each entry in her reminiscences of Akhmatova. The virtual absence of a documentary apparatus in these memoirs increases their immediacy; there is one less layer of modality to penetrate. But it also endows Nadezhda Mandelstam's account with a distinctly *rhetorical* authority: there is no appeal beyond the word of the author.[13]

These remarks may serve as a transition to Nadezhda Mandelstam's poetics more generally. Contiguity figures, that is synecdoche and metonomy, offer a key to the manner in which her language embodies a world view. From another perspective, that of logic (or metalogic), the main figure is irony. Readers familiar with the book will probably agree that it has one of the most effective hooks in Russian literature: "After slapping Alexy Tolstoy in the face, O. M. at once returned to Moscow, and from there he telephoned Anna Akhmatova daily and implored her to come" (7). Certainly an *in medias res* beginning if ever there was one, this opening evokes the epic tradition—ironically, perhaps, if we recall Osip Mandelstam's claim in the 1920s that the epic could not be a resource for him and his contemporaries. However, Nadezhda Mandelstam's hero does not articulate the origin and destiny of a people but

---

[13] The novelistic vantage point is present already in the first paragraph. It enters when the writer describes how Anna Akhmatova, in far-off Leningrad, hesitates to come to Moscow in response to Osip Mandelstam's urgent summons: "Uzhe sobravshis' i kupiv bilet, ona zadumalas', stoja u okna. 'Molites', chtoby vas minovala eta chasha?'—sprosil Punin, umnyj, zhelchnyj i blestjashchij chelovek" ("With the preparations for the trip already made and the ticket already bought, she lost herself in thought, standing in front of the window. 'Are you praying that this cup will pass you by?' asked Punin, an intelligent, irascible, and brilliant man").

of a social formation: the Russian intelligentsia or at least its creative wing, viewed from the perspective of a period of crisis and collapse.

The very first sentence establishes the tie between Mandelstam and Akhmatova, and the durability of this friendship is one of the first themes to enter the book: "Upon meeting each other they would become as gay and carefree as the boy and girl who had met at the Poet's Guild. "Stop it!" I would shout, "I can't live with a couple of parrots!" But in May of 1934 they had no time for joking" (7).

Nadezhda Mandelstam's first quotation of her own speech presents her as a third party, annoyed at the "boy" and "girl" poets. (Along the same lines, later in her narrative she will recall them teasing her as their "mama" [237].) But in the space of two sentences she also shuttles us from the heyday of the guild in the 1910s to May 1934, the time of Mandelstam's first arrest, which is what the story is building toward. Because there two time levels are viewed from the perspective of the late 1950s to early 1960s, the time of writing, a tripartite temporal frame is established in which everything earlier and later will be related to Mandelstam's final years, 1934 to 1938. If we think of chronology as the neutral principle of narrative structure in a memoir, the main figure of narration in Nadezhda Mandelstam's first volume is disclosed as a particularizing synecdoche: a slice of roughly five years condenses the drama of half a century. Everything outside this culminating phase of Mandelstam's life, which coincides with the Great Terror, becomes in effect a flashback or a flash forward. Her husband's last years are placed at the center in part because Osip's death gives Nadezhda her aim in life from midlife on and thus empowers her as an artist. To put it another way, the death of the poet Mandelstam is represented as the originary act that brings the writer Nadezhda Mandelstam into being.

Beyond establishing a line of succession, Nadezhda Mandelstam requires a temporal recursiveness because during these pivotal years she was in no position either to formulate what was happening to her and to Osip or to speculate about the thirties as a culmination of earlier developments. She tends in general to place thematic culminations in a chain of anticipation and aftermath, which tendency is often associated with an acute sense of drama and of those ritually significant moments that initiate or end some phase of life.[14] For example, in connection with the stratagem used to set up Osip in 1938, Nadezhda recalls his reaction to a story told by Georgian party boss Nestor Lakoba during an earlier stay at a rest home, in 1931. The story concerns one of Lakoba's ancestors who invited an enemy to his home and then murdered him. According to Nadezhda Mandelstam, "Lakoba's story made a big impression

---

[14] Other examples include the writer's many observations on the time-honored rituals of arrest and on the elements of the "ritual for bringing the writers who perished in the camps back to life" (393).

upon Osip Mandelstam; he sensed that it had some second level of meaning" (344). Here we have Nadezhda, looking back from a post-Stalinist perspective, portraying Osip in 1931 experiencing a murky premonition of his fate, which is to be seized in violation of guest right, rather like the victim in Lakoba's story.

The foregrounding of Mandelstam's last years undoubtedly also has an ideological motive. Rightly or wrongly, Nadezhda Mandelstam portrays her husband as a man largely constrained by what he has written. In this connection, it is Mandelstam's youthful lecture and essay "Pushkin and Scriabin" that authorizes the narrative strategy of the memoirs. Nadezhda Mandelstam recalls this essay in the opening lines of the chapter entitled "The Road to Destruction" ("Gibel'nyj put' "): "The artist's death is not a matter of contingency but is his final creative act, illuminating his life's course as if with a cluster of rays" (165; cf. also 182, 270–71). If this is to be the standard, then it makes sense to tell the story outward from the chain of events leading up to the poet's death.

This retrospective illumination can be construed as essentially a form of dramatic irony: the author (and audience) enjoy an understanding of the implications of the interplay of actors, actions, and motives not shared by the actors—including the younger Nadezhda Mandelstam—in the time of the narrated events. Yet if the author's irony is a reflex of hindsight, as it is, for example, in her bitter comment as to how a double suicide in 1934 would have shared them the agonies of Osip's second arrest and Nadezhda's widowhood, it is not a general and undifferentiated reflex. Rather, the writer's irony is a rich field for the study of how rhetorical effects can be moves in a contest for authority. To begin with, the writer holds a set of beliefs—in the ineradicability of kindness and its subsistence in the Russian people, in the self-extinguishing quality of evil—that are *not* treated ironically. These are points of reference for her critique of her principal target, the postrevolutionary intelligentsia, which has preserved its traditional pieties but has emptied them of their moral content. The writer's ironic stance is already evident in her choice of chapter titles whose ironic relationship to the chapters they head parodies the Stalinist "transvaluation of values" she is exploring. Consider, for example, the first and third chapters, "A May Night" ("Majskaja noch") and "Morning Reflections" ("Utrennye razmyshlenija"), titles that provide a view of the night of Mandelstam's first arrest by suggesting its tremendous distance from the worlds of Gogol's Dikanka or Lomonosov's spiritual ode, which are evoked here as subtexts. Or consider the multiple ironies in "Our Literature" ("Nasha literatura"). The shifter "our" "nasha" has never been shiftier; there are at least three pronominal referents involved: those who share Nadezhda Mandelstam's values, those who share the values of the old Bolshevik who heads the Office of Marxism-Leninism at Tashkent University, and a referent that actually has no existence, based as it is on the false presupposition of the old Marxist that she and Nadezhda are kindred spirits. By the same token, while each has her own "literature," they have none in common. As examples of sustained ironic discourse, consider the portraits of Larisa Rejsner, fascinated by the cult of force (115–19); of Nikolay Bukharin, a kind man who struggles to suppress his awareness of the deadly consequences of his own theorizing (119–25); or of Tanya Grigoreva, Nadezhda's sister-in-law, skewered by one of the author's most telling ripostes: "Leaving, I said, 'If one night Fascists are substituted for the Bolsheviks, you won't even notice.' Tanya responded that this couldn't happen" (331).

The memoirs allow the reader to surmise that the quality of the sarcasm directed at Tanya Grigoreva is influenced by the respective positions of the two women in the Mandelstam family system as much as it is by Tanya's Stalinism. Osip and Nadezhda were in conflict with Evgeny and Tanya over who should have the responsibility of caring for the brothers' father, over Evgeny's failure to aid Osip in 1934 and later, and over Tanya's treatment of her stepdaughter Tatka, Osip and Nadezhda 's beloved niece. While most of the writer's irony has a retaliatory quality, serving as a symbolic summoning unto judgment, there is also a preemptive variety, aimed at potential challenge to Nadezhda Mandelstam's authority. A good example is her attack upon "some bright editor,"[15] a hypothetical representative of the Soviet variety of the species, who would explain to her "with perfect clarity" why the poet's wishes concerning the selection and ordering of his verses for publication should be ignored as a matter of principle (209).

The deviation from chronological history entails other figures of narration, most strikingly what seems to the reader like a refusal to get on with the story. A number of currents in the text yields this quality of indirection. For instance, if everything must be anchored to a five-year period, there are bound to be lots of satellite episodes that will have to be threaded in. On a less formal level, the author clearly seeks to make both herself and her husband representative figures, capable of instancing the crisis of the intelligentsia. At the same time she wants to distance Osip Mandelstam and herself, in order to underline their uniqueness. Both these drives locate Nadezhda Mandelstam's discourse with respect to the values of Stalinism. And both, again, can be construed as synecdoche. Thus the poet becomes just another *intelligent* caught up by the Terror, his representative quality enhanced by his wife's belief that a love of poetry is *the* distinctive feature of an authentic intelligentsia. Her own fate she depicts as a particularization of the fate of the women of her generation (142), the widows "repeating in the night the words of husbands who have perished" (295).

---

[15] "Kakoj-nibud' umnyj redaktor," perhaps an echo of "kakoj-nibud' chestnyj predatel" ("some honorable traitor"), a phrase from Mandelstam's bitter lyric "Kvartira" ("The Apartment"). The allusion would suggest that for Nadezhda a "bright editor" is as much an oxymoron as "an honorable traitor."

It is a common enough poetic device to substitute one synecdoche for another; Nadezhda can tell Osip's story by writing instead about Mikhail Zenkevich. By the same token she can generalize her own widowhood by talking about her friend Alisa Usova instead of herself. This particular substitution is also a device for handling the delicate issue of emphasizing one's own heroism. But the same rhetorical device is at work in her characterizations of the worst capitulationists. To portray what a Nikolay Tikhonov or Tanya Grigoreva is like is a way of showing what Osip and Nadezhda Mandelstam are *not* like.

This substitution of images drawn from the same paradigm makes motif structure an important source of coherence. It is the reader who must produce the intersections of meaning that bridge the gap from kernel to satellite episodes. The motif structure of *Hope Against Hope* depends not only upon synecdoche but upon metonymy, that is, upon figures that evoke a pattern because they stand in some existential relationship to the whole, rather than in an attributive or distributive relationship. The logic of metonymy is a way of getting at the poetic effects associated with the author's predilection for capturing a complex condition in a bare statement or even a single detail.[16] The more obvious of these two techniques is the tendency of a normally unadorned prose to become, if anything, even more spare at the moments of greatest emotional or dramatic intensity. The opening sentence is a good example of this process. Another comes at the very end of the chapter "Preparations and Leavetakings" ("Sbory i provody"), where the merest trace summons up a world of thought and feeling. The Mandelstams are looking out the window as the train taking them into exile leaves the station: "A barrier was taking shape between us and that world. As yet a glass one, as yet transparent, but already impenetrable. And the train left for Sverdlovsk" ("Mezhdu nami i tem mirom obrazovalas' peregorodka. Eshche stekljannaja, eshche prozrachnaja, no ushe nepronitsaemaja. I poezd ushel na Sverdlovsk,"44)

Why is this so effective? I suspect that it is partly a matter of the management of rhythmic sequences, reminiscent of Pushkin's prose, with the final brief phrase serving as a cadence. There may also be something in the functional word order (aktual'noe chlenenie) creating an ominous linkage between the final elements in each rheme: *peregorodka—nepronitsaemaja—Sverdlovsk* (*barrier—impenetrable—Sverdlovsk*). The three stressed o's of the third sentence add their own negative overtones. There is also the elliptical quality of the second sentence, which is set off by being a nominative sentence (nazyvnoe predlozhenie) and also by the balance and contrast of its three nominative, singular, feminine adjectives, the third of which is semantically opposed to the first two. And then there are the echoes of word signals from Osip

---

[16] My approach to the figures of synecdoche and metonymy is based on the distinctions made by the Group μ authors in chapter 4 of their *General Rhetoric*.

Mandelstam's early verse: *steklo, prozrachnaja* (glass, transparent). But all these implications are assimilated to the writer's sense of the ritual moment and her use of the mundane as a way of making connections so that the view from the train becomes a valedictory experience.[17]

The same metonymic impulse operates on the level of individual images. Consider, for example, Nadezhda Mandelstam's use of foods as a kind of shorthand for the experience of arrest, imprisonment, and exile: an egg, mentioned twice, is the only food in the house at the time of Mandelstam's first arrest. During the search of their apartment that accompanies the arrest, a young Chekist offers them hard candies (*ledentsy*). Nadezhda Mandelstam generalizes this gesture as first a ritual of the arrest procedure and second, when she sees it repeated in the 1950s by a former Chekist turned writer, as part of an expressive totality that, as she comments, makes itself felt in every trivial detail (110). There is also the opposite of the hard candy, the chocolate. Tossed into a prison-train car by the writer's working-class landlady in Struino, the chocolate evokes the tradition of popular compassion for all prisoners and is part of a pronounced democratic pathos.

A richer pattern, which penetrates the whole text, is connected with the motif of masks and masking. An odd conjunction on the second page initiates the development. Describing the unfinished kitchen that becomes Akhmatova's domain during her visits from Leningrad, Nadezhda Mandelstam mentions the disconnected gas stove, which, out of deference to their guest, is covered with an oil cloth (*kleenka*) and disguised as a table (*maskirovalas'pod stol*). A few sentences later, apropos of the agents who have come for her husband, she says that their civilian coats "served as a uniform, only a disguised one" (*maskirovochnaja forma*). This juxtaposition of the "masked" stove and the "masked" uniforms may appear so unmotivated as to escape notice, yet as the pattern crystallizes over hundreds of pages, the two images acquire upon rereading the power to bracket a whole world where survival depends upon a language and a decorum that function as masks rendering private feeling invisible and almost inexpressible. Nadezhda Mandelstam is an acute field anthropologist describing a discursive system in which the rulers have their code and the victims theirs, and decorum becomes largely a system for regulating social intercourse between these two groups, with terror as the constructive factor in what the writer calls "the peculiar codex of Soviet polite behavior" (305). The field of "masked utterances" ("*zamaskirovannye vyskazyvanija*") is suffocatingly inauthentic, but, at least in public, the mask is mandatory. Recalling the episode of her expulsion from the Ulyanovsk Pedagogical Institute in 1953, Nadezhda Mandelstam uses the institute's director, whose remarkable resemblance to Chekhov facilitates his work as a leader of

---

[17] The quoted passage also sets up the metaphor of the past as the world behind the mirror (*zazerkal'e*, 44), a figure that links *Hope Against Hope* with Akhmatova's *Poem Without a Hero*.

anti-Semitic pogroms, to illustrate a more general perception: "There is a degree of barbarization when all the veils, invented by a hypocritical society to hide the true essence of things, slip off people. But what distinguished us was that we should never remove our attractive and affectionate civic mask" (332).

In this instance the use of the first-person plural pronoun is dictated by the fact that the agents of evil obliged their victims and potential victims to adopt masks also. The wives of those who vanished, for example, had to go on smiling to their neighbors and coworkers. Speaking of the roughly twenty years from the time she received the news of Mandelstam's death to the time she decided to begin the work of resurrecting him, Nadezhda Mandelstam says: "I was someone else, and I wore, so to speak, an iron mask" (233). Viewed in this light, *Hope Against Hope* becomes an act of radical unmasking. By calling things by what she considers to be their proper names, by restoring her husband's work and memory, she is also restoring herself to herself.

CHAPTER 11

Lydia Ginzburg and the Fluidity of Genre

Sarah Pratt

THE RAW MATERIAL of Lydia Ginzburg's life could certainly provide the basis for a substantial memoir.[1] Born in Odessa in 1902 but an inhabitant of Leningrad for most of her adult life, Ginzburg represents the vibrant generation of the intelligentsia that kept Russian culture alive, indeed injected it with a new intellectual vigor in the 1920s. Having studied with Tynjanov and other members of the formalist school, she has contributed much to the continuing resonance of formalism in Russian culture. As Ginzburg established herself as a scholar, eventually producing seven books and more than fifty articles,[2] she also moved easily between the realm of literary scholarship and its object, becoming a friend and colleague of such major literary figures as Akhmatova and Zabolotsky. Her physical and mental fortitude were, no doubt, severely tested during the difficult Stalin years, the siege of Leningrad during World War II, and the shifting winds of cultural thaw and freeze that have blown since them, but she has survived and continued to develop intellectually, gradually taking on the role of mentor for the younger generation of the literary intelligentsia.[3]

Yet in spite of the intrinsic interest of her life history and her multi-faceted contributions to the field of literary studies, Ginzburg for the greater part of her career has not received the same degree of recognition as many of her peers. It is only in the last two decades or so—after nearly five decades of work—that she has begun to achieve visibility on an international scale. Since the early 1970s every two or three years has seen the publication of a new

---

[1] An earlier version of this article appeared in the *Slavic and East European Journal* 30, no. 1 (Spring 1986): 45–53.

[2] The books are *Tvorcheskij put' Lermontova* (Leningrad: G.I.X.L., 1940); *Byloe i dumy Gertsena* (Leningrad: G.I.X.L., 1957); *O lirike* (Leningrad: Sovetskij pisatel', 1964; expanded edition 1974); *O psikhologicheskoj proze* (Leningrad: Sovetskij pisatel', 1971; republished by Khudozhestvennaja literatura, 1977); *Psychological Prose*, English translation by Judson Rosengrant (Princeton: Princeton University Press, 1989); *O literaturnom geroe* (Leningrad: Sovetskij pisatel', 1979); *O starom i novom* (Leningrad: Sovetskij pisatel', 1982); *Literatura v poishakh real'nosti* (Leningrad: Sovetskij pisatel', 1987).

[3] A remarkable semifictional memoir was published in the January issue of the Leningrad magazine, *Neva* dedicated to fortieth anniversary of the defeat of the Germans and the end of the Leningrad blockade; see Lydia Ginzburg, "Zapiski blokadnogo chekoveka," *Neva* 1: 84–108; reprinted with some additions in Ginzburg, *Literatura v poiskakh real'nosti*, 334–92.

book or a revised version of an old one. In 1971 she published *Psychological Prose (O psikhologicheskoj proze)*. In 1974 came the publication of an expanded version of her book first published ten years previously, *The Lyric (Olirike)*, with a new chapter on Mandelstam. Then in 1976 came the translation of an essay based on the same material, "The Poetics of Osip Mandelstam," in Victor Erlich's anthology of twentieth-century Russian literary criticism, and 1977 saw the republication of *Psychological Prose*. A new book, *The Literary Hero (O literaturnom geroe)*, appeared in 1979. In 1982 and 1987 Ginzburg published collections of selected works entitled *The Old and the New (Ostarom i novom)* and *Literature in Search of Reality (Literatura v poiskakh real'nosti)*. In 1985 Alexander and Alice Stone Nakhimovsky's anthology *The Semiotics of Russian Cultural History* made Ginzburg's essay, "The Human Document and the Formation of Character" (essentially a translation of the first chapter of *Psychological Prose*) accessible to English-language readers. The same year Ginzburg herself became the object of American scholarship with the appearance of a special issue of *Canadian-American Slavic Studies* devoted to her contribution to literary criticism. A translation of *Psychological Prose* is scheduled for publication by Princeton University Press.[4]

The most significant element in this trend is surely the publication of *The Old and the New*, a collection that can, and I believe should, be viewed as a form of autobiography. The publication of a volume of Ginzburg's selected works ranging in date from the 1920s to the 1980s and ranging in category from relatively abstract articles on literary theory to detailed studies of specific poets, memoirs or literary acquaintances, and excerpts from Ginzburg's own notes on her daily life and thoughts indicates that in 1982 the Soviet literary establishment was finally ready to admit Ginzburg as a major literary figure in her own right. But more important for our present purpose is the fact that through this book, Ginzburg herself constructs a summary statement of her own identity—and this is the basis for the claim that *The Old and the New*, taken as a whole, is an autobiographical work.

The volume is divided into three main subsections. Part 1 contains theoretical studies in the form of two long articles and the text of an interview. These are perhaps the essence of the new (novoe) in the title for they are all attributed to the period 1975–1980. In the first article, "On Historicism and Structure" ("Ob istorizme i o strukturnosti"), Ginzburg offers a credo defining her own theoretical position in relation to formalism, reader-response theory, and se-

---

[4] Ginzburg, *O psikhologicheskoj proze; O lirike; O literaturnom geroe; O starom i novom; Literatura v poiskakh real'nosti*. Victor Erlich, ed., *Twentieth Century Russian Literary Criticism* (New Haven: Yale University Press, 1975); Alexander D. and Alice Stone Nakhimovsky, eds., *The Semiotics of Russian Cultural History* (Ithaca: Cornell University Press, 1985); Sarah Pratt, guest ed., *Canadian-American Slavic Studies Special Issue: Lidia Ginzburg's Contribution to Literary Criticism* 19, no. 2 (Summer 1985)

miotics, with reference to such critics as Tynjanov, Vinokur, Sollers, Barthes, and Taranovsky. The direction of her argument may at first baffle the uninitiated, for Ginzburg is not one to take her readers gently by the hand and guide them through the intricacies of her thought. Or, to put it another way, she does not provide her readers with the intellectual equivalent of a TV dinner, fully prepared, neatly compartmentalized, and ready to be warmed over and served. Rather, she supplies ingredients—deftly chosen examples from poetry, prose, and criticism—and an excellent recipe in the form of her own hypotheses and commentary, which give directions with a kind of laconic logic; but the reader must always work to put the whole together. Thus in the article under discussion she begins with the assertion that interest in the interrelation between historical and structural aspects of a literary work is now replacing the Saussurian assumption of a dichotomy between synchronic and diachronic modes of analysis. She then moves on to note the uses and limitations of a historical approach, and in a concluding section on the nature of biography, she touches upon a premise that has been central to her thinking since the beginning of her career: that there is no definite boundary between historically determined fact and "aesthetically determined fiction, that "documentary literature"—historical material organized in accordance with certain "aesthetic principles—exists as a bridge between the two realms. This notion of a continuum of genre will eventually serve our argument about *The Old and the New* as autobiography, but for now we must turn again to a description of the book's contents.

In the next article in Part 1 of *The Old and the New*, "The Personal and the Universal in Lyric Poetry" ("Chastnoe i obshchee v liricheskom stikhotvorenij"), Ginzburg goes beyond her studies in *The Lyric* to make a broad theoretical statement about the relation between "inductive" lyric poems, in which movement toward a basic lyrical theme has its starting point in the expression of a personal experience, and "deductive" lyric poems, in which the theme itself is the starting point. As in *The Lyric*, Ginzburg's choice of examples demonstrates her profound and wide-ranging knowledge of Russian poetry from eighteenth-century neoclassicism down to the poetry to Alexander Kushner, who lives and writes in Leningrad today.

The interview "Conversation about Literary Studies" ("Razgovor o literaturovedenii"), which rounds out the theoretical section of the volume, both introduces new ideas and touches on a number of themes discussed in the opening article. Ginzburg again addresses the issue of her relation to various literary schools, particularly formalism and the numerous subspecies of structuralism. While clearly dissociating herself from most established literary schools, she nonetheless argues for the necessity of selective vision (as opposed to an attempt at all-embracing objectivity) in original scholarship. The broadest area of concern in the interview, however, is an investigation of the nature of literary studies (literaturovedenie). Here Ginzburg notes the generic fluidity of literary studies, citing their role as a discipline mediating between art (iskusstvo) and science (nauka) and noting the fluctuating vocabulary used to define the discipline in various languages—*filologija, istorija literatury, literaturovedenie; Kunstwissenschaft, Literaturwissenschaft*; literary criticism, literary theory, and the like. Much as the interview opens with a discussion of the "intermediate" position of literary studies, it closes with a statement of Ginzburg's special interest in "intermediate genres" (promezhutochnye zhanry) of literature, forms like memoir and autobiography that link history and belles lettres.

Moving from broad statements of theory to its application, part 2 of *The Old and the New* contains eight articles, most reprinted from earlier publications, on specific poets and literary problems. Vyazemsky's notebooks, Pushkin and realism, and Decembrists' poetry, the philosophical lyric, Belinsky and romanticism, and Mandelstam's poetics are among the topics investigated in this section.

Part 3 includes article-length reminiscences of Tynyanov, Akhmatova, Bagritsky, and Zabolotsky and a long section of fragmentary diary notes entitled "From Old Notebooks" ("Iz starykh zapisej"). Like much that has come before, both the reminiscences and the notes focus on connections between life, literature, human nature, and various forms of knowledge. The volume concludes with a chronological bibliography of Ginzburg's scholarly works.

Some of the individual pieces in part 3 are so obviously autobiographical as to preclude any possibility of argument about their genre. Take, for instance, the diary entry in which Ginzburg gives an account of her college years, mixing gentle self-irony with vaguely sweet nostalgia, even displaying a certain pride in her admission that she "did abominably" in chemistry:

> When I was eighteen years old, I believed that everyone should first of all acquire a general background in the natural sciences; therefore I matriculated in the department of chemistry, where I did abominably (gde uchilas' preskverno). Then I assumed that I should make a thorough study of philosophy before I went on to the subjects that directly interested me. That was youth; it seemed to me that I was standing at the threshold of an inexhaustible span of time.[5]

This kind of writing provides the basis for most critical studies of autobiography[6] and indeed for the "rules" of autobiography put forward in

[5] Ginzburg, *O starom i novom*, 394.

[6] See, for example, Francis R. Hart, "Notes for an Anatomy of Modern Autobiography," *New Literary History* 1, no. 1 (Fall 1969): 448–511; William L. Howarth, "Some Principles of Autobiography," *New Literary History* 5, no. 2 (Winter 1974): 363–81; James Olney, ed., *Autobiography: Essays Theoretical and Critical* (Princton: Princeton University Press, 1980); James Olney, *Metaphors of Self: The Meaning of Autobiography* (Princeton: Princeton University Press, 1972); Roy Pascal, *Design and Truth in Autobiography* (London: Routledge & Kegan Paul, 1960); William C. Spengemann, *The Forms of Autobiography* (New Haven: Yale University

one of the major theoretical works on the topic, Elizabeth Bruss's *Autobiographical Acts: The Changing Situation of a Literary Genre*. Bruss's rules require that the author of the autobiography claim individual responsibility for the creation of the text, that the text refer to the author, that the author actually exist, and that the events reported be presented as true by the author and essentially accepted as true by the reader.[7]

A few passages in part 3 of *The Old and the New*, like that cited above, meet these criteria in a way that leaves no room for equivocation, but others seem to exist in a no man's land of genre somewhere between autobiography, memoir, literary history, and literary theory. Articles of this hybrid type include "Tynyanov as Literary Critic" ("Tynjanov—literaturoved"), "Akhmatova: A Few Pages of Memories" ("Akhmatova, neskol'ko stranits vospinanij"), "Encounters with Bagritsky" ("Vtsrechi s Bagritskim"), and "Zabolotsky in the 1920s" ("Zabolotskij dvadtsatykh godov").

The piece on Akhmatova, for example, opens anecdotally as Ginzburg describes her first meeting with the poet. A friend introduced the twenty-four year-old Ginzburg to Akhmatova by referring to Ginzburg's first published article, "Vyazemsky as litérateur" ("Vjazemskij—literator"), and Ginzburg reports her joy at Akhmatova's reaction:

> Natalya Viktorovna introduced me: "Here's the one whose article . . ."
>
> "A fine article," said Anna Andreevna.
>
> This was the first phrase I heard from Anna Andreevna, and I was very proud of it. After that we met on and off for forty years, to the very end [of Akhmatova's life].[8]

From this beginning Ginzburg goes on to discuss Akhmatova's "system of gestures" and asserts that in daily life Akhmatova reflected not so much the heroines of her poetry as her poetic method. In this connection she characterizes Akhmatova's mind as "sober, observant, and somewhat rationalistic" and notes: "Akhmatova never thought of the lyric as the spontaneous overflow of the soul. She saw the necessity of poetic discipline, self-constraint, self-limitation by the creative individual. . . . For Akhmatova the lyric was not the raw material of the soul but a deep transformation of internal experience."[9] The analysis of Akhmatova's approach to the lyric leads to further musings on the indelible change wrought by the symbolists on the Russian poetic tradition and on the paradoxical nature of lyric poetry. The lyric is, according to Ginzburg, "the most subjective genre of literature" yet more than any other

---

Press, 1980); A.O.J. Cockshut, *The Art of Autobiography in 19th and 20th Century England* (New Haven: Yale University Press 1984).

[7] Elizabeth Bruss, *Autobiographical Acts: The Changing Situation of a Genre* (Baltimore: Johns Hopkins University Press, 1976), 10–11.

[8] Ginzburg, *O starom i novom*, 328.

[9] Ibid., 329.

"strives toward generalized experience," because the reader of lyric poetry "seeks not so much the poet, but himself."[10]

On the one hand, *The Old and the New* seems to fit Bruss's criteria: Ginzburg does claim individual responsibility as the writer; she is referred to in the text; she does, in fact, exist; and she presents her case as true, and we presumably accept it as such. Yet on the other hand these qualifications somehow miss the point. They fail to deal with the kind of intellectualization that is an intrinsic and absolutely essential part of Ginzburg's autobiographical writings. In terms of Bruss's vision, Ginzburg's analyses of literary matters are merely side issues, when in truth these discussions carry the main thrust of the piece. And although Bruss disparages the view that autobiography can and should be based on absolute fact,[11] her rubrics exclude the scholarly articles in parts 1 and 2 of *The Old and the New* from the realm of autobiography altogether.

The argument in favor of defining *The Old and the New* as autobiography must obviously be based on a more flexible concept of the genre, the kind of definition put forward by Roy Pascal, one of the first modern scholars to study the genre seriously. Pascal creates a definition that not only allows for the intellectualization and quasi-literary structuring of life characteristic of most of the pieces in *The Old and the New* but includes them as essential aspects of autobiography. In his book, *Design and Truth in Autobiography* he writes:

> Autobiography is a shaping of the past. . . . It establishes certain stages in an individual life, makes links between them, and defines, implicitly or explicitly, a certain consistency of relation between the self and the outside world. . . . The coherence implies that the writer takes a particular standpoint, the standpoint of the moment at which he reviews his life, and interprets his life from it. The standpoint may be the social position of the writer, his acknowledged achievement in any field, [or] his present philosophy; in every case it is the present position which enables him to see his life as something of a unity, something that may be reduced to order.[12]

All of these statements apply to *The Old and the New*. Using her position as an established figure in Russian literary life, Ginzburg, through the very creation of *The Old and the New* as a single volume, shapes the past, unifies the various aspects of her literary endeavor, and defines a "certain consistency of relation" between herself and the outside world. The ordering of the past is suggested by the book's title, made explicit by the dates carefully appended to the end of each article (in some cases even two dates, one indicating an original version, the other a revised version), and reinforced by the chronologically arranged bibliography that closes the volume.

Moreover, the book establishes links between the stages of the past as, for

---

[10] Ibid., 329, 333.
[11] Bruss, *Autobiographical Acts*, 127–28.
[12] Pascal, *Design and Truth in Autobiography*, 9.

example, Ginzburg's recent theoretical work on the lyric is juxtaposed to her early studies of Pushkin, or as her continuing interest in autobiographical genres is shown in her early work on Vyazemsky's notebooks, in her own diary entries from the twenties and thirties, and in her memoirs of encounters with other literary figures written in the sixties and seventies. With its clearly marked tripartite division by category (theoretical works in part 1, articles on specific poets and problems in part 2, and reminiscences in part 3—a division further underlined by Ginsburg in her preface to the volume) and with its ever-present set of dates and notes on publication, *The Old and the New* provides both a logical and a chronological ordering of Ginzburg's life.

Yet what Pascal actually had in mind were standard autobiographical works like Saint Augustine's *Confession*, Rousseau's *Confessions*, and Goethe's *Poetry and Truth*, for in Western scholarship the notion of autobiography as an inherently flexible genre has become popular only rather recently. For example, in a study published in 1980 William Spengemann accepts certain poems, novels, and plays as autobiography on the grounds that the works "do seem, despite their fictiveness, to address the same problems of self-definition that have taxed autobiographers ever since Augustine discovered that the self is a hard ground to plow."[13] Admitting a similar elasticity but describing a movement in the opposite direction, Jane Gary Harris notes that Mandelstam's *Noise of Time (Shum vremeni)* "may be read simply as autobiographical reminiscences" but that in fact "on a deeper level Mandelstam's theoretical statements, hypotheses about the poet, philology, and esthetics are sifted through a peculiar new syntax which transforms autobiography into literary prose."[14] It is here that we begin to approach the essence of the problem as it relates to *The Old and the New*, and appropriately enough, it is here that Ginzburg's own scholarship emerges as the ultimate source in our search for a solution to the problem of the genre of the work.

Throughout her oeuvre, Ginzburg describes the world in terms of three primary functions: aesthetic structuring, logical-cognitive structuring, and definition of individual character or personality. The greater part of her work focuses in one way or another on problems of aesthetic structure, and it is in this context that she, more than any other major modern critic, has contributed to the notion of the capaciousness of the autobiographical genre. She first approached the problem in her work on Vyazemsky's notebooks in the 1920s and 1930s, continued it in her studies of Herzen in the 1940s to 1960s, and then worked her ideas into fully developed theories in her studies of the 1970s, *Psychological Prose* and *The Literary Hero*.[15] These works all rest on the

[13] Spengemann, *The Forms of Autobiography*, xiii.

[14] Jane Gary Harris, "Introduction: The Impulse and the Text" in Osip Mandelstam, *The Complete Prose and Letters* (Ann Arbor: Ardis, 1979), 20.

[15] See among other works: Lydia Ginzburg, "Vjazemskij—literator" in *Russkaja proza* (Leningrad: Academia, 1926), 102–34; idem, "Vjazemskij" in P. Vjazemskij, *Staraja sapisnaja*

fundamental assumptions finally articulated in *Psychological Prose* that "esthetic activity goes on continuously in the human mind" and that "art is merely the ultimate or final stage" of this aesthetic activity.[16] Accordingly, there exists a continuum of aesthetic function that ranges from "everyday human documents" such as letters, diaries, and notes, which, being directly linked with life itself, reflect only a minimal degree of aesthetic structuring, to novels and other forms of artistic literature in which esthetic structuring is a dominant element. According to Ginzburg, autobiography, like the memoir, history, and biography, exists as an intermediate form between the continuum's two extremes. It is a mélange of documentary and artistic qualities— the raw material of life is given a greater or lesser degree of aesthetic structure, depending on the whim and skill of the autobiographer, sometimes moving closer to the aesthetic artifice of the novel, sometimes closer to relatively unstructured "human documents."

While this aspect of Ginzburg's thought explains and underscores the general flexibility of the genre, it is her observations on logical-cognitive structuring and definition of individual character that allows us to integrate the theoretical and scholarly articles in parts 1 and 2 of *The Old and the New* with the notes and memoirs in part 3. According to Ginzburg, both logical-cognitive activity and character defining activity take place in a manner analogous to the aesthetic function. Just as art evolves from a constant human tendency to view life in terms of aesthetic structures, so scholarship or science (nauka) evolves from a constant human tendency to engage in logical-cognitive evaluation of the unstructured material presented by life.[17] Again the function creates a continuum, simple cognitive observations forming one pole and comprehensive scholarly studies the other. In similar fashion, human character or personality is defined, or defines itself, through a kind of "creative structuring" that begins with life's basic events and selects, filters, and interprets them until a distinctive formulation of character is achieved. This process involves both aesthetic structuring related to artistic endeavor and logical-cognitive structuring related to the science of sociology or psychology.[18] A similar point is made in a different context in *The Literary Hero*. In a discussion of the role of the spoken word in the definition of character Ginzburg asserts that the spoken word serves not only as a form of self-assertion but also as the "prototype for the individual's artistic and scholarly activity."[19]

---

knizhka (Leningrad: Izdatel'stvo pisatelej, 1929), 9–50; idem, "Gertsen—sozdatel' 'Bylogo i dum,' " *Zvezda* 1 (1944): 125–38; idem, *"Byloe i dumy" Gertsena; O literaturnom geroe*.

[16] Ginzburg, O psikhologicheskoj proze, 6, 12–13. I am grateful to Judson Rosengrant for allowing me to use the manuscript version of his translation of this work. The page numbers given here refer to the 1977 Russian text.

[17] Ibid., 6.

[18] Ibid., 12–14.

[19] Ginzburg, *O literaturnom geroe*, 164.

It is particularly significant that each of Ginzburg's three functions—aesthetic structuring, logical-cognitive structuring, and definition of individual character—has its starting point in life rather than in an abstract intellectual precept and that the aesthetic and logical-cognitive modes are, as often as not, bound together. As Ginzburg herself puts it, ''Art is sealed off neither from logical cognition nor from life.''[20] Sometimes this bonding results from the process of definition of character discussed above; sometimes art simply absorbs scientific principles, as was the case in French prose of the second half of the nineteenth century;[21] and sometimes the merging simply reflects the nature of a particular discipline, for instance, literary studies (literaturovedenie). In this connection Ginzburg observes:

> I must confess that the question of whether literary studies are a science or not has never bothered me. . . . It seems to me that literary studies are a borderland between art and science, and it would be difficult to establish any exact boundary. . . . The methods of literary analysis lie at the intersection of two planes. The proportions can change from total dominance by art to total dominance by humanistic, scientific—but truly scientific—thought.[22]

If we extract the essence of these statements—namely, that art can include science or scholarship and that literary studies straddle the boundary between art and scholarship—and combine them with Ginzburg's concept of autobiography as an extremely capacious genre, then we must consider the possibility that the scholarly articles, works of and about literary criticism, in parts 1 and 2 of *The Old and the New* contribute to the ''art'' of Ginzburg's own loosely-defined autobiography.

But perhaps more significant than this theoretical argument is the simple fact that the ''creative structuring of character'' in *The Old and the New*, Ginzburg's re-creation of her own character, lies as much or more in the scholarly articles and in Ginzburg's ruminations on the nature of Zabolotsky's art or Akhmatova's relation to Pushkin as in the more obviously autobiographical parts of the volume. It may be that in other individuals' lives the aesthetic and logical-cognitive elements are more seamlessly integrated. Certainly most modern autobiographers describe a process of self-definition that seems to be more or less homogeneous, whereas Ginzburg in *The Old and the New* seems at first glance to separate and emphasize the scholarly or logical-cognitive element, the more so because of the clearly marked divisions within the volume itself. Yet the fact is that Ginzburg's own life, her own ''creative structuring of character,'' has evolved in an environment in which life, literature, and scholarship exist as parts of a single, integrated phenomenon. Her relations to

---

[20] Ginzburg, *O psikhologiceskoj proze*, 8.
[21] Ibid.
[22] Ginzburg, ''Razgovor o literaturovedenij'' in *O starom i novom*, 46.

literature and ideas are no less a part of her real life than her relations to people and historical events. This can be seen, for example, in her relations to her teachers, her *maîtres*, as she calls them:

> Many people modify us a little bit. . . . But they, the *maîtres*, they themselves changed life in its purest aspect. . . . If there had been no Eikhenbaum, no Tynyanov, life would have been different, that is, I would have been a different person with different capabilities and different ways of thinking, feeling, working, relating to people, and seeing things.[23]

The ultimate literariness of her life becomes even more obvious in another passage as she sets up what might be called a basic grammar of perception, a way of perceiving life and reacting to life based entirely on the activating force of the word:

> Anything that is not expressed in words (either spoken aloud or said to oneself) has no reality for me; or more accurately, I lack the organs of perception for it. To express a thing in words does not mean simply to name it by citing the appropriate terms. With any given incident it is necessary to work out a formula, a little structure, a microcosm of a plot with its own denouement. When I see a beautiful landscape and lack a formula for it, I experience a sense of pointlessness connected with that event—as if I had been doing nothing but sitting on a bench in some dusty square chewing on sunflower seeds. All the joys and sorrows of life reach us through clots of words, which, like quotations that run through one's head again and again, seem to congeal in one's conscious mind, remaining there for a long time.[24]

It is this intermingling of life and literature, this sense of the word as the catalyst and fixative of our perception of reality, that makes Ginzburg's article on Pushkin, Vyazemsky, lyric poetry, historicism, and structuralism—in short all the articles in parts 1 and 2 of *The Old and the New*—not only legitimate but essential aspects of her autobiography.

---

[23] Ginzburg, ''Iz starykh zapisej'' in *O starom i novum*, 46.
[24] Ibid., 396.

CHAPTER 12

Roman Jakobson: The Autobiography of a Scholar

Krystyna Pomorska

THE AUTOBIOGRAPHICAL SKETCH of Vladimir Mayakovsky "I—myself" (1926–29) begins with the words: "I am a poet. This is what is interesting about me. I am writing about this here. About the rest . . . only if it became fixed in the word." Another autobiography of a poet, *Safe Conduct* by Boris Pasternak, contains a similar statement, which can be summarized as follows: if we try to present the life of a poet as a sequence of everyday facts, we would end up with trivialities.

During a discussion after his lecture at Moscow University in October 1979 somebody asked Roman Jakobson "to summarize briefly" his biography.[1] He answered: "I do not like to turn to my past. I am living by my future." And he added: "Although there is not much of it left for me, yet I am living by the future." When asked about writing his memoirs of a life "so rich and adventurous," he would shrug with disgust ("To sit and 'write memoirs': I can't even stand the idea!"[2]). This attitude toward the value of life and toward the past as opposed to the future is as characteristic of Jakobson as it was of both poets.

The evidence thus far might suggest that Jakobson was opposed to the very idea of writing his own biography. Nevertheless the corpus of his work contains at least three distinct though unostentatious autobiographical genres: the *Dialogues*, a detailed account of his life as a scholar; the "Retrospects," each one of which contains reflections on the issues involved in one of the seven volumes of his *Selected Writings*;[3] and finally the numerous interviews in which he discusses his scholarly life and other matters, but only "if they became fixed in the word," to use the phrase of Mayakovsky he was fond of quoting.

The Italian scholar Lorenzo Renzi in his recent study on Jakobson expresses

---

[1] This essay first appeared in *Language, Poetry and Poetics. The Generation of the 1890s: Jakobson, Trubetzkoy, Mayakovskij. Proceedings of the First Roman Jakobson Colloquium, M.I.T., Oct. 5–6, 1984*, ed. K. Pomorska et al. (Amsterdam: Mouton de Gruyter, 1987). The reprinting of this article is offered as a tribute to Krystyna Pomorska, whose untimely death deprived the scholarly community of a major Slavicist and extraordinarily perceptive reader of "autobiography." I would like to thank Professor Stephen Rudy for bringing this article to my attention and Professor Stanislaw Pomorski for giving permission to reprint it in this volume [Ed.].

[2] "Terpet' ne mogu etu ideju: sidet' i 'pisat' vospominanija'!"

[3] Roman Jakobson, *Selected Writings*, 7 vols. (Amsterdam: Mouton Publishers, 1966–85).

a similar opinion, calling both *Dialogues* and "Retrospects" "[il raconto] della vita intellettuale" of the scholar. He names the life account *res gestae*, the biography "priva di aspetti futili . . . dove le impresse sono naturalmente impresse scientifiche."[4] A scholarly autobiography thus conceived coincides with that of both poets. Taking all this into consideration, the paradox between refusing to write one's autobiography and leaving behind an account of one's life is resolved: not a biography in general but a specific *type* of biography solves the apparent contradiction.

Jakobson's negative attitude toward memoirs was based on several key premises. Traditionally one expects from memoirs a certain number of facts, heterogeneous in nature and "sensational" in function. It is precisely this feature of a biography that Pasternak refers to when he mentions the "horrors, revelations, and plots" ("strakhi, fabuly i vvedenija") expected by the reader.[5] The element obviously unacceptable to Jakobson was the tense of this genre: memoirs belong to the past tense; they push one's life into the past, thus putting an end to one's biography and, consequently, to one's life. Finally, memoirs presuppose an idle monologue without a clear addressee and a definite function.

Jakobson's concept of the res gestae is diametrically opposed to all traditional notions of autobiography. He selected facts according to one principle: the extent to which they were results or stimuli of his work. The selection is patterned into a system. One of its features is the obliteration of the gaps between the three dimensions of time in his narration. Accordingly, each of the "Retrospects" ends with a program for future work not yet done but already planned.[6] Similarly, the last chapter of the *Dialogues* contains an appraisal of semiotics as an important and still evolving branch of science: "*We must now clearly undertake* the comparative study of language and all other groups of signs, a study that has been planned over the course of centuries."[7] Almost none of the interviews ends with a traditional formula. None of them has a finished ending; rather, they break off abruptly.

Instead of monologue, Jakobson chose *dialogue* as his mode of expression. In his theory he emphasized the dialogic character of language itself, as he did in praxis: he would state at the first meeting of a course that he expected not to deliver a monologue but rather to have a discussion, questions, even inter-

[4] Lorenzo Renzi, "Roman Jakobson: Verso l'ultima Thule del linguaggio," *Nuova Corrente* 30 (1983): 206. "[The story] of intellectual life of a scholar"; the biography "without anything futile . . . where works undertaken are naturally all scientific undertakings."

[5] Boris Pasternak, *Okhrannaja gramota* in *Sochinenija* 2, ed. G. Struve and B. Filippov (Ann Arbor, Mich.: University of Michigan Press, 1961), 205. And, see in this collection, "Boris Pasternak's *Safe Conduct*."

[6] Characteristically, the topic of the last public lecture by Jakobson at Moscow University was: "Ocheredyne zadachi nauki o jazyke."

[7] Roman Jakobson and Krystyna Pomorska, *Dialogues* (Cambridge, Mass.: Harvard University Press, 1983), 157.

ruptions—a genuine dialogue. Even in the setting of a public lecture he created the impression of a similar approach. A Spanish reviewer of one of his large talks observed that he lectured ''as if conducting a huge orchestra.'' Even the ''Retrospects'' are partially dialogic because of their strongly polemical character (especially those in volumes 3 and 4). The dynamic, active character of the ''Retrospects'' is further enhanced by the fact that they are attached to the *material product* of the life: the oeuvre itself. To use Jakobson's semiotic categories, the ''Retrospects'' have a *deictic function* with respect to the work of their author.

As indicated before, Roman Jakobson presented his life exclusively in terms of his work. Thus he did not follow the traditional dichotomy between facts of life and creativity. This was no doubt caused by the author's particular attitude to life and by his temperament. C. Lévi-Strauss, a keen observer, put it succinctly in the *Tribute to Roman Jakobson*: ''What struck those who approached Roman Jakobson was, above all, the extraordinary kinship between the man and his work. In harmony with his writings, his personality radiated a prodigious vitality. The same generosity, the same demonstrative strength, the same effervescent spirit defined one's contact with him as well as the perception that in reading his works, one was in touch with an oeuvre that gave definitive foundation to linguistic theory.''[8]

There is yet another, perhaps more important factor responsible for the shape of his self-presentation. Jakobson belonged to the generation of scholars and poets who broke with the traditional, especially nineteenth-century, approach to the biography of a creative man as ''Dichtung und Wahrheit.'' The idea underlying this dichotomy presupposes a distinct separation between reality—''hard facts''—and the mind. Such a separation, however, was proclaimed erroneous by philosophers two centuries before our time, notably by Kant and his followers. The philosophers' pronouncements were later proved by the psychophysiological tests of the Gestaltists (Koffka, Kohler, and Wertheimer) around 1910. Thus it was demonstrated that conscious sensations are not mere copies of the external world of ''real objects'' but rather *homologous constructs* of these objects. These scientific findings paved the way for a fresh approach to human creativity in its relation to reality. A writer's biography thus presented the most confusing and challenging realm in which to resolve this dichotomy. The traditional belief that the facts of a writer's life are in direct causal relationship to his creative work now seemed questionable, if not wrong. The issue was immediately pursued by the Russian formalists, who were directly influenced by Gestalt psychology. With characteristic radicalism the formalists at first simply discarded biography altogether from the area of scientific investigation as irrelevant. Gradually they reconsidered and

[8] Claude Lévi-Strauss in *A Tribute to Roman Jakobson: 1896–1982* (Amsterdam: Mouton Publishers, 1983), 71.

drew back from their rebellious attitude,[9] but it was Jakobson who, in the 1930s, elaborated the most complete concept of the biography of a poet. He insisted that in the authentic life of the poet the two realms—external reality and creativity—merge into an indissoluble whole: the poet's own mythology. Jakobson's works on Mayakovsky, Pushkin, Macha, and Erben demonstrated and developed this proposition. In a later period he repeated his idea in a condensed form in the *Dialogues*. He restated that the only authentic life of the poet can be found in his poetic word, that the poet's work anticipates the future and thus belongs to the future. Therefore the poet, according to Pasternak's dramatic statement, is always "displaced" in his own time.[10]

Jakobson emphasized his affinity with poets rather than with the academic scholars of his time.[11] V. V. Ivanov carried this point further and noticed that Jakobson wrote about and identified with those innovative scholars who were "displaced": "Whether he speaks of Peirce as a genius for whom no American university was able to find a place, or of Baudouin who . . . [was] geographically cut off from . . . accepted theories . . . Jakobson had always his own experience in mind."[12]

A twofold conclusion follows from this juxtaposition: in Jakobson's view there is no difference between the poet and the innovative scholar. Consequently, we can examine his own autobiography with the tools that he himself created to analyze the biographies of poets. Thus the only authentic life of the scholar is to be found in *his* word. Indeed, instead of a mechanically causal connection between life and work, Jakobson presents a set of mutual relations between his creativity and external facts.

The first relation is the link betwen tradition and innovation. A revolutionary in his linguistic quest, Jakobson never failed to emphasize his indebtedness to his teachers, paying particular attention to those scholars of the past whose work he considered his proper heritage.[13] His autobiography contains the explication of this dialectical tension, the main example being the Saussurean tradition. As Jakobson became acquainted with the *Cours de linguistique generale*[14] in 1920–21, he gradually adopted such Saussurean oppositions as sysnchrony/diachrony, *langue/parole*, and *signans/signatum* and incorporated them into his metalanguage. Developing these ideas, he simultaneously re-

[9] See especially Boris V. Tomashevskij, *Russkoe stikhoslozhenie. Metrika* (Petrograd: Academia, 1923).

[10] See Boris Pasternak's letter to Roman Jakobson (1943), discussed in Jakobson and Pomorska, *Dialogues*, 142–43.

[11] Ibid., nn. See also "A. J. Liehm interviews Jakobson" in *Red Letters* 6 (London).

[12] Vjacheslav V. Ivanov, "Roman Jakobson: The Future" in *A Tribute to Roman Jakobson*, 56.

[13] See Edward Stankiewicz, "Roman Jakobson: Teacher and Scholar" in *A Tribute to Roman Jakobson*, 17–26; also Roman Jakobson, "Acknowledgements" in *Selected Writings* 2.

[14] Ferdinand de Saussure, *Cours de linguistique generale* (1906–11); cited after the English translation, *Course in General Linguistics* (New York–Toronto, 1966).

worked them critically, one by one. The Saussurean tradition in Jakobson's theory should thus be viewed as a functional parallelism between the two and not as a direct teacher-student relation (linear causality). The Saussurean system came into contact with a creative mind and not merely with a responsive instrument that absorbed and reproduced it. A contact of this sort necessarily involves the element of a significant contrast (contrastive juxtaposition). Another such contact is represented by an episode recounted in the "Retrospect" to *Selected Works* 1: the freshman Jakobson consults with his professor D. N. Ushakov as to his reading list in linguistics. Ushakov "appoved all the many titles except the 1912 monograph on Russian vowels by L. V. Shcherba . . . alien to the orthodox disciples of the Moscow linguistic school. *Naturally it was just this forbidden book which I read first*, and I was captivated . . . by its . . . glosses to the concept of the phoneme"[15] (italics mine). This is an exemplary case of how one can learn not only by following advice (similarity) but by disobeying it (contrast). Naturally, to profit from disobeyed advice one has to have exceptional qualities of judgment regarding one's choices.

Another relation, particularly involved in Jakobson's work, is that of linguistic science versus poetry and art. Traditionally, linguists declare their noncommitment to poetry and art, considering it merely another area of study, if not an ascientific field altogether. In the *Dialogues* Jakobson says: "Poetry was my first passion during the years I spent in high school. . . . My first attempts at writing verse were losely tied for me to the investigation of verbal art. . . . At the age of nine or ten I was trying to represent the verse that I read, as well as my own feeble efforts at poetry, through pecliar metrical schemes that I would invent on the spot for the purpose."[16] An even more pertinent example of this activity is given in the "Retrospect" to *Selected Works* 4: "A passion for gathering proverbs possessed me as soon as I learned to scrawl letters. Proverbial sayings were zealously seized upon to cover empty calendar sheets. Discussions with specialist in childhood psychology, Charlotte Buhler and Rosa Katz, have reinforced my conviction that such infantile predilections are neither fortuitous in their choice nor without consequence for the later line of mental development."[17] The author then speaks about the twofold character of this particular "infantile predilection": "The proverb pertains simultaneously to daily speech and to verbal art. . . . The proverb is the largest coded unit occurring in our speech and at the same time the shortest poetic composition. . . . The six-year-old boy, fascinated by these intermediate forms between language and poetry, was compelled to stay on the watershed of linguistics and poetics."[18]

The same considerations and relations continued in Jakobson's life when he

---

[15] Jakobson, *Selected Writings*, 2:631.
[16] Jakobson and Pomorska, *Dialogues*, 2
[17] Jakobson, *Selected Writings* 4 (1966), 637.
[18] Ibid.

met the avant-garde poets Velimir Khlebnikov, A. E. Kruchenykh, and, later, Vladimir Mayakovsky. Especially his contacts with Khlebnikov (in 1914, when Jakobson was seventeen) and "the phonic analysis of Khlebnikov's poetic texture prompted use of linguistic data about the sounds of speech. On the other hand, the new light that the original work of this poet shed on the sounds of languages led me to question willy-nilly the habitual conception of phonic material in linguistics and to subject it to a fundamental revision"[19] (italics mine). Similarly, the pictorial discoveries of Picasso, Braque, and the entire postimpressionist avant-garde trend in visual art, according to the "Retrospect" to *Selected Works* 1, contributed greatly to the relational approach to linguistic phenomena. This correlation was carried over from the abstract realm to human relationships and to intellectual interdependence. For example, Kasimir Malevich, one of the greatest innovators in the visual arts, took a number of ideas from the conversations he had with the young adept of the Moscow school of linguistics. Another eminent painter, the Czech Josef Sima, speaks in his still unpublished diaries about the role Jakobson's theories played in his painting. The interest in and participation of Mayakovsky in the gatherings of the Moscow Linguistic Circle and Jakobson's works on his poetry is yet another example of this correlation.[20]

The interdependence of linguistics and poetry can serve as the most important example of the range and form of these correlations. Not only is linguistics allied to poetry as a tool of investigation, poetry itself is treated as a specific source of knowledge for linguistics. Poetry was approached phenomenologically, in its specific modality, and exploited as an important part of scientific metalanguage. Not the linear concept "linguistics plus poetry" nor the disjunction "scholar or artist" but the "poetry of grammar *and* the grammar of poetry": this was the feedback system on which Jakobson insisted.

At the end of chapter 4 of the *Dialogues* Jakobson refers to the devastating loss of Trubetzkoy, which coincided with the catstrophe of World War II: "For me the years of homeless wanderings from one country to another had begun."[21] The very title of the next chapter, "The Effects of the International Experience on the Development of Linguistic Theory," signals how the author himself perceived those homeless wanderings. Typically, a seeming interference with his work is transposed into creative results. Thus the antinomy proper conditions/interference is abolished. In each country where the war drove Jakobson to find refuge, regardless of how short the span of time or the impending danger, he carried on his research and left his creative imprint. On

[19] Jakobson and Pomorska, *Dialogues*, 21.

[20] See the "Retrospect" in *Selected Writings* 1; also Jakobson and Pomorska, *Dialogues* and "Linguistics and Poetics" in *Language in Literature*, ed. Krystyna Pomorska and Stephen Rudy (Cambridge, Mass.: Harvard University Press, 1987), 62–94.

[21] Jakobson and Pomorska, *Dialogues*, 34.

the other hand, he knew how to use the resources available in each country in which he happened to be: "I must admit," he says, "that the succession of scientific environments, each with its own particular interests and local watch-words, allowed me to reformulate my own questions and to enlarge their scope."[22] The scientific environment and its particular interests took on various shapes: it could be a congenial group of scholars, as for instance the Norwegian linguists, with their expertise and "deep interest in a multilingual comparison" that "spontaneously" led to a "collective work in comparative phonology" and to the preparation of a phonological atlas of the world's languages.[23] It could also happen that the local tradition was opposed to Jakobson's ideas and that he, on his part, questioned the approach of some theoreticians, as for example those of the Copenhagen Linguistic Circle or, later, of the behaviorists in the United States. Yet "at the same time these discussions led [him] to carry to its logical conclusion the principle of relativism in phonological analysis" and "taught [him] to maintain a greater rigor in [his] definitions."[24] Sometimes the congenial environment presented itself in the form of a local institution, specialized in a seemingly unrelated area, which he discovered by a "strange concurrence of events." In Sweden, for example, such an institution was the Uppsala psychiatric clinic, headed by V. I. Jacobowsky, and the "wealth of medical libraries" of Stockholm. The final result of this "concurrence of events" was the publication of the monograph *Kindersprache, Aphasie und allgemeine Lautgesetze*.[25] Jakobson also credits his sojourn in Sweden with the possibility of learning "how to convey new ideas in a widely accessible form, avoiding . . . the use of new technical terms" when addressing an audience that, at that time, was "not interested in phonological analysis of linguistic structure."[26]

V. V. Ivanov, in his speech for the *Tribute*, noticed one of the most characteristic features in Jakobson's life and personality: not only was he not afraid of catastrophes but he *worked best* in times of disaster.[27] Jakobson's own account of the central catastrophe of his life—the Second World War—and his assessment of its results quoted above confirm unequivocally Ivanov's observation. Ivanov recalls Jakobson's own words: that he could bear the difficulties of each day "because he was already thinking about the future, about what would happen tomorrow, and the day after, and the next."[28] He belonged

---

[22] Ibid., 35.

[23] Ibid., 37–38.

[24] Ibid., 35–36.

[25] *Kindersprache, Aphasie und allgemeine Lautgesetze* (1941) is translated as *Studies on Child Language and Aphasia* (The Hague: Mouton Publishers, 1971).

[26] Jakobson and Pomorska, *Dialogues*, 39.

[27] It was not by chance that Jakobson took a deep interest in the mathematical theory of catastrophes advanced by René Thom.

[28] Vyacheslav Ivanov in *A Tribute to Roman Jakobson*, 50.

wholly in the future and "did not fit" into the present. He used the present to go out into the future, drawing upon his formative years, which coincided with "the turbulent artistic movement of the early twentieth century," that extraordinary past that provided "the strongest impulse towards a shift in the approach to language." The "great men of art born in the 1880s" who created this artistic movement were able to complete their schooling, Jakobson commented, "in one of the most placid spans of world history, before that . . . last hour of universal calm (*poslednij chas vsemirnoj tishiny*) was shattered by a train of cataclysms."[29] Ivanov wisely calls this epoch a "renaissance that began the century, but had no continuation."[30] Jakobson lived between the great past without continuation and the future, and simultaneously between the "last hour of universal calm" and the global catastrophes of our times. Although seemingly contradictory, these historical and psychological crossroads made it possible for him to resolve antinomies, especially the fundamental antinomy of time.

The unity of time was the chief preoccupation of Jakobson and his entire generation.[31] All his life he returned to this question, frequently and in various ways. In one of his last papers, on Einstein,[32] Jakobson insists that we should always keep in mind what Einstein emphasized shortly before his death: that the distinction between past, present, and future is illusory. In his reminiscences of Yury Tynjanov[33] he remarks that Tynjanov's historical novels apparently testify to the author's belief in the unity of past and present. When analyzing Norwid[34] he chooses a poem, "Przeszłosc," in which the attempt to disjoint time is presented as an act of the devil. In the 1920s and 1930s, in his revision of the Saussurean oppositional concept of synchrony as static versus diachrony as dynamic, Jakobson was governed by the same consideration. Thus the unity of time in the form of simultaneity and dynamic creativity in the life of language was formulated. A similar unity applies to the life of any organism, including human life. As we have attempted to show, Jakobson pursues the same principle in his autobiography. Resolving the antinomy between tradition and innovation, and also between the present and the future, he factually abolishes the sharp delineation of time into three disparate sequences. As one of the reviewers of the *Dialogues* observed, "It is a descrip-

---

[29] Jakobson, *Selected Writings*, 1:631–32.

[30] Vyacheslav Ivanov in *A Tribute to Roman Jakobson*, 49.

[31] See Roman Jakobson, "On a Generation That Squandered Its Poets" in *Language in Literature*, 277–90; and Jakobson and Pomorska, "The Utopian Future of the Russian Avant-Garde" in *Dialogues*.

[32] Jakobson on Einstein in Roman Jakobson and Linda Waugh, *The Sound Shape of Language*, (Bloomington: Indiana University Press, 1979).

[33] Roman Jakobson, "Life and Language," *Linguistics* 138 (1974): 97–103.

[34] Roman Jakobson, "Preszłosc' Cypriana Norwida," *Selected Writings* 3 (1963), 499–507.

tion and analysis of serious *work in progress*, filled with all the excitement, polemics and evolving potential."[35]

It is worth noting that in the oeuvre of Jakobson's peer Boris Pasternak the life of the creative personality is presented in a similar ways. In his early novella *The Childhood of Ljuvers*, in *Safe Conduct* from the middle period, and in the last novel *Doctor Zhivago* Pasternak rejects mechanical causality and simple linearity in both the external and psychic life of his heroes. Instead, he shows chords of happenings and impressions that govern the life of a unique personality.[36]

The problem of time has a direct connection with the formal representation of the speaking subject in Jakobson's autobiography. A striking feature of his discourse is a strong tendency to avoid the first-person singular. The most demonstrative example appears in the "Retrospect" to *Selected Works* 2. In the summary of the impact of philosophy and psychology on his work, and especially in the discussion of his revision of Saussurean theory, not once does the author use the first person. He either refers to "*linguistic theory of our time*"[37] or employs impersonal constructions, for example "this assumption *has been submitted* to a gradual revision."[38] Ending his statement he says: "*The assiduous fieldwork of contemporary linguistics has prompted* the conclusion."[39] Thus a remarkable feature of the various pieces of the scholar's autobiography is the inclusion in the author's point of view of all the opinions of his coworkers in linguistics, which constitutes an expression of their collective effort. While the "Retrospects" by their very character permit the author to dissolve his "I" in the collective effort or directly in the subject matter, the issue assumes a different aspect in the *Dialogues*. He is confronted with questions aimed directly at him. And yet he manages to use a similar strategy. Example: "This was one of the main stimuli that *forced us* to overcome the separation between" or: "The phonic analysis of Khlebnikov's poetic texture *prompted use* of linguistic data,"[40] etc. In the "Acknowledgements" to *Selected Works* 2 he gives a clue to this principle: "Young unorthodox linguists heeded the rallying slogans of the avant-garde poets, and we were at one with the brave and moving call jointly launched by Khlebnikov, Kruchenykh, Burljuk, and Mayakovsky: "To stand on the rock of the word WE amid a high sea of catcalls and hatred.' " Indeed, collective efforts and anonymous creation, aimed at the future, were among the fundamental tenets of the futurists and

---

[35] Michael Sosa, "Dialogues" in *World Literature Today* (Spring, 1984).

[36] See Krystyna Pomorska, *Themes and Variations in Pasternak's Poetics* (Lisse: The Peter de Ridder Press, 1975) as well as her essay "Boris Pasternak's *Safe Conduct*" in this volume; and Boris Gasparov, "Vremennoj kontrapunkt v romane *Doktor Zhivago*" (forthcoming).

[37] "Retrospect" to *Selected Writings*, 2:712.

[38] Ibid., 717.

[39] Ibid., 722.

[40] Jakobson and Pomorska, *Dialogues*, 20–21.

central to their avant-garde mythology. The avoidance of the personal "I" in favor of the collective in the autobiography of the scholar has a similar philosophical significance. In this framework it is only logical that Jakobson was the proponent of a new approach to the poet's biography understood as myth. According to his proposition, discussed above in a different connection, myth is the primordial and eternal truth about the poet's life, and as such it is always aimed toward the future. Thus the necessary condition for the preservation of myth is that it be adopted by the collective. This condition, in turn, makes individual creation relative to collective creation, since preservation by the community requires a constant collective/individual recreation.[41] In sum, the individual work must reach a state of generalization in order to be preserved. This is the awareness that governed the scholar in forming his discourse.

This issue has further implications in the framework of Jakobson's linguistic theory. One of the most renowned among his works on grammatic categories ("Shifters, Verbal Categories and the Russian Verb")[42] discusses the personal pronominal system. He returned to the same question later in his analysis of Louis Aragon's novel *Blanche ou l'oublie*,[43] which addresses the issue of personal pronouns from the point of view of the psychology of writing. Jakobson considers the first-person singular, the "I" pronoun, the most enigmatic and difficult in that it "signifies the same intermittent function of different subjects."[44] Therefore it immediately poses the question of the self "as a point relative to other points," to use the metalanguage of Lévi-Strauss. Thus in a discourse directed toward the human collective, which both adopts and recreates it, the encoder and decoder should approximate equality. This procedure becomes even clearer when set against the basic principle of Jakobson's theory of communication: "The more closely the addressee approximates the code used by the addresser, the higher is the amount of information obtained."[45] To reverse it we may say that in the case discussed here the addresser approximates the code of the addressee to provide the highest information obtainable.[46]

[41] See the discussion of this matter in Claude Lévi-Strauss, *The Naked Man* (New York: Harper and Row, 1981).

[42] Jakobson, "Shifters, Verbal Categories and the Russian Verb" in *Selected Writings*, 2:130–47.

[43] Roman Jakobson, "Le métalangage d'Aragon" in *Selected Writings*, 3:148–54.

[44] Jakobson, "Shifters, Verbal Categories and the Russian Verb," 132.

[45] Ibid., 130.

[46] I wish to thank Professor Elzbieta Chodakowska for valuable discussions that led me to reshape the first version of this paper and Professor Stephen Rudy for a number of important suggestions.

CHAPTER 13

In Search of the Right Milieu: Eduard Limonov's Kharkov Cycle

Patricia Carden

> No malo, malo
> Ljubvi i slavy za spinoj.
>
> —Eduard Bagritsky, "Golubi"

EDUARD LIMONOV came to general notice in the West with the publication of *It's Me, Eddie!* (*Eto ja—Edichka!*), his rambunctious account of his life down and out on the streets of New York.[1] A Russian émigré whose transit to the West had been aided by the eagerness of the Russian police to rid themselves of a troublemaker, Limonov gleefully thumbed his nose at his American hosts, flauting his use of the welfare system to support his vocation as writer, while taking aim at many sacred cows of American liberal ideology. The book also told a dark story of his beautiful young wife's seduction and destruction in the shaky, glamorous world of publicity and fashion, where her job as a model led her, and of the poet's own despair, attempted suicide, and final reversion to New York street life for consolation. Although Limonov had been known before to a few people who followed Russian poetry, it was only with his conceptualizing and presenting of himself in an autobiographical novel that he reached the larger audience he sought. The book's rafiné, even obstreperous tone of voice made it hard to sell to the American audience, which felt that it had nourished a viper in its bosom, but the translations into European languages (under such provocative titles as *Le poet russe aime les grands negres*) were popular successes. The autobiographical hero fit easily into a European conception of the *poet maudit*, and indeed it was clear from the book that Limonov conceived himself in a romantic tradition fed by these very legends.

The success of his autobiographical novel led Limonov to seize his chance. He began writing a series of works that mined his personal experience. Perhaps the most compelling of these are the two books that form the "Kharkov cycle" and deal with his boyhood and youth growing up in a large city of the Soviet Ukraine. These two works, *Adolescent Savenko* (*Podrostok Savenko*) and *Young Rascal* (*Molodoj negodjaj*), not only tell the story of the poet's

---

[1] *Eto ia—Edichka!* (New York: Index Publishers, 1979); English translation by S. L. Campbell, *It's Me, Eddie: A Fictional Memoir* (New York: Random House, 1983).

early life, they create a panorama of Soviet urban provincial life that is unparalleled in recent Russian literature.[2] Oddly enough, it takes its cue from Gorky's autobiographical cycle, which depicted life at the turn of the century in the towns along the Volga. Limonov's cycle is similarly rich in the characters and details of a milieu far from the capitals. Like Gorky Limonov depicts a life much more the norm of Soviet experience than that lived and described by the Moscow and Leningrad intelligentsia. If truth be told, the Russian intellectual and professional classes are uncommonly snobbish, uncommonly given to drawing a sharp line between themselves and people of the working class. Like the Russian nobility of the nineteenth century they can stretch themselves to accommodate some romantic vision of "country people," the more archaic in their habits the better, but they have little truck with the teeming life of modern cities. This predilection has no doubt been reinforced by the way official culture force feeds the populace with a glorified image of the worker. The reaction has led to an impoverishment of the underlying reality in Russian writers' depictions of their lives. Only recently has a new "city prose" begun to show a wider, if still limited, variety of situations and professions. Limonov to his credit deals with the whole range of people who make up his city.

The bare facts of the life recounted in the Kharkov cycle are these: the autobiographical hero, young Eddie, is the son of Benjamin and Raissa Savenko, people living an ordinary life in Saltovka, a workers' suburb of Kharkov. Benjamin works as an officer in the MVD, but except for his frequent absences from home nothing about his profession singles the family out from the gray routine of petty bourgeois life. Benjamin is a member of the rank and file, first a senior lieutenant and then a captain, whose responsibility is to transport prisoners. A man of strict integrity within narrow limits, he has been unwilling to use his position to achieve any benefits for himself and his family, in particular to find them a nice apartment in a better neighborhood. His wife has a technical education, but she long ago resigned herself to being a housewife, settling down, and making a life for herself among the working class and petty professional people of her neighborhood. Nevertheless she clings to standards of bourgeois respectability and voices her dissatisfaction with her husband's fecklessness.

Eddie is a model boy whom teachers choose to lead the class unit of the Young Pioneers. He lives largely in a world of fantasy constructed from the accounts of adventurers and explorers. He occupies himself making elaborate classifications of geography, history, flora, and fauna and dreams of becoming an explorer himself and going to Brazil. But as he grows conscious of his father's weakness, of his father's powerlessness to protect him in the rough-and-tumble of Saltovka life, his allegiances change. Seeking to be with those

---

[2] *Podrostok Savenko* (Paris: Sintaksis, 1983); English translation by Judson Rosengrant (New York: Grove Press, 1989); *Molodoi negodiai* (Paris: Sintaksis, 1986).

who can take what they want, he turns to the *shpana*, the delinquent working-class youths of the Saltovka streets, whose respect he earns by carousing and thieving with them. This new style of life brings him into sharp conflict with his parents, who have envisioned a proper, upwardly mobile life for him. This conflict is the subject of the *Adolescent Savenko*.

Young Rascal takes up at a slightly later period after Eddie has left school and worked in a factory for a time (where once again he was a model worker until he grew bored with it). Eddie drifts into a job as a bookseller in the center of Kharkov. Here he comes into contact with the city's literary bohemia. He moves in with a vivid and physically lush Jewish woman some years older than himself, the muse and mistress to Kharkov's poets. He has written verse since adolescence, but he now conceives a fierce determination to become a poet. He begins to train himself by a rigorous regime of writing, under the tutelage of a student from the university. At the same time he takes up the trade of tailor to support himself, fashioning jeans and modish trousers for Kharkov's cultural avant-garde. By good fortune Eddie discovers Kharkov's artistic bohemia just at the season of its brief flowering. He achieves the recognition as a poet that he craves, is renamed Limonov ("Mr. Lemon") in honor of his love for tropical climates, and settles into a comfortable menage with Anna. But his restless nature makes him impatient with his new milieu once he has conquered it. He sees that Kharkov bohemia is beginning to fade after its short period of bloom, and he conceives a plan to move on to Moscow, the true center of literary life.[3]

As I have presented the story thus far, one might get the impression of a leisurely chronicle, but Limonov's sensibility is one of crisis, of the extreme moment, and each of the books centers on a single day that proves decisive in the autobiographical hero's development. Stories from the remembered past weave in and out of the present-centered narrative, but the plot leads up to a single decisive event, a manifestation of the hero's will.

The present events of *Adolescent Savenko* occur when Eddie is fifteen, on the 1958 anniversary of the Revolution. He is caught up in a conflict with his parents, who in their desire to educate him to sobriety and moderation have not given him the customary present of cash for the holidays. Eddie has made plans to take his girlfriend Svetka to a party with a well-to-do and fashionable set of young people, but each member of the party is expected to kick in a sum to help pay for the entertainment, and Eddie finds himself embarrassed by the

---

[3] An overview of Limonov's career with substantial biographical detail is provided by Olga Matich in her article "The Moral Immoralist: Edward Limonov's *Eto ja—Edička!*" *SEEJ*, no. 4 (1986): 526–40. Matich's bibliography includes many examples of Russian émigré responses to Limonov's work. For a shrewd assessment of Limonov's literary posture see Edward Brown's remarks in "The Exile Experience" published in a volume of essays edited by Olga Matich and Michael Heim: *Russian Literature in Emigration: The Third Wave* (Ann Arbor: Ardis, 1984), 53–61.

lack of funds. Increasingly desperate, he goes from place to place trying to raise the money by one means or another. Meanwhile Svetka proves elusive, and he begins to suspect that she has betrayed him by going off with an older boy who has a regular job, ready cash, and nice clothes. At the end of the evening he goes to her apartment intending to confront her with her lover, but instead he bursts in upon a sober Svetka, who reveals to him that she has been sleeping with men for a long time and that he seems a baby to her. The book ends with Eddie's attempt to run away from home and his ignominious return.

In *Young Rascal* the foregrounded events take place on August 26, 1967, when Eddie is twenty-four. The narrative ranges over events from 1964, when Eddie first meets Anna Rubenstein and becomes a member of Kharkov's literary bohemia to the present day of the story. The conflict now is with Anna, his "wife," who interferes with his free enjoyment of his own pleasure: wandering about the city with his pals, flirting with women who catch his eye, and drinking. Like a comical fury she pursues him from one haunt to another. Late in the evening, while accompanying a friend's girl to her door as a polite gesture, he recognizes in one of her neighbors an ancient enemy who once put a move on Anna at the cinema. Eddie feels that he did not act to defend his woman and his own honor with the requisite speed and firmness. Now he conceives a plan for revenge. Ascending to the floor where his enemy lives, he builds a fire outside the door of his apartment. He returns to the sleeping Anna full of creative mania and paints his unsuspecting "wife's" body in an elaborate tatoo of designs.

This account is paralleled by two accessory stories. The day is singled out not only by Eddie's criminal act but by the suicide of a leading Kharkov poet, an event that crystallizes Eddie's own fears and ambitions and leads him to decide to abandon Kharkov and make the big move to Moscow. The accounts of the day's events is interwoven with the story of how he first claimed Anna, when coming to Kharkov as a working-class lad from the dingy suburbs he sat timid and silent at her bohemian parties, unable to enter into the discussion of literature and painting. Having served his apprenticeship, he decides to take the decisive step and seduce her. Certain that she is sleeping with a former lover, he crosses Kharkov in a blizzard and stands under her window shouting imprecations. She turns him away that night and leaves the next morning for a resort in the Crimea. He follows her there, gets admission to her sanitorium by posing as her brother, and persuades her to take him into her room for the night. But Anna's incidental roommate, an imposing woman from Leningrad, finally loses patience over the muffled scramblings and groanings of the pair and summons the authorities. Eddie is banished into the night, and Anna has to leave the next day with a charge of "amoral behavior" on her record. The structure of the book thus depends on the interweaving of three narratives about moments of decision that change the course of Ed's life.

The story of Eddie and Anna is robust, even Bocaccian (one wishes that these characters could find their Fellini to recreate their adventures on film), and indeed Limonov's world view is essentially comic, earthbound, and centered in the body.[4] Even his moment of "transcendence," when drunk in a snowstorm he climbs the belltower of the Orthodox cathedral and challenges God and Satan, is comic and anticlimactic. He retains a childish, magical attitude toward authority. As an adolescent, disillusioned by the images of political leaders he sees on TV, he keeps a secret notebook of members of the Politburo who are to be eliminated when the *shpana* comes to power. Years later, meditating on the existence of God, he pictures him as a kind of super KGB agent, spying on everyone's thoughts every minute (*YR*, 190). Never having set foot in a church, he decides to try his luck with God: "They say that a novice at cards always wins the first time." From the cathedral's tower he calls upon the Deity to give him an exceptional fate, but thinking better of it he decides instead to make a pact with the devil and asks him to remove his rival from his path to Anna and—if more can be granted—to let him become a hero (193).

An autobiography begins from an implicit or explicit claim about the interest of the life to be examined—it is representative, it is exceptional. The tone of Limonov's autobiographical writings is subtle and cunning. Often we hear the voice of the "hero," a braggart of fairy-tale proportions, reveling shamelessly in his own adventures. "We are the National Hero" proclaims the title of a Limonov prose poem.[5] But there is a second self, a narrator-author, who is shrewd and observant. Scanning reality with a calculating and even cold eye, he stores up impressions for future use. And over both voices presides the bard, celebrating these unsung places and people, *their* bard, recognized as such even in his teens when the *shpana* from Saltovka cheered him at the poetry contest on Kharkov's Victory Square. He is the namesake of the poet Eduard Bagritsky, a songster from the south of Russia who conceived himself in a romantic, outlaw vein. And Eddie willingly takes on his destiny as poet-adventurer.

A.O.J. Cockshut has written that "Any autobiographer who survives his book by many years is leaving a poignant hostage to fortune," but with Limonov one feels that is not the case.[6] His autobiographical writings are informed by a restless uncertainty. He seeks meaning together with the reader

---

[4] Irwin Titunik associates *Edichka* with a tradition of Russian erotic literature dating to Trediakovsky: "The models of created worlds signalized by Ovid and Catullus are precisely the contexts in which we can—and must—understand the artistic meaning of the efforts brought to bear in Russian literature by Trediakovskii and Limonov." Titunik, "Vasilii Trediakovskii and Eduard Limonov: Erotic Reverberations in the History of Russian Literature" in Kenneth Brostrom, ed., *Russian Literature and American Critics*, Papers in Slavic Philology 4 (Ann Arbor: Department of Slavic Languages, University of Michigan, 1984): 399.

[5] "My natsional'nyi geroi" in Mikhail Shemiakin, ed., *Apollon—77* (Paris: Les Arts grafiques de Paris, 1977).

[6] A.O.J. Cockshut, *The Art of Autobiography* (New Haven: Yale University Press, 1984), 5.

and this leaves everything open to revision. He conceives himself as a multi-layered being: the working-class, criminal lad from Saltovka; the lion of the provincial literary circle, commanding its desirable woman; the present-day writer, informed by the sophistication of wide reading, travel, contacts, and exposure to Western culture. There remains one stage in the transformation yet to be examined, the provincial aspirant storming the capital, a role that has been anticipated in Limonov's poetry and that serves as background to *It's Me, Eddie*. It's easy to anticipate that this experience will form the core of the next volume in the autobiographical cycle.

In Limonov's books we find a willful looseness of construction that keeps the parallels in sight while not drawing the plot too tightly together, an impressionistic method recalling his favorite Apollinaire or even his namesake Bagritsky. Paradoxically the trying on of many roles is a gauge of sincerity. The supercritical and penetrating mind of the protagonist is always alert to the element of the theatrical and its attendant bad faith. There is an almost Tolstoyan psychology of self-analysis with the same acute sense of the "false." But Limonov treats this human frailty with humor and worldly wisdom. He is not so quick as Tolstoy to signal his authorial distance from the vainglorious or self-pitying moment. Usually he first enlists our emotional cooperation, then allows us to readjust our response in company with his own ironic revision.

Limonov has a keen sense of the self as object as projected by others. At one point after having remarked on his low opinion of an acquaintance, he turns the tables and muses on how phoney the acquaintance must find him. The constant interplay of internal and external points of vantage is embodied in the text in the liberal use of epithets. People are summed up in nicknames and epithets that may or may not express the essence of the character but do truly embody the gorup's vision of them. The very titles of Limonov's own prose works consist of such designations, part of the provisionality of the view of the self that informs his work. The interplay of self and group provides the motivations for the actions that shape the protagonists' lives, in particular that of the author-protagonist but indeed of all the personages who occupy his stage. They conform to roles that have clear public valuation. The author has his own striking vision of his future, of his destiny as poet, when he sees the Kharkov poet Motrich reciting his verses to an admiring company.

Theater is gregarious, both for performer and audience. As a kid running away from home with the romantic idea of a self-sustaining life in the wilderness, Eddie is driven back to the village where he has been sent for the summer not by hunger but by loneliness: "Eddie-baby had discovered that he was a social creature" (*AS*, 118). Gregariousness was enforced in Soviet life of the fifties and sixties among people living in workers' dormitories or in single rooms in communal apartments. But Russians have a taste for communal life. As a rejector of the family life Eddie seeks his company in the streets. In

Saltovka he becomes a member of the "society of the benches under the lindens"—the hangout at the bus stop on the Saltovka highway, where the rowdies congregate to drink and talk. In youth he graduates to the benches in Shevchenko Park in the center of Kharkov, where the different intellectual factions have their own corners staked out. Both societies greatly value the ability to prattle (trepat'sja). The poor student Bokarev is admitted to the society of young workers and thieves because "he can talk about anything you might ask." His conversation, informed by his technical education, has "the romanticism of mathematics and figures" savored by the uneducated (*AS*, 111).

Like the audiences of the park benches, Limonov is attracted by his characters' theatricality, by their ability to envision interesting roles for themselves and perform them successfully. His wife Anna is particularly successful at self-projection. Limonov speculates that the discourse in his wife's Jewish family with its extravagant rhetoric was more influential on his development as a poet than his wide reading. Those who cannot bring off the roles they attempt are subjected to ridicule. For example, there is the kindhearted police officer Captain Zilbermann, who oversees the cases of juvenile offenders: "Obviously he imagines that he is inspector Maigret; it's revealing that he is eternally clothed in an idiotic leather coat that reaches his heels and smokes a pipe. . . . Charlie Chaplin, not Inspector Maigret—that's who he is" [or Peter Sellers, perhaps?] (*AS*, 6). Zilbermann is a complex of inappropriate responses. He is a Jew: "A Jew-policeman is some kind of joke. The only thing funnier would be a Jew-doorman." Hoping to save Eddie by exercising a good influence on him, Zilbermann encourages him to pursue his literary endeavors. In his ridiculous leather coat he pursues the desperate adolescent around the city, seeking him out on dancefloors and in teenage hangouts.

The essentially theatrical evaluation of the individual role leads to the constantly shifting perspective from performer to observer that is characteristic of the Limonovian narrative. If all the world's a stage, then each of us is both actor and audience. Time plays an important part, the medium in which the self finds his own authentic roles. One role displaces another in the process of self-definition. This fluidity doesn't seem to be particularly disturbing for Limonov as it was for Rousseau (and to a lesser degree for Tolstoy). He has a kind of mental good health, almost synonymous with good humor. Although there is a nasty side to his temperament, as he acknowledges, his fundamental quality is one of cheerfulness, curiosity and equanimity. Self-doubt and pain are acknowledged but subsumed.

Perhaps there is some loss of intensity in Limonov's work because of this underlying equanimity. The reader has the sense that Limonov will use everything to his literary purposes; nothing is withheld. At the same time no significance is really delayed. The use of "roughening" or "deferment" so central to formalist poetics is quite rudimentary. Time brings each process to its fruition. The discovery of falsity does not lead to prolonged bereavement as in Tolstoy. Limonov may lash out, but then he sheds his old skin and moves on to a new life. The former life is integrated as nostalgia. Self-transformation becomes a ritual occurring cyclically and accepted as a natural phenomenon. If transformation also means abandonment of past ties, this is accepted without guilt. At the end of *Young Rascal* he begins to receive letters from Anna, who has learned of his fame and writes to him in Paris. He refuses to acknowledge these letters because they reopen a past that has already been conceived by him as literature. Perhaps to this degree he has left a hostage to fortune, even if not in Cockshut's sense. Although there is nothing that needs to be hidden for Limonov, there are certainly things that must not be rewritten. At one point Eddie thinks of his role thus: "He is an organizer of chaos, he is chaos' vanquisher. People of his stripe are cutting down chaos all their lives and stacking it up in orderly piles. True, chaos quickly springs up again like a jungle on the very ground that was cleared" (*YR*, 144). Hence Eddie's self-chosen epithet: the "commonsense commando" ("borets s chush'ju sobach'ej"). "Chush' sobach'ja" is the term Eddie applies to the world of conventional life, which paradoxically is the arena of the unordered, cluttered—hence unaesthetic— life.

The breaking of images from conventional conceptions of life is radical in Limonov. For example, the conventional image of the MVD officer, full of power, dangerous, and glamorous, like a Nazi officer in a film, is submitted to radical revision. At night he overhears his father telling his mother about transporting a prisoner who is said to have attempted to assassinate Khrushchev. The father clearly feels sympathy for the prisoner, "a manly fellow, still young, perhaps thirty-five at most. Red-haired, tall." The father is impressed by the prisoner's fortitude. Although he is being transferred to be shot, he holds to his daily regime, doing his exercises and reading. Benjamin has violated the rules to allow his prisoner to read (129). The reader expects the news that his father has met an important political prisoner to be highly charged. He reads with curiosity and savors the "insider's" information about how executions are carried out. But Limonov defuses the tension and directs the reader's attention elsewhere. The father tells the story primarily as a piece of curious information that will have no impact on his own life. The parents fall asleep and so does Eddie (130). Transporting prisoners is just more *byt*— boring everyday experience that Eddie wants to put aside in favor of a more exotic world. The presentation challenges the reader's assumption that the event is important. The brave prisoner is reevaluated not as a political hero but as one more victim of a stultifying and conventional reality. The father's kind gesture is subtly devalued, too, as inadequate to the circumstances, even while its positive bearing on the father's character is acknowledged.

It is a sad fact of Eddie's biography that his father, a very ordinary, meek, and powerless man, has been drawn into a dirty business. His biography must be edited from time to time by Eddie's mother and relatives to eliminate embarrassing details, like the mandate Benjamin received in youth from Lavrenty Beria himself to seek out deserters in the taiga. Once a source of gratification, after the fall of Beria it must be suppressed. The mandate thrills Eddie as a source of power, which he misses in his father. "Why doesn't he have such a mandate now?" The two Kharkov books are set in a foregrounded era of Brezhnev. There is a vague sense of a more ominous early time, but it doesn't bear much on Eddie's mentality or the mentality of his generation. They know that there were people whom Stalin persecuted, but they admire more the genuine criminals in their milieu who have returned from prison. Criminality is viewed as a large field for action. Eddie admires the criminal-dreamers who invent imaginative schemes, like the technical student Bokarev who dreams of becoming a millionaire selling photo cribsheets for exams. He envisions a nationwide system of distribution in which thousands of kids organized into well-disciplined units will sell his cribsheets outside schools, universities and technical institutes (*YR*, 110).

In spite of the diffused "philosophical" tone of the narrator's voice, there are moments in the books that are highly charged. These are variants of the primal scene in which the protagonist, as outsider-voyeur, seeks to spy upon the tryst of a man with a woman, suspected and confirmed. The least significant of these is the classical primal scene of father and mother that Eddie discusses willingly enough but with little passion.

> Eddie-baby enters the room and fully dressed lies down on his couch. One side of the couch is against his parents' big iron bed. The bed's headboard and footboard are high and nickleplated and made up of a whole collection of spheres and columns. When Eddie-baby was little it was all the same to him where he slept. Now the proximity of their bed upsets him. His friends tell him laughing that they caught their parents "fucking" (as they say), but Eddie-baby never caught his. Sometimes when he was a kid, at night he could hear some sort of sighs and groans from the bed, but he attributed them to bad dreams. (*AS*, 123)

Eddie's failure to discover his parents in the primal act is partly a matter of class: his modest and discreet bourgeois parents are careful to avoid discovery, while the working-class parents in the neighborhood take the facts of life in stride and aren't too careful around their children. But perhaps more importantly, Eddie's parents have fewer opportunities. His father's job necessitates long absences while he escorts prisoner convoys. And indeed the discovery of his father's occupation is far more highly charged for Eddie, his real "primal scene." It is striking that the passage describing his parents' sexual life leads directly into the revelation of his father's occupation. In chapter 30 of *Adolescent Savenko* Eddie both speculates about his parents' sexual life and recounts his own version of the primal scene when he discovered his father's true occupation.

His parents' sexual life is a mystery: "When, then, do they fuck?" Eddie can't help thinking. They in fact have little shared domestic life, given Benjamin's long absences and his long hours at work when he is in Kharkov. But all this is told from the objective stance of the present-day Eddie: "His parents' sexual life doesn't interest him very much." In the present of the narrative his father's occupation too is only an occasion for mild distaste and fundamental indifference. He recalls that his father is spending the holiday on a train somewhere escorting a convoy of prisoners, but it is of no importance to him. He thinks back to a time of childish innocence when "he still somehow missed his father and expected his return from Siberia every day."

This is an important moment in Eddie's development: when he discovers and draws a line between two worlds. Missing his father, he goes to the station to meet his train. He is puzzled when his father doesn't arrive on the train as scheduled. The father is somewhere else with special prison cars that have been drawn off onto a distant siding. Wandering about the station, Eddie chances upon this remote siding and there sees a new version of the primal scene, a new kind of paternal betrayal.

> The scene before him was extremely laconic and stern. From under his wagon Eddie-baby saw a circle of soldiers with rifles to which bayonets were attached. The soldiers held the rifles with their bayonets forwards and slightly inclined towards the ground. On boards which had been laid down from a freight car with barred openings, there descended a wary chain of some persons or other. The chain poured into the "Black Mariah"—a black, enclosed van. The ring of soldiers, still wearing overcoats (after all, it was only April), was broken in only one place—where an officer stood. In one hand the officer held a sheaf of papers, the other rested on his holster, which had been unfastened in case of need. It was Benjamin Ivanovich (AS, 126).

Eddie is shocked. He has already gone over to the *shpana*. Now he thinks, "He delivers the *shpana* to camps and prisons" (127). Although Eddie had known that his father was an MVD officer, it had never occurred to him that that fact impinged upon his life. Now "that his father was a pig became his private secret; he kept his secret to himslf, for Eddie-baby's place in the world of the Saltovka neighborhood and in the cosmos would have changed at once if his friends had found out that he was the son of a pig." Eddie's identification with "those who do what is forbidden" is political only in an elemental sense. That his father might be an instrument of political oppression in a larger sense is a matter of indifference to him. He has already conceived his cosmos in a way that goes counter to even the official paradigm of dissent. This new conception will take him further and further away from the middle-class life of conformity or dissent.

The cycle shows Eddie defining himself more and more in terms of "the forbidden openly flouted." At fifteen he prides himself that "he has fucked them all over," that he has established his specialness and his dominance. When he takes up the folkways of the *shpana*, it has a significance for him that it cannot have for them: he has a choice. Literature in turn becomes a ratification of the forbidden. At the age of fifteen, reading Bagritsky, "to his amazement he found indecent lines" where contraceptives are openly mentioned (*AS*, 9). He copies forbidden books, like the first volume of Freud to come into his hands, line by line. In *Young Rascal* the forbidden world of criminality is changed for the world of bohemia, which is equally contemptuous of conventional life. At the end of this book he makes a symbolic gesture of rejection of this world in turn. He paints the sleeping Anna's naked body all over with an indelible pencil, drawing elaborate and obscene designs. He is ready to depart: "For almost three years our youth had lived among these people and among them and with their help he had become the poet Ed Limonov. Now the complex communal life of these several hundred idlers, prattlers, wits, alcoholics, bad but sincere poets and artists, which had been created by time and nature, is due to dissolve and die."

CHAPTER 14

Literary Selves: The Tertz-Sinyavsky Dialogue

Andrew J. Nussbaum

> Where does it eventually get to, this all-pervasive particle ''I''?
> Abram Tertz, *A Voice from the Chorus*

ANDREY SINYAVSKY first came to the West as Abram Tertz, a mysterious personality who sent his literature abroad in his search for artistic freedom.[1] Smuggled from the Soviet Union, this literature arrived in the West ''faceless,'' its author not merely unknown but relying on that anonymity to continue his literary endeavors. Tertz represented an incorporeal identity whose aesthetic opinions challenged Soviet literary authority. The entire drama of Soviet pursuit of this renegade writer, who almost magically evaded the authorities for over six years, has a romantically heroic quality. Using Tertz as a literary costume, the Moscow teacher and writer with a modest reputation secretly transfomed himself—ironically to address his own tradition. Sinyavsky's arrest was Tertz's unmasking.

Although emigration has freed Sinyavsky of the political necessity that led to Tertz's invention, Tertz remains a vital part of the author's creations. The three texts relevant to this essay, *A Voice from the Chorus* (*Golos iz khora*), *Kroshka Tsores*, and *Good Night* (*Spokojnoj nochi*), are attributed on the title page to Tertz.[2] Tertz's contemporary role in Sinyavsky's creative life, particularly in these autobiographical works, obviously surpasses his initial use as a vehicle for transmitting literature across the Soviet border. Through a detailed reading of *Good Night* and brief analysis of the two earlier books this essay seeks to engage both Sinyavsky and Tertz in a discussion of autobiography.[3]

[1] The author of this essay would like to thank Stanley J. Rabinowitz, who advised the Amherst College thesis leading to this article, Dale Peterson for his insightful comments, and Viktoria and Mikhail Schweitzer for personal accounts of Sinyavsky and the Soviet prison world.

[2] Abram Tertz, *A Voice from the Chorus*, trans. Kyril Fitzlyon and Max Hayward (New York: Farrar, Straus and Giroux, 1976); idem, *Kroshka Tsores* (Paris: Sintaksis, 1980); idem, *Spokojnoj nochi* (Paris: Sintaksis, 1984).

[3] For another treatment of the role of Tertz in Sinyavsky's literature, particularly as revealed in Sinyavsky's critical works on Gogol (*In the Shadow of Gogol; V teni Goglja*) and Pushkin (*Strolling with Pushkin; Progulki s Pushkinom*), see Donald Fanger, ''Conflicting Imperatives in the Model of the Russian Writer: The Case of Tertz/Sinyavsky'' in *Literature and History: Theoretical Problems and Russian Case Studies*, ed. Gary S. Morson (Stanford, Calif.: Stanford University Press, 1986). Fanger's observations about Sinyavsky's questioning of traditional Russian

Sinyavsky's autobiographical triptych investigates the genre from three perspectives: the memoir from *A Voice from the Chorus*, a fictional rendition of the autobiographical act in *Kroshka Tsores*, and a provocative reformulation of autobiography in Tertz's "recounting" of Sinyavsky's life in *Good Night*. In all three texts Sinyavsky challenges traditional notions of autobiography, revealing the author's elemental struggle with language and form in the autobiographical act. Sinyavsky discovers only deception in the apparent simplicity and authority of "I," and these texts highlight, even revel in, the deception. In *Kroshka Tsores* Sinyavsky's hero is ultimately silenced by his inability to appreciate the inadequacies of the traditional autobiography. In Sinyavsky's most recent experiment with autobiography, however, these inadequacies become a source of liberation for Tertz, who abandons the conventional form in favor of a more fundamental engagement of language, his literary tradition, and the nearly catholic principles of the contemporary witness tale.

Modern literary scholarship has repeatedly attempted to grasp the term "autobiography"; the interest in the subject is shown by abundant disagreement and continual reevaluation. An abbreviated history of autobiography might look like this: St. Augustine wrote the exemplar, Rousseau expanded it, and Joyce exploded it by dissection. Writers of modernist autobiographies have removed the reader's innocent faith in the self-revelations created by the genre. The careful reader questions the reliability of language as a conveyor of authentic selfhood. The search for the autobiographical atom has turned scholars into literary psychoanalysts, readers of the writing of a life, not of the life itself.

In the traditional autobiography "self" is a progressive term. Through a cohesive, frequently chronological presentation of selected events an author attempts to develop a self that might reasonably be extended from the past to the writer's present image of himself. The resulting text may exhibit, and St. Augustine's *Confessions* certainly does, moments of crisis, the autobiographer's own doubts of the viability of his task, but these episodes are crises within a plot. The autobiographical structure itself is never allowed to collapse. These writers assume that beginning with birth and leading into the present there exists a single continuous "I"; writing a traditional autobiography involves recording that "I" 's development, not creating a fictional character.

Modern autobiographers, especially literary ones, deny the apparent lack of artifice in the conventional autobiographical act. Thus Vladimir Nabokov in *Speak, Memory* personifies memory, treating Mnemosyne as both character and muse. Many modern writers highlight the author's role in the creation of an autobiography. The notion of an extant "life" is demystified to expose the

---

attitudes toward these two parents of modern Russian literature are echoed in Sinyavsky's latest prose.

hand of the autobiographer as creator, like the voice of the timid figure hiding behind the omnipotent Wizard of Oz.

What perhaps unites conventional and modern autobiographies is their illustration of consciousness.[4] Whether St. Augustine or Nabokov is the author, a reader can learn from the text's structure as well as from the facts recounted. The life events presented would be little more than historical data without the author's supplying their meaning through his narration. A writer produces the "I" by connecting selected events; that "I," in its traditional coherance or modern chaos, reflects the consciousness behind it. Contemporary literary criticism has in at least one respect echoed modern autobiographers; neither regards the construction of such a text as a naive act.

. . .

Sinyavsky's first venture into the autobiographical field, *A Voice from the Chorus*, provides an introduction to his latest works. This book represents the purest example of the autobiographical mode because the author presents the letters as documents without commentary. Yet even here, in memoir form, Sinyavsky's idiosyncratic approach to the genre is evident. Italicized quotations from other inmates are interspersed with the letter entries. At times these snatches of prison conversation relate to the letter's topic, often they appear to be simply idle chatter. But Sinyavsky's desire to include this other voice signifies two important aspects of his style: first, his avoidance of any form that has not been previously altered to suit his tastes, and second his need to depict for the reader the environment in which he wrote the letters. Sinyavsky uses the prisoners' reported speech, anecdotes, and camp songs to build a linguistic realm against which he sets his consciousness, reported in the letters. The reader gains a sense of this world through synecdochic representation of it. The title reflects a fundamental autobiographical need; illustration of a consciousness necessitates the positioning of it against an external voice.

The concerns Sinyavsky raises in the letters show the significance he attributes to his camp years. The subject is not suffering or any other physical condition but creative emotion; these are notes of a highly artistically self-conscious being, not a physical toiler. Sinyavsky writes about art, language, fairy tales, other artists, dreams, and existential questions. He regards language as a diabolical force. The act of literary composition is for Sinyavsky all-enveloping:

> From the start, from the very first paragraphs you must write in such a manner as to cut off every way of retreat and thereafter live only by the law of the train of words now set in motion as being the only course available to you, not giving way to any

[4] Roy Pascal, *Design and Truth in Autobiography* (Cambridge, Mass.: Harvard University Press, 1960), viii.

hopes for some world other than this self-sufficient text which is henceforth wholly in command of both theme and language, and you must cast aside all mental reservations and burn all your boats in order to act with uncharacteristic self-assurance. Artistic creation is a desperate posing of the question: to live or not to live? (258)

This expression of the text's arresting its creator will produce Sinyavsky's central dilemma, to be discussed later, in the autobiographical act. The intensity he attributes to writing, its proximity to life and to death, and the mystery of its powers form an autonomous environment belonging to the text rather than to the author.

A Voice from the Chorus must be regarded as only an intermediate stage in Sinyavsky's treatment of autobiography; the prose is too controlled, too comfortably poetic, because of the author's distance from it. We are told to read each letter as an accomplished fact, separate from the man whose name appears on the cover. Recalling the notion that "artistic creation is a desperate posing of the question: to live or not to live," which will serve as a credo for the narrators in Sinyavsky's later books, we must finally regard *Voice* as a less than artistic work by its author's own definition. The book lacks the aura of instability and danger that the reader feels in the literary acts producing, and reproduced in, *Kroshka Tsores* and *Good Night*. *Voice* provides the reader interested in Sinyavsky the raw material of his aesthetics without the actual literary drama.

In *Kroshka Tsores* and *Good Night* Sinyavsky develops the authorial drama he articulates in this work. The later prose not only builds a world but conveys the narrator's subjection of himself to the textual universe he paradoxically is alleged to create. Unlike the pseudo-memoir of *Voice*, these texts are not "clean"; the pages produce a scent of creative perspiration, the sweat of the narrator's dramatic relationship with his evolving book, in each case an autobiography. The author immerses himself in this fantastic world to write, and the reader must perceive the text's cosmology to understand the author. Sinyavsky explores as he writes, weaving his way through a linguistic labyrinth he is not sure that he can ever master.

. . .

In *Kroshka Tsores* Sinyavsky's narrator attempts to develop an autobiography. This "small crumb of a man" ("kroshka") opens his tale with the paradigmatic introduction to a traditional autobiography: "I was born and raised." The book begins with the narrator's literal beginning, described as "completely normal," and closes at the moment of the text's composition. With its neat cover and small size, the text's shape itself connotes a tidy story. Everything looks in order here, and the first sentence ostensibly assures the reader of the text's simplicity.

By the end of page one, however, the reader should begin to regard the opening as more of a ploy or false start than an accurate indication of the tale's complexity. Kroshka begins his story with a false enticement, provoking expectations he will not fulfill.[5] His self-professsed normality gives way to an account of his childhood stutter, induced by the screams of an old woman dying in the next room. Oppressed by this defect, the young Kroshka dreams of a fairy (feja), Dora Alexandrovna, who cures him of his speech disorder, literally giving him language, in exchange for a pact with the devil. But Dora Alexandrovna is also the name of a pediatrician who visits the ill Kroshka. Her double identity is never resolved by the narrator. After only four pages the first chapter ends with a reversal; Dora stutters but Kroshka does not, and Kroshka's Faustian commitment to the devil supercedes his claim of normality.

The beginning is extremely complex; Kroshka presents a direct autobiographical intention in a markedly romantic environment. The dedication to E.T.A. Hoffman, the Faustian motif, and Dora's appearance suggest myth or legend, not traditional autobiography. The romantic elements reshape the world in which Kroshka attempts to place himself. His desire to fix himself is disrupted by the inherently destabilized realm he depicts early in the text. The reader cannot help but marvel at the rapid and complete discrediting of the opening assurance of a traditional autobiography.

In the next chapters Kroshka relates his unwitting role in the deaths of his five brothers. Dora occasionally reappears, although her identity becomes increasingly ambiguous. At different times Kroshka refers to the fairy or muse who inspires him to fluency, the pediatrician, his first love, his mother, his alleged wife, and even his dog all as "Dora."[6]

Each successive family disaster causes Kroshka to withdraw further into his nocturnal world, the literary realm. Kroshka Tsores diminishes as his text grows. He perceives his life as split into two halves: "The day—to live, the night—to write" ("Dnem—zhit', noch'ju—pisat'," 10).[7] While he continu-

---

[5] Sinyavsky enjoys such deceptions. Note his discussion of his son's letter in *A Voice from the Chorus*:

> Yegor writes in his letter:
> "I want you to make me a picture of me and I shall make you a picture of a ball."
> A sentence superb in the elegance of its composition. One expects: "and I shall make you a picture of you." But not a bit of it—not "you" but a "ball!" The way that ball bounces back and forth from one end of the sentence to the other. (298)

[6] I resist the temptation to invoke Freud here, but Sinyavsky may be intentionally teasing his post-Freudian reader by his name choice.

[7] Translations provided in this essay are mine. Because Sinyavsky's prose is at times more influenced by linguistic devices than by any narrative logic, I have transliterated some critical passages for those who read Russian.

ally seeks more desperately to establish some link to historical reality, Krosh-ka's confinement to his own nights of writing increases. The text has a her-metic quality, closing inward as its hero's life deteriorates.

This movement foreshadows the futility in Kroshka's autobiographical ef-fort to find his self in his external life. His curse is the antithesis of Midas's; all disappears with his touch—his brothers, his dog, and ultimately the lan-guage used to tell, indeed to form, his life. In the book's closing scene Dora's powers allow Kroshka to witness a meeting of his five dead brothers in which each attributes the cause of his death as the cause of Kroshka's. They end by denouncing with Soviet slogans both father and son as writers. Kroshka's per-ception of this scene fades as Dora departs, and the text decomposes—sen-tences evaporate first into phrases, then into words, and finally into a string of letters. In the last paragraph Kroshka awakens at dawn, as though the whole text has been a nightmare for the author, who ends his book a stuttering old man. The story concludes in linguistic dumbness; Kroshka leaves his autobi-ography as he began it.

Kroshka's autobiographical act undermines itself. His text betrays and de-stabilizes his intention to construct a cohesive autobiography. Structurally, the final seventh chapter comprises nearly one-third of the book; linguistically, Kroshka is overwhelmed by ineffability and ultimately is unable to compose. He suffocates in his metaphors, which become symbols without referents. The tale's "I," contrary to conventional autobiographical and fictive modes, does not evolve but dissolves: "Does she realize what is happening with me, that I am shrivelling into a little lump, dissolving, devolving, turning into the ill, helpless child who lay before her forty and some years ago, a naked child in my squeaky little bed?" (84).

Dora's gift, language, brings Kroshka only misery and frustration. By the end of the autobiography he has shrivelled, not grown. *Kroshka Tsores* be-comes antiautobiography, the chaotic decomposition of an "I" instead of its logical development. At the end Kroshka is a lonely, small, placeless man who can only stutter like gogol's Akaky Akakievich.

A second level to Kroshka's narrative exists, however. Kroshka Tsores, invented by Abram Tertz, is also identified as Andrey Sinyavsky, *Kroshka Tsores* offers a few genuine autobographical credentials—Kroshka and Sin-yavsky studied at Moscow State University, and the address given in chapter 7 as Kroshka's childhood home was Sinyavsky's parents' address in Moscow.[8] Both narrator and author are writers by profession, and the importance

---

[8] See *Kroshka Tsores*, 104. According to Viktoria Schweitzer, a friend of Sinyavsky's familiar with his life in the Soviet Union, the author and his parents lived at number 9, Khlebnij. From a personal conversation.

Kroshka attributes to his father by searching for him in his autobiography closely mirrors the critical role Sinyavsky's father will play in *Good Night*.

In his creative predicament Kroshka's relationship to Sinyavsky becomes more apparent. His text portrays the growing internal exile of a writer confined to an environment restricting his literary consciousness. The double set of problems Sinyavsky confronted when he discovered his other self, Abram Tertz, while still in the Soviet Union plague and eventually silence Kroshka. Tertz's creativity demanded liberation, but Sinyavsky was trapped in a society antipathetic to his notion of fiction. As we will see in *Good Night*, Sinyavsky develops his autobiography in the novelistic form because his self, to the extent that he believes in the existence of any single self, includes Sinyavsky and Tertz. Kroshka combines the dilemma of both egos. Externally, he is isolated in society; inwardly, his aesthetic capability proves elusive, frustrating his efforts to construct an autobiography according to traditional precepts. Kroshka is a paradigm of modern literary problematics whose dilemma lacks a solution. He is both discontent with his world and dissatisfied with the limitations of his medium.

As frequently occurs after reading any modernist work, the reader senses desolation, not victory, in the conclusion. Kroshka's own failure to construct a self, to come to terms with his experience, the experience of language he begins on page one, reflects Sinyavsky's ambivalence toward his character. We too are torn between sympathy for Kroshka, the deprived progeny of Gogol's small men, and rejection of his autobiography as an act of supreme self-indulgence and self-pity.

Were Kroshka Tsores purely fictional, the reader could dismiss him as a pathetic antihero. But Kroshka is Sinyavsky, not in a traditional historical sense but in a modernist allegorical construct of self and consciousness. Sinyavsky develops Kroshka to imitate his own creative mind, to illustrate Tertz rather than a set of historical events. In fact, the events are purposely made transparently fictional to prevent the reader from judging Kroshka's, and hence Sinyavsky's, ''I'' in conventional autobiographical terms. Sinyavsky's method expands Nabokov's understanding of autobiography as the discovery of patterns in memory, the creation of texture in the life fabric. Sinyavsky highlights the design, his consciousness, by using it to fabricate the life itself. With his emphasis on the self as cognitive rather than active, autobiography suddenly becomes profoundly creative, true only to the author's own autobiographical sensibility. Truth and fiction cease to be mutually exclusive.

At the same time we realize that Sinyavsky's exploration of the autobiographical terrain cannot end in this work. Just as Kroshka's nocturnal world depends on the oppressive nature of its daytime counterpart for its vibrancy, Tertz, we assume, must somehow rely on Sinyavsky's life events. Apparent in *A Voice from the Chorus* is prison's impact on the author's literary mind, Tertz's benefit from Sinyavsky's fate. *Kroshka Tsores* allows Tertz to experiment with his creative approach to autobiography. What remains, and what Sinyavsky attempts in *Good Night*, is to apply Tertz to Sinyavsky himself.

. . .

Good Night comprises the third and most recent portion of Sinyavsky's autobiographical tryptich, all produced since Sinyavsky's emigration from the Soviet Union. By focusing on the writer's history of persecution in the Soviet Union, this latest book appears to be the novel Western readers have come to expect from Russian writers hostile to the Soviet system. Conditioned by works such as Solzhenitsyn's *Gulag Archipelago*, we anticipate Sinyavsky's story: the "show trial," the persecution of a man for his ideas, the subhuman life of the prison world. What else but realistic portrayal of a life could emerge from such a sobering history? But the title itself should create doubt in the reader's preconceived version of *Good Night*. It carries neither the heavy fist of "labor camp" ("gulag") nor the somber tone of a memoir. *Good Night* might imply reconciliation, resignation, or indifference. Whatever its meaning, and there may be several, the book signals a new type of life history in the series of dissident Russian writers' accounts of Soviet existence.

Tertz has "rewritten" Sinyavsky's life into a profoundly fictive work that addresses fundamental literary, rather than historical, concerns, as this discussion and some close textual readings of *Good Night* will show. The text of *Good Night* enacts a literary discourse encompassing the autobiographical genre, modernist notions of consciousness and the self, the ancient Russian literary form of the fairy tale (skazka), and Sinyavsky's exploration of the limits of his medium, language. *Good Night* is the most wildly experimental and provocative work of the triptych.

The mere physical appearance of the work suggests the author's multiple creative impulses. When referring to the text as a text, the reader must include not only the black type dominating the five chapters but also the red type that occasionally transports the reader to another narrative level and the drawings, carefully chosen from letters of Mariya to her husband Sinyavsky while in a Soviet labor camp. One reviewer attempts to encompass this multimedia presentation in the phrase "polygraphic *poema*."[9] Describing the book as a "poema" appropriately evokes one of Sinyavsky's literary ancestors, Gogol, who used this term to subtitle *Dead Souls*. In this work "text" signifies the words on the page and also the look of the pages, the alternations in ink color, the occasionally wild punctuation, and those caricatures. All combine to envelop the reader in a textual aura, not only in an act of reading. Tertz writing in Paris treats Sinyavsky's history in a variety of forms. The result, *Good*

---

[9] S. Maksudov, "*Spokojnoj nochi* s Dobrym Utrom," *Strana i mir* 10 (1984): 94.

Night, represents a thickly textured work, more like an oil painting with impasto than a smooth watercolor surface.

What, then, is the self presented here? In contrast to the traditional autobiography's movement, to Augustine's sense of a developing self through time, Sinyavsky's self does not mature. This avoidance of the progressive self is evident in the novel's structure. Chapters 2, 3, and 4 seem to float autonomously; each is dislocated from the text as a whole and from the preceding and subsequent chapters, while chapter 5 gives the causes (smuggling literature and Serezha the informant) for the result (Sinyavsky's arrest) detailed in chapter 1. In traditional autobiography, in fact, the first chapter would be the last, the culmination of the author's "I" realizing it will have to suffer for its attachment to literature. But there is no such moral to Sinyavsky's personal history, no clear direction because "in a book, in a true book, the horseman is always headless."[10] The chapters suggest an author who does more wandering in search of a self than cohesive self-development.

The question posed is deceptively simple because it implies a single, definable, and hence identifiable self. Sinyavsky chooses to explore the autobiographical terrain, not to settle a single self there. The growth is perhaps more horizontal than vertical; his self does not grow up, it expands. in chapter 1 the reader has one sense of the narrator, but chapter 2's opening breaks the reader away from the first chapter, presenting the voice as a new, independent one: "Did it ever happen for you, kind reader, to be in the Meeting House? If not, allow me for the beginning, for the comfort of the narration, to describe'to you this modest hotel of a barrack sort, adjacent to the watch and entrance area, on the border of the prison-camp zone and the unrestricted public road" (107). Chapter 2 is introduced to emphasize its strictly coincidental relationship to chapter 1. Sinyavsky's self speaks in several voices; his consciousness is articulated not by a coherent, unified self but by several narrative voices.

The text at all levels illustrates continuous bifurcation and plurality of sensibility rather than delineation of a single persona. Interrupting the black text of chapter 1, the (feerija) provides a motif for Sinyavsky's difficult in grasping any single representation of his self. Normally a ballet using a fairy-tale's story, Sinyavsky's feerija is based on a KGB interrogation. Literally, the interrogation is a search for "Who are you?"—an effort to expose Sinyavsky's hidden self, Abram Tertz. But Sinyavsky treats this scene fantastically, including a round dance by the interrogator's henchmen and a linguistic battle between third and first person (between "On" and "Ja") over Chekhov and Pushkin, who become "Pekhov" and "Chushkin."

Thus, the process of discovering self is completely destabilized to remove the possibility of any facile answers to the identity question. The historical importance of the interrogation becomes not drama but comedy, play, the au-

---

[10] "V knige, v istinoj knige, vsadnik vsegda bez golovy" (245).

thor's farce at the expense of his interrogators. Each chapter provides Sinyavsky another environment against which to juxtapose his self, but because the chapters are not connected the reader perceives many self-images. Kroshka Tsores, although his sense of self ultimately explodes, attempts to develop himself by connecting the incidents of the five brothers' deaths. In *Good Night* Sinyavsky tackles the autobiographical process one step closer to its root by not assuming any self-coherence.

Events in the Sinyavskian consciousness lead more to numerous echoes than to a single reverberation. Each chapter can be treated as a moment, a separate unit around which Sinyavsky collects a variety of impulses. For example, chapter 4, "Dangerous Connections" ("Opasnye svjazi"), focuses on an event, Stalin's death, to portray Sinyavsky's consciousness. "Dangerous connections" probably refers to the associations Tertz's mind develops in this chapter. Tertz weaves an account of Sinyavsky in Moscow at the time of Stalin's death with two story lines presented in red type: the Time of Troubles told from the torturer's perspective, and the Second Coming, complete with Christ "looking like a gorilla' and John the Baptist's head carried on a platter by the beheaded John. The entire chapter evokes a mood of defamiliarization (ostranenie), which combines Bulgakov's fantastic parody of, and Tolstoy's interest in, history into what can only be called historical unreality. One should not read the term too somberly; Tertz is playing here, as elsewhere in the text. He laughs wildly, not viciously.[11]

Instead of using an event, the final chapter, "In the Belly of the White Whale" ("Vo chreve kitovom"), forms around a location. This chapter provides the reader with the background to the arrest that occurs in the book's opening sentence. Here the cycle is completed with analysis of the informer Serezha and the Frenchwoman Hélène who smuggles out Tertz's literature. Sinyavsky praises Serezha as an artistic genius and destroys him for his hollow soul feeding on the power derived from others' destruction. Yet Sinyavasky cannot treat even this subject conventionally. He denies himself the moral judgment by reversing the situation *and* the reader's expectations: "I used him. Yes, used him—in the capacity of an informer, and this, as you will further read, saved me. My informer, in retrospect, under control, in certain terms, was a godsend. And although friendship subsided, we continued to meet, and, it seems, he in his warm-hearted simplicity trusted me, but I, like a devil, began to deceive him" (381).

Tertz revels in those convolutions of reality. He can express pity for Pa-

---

[11] For his unconventional treatment of an event few Russians, Soviet or émigré, dare to laugh at, Sinyavsky has been reviled both inside and outside the Soviet Union. Emigré contempt for him has even led to accusations that he was planted by the KGB in the West to upset and divide the émigré community. Sinyavsky himself refers to his period in emigration as "the second judgment of Abram Tertz." See Andrey Sinyavsky, "Andrey Sinyavsky o sebe" in Olga Matich, ed., *The Third Wave: Russian Literature in Emigration* (Ann Arbor: Ardis Publishers, 1984), 108.

khomov, his interrogator, or apologize for baiting Serezha into acting as his informer. He is, really, playing with his alter ego's life. But more importantly, Tertz is laughing at his audience's canons, whether historical, religious, or autobiographical. The laughter expresses the author's exhilaration at escaping the confines of the traditional camp epic. Tertz perpetually guards Sinyavsky's text from solidifying into conformity. Only in the book's closing paragraph does this continual, almost desperate instability of reality in the consciousness seem to recede. Returning from Venice with his "escorts," Sinyavsky falls asleep on the train—or perhaps Tertz comes to terms with Sinyavsky—with an extended reverie to the night's long-awaited peace.

The highly allusive narration in each chapter complements the chronologically and visually frenetic nature of the text. The frequent ellipses suggest transitions the author cannot stop to write on his literary flight from, for example, Moscow to "In France I now have . . ." ("U menja sejchas vo Frantsii . . ."). Each successive association relies on the previous one for its impetus; episodes unfold within scenes, thoughts within reflections that are themselves moments in other events. The reader has to climb continually in and out of these many levels of text to keep pace with the author.

. . .

Language in Sinyavsky's narration becomes a dynamic medium as diverse thoughts commingle in the author's mind. The autobiographical act, for Sinyavsky, finally must be an engagement with language. His metaphors are as elaborate as Kroshka's, and sometimes Sinyavsky appears to drown in them. An example of this occurs in chapter 2, where a casual remark about the *Macbeth* witches made in a banquet toast at the Prague Restaurant transforms itself into a lengthy paragraph analyzing Macbeth's and Prince Oleg's fates, which in turn leads Sinyavsky to an extended description of the Swiss Alps.[12]

Although perhaps related to Sinyavsky's efforts to discover the authorities' information about Tertz's identity described earlier in the chapter, the choice and development of these literary allusions exceeds any simple analogy to Sinyavsky's life. Shakespeare and Pushkin can only spectate as Tertz highlights the surreal elements in their heroes' downfalls. He reveals not Macduff's role in Macbeth's death but the forest's approaching Macbeth "like a wall" ("pojdet stenoju"). Appropriately, the section itself creates a linguistic labyrinth; the sentences are long and extremely complex.

Emerging from this dense section of the passage, Sinyavsky turns a literary forest into an actual one in the Swiss Alps, which quickly becomes another

---

[12] The passage discussed in this section appears on pages 142–46 of the novel. See *Macbeth*, act 4, sc.1 and, for the Pushkin poem, "Pesn' o veshchem Olege," *Izbrannye proizvedenija v dvukh tomakh* (Moscow: Izdatel'stvo Khudozhestvennaja literatura, 1965).

metaphor. Tertz moves the reader to this paragraph with one of his character-istic ellipses, leaving the transition to the reader. In this paragraph the forest takes on another role, representing not man's fate but the man who tries to surpass his limits. The Alps serve as a symbol for the unattainable heights that the individual, caught in a Sisyphean predicament, nonetheless must attempt to reach in his own way. As these figures develop, it becomes apparent that Sinyavsky is referring to the writer and his encounter with language, his strug-gle to overcome its boundaries. Initially the forest attempts to move against the mountain, climbing up it:

> The forest could not prevail; it was not within his strength, and he was falling in battle, he sacrificed himself for the sake of the maintenance of the aforesaid burst, executed, it seemed, in agreement with the mountain, who owed him an easy, feath-ered ascent to the heavenly hall, from whence, suddenly turning, baring her teeth, she [the mountain] threw him back with cold indignation, like a feeble literature no longer needed by her and unstitched by her height. (145)[13]

"Literature" ("slovesnost' ") is the critical word here, suggesting that the for-est represents the literary act, an expression that seeks to overcome its moun-tainous obstacle, namely language.

The function of "forest" in this section seems to illustrate the point. Not only does this word occur frequently in the rest of the text, especially in the sections on the fairy tale and the father, but within these few pages it con-stantly evokes new meanings. First it represents Birnham Wood, then the hand of fate, then a force that seeks to defy human limits, and ultimately a specific subject, literature. We cannot say what the forest is in this section; it meta-morphoses to accommodate Sinyavsky's fluid sense of language. The rhetoric is as intricate as the prophecies, whose subtleties escape Oleg and Macbeth. The author even joins the reader in his utter desperation after attempting to understand the allusive powers of speech.

> But here it was revealed to me, as if it were my sorrow, the impertinence and incon-clusiveness of speech, on which hangs, clings, and is lost for nothing every authorial design. And that which we from want of habit take for style, for artistic peculiarities, is all only an attempt, in turn doomed to failure, to go beyond the boundaries of language and space allotted to us and either by frontal attack or roundabout maneu-ver to speak, at last, about things not subject to disclosure. The discourse is about the inaccessible. (146)[14]

---

[13] "Les ne mog odolet', emu bylo ne pod silu, i on lozhilsja kost'mi, on zhertvoval soboju radi podderzhanija oznachennogo ryvka, proizvedennogo, kazalos', v soglasii s goroj, objazannoj emu legkim, operennym voskhozhdeniem v nebesnyj chertog, otkuda, vnezapno oborotjas', oskoljas', ona otbrasyvala ego s kholodynm negodovaniem, kak nenuzhnuju ej bol'she i podporchennuju ee vysotoj nemoshchnuju slovesnost'."

[14] "No tut zhe mne otkryvalis', slovno eto moja pechal', derzost' i neokonchatel'nost' rechi, na chem visit, lepitsja i propadaet vpustuju vsjakij avtorskij zamysel. I to, chto my s neprivychki

At these moments the multilayered prose nearly suffocates the possibility of meaning, and Sinyavsky becomes a more sophisticated version of Kroshka in the imminence of death, silence from a stuttering pen. We feel the intensity of the battle, at times Pyrrhic, with language, in addition to Tertz's refined literary sense, as he tries to report what begins as a simple episode.

The discussion is indeed about the inaccessible and is itself remote. But these textually opaque portions of the book are the most exciting passages for the reader who can afford to climb the mountain because they illustrate the complex hybrid mentality, combining the reality of literature and fictiousness of reality and the ripples of significance any event can have in Sinyavsky's consciousness. Sinyavsky manipulates two classic literary events to show the arbitrary quality of truth. Like writers of literary fairy tales, especially Gogol, Sinyavsky plays with his material directly in front of the reader.[15] Macbeth and Prince Oleg are used to begin Sinyavsky's own fairy tale, replete with moving forests and evil mountains. One cannot accurately describe the reference to *Macbeth* as merely an allusion to Shakespeare because Tertz openly imposes his voice on Macbeth's story.

A toast specifically located at the Prague Restaurant in Moscow thus devolves, becoming more abstract until it is finally inaccessible even for the author, who never returns to the scene he left so abruptly. The banquet is itself removed from the chapter's location in the Meeting House. Folklore, literature, nature, and reality are intertwined, and the passage is as provocative as it is difficult. Meanwhile, stunned by this "logic," the reader is left back in Moscow waiting for the speaker to finish his toast and wondering where narrator and character, Tertz and Sinyavsky, have gone. Sinyavsky does not outline the rules of his autobiography's universe; the closest he comes to explaining his method of self-construction is in defining the literary process itself, which to him is essentially mysterious. Sinyavsky's creativity works in the text without exterior boundaries. Even language may succumb to his imagination: "To devise, in the extreme event, if necessary, a language intelligible to no one. . . . And, while dying, to know that all the words were placed correctly" (86). The reader is left with a text that alternates between comprehensibility and confusion, articulation and ineffability. Language, as it does in the *Macbeth* passage just discussed, intrudes as an independent force, a

---

prinimaem za slog, za khudozhestvennye osobennosti, vsego lish' ocherednaja i obrechennaja na neudachu popytka vyjti za predely otvedennogo nam jazyka i prostranstva i v lob ili obkhodnym manevrom skazat', nakonets, o veshchakh, ne podlezhashchikh razglasheniju. Rech' idet o nedostupnom."

[15] James M. Holquist in an insightful article, "The Devil in Mufti: The *Marchenwelt* in Gogol's Short Stories," *PMLA* 82 (1967): 352–62, uses the German tradition to propose that literary fairy tales rely on an unsettled reality and the author's often arbitrary transformations of it. See particularly page 354. The fairytale (skazka) in Sinyavsky's work will be discussed later in this essay.

visitor who upsets Tertz and the reader as often as he consoles them. The self, we are told, is there, but can we ever really reach it?

Sinyavsky treats the autobiographical act as literal self-creation. Any unified, graspable self that either reader or writer discovers in the text is exclusive to that text. The book thus becomes fiction, in contrast to traditional autobiography. No stable definition of self is accepted; self only exists in the text. To the question "How, let us ask, can you make certain, before you have died, that you are a person, a person in truth, with your own irreplaceable soul and original body?" (375), Sinyavsky insists that "There are no criteria" ("Net kriteriev"). Any problem that the reader has in trying to search for Sinyavsky's self stems from an expectation that the self is not exclusively literary but something extrinsic to the autobiographical act, extant in the universe outside the text. Just as a novel presents a world of its own, Sinyavsky's self is constituted by his book; in fact, that self depends solely on the moment depicted in *Good Night*, not on any external construct.

These are all transitory images of a self, not absolute self-definition. They are poses of a consciousness not unlike the two masks that intellect dons in Sinyavsky's life—Abram Tertz and Andrey Sinyavsky. Throughout the text bifurcation of impression disrupts the narrative. Images slide together in Sinyavsky's consciousness, unconstrained by logic.

The Meeting House (Dom svidanij) chapter provides an illustration of this multileveled consciousness. Sinyavsky and his wife speak of trivial matters because they sense the guards' eavesdropping; meanwhile they write notes in the air to each other, and Sinyavsky simultaneously intersperses conversations he overhears in the other rooms of the meeting house. Multiplicity of perception characterizes the entire section.

> Or had she simply tired of this compulsory game on two, on three, levels of consciousness, where the mouse and the serpent alternate, changing places, and the zone with its phantoms constitutes not a surrounding but, if you like, a style and stimulus for a still unwritten book. . . .
>
> I recognize that whether I am telling about the Buchenwald alarm, or about Postnikov with his mysterious film, which I attempt to catch—about anything—everything, absolutely everything, assumes in my exposition a mocked and bifurcated form. (169)

This sharpened perception does not clarify a moment but splits it. Sinyavsky's life and Tertz's creativity produce double vision, a perpetual fission of impressions in the consciousness. Instead of a single meaning. Sinyavsky divines rhythm in his life, the pace of these collisions sparked by a single event in his consciousness. The Meeting House chapter highlights the simultaneity of these impulses and also the difficulty of recreating such an intellect on paper. Truly this chain of mental impulses is Tertz's creative stimulation from an external event, his mocking of Sinyavsky's life. And prison, for which

Sinyavsky says he is grateful, provides a fertile environment for such a consciousness submerged in association and allusion. "I have never encountered this style, this rhythm, this life-stimulus, as terrible, alluring, and gratifying as prison" (40). This assertion reflects Tertz's fascination with the Soviet prison's otherworldliness. Authors such as Bulgakov also found a fantastic chord in the harsh melody of Soviet reality. Sinyavsky, however, uses his statement as much for its provocative negation of the camp-story genre. He becomes all the more modernist because the tradition he flaunts is well-established despite its youth.

Sinyavsky replaces the traditional autobiographer's "meaning" of life with this rhythm, offering not conclusion but association, metaphor. The "Meeting House" can in fact be seen as Sinyavsky's mind, which serves as a meeting house for divergent images, distinct moments in time drawn together by the pen. Such a consciousness is not solid but amorphous, such a self is not fixed but elusive. The reader must abandon his desire to establish the author's self as a point in time; rather, Sinyavsky treats his consciousness as an expanse unfolding in space. Sinyavsky struggles in *Good Night* because he has too many sensibilities to unite. His self spills out across the pages, defying coherence and confinement.

Sinyavsky does not deny the existence of his life, instead he rejects the identification of a single self with that life. In reading the chapters as individual vignettes of the self, images that depend for their illumination on the setting, the very individuality of these portraits distinguishes *Good Night* as a modern autobiography. Growth of the self, implying progression, is replaced by movement from one pose to the next not necessarily for the sake of development of a cohesive self but simly for that motion.

Starting with an investigation of the sense of identity articulated by the author in his work, we have either come very far or gone nowhere. Either these disparate images, related without transitions to connect them, form a whole, a self, which the reader must piece together much in the way that he might reconstruct Picasso's cubism to create a recognizable figure, or they remain disparate and fundamentally irreconcilable. There seems little justification in a reader's supplying meaning where the author has deliberately refrained from doing so. Picasso's motivation in abandoning traditional practices was not to test the viewer's ability to reconstruct in traditional terms of perspective but to challenge the viewer to be aware of the artifice of those terms and of his dependence on them by proposing another system. On the other hand, do we simply abandon these five vignettes to irreconcilability when we know that a single, nonschizophrenic persona lies behind them? Either we have discovered a self that is profoundly complex or that very complexity confounds any possibility of definition as "self."

These doubts reflect Sinyavsky's own anxiety over any stable definition of self and an accompanying modern distrust of the traditional autobiography's tenets. *Good Night* is structured around a series of reversals undermining the authority of the ostensibly self-obvious autobiographical axioms: fantasy vs. history, fiction vs. autobiography, imagination vs. memory. Juxtapositions of the unreal with the real pervade every level of the text, from the red and black type to the narration of an episode.

Sinyavsky plays the literary alchemist, pouring fantasy into reality instead of acknowledging their separate domains. The one envelops the other; the novel's world is just that—unique to the novel, neither exclusively literary nor literal. Thus, although no inaccuracies whatsoever of Sinyavsky's historical life are reported in *Good Night*,[16] the reader soon realizes that history is not the only factor here, that events in any autobiography are subject to interpretation, and Sinyavsky exploits this freedom to interpret. The opening sentence, "I was taken" ("Menja vzjali"), arrests Sinyavsky into the Soviet prison world and seizes the reader, confining him to the world of Sinyavsky's consciousness. Tertz's creativity, on the other hand, is stimulated, not incarcerated, by its alter ego's travails.

. . .

Unable to accept the conventional view of a stable self, Sinyavsky turns to a more primitive form of art, the fairy tale, to find his literary roots. It is important to note that the author's discovery of the fairytale as a literary ancestor occurs in the book's central chapter, "Father." This chapter is noticeably different in tone and difficulty from the others. Although the chronology is typically Sinyavskian, the narration is almost nostalgic and comprehensible on a first reading. Chapter 3 occurs in the forest—the father remains largely anonymous and distant. In fact, the discovery of his literary sensibility pulls Sinyavsky away from his father. The chapter ends on a note of separation, a communication gap between the emerging writer and his parent, who fears the KGB listens to his thoughts. In turning to his own literary world, to the fairy tale, Sinyavsky seems to cut himself off from any definitive link to his own roots, just as Kroshka's nighttime exploits continually displaced him from his family.

Sinyavsky relishes the fairy tale's authority to create its own reality and its own truth:

> The fairy tale imparts to everything order and foundation. It is in no way a dream. It starts like Volodya, from the ordinary, like it happens in life, like you and I live, eat bread. Once upon a time there lived. An old man and his wife. It's always good for the rich. The pauper appears everywhere in a bad way. The rich man has a castle.

---

[16] Viktoria Schweitzer can even identify the woman who in chapter 4 has the dream about Stalin's ghost visiting her to ask forgiveness. From a personal conversation.

The pauper lives in squalor. The rich man has a wife in pearls. The pauper—a frog. The rich man is as wise as Solomon. And the poor man is a fool's fool.

—No—says the fairy tale—not true, not right. All this seems so to you. And I pretended. This is only the preparation, the introduction. We haven't even reached the middle. In any event, you will see, everything will not be this way. (273–74)

The authority of that denial and the emphasis on "seeming" over "being" assert the fantastic not as impossible but as real and more provocative than factual reality. The fairy tale relies on reality, on the rich man and the poor man, in order to restructure it. The fairy tale responds to reality with its own terms, not unlike the relationship between Kroshka's noctural fantasies and his daytime world or between Sinyavsky's modern treatment of autobiography and the autobiographical tradition. The fairy tale represents not so much escape as a different means of treating the same environment, a new perspective and hence a new truth system.

Sinyavsky's emphasis on the power of the fairy tale allows him to challenge canons of both Soviet dissident literature and autobiography. Even the most harsh reality can be mitigated; a KGB interrogation becomes a fairy-tale ballet (feerija), Stalinist Russia is parodied in juxtaposition to the Second Coming, and Lefortovo Prison, the "belly of the whale," is a creative enigma for Tertz. In each case symbols of absolute terror mingle with the author's vivid humor.[17] Tertz's creative consciousness rebels against the somber morality traditionally used in émigré literature when depicting these images of Soviet power, and he rebels because that morality has itself amassed a degree of authority in Western émigré literature. Similarly, his textual world demystifies the autobiographical absolutes of "truth," "self," and "life" by playing with all three.

Sinyavsky expands his rejection of the common autobiographical sensibility by incorporating into *Good Night* not only a text but discussions of the creation of that text. These passages undermine the authority of the author himself by depicting art as possessor of people, not vice versa. In the course of writing his novel, Sinyavsky addresses it in the intimate "you" form, coaches it, begs it, and even walks with it.[18] The book in conception consumes the personality composing it:

And it is also important to have time to say: when you write, you must not think. It is necessary to exclude yourself. When you are writing, you get lost, stray, but mainly you forget yourself and live, not thinking about anything. And how fine this is! At last you are not, you—died. Alone is the forest. And we sink into the forest. We sink into the text.

---

[17] This fluctuation is another quality that Holquist identifies as a characteristic of the literary fairy tale. See Holquist, "The Devil in Mufti," 352.

[18] See, for example, 87 in *Spokojnoj nochi*.

Because of this it is most important that in the book you are writing there exists
mystery. For the author, for you. She [the mystery] somehow awakes, she somehow
departs and quietly does her invisible task. (262)[19]

The novel creates its own world and takes on its own life. The powers of art,
but primarily Sinyavsky's insistence that his self is lost, confused, excluded,
even, perhaps, nonexistent when he writes, finally destroys the possibility of
traditional autobiography in literature. Literary creation demands defacement
of the author, the receiver of its impulses who is himself consumed by the
world created in the text.

Traditional autobiography more than other types of literature relies on the
author's ability to control his material—to select experiences from his life that
create and sustain a logical self. Sinyavsky's art, however, precludes such a
conscious selectivity because it is not subject to any external restraints, even
the will of the artist. The integrity of the text must not be violated by an author
imposing his system, his desires, or his goals on it. Indeed, the reader senses
himself closer to the Tertz who struggles with the text in Paris than to the "I,"
Sinyavsky, who acts out the drama, because this question of narrative control
continually arises. Tertz interrupts himself, warning "not all at once," wor-
rying that "I won't succeed," confessing that "all these camp stories burst
me open," and even when fewer than thirty pages remain, realizing that "I
keep running ahead."[20]

The autobiographical act reproduced in *Good Night* expands as the text develops. The identity question "Who am I?" cannot be resolved without Tertz
investigating other questions: "What is a writer?" and "Whose book is this?"
The process of articulation proves difficult at best; we have an image of Sinyavsky as the linguistic Don Quixote, slaying word-dragons, attacking for-
tresses that are actually sentences.

These complexities rapidly emerge in a book that begins with the simple
declarative, "It was at the Nikita Gates, when I was taken" ("Eto bylo u
Nikitskikh vorot, kogda menja vzjali"). *Good Night* contains an expansive
interior architecture, not unlike the design of Lefortovo prison:

But in the image of prose, this is Lefortovo. . . . Excuse me, I am sure that nobody
appreciates the reserves of the structure. Nobody guesses how great is its cage, hidden from the observer. Is it really possible, you will ask, for that which is within to

---

[19] "Eshche tozhe vazhno uspet' skazat': kogda pishesh', nel'zja dumat'. Nuzhno vykljuchit'
sebja. Kogda pishesh'—terjaesh'sja, putaesh', no glavnoe—zabyvaesh' sebja i zhivesh', ni o
chem ne dumaja. I kak eto prekrasno! Tebja net nakonets, ty-umer. Odin les. I my ukhodim v les.
Ukhodim v tekst.

Poetomu samoe vazhnoe, chtoby v knige, kotoruju pishesh', byla tainstvennost'. Dlja avtora,
dlja tebja. Ona-to i pobuzhdaet, ona-to i tjanet ukhodit' i tikho delat' svoe nevidimoe delo."

[20] The last expression occurs on 418.

be immeasurably more vast than that which you survey from the outside? In Lefortovo I became convinced: it's possible. (371–72)

Submerging oneself in the belly of the whale to better comprehend the beast is no less terrifying than the exploration of Lefortovo's inner walls—or the infrastructure of language. Kroshka's autobiography represents a hollow shell, a structure he attempts to build but of which he is too literarily pristine to detect the faults; his autobiography collapses. *Good Night* at first glance appears to be a typical camp memoir; its author, however, embarks on a more fantastic journey through his own interior, his consciousness, once the text begins. Both Kroshka and Sinyavsky promise simplicity and conformity in their autobiographies' openings; neither sustains these expectations.

We have, then, turned an investigation of a text's autobiographical notion into an exploration of an author's coming to terms with a nontraditional, highly fluid sense of self that eludes both reader and writer in the text. In this sense Sinyavsky fails as a traditional autobiographer; he seems unable to control both form and content—the literary act and his own memory threaten to burst him at any time. But the failure rests more accurately in the reader's search for the autobiography, in the desire to separate Andrey Sinyavsky from the novel in which Tertz places him. By attempting to extract the self from the text's world, the twentieth-century reader repeats the mistake of those nineteenth-century literary heroines who, having read romantic novels, sought to act them out in reality. Remember, Sinyavsky warns us in bold print on the title page, this is a *novel*.

Yet why does this writer confront the autobiographical mode at all? The intent for Sinyavsky in writing *Good Night* is not to find a stable self; both he and Kroshka Tsores avoid stability. Instead the text and the act of writing become meaningful for the process, the creative endeavor allowing the author to redefine reality—Sinyavsky to experience other lives and Tertz to experiment linguistically. Such an exploratory desire leads Sinyavsky in chapter 4 to multivolume history books at the Lenin Library:

With them you experience long life, having forgotten about your transitoriness. Vasco da Gama rounds the Cape of Good Hope. Magellan. Oh, how long this drags on! You rest contentedly, reading. You resolve to live forever. And calming myself, I fall asleep: he rounds, Magellan! . . .

These are books exclusively about the duration of the voyage. In the duration is the sense and style. (292)

The opening sentence, "I was taken" ("menja vzjali"), assumes another meaning for the author imprisoned in this text, confined until some expression is found. Tertz is, in fact, "taken," not by the KGB but by his own writing. In such a creative world the author becomes a literary explorer of the universe.

In the exploration lies the significance of the act. And exploration brings liberation for the traveler from all that which previously constrained him. *Good Night* is for its author a liberating act; autobiography becomes not confinement of a persona to a single self but liberation of consciousness. Tertz the writer defies all generic conventions. He disrupts his text with two-color type, the violated fictional forms contained in the red sections question assumptions about the appropriateness and relevance of literary canons, and the autobiographical and novelistic modes are so finely woven together that they become inseparable. History cannot be distinguished from personal vision in Sinyavsky. Similarly the Soviet dissident liberates himself from the necessity of recording his life, of becoming only another witness of his era, instead of remaining the artist that he is.

Good Night concludes with a modern hymn to the night, suggesting a writer at last at peace with his text. As Sinyavsky returns to Moscow on, of course, a train, the writer, soon to be arrested, ironically feels himself released. The title's significance becomes apparent when Sinyavsky finally sleeps, departing from the literary womb and returning to humanity, "to be like all people" ("Byt' kak vse ljudi," 444). Perhaps the night becomes calm because Tertz succeeds in reshaping Sinyavsky's experiences, in exorcising them from history by subjecting them to his creative consciousness. This apparent last word, however, lacks the sense of a definite conclusion to Sinyavsky's journey. Immediately preceding this passage Sinyavsky refers several times to the cognac he has drunk with his escorts on the train and its effort on his thoughts, even imagining that fire comes from his mouth. We want to read the closing image in terms of salvation or resurrection, not alcoholic hallucination; we want to regard the final ellipsis not as Kroshka's muteness but as Sinyavsky's tranquillity. And we can do this; Sinyavsky extends the last paragraph's poetic prose to remove it from the setting. Still the doubt lingers, especially in light of all the questions the previous 450 pages have posed. If Sinyavsky requires one task of his readers, it is to be aware, and wary, of the conventions readers bring to texts.

At the end Tertz and Sinyavsky leave the book much as Gogol departs from the first part of *Dead Souls* on his fiery troika. Kroshka too distinctly removes himself from his narrative as he becomes a stuttering old man. But the departure in *Good Night* represents more release from confinement than desperation; the freedom lies in Sinyavsky's not containing his self in a single text. The author, like a vapor or the evening mist, vanishes from his romantic world of the fairy tale, whose linguistic demons have pursued him throughout the text, as spontaneously as he was taken into it.

.   .   .

From this study of Sinyavsky's most recent work, one can see that the continued importance of Tertz, initially a political necessity to escape arrest, suggests an existential and an aesthetic reality in Sinyavsky's literature. The two names help the reader to comprehend a bifurcated self, the dynamic between a more factual historical world and the writer's creative energy. Tertz is a metaphor, a device for conveying to the reader a more complex Sinyavskian view of the self and reality. The convenience lies in the license Sinyavsky gives to Tertz to roam the literary terrain, rewrite history, predict the future, and compose fairy tales. Ultimately, there are not two of Andrey Sinyavsky but a single "I," constantly changing, who mediates the Tertz-Sinyavsky exchange internally. "The 'I' is a particle which, while endlessly crying out 'Give! Give!' at the same time searches mutely for a way to get rid of itself. The personality hovers in an unstable balance between life and death."[21] For Sinyavsky, confinement to a permanent, supratextual "I" would paralyze his literary agility; thus Kroshka's efforts to find his father end only in linguistic decay. Yet paradoxically the "I" cannot be avoided; that delicate balancing of the "I" between life and death is the same tenuous quality Sinyavsky attributes to the act of composition. Like other modern writers, he realizes that to engage in the literary act is inevitably to attempt the autobiographical act in some form.

In the end Tertz and Sinyavsky seem to coexist in a state of wary equilibrium within this author. Tertz began in the 1960s with fantastic stories, tales only allegorically referring to their author's life. But the nature of this contemporary autobiographical trilogy in emigration, beginning with *A Voice from the Chorus*, clearly suggests a more conscious engagement with the author's own fate, Sinyavsky's personal history. *Kroshka Tsores* and *Good Night* are, in fact, this author's witness tales. The student of Tertz's creativity, however, rebels against the word "witness" because of the names it evokes, with Pavlovian immediacy, for most Western readers: Aleksandr Solzhenitsyn, Nadezhda Mandelstam, and Lydia Chukovskaya. Although the *gulag* cliché of freedom in captivity may very well apply to Sinyavsky's camp years, this author's creative stimulation from imprisonment remains quite distinct from the moral conclusions others have drawn from similar fates.

Yet despite Sinyavsky's radically different presentation, he belies a commitment to his tradition in a broad sense. Tertz writes about Sinyavsky, about Russia in its Soviet context. The implicit model of this essay parallels Sinyavsky's own metaphor, picking his voice from the chorus of his émigré and Russian literary traditions. But the metaphor finally undermines itself. Sinyavsky remains vitally linked to these two, a commitment suggested by his return to Moscow in the last scene of *Good Night*. Kroshka's autobiography might be described as the imposing of Gogol's "Diary of a Madman" on a modern literary and historical context: both main characters are writers, both are small men, the romantic one goes insane, his modern counterpart's self deteriorates.

---

[21] *A Voice from the Chorus*, 73.

Sinyavsky's provocative treatment of many conventions—autobiography, the émigré tradition, and Russian literature—suggest a desire to establish his place in each of these. Yes, his voice projects from its background, but it simultaneously broadens the range of the chorus to include the author's aesthetic.

We are left with several echoes, the literary poses of a consciousness, each true in its unique environment. The multiplicity of presentations of the self is more important than any progression one might read in them. To propose that Sinyavsky in *Good Night* realizes an autobiographical sensibility would be to attempt what this author demands that we not do—confine his consciousness. Any final autobiographical method necessarily establishes one position of the consciousness, one self; such a static position implies death, because, for Sinyavsky, statis is death. *Good Night* is not an epitaph; it signals freedom instead of conclusion because the intellect succeeds in treating the life without becoming consumed by it. Tertz the explorer wanders through Sinyavsky's history, evading its envelopment. Tertz is a ghost; neither the Soviet authorities nor any one text can catch him. In stark contrast to the centralized monstrosity of official Soviet literature, a Leviathan trudging along, at best, ever so slowly, Tertz is whimsical and vibrant. The consciousness exceeds the historical life in which it resides, even if it always relies on that life, as Tertz does in these books.

Select Bibliography

The following includes works cited in this volume plus a list of books and articles that may help to illuminate some of the theoretical or critical issues raised in this volume or suggest new avenues of research. When available, English translations of works cited in the essays are given along with the references to the original texts.

Aichinger, Ingrid. "Probleme der Autobiographie als Sprachkunstwerk." *Öesterreich in Geschichte und Literatur* (Vienna) 4 (1970): 418–34.

Amelia, Antonella d'. "Avtobiograficheskoe prostranstvo' Alekseja Mikhajlovicha Remizova. *Uchitel' muzyki*, i-xxxiii. Paris, 1983.

———. "K istorii sozdanija 'Uchitelja muzyki.' " *Uchitel' muzyki*, 555–67. Paris, 1953.

Appel, Alfred, Jr. *Nabokov's Dark Cinema*. New York: Oxford University Press, 1974.

———. The Annotated Lolita. New York: McGraw-Hill, 1970.

"L'Autobiographie." *Revue d'histoire littéraire de la France* 6 (1975).

"Autobiography." Edited by Christie Vance. *Genre* 6, nos. 1–2 (March and June 1973).

Avvakum. *Pustozerskij sbornik: Avtografy sochinenij Avvakuma i Epifanija*. Leningrad: Nauka, 1975.

Axthelm, Peter M. *The Modern Confessional Novel*. New Haven: Yale University Press, 1967.

Bakhtin, Mikhail M. "K metodologii literaturovedenija." *Kontekst* (1974).

———. "Forms of Time and the Chronotope." In *The Dialogic Imagination*, edited and translated by J. M. Holquist and C. Emerson. Austin: University of Texas Press, 1981.

Balburov, E. A. *Poetika liricheskoj prozy: 1960–1970g*. Novosibirsk: Nauka, 1985.

Ball, Hugo. *Flight out of Time: A Dada Diary*. Edited by J. Elderfield. Translated by A. Raimes. New York, 1974.

Barthes, Roland. "Introduction à l'analyse structurale des récits." *Communications* 8 (1966).

———. "The Death of the Author." *Image-Music-Text*. Translated by S. Heath. London: Fontana, 1977.

———. *Camera Lucida*. New York: Hill and Wang, 1981.

———. *A Barthes Reader*. New York: Hill and Wang, 1982.

———. *Roland Barthes*. New York: Hill and Wang, 1977. Original: Paris: Editions du Seuil, 1975.

Bates, Ernest S. *Inside Out: An Introduction to Autobiography*. 2 vols. Oxford: Oxford University Press, 1936–37.

Beaujour, Elizabeth K. *Olesha: The Invisible Land*. New York: Columbia University Press, 1970.

Beaujour, Michel. *Miroirs d'encre: Rhétorique de l'autoportrait*. Paris: Editions du Seuil, 1980.

Bely, Andrey. *Peterburg*. Edited by L. K. Dolgopolov. Moscow: Nauka, 1981.

―――. *The First Encounter*. Translated by G. Janacek. Princeton: Princeton University Press, 1979.

―――. *Selected Essays of Andrey Bely*. Translated by S. Cassedy. Berkeley: University of California Press, 1985.

―――. *Vospominanija ob A. A. Bloke. Zapiski mechtatelej* (Leningrad) 6 (1922): 5–122. Expanded version in *Epopeja* (Berlin)1–4 (1922–23). Reprint. Munich, 1969.

―――. *Nachalo veka*, partially published in "Iz knigi 'Nachalo veka' (Berlinskaja redaktsija)." *Voprosy literatury* 6 (1974): 214–44. Revised edition. Moscow: Khudozestvennaja literatura, 1933.

―――. *Mezhdu dvukh revoliutsii*. Leningrad: Izdatel'stvo Pisatelej, 1934. Reprint. Chicago: Russian Language Specialities, 1966.

―――. *Na rubezhe dvukh stoletii*. Moscow: Zemlja i fabrika, 1930. Reprint. Chicago: Russian Language Specialties, 1966.

―――. *Stikhotvorenija*. Edited by John Malmstad. 3 vols. Munich: Fink Verlag, 1969.

―――. *Petersburg*. English translation by R. Maguire and J. Malmstad. Bloomington, Ind.: Indiana University Press, 1978.

Berberova, Nina. *The Italics Are Mine*. Translated by P. Radley. New York: Harcourt, Brace and World, 1969.

Bergson, Henri. *Introduction to Metaphysics*. Translated by T. E. Hulme. New York, 1949. Original: Paris, 1903.

Berkovskij, N. "O proze Mandelstama." *Tekushchaja literatura*. Moscow: Federatsija, 1930.

Berthoff, Warner. "Witness and Testament: Two Contemporary Classics." *New Literary History* 2, no. 2 (Winter 1971): 311–27.

Belinkov, Arkady. *Sdacha i gibel' sovetskogo intelligenta: Iurij Olesha*. Madrid: private publisher, 1976.

Björling, Fiona. "Morality as History: An Analysis of Yuri Trifonov's Novel *Starik*." *Text and Context: Essays to Honor Nils Åke Nilsson*. Edited by Peter Alberg Jensen and Barbara Lönquist et al. Stockholm Studies in Russian Literature, no. 23. Stockholm: Almqvist and Wiksell, 1987.

Bloom, Harold. *Romanticism and Consciousness: Essays in Criticism*. New York: W. W. Norton, 1979.

Bocharov, A. "Energija Trifonovskoj prozy." *Jurij Trifonov. Povesti*. Moscow, 1978.

Bode, Ingrid. *Die Autobiographien zur deutschen Literatur, Kunst und Musik 1900–1965: Bibliographie und Nachweise der Personlichen begegnungen und Charakteristiken*. Stuttgart: J. B. Metzlersche Verlagbuchhandlung, 1966.

Booth, Wayne "Distance and Point of View: An Esssay in Classification," *Poetique* 4 (1970).

―――. *The Rhetoric of Fiction*. Chicago: University of Chicago Press, 1961.

Borel, Jacques. "Problemes de l'autobiographie." *Positions et oppositions sur le roman contemporain*. Edited by Michel Mansuy. Klincksieck: Actes du colloque de Strasbourg, 1971, 79–90.

Bottrall, Margaret. *Every Man a Phoenix: Studies in Seventeenth Century Autobiography*. London: J. Murray, 1958.

Bourgeois, René. "La signification du premier souvenir." *Actes du colloque sur l'autobiographie organisé par le Centre stendhalien de l'Université de langue et lettres de Grenoble*. Grenoble: Presses Universitaires de Grenoble, 1974.

Bree, Germaine. "The Breakup of Traditional Genres." *Bucknell Review* , 21, no. 2 (1973): 3–13.

Brignano, R. G. *Black Americans in Autobiography: A Bibliography*. Chapel Hill: Duke University Press, 1974.

Brooks, Jeffrey. "Readers and Reading at the End of the Tsarist Era." *Literature and Society in Imperial Russia: 1800–1914*. Edited by William Todd. Stanford, Calif.: Stanford University Press, 1978.

Brown, Clarence, ed. and trans. *The Noise of Time: The Prose of Osip Mandelstam*. San Francisco: North Point Press, 1986.

———. *The Viking Portable Twentieth Century Russian Reader*. New York: Viking Penguin Inc., 1985.

Brown, Edward J. *Russian Literature since the Revolution*. Revised edition. Cambridge, Mass.: Harvard University Press, 1982.

———. "The Exile Experience." In *Russian Literature in Emigration: The Third Wave*, edited by Olga Matich and Michael Heim, 53–61. Ann Arbor: Ardis, 1984.

Bruss, Elizabeth. "L'autobiographie considérée comme acte littéraire." *Poétique* 17 (1974).

———. *Autobiographical Acts: The Changing Situation of a Literary Genre*. Baltimore: Johns Hopkins University Press, 1976.

Buckley, Jerome. *The Turning Key: Autobiography and the Subjective Impulse since 1800*. Cambridge, Mass.: Harvard University Press, 1984.

———. "Towards Early-Modern Autobiography: The Roles of Oscar Wilde, George Moore, Edmund Gosse, and Henry Adams." In *Modernism Reconsidered*, edited by R. Kiely and J. Hildebiddle, 1–16. Cambridge, Mass.: Harvard English Studies, Harvard University Press, 1983.

Bugaeva, K. N. *Vospominanija o Belom*. Berkeley: Berkeley Slavic Specialties, 1981.

Bugaeva, K. N., and A. Petrovskij. "Literaturnoe nasledstvo Andreja Belogo." *Literaturnoe nasledstvo*, 27–28. Moscow: Nauka, 1937.

Burr, Anna Robeson. *The Autobiography: A Critical and Comparative Study*. Boston: Houghton Mifflin, 1909. Reprint. Norwood, Pa.: Norwood Editions, 1977.

Butler, Richard. *The Difficult Art of Autobiography*. Oxford: Clarendon Press, 1968.

Butor, Michel. *Essais sur le roman*. Paris: Editions Gallimard, coll. Idées, 1969.

Calvet, Jean. *L'Enfant dans la littérature française*. 2 vols. F. Lanore, 1947.

Carlock, Mary Sue. "Writings about the Autobiography: A Selective Bibliography." *Bulletin of Bibliography and Magazine Notes* 26 (1969): 1–2.

Castellano, Charlene. "The Many Faces of Truth in Andrey Bely's *Petersburg*." *West Virginia University Philological Papers* 30 (1984).

———. "Synaesthesia: Imagination's Semiotic in Andrey Bely's *Petersburg*." Ann Arbor: University Microfilms, 1980.

Chapman, Seymour. *Story and Discourse: Narrative Structure in Fiction and Film*. Ithaca: Cornell University Press, 1978.

Chudakova, Marietta O. *Masterstvo Jurija Oleshi*. Moscow: Nauka, 1972.

———. *Poetika Mikhaila Zoshchenko*. Moscow: Nauka, 1979.

Chukovskaja, Lidija. *Zapiski ob Anne Akhmatovoj*. 2 vols. Paris: YMCA Press, 1976 and 1980.

Chukovskij, Kornej. "Zoshchenko." *Sobranie sochinenij v desjati tomakh* 2. Moscow: Khudozhestvennaja literatura, 1965, 484–552.

Clark, Arthur Melville. *Autobiography, It Genesis and Phases*. Edinburgh: Oliver and Boyd, 1935. Reprint. Folcraft, Pa.: Folcraft Library Editions, 1976.

Clement, Catherine B., and Bernard Pingaud. "Roman—Analyse." *Revue française de psychanalyse* 38 (January 1974): 5–24.

Clifford, James L., ed. *Biography as an Art—Selected Criticism, 1560–1960*. New York, 1962.

Cockshut, A.O.J. *The Art of Autobiography in 19th and 20th Century England*. New Haven: Yale University Press, 1984.

Coe, Richard. *When the Grass Was Taller: Autobiography and the Experience of Childhood*. New Haven: Yale University Press, 1984.

Coirault, Yves. "Autobiographie et mémoires. XVIIe–XVIIIe siècles: Ou existence et naissance de l'autobiographie." *Revue d'histoire littéraire de la France* 6 (1975).

Courcelle, Pierre. *Les Confession de saint Augustin dans la tradition littéraire, anté- cédents et postérité*. Etudes augustiniennes, 1963.

Cox, James M. "Autobiography and America." *Aspects of Narrative*, edited by J. H. Miller, 143–72. New York: Columbia University Press, 1971.

———. "Recovering Literature's Lost Ground Through Autobiography." *Autobiog- raphy: Essays Theoretical and Critical*. Edited by James Olney, 123–45. Princeton University Press, 1980.

Crone, Anna Lisa. *Rozanov and the End of Literature*. Wurzburg: JAL Verlag, 1978.

Crone, A. L. and C. Chvany, eds. *New Studies in Russian Literature*. Festschrift for Bayara Aroutunova. Columbus, Ohio: Slavica, 1987.

Dawson, Carl. *Prophets of Past Time*. Baltimore: Johns Hopkins University Press, 1988.

de Man, Paul. "Autobiography as Defacement." *Modern Language Notes* 94 (1979): 918–38.

———. *The Rhetoric of Romanticism*. New York: Columbia University Press, 1984.

———. "The Rhetoric of Temporality." In *Interpretation Theory and Practice*, edited by Charles S. Singleton, 173–209. Baltimore: Johns Hopkins University Press, 1969.

Delany, Paul. *British Autobiography in the Seventeenth Century*. London: Routledge and Kegan Paul, 1969.

Démoris, René. *Le Roman à la première personne: Du Classicisme aux Lumières*. Paris: Editions A. Colin, 1975.

Derrida, Jacques. *The Ear of the Other: Otobiography, Transference, Translation: Texts and Discussions with Jacques Derrida*. English edition edited by Christie McDonald; translated by Peggy Kamuf. New York: Schocken Books, 1985. From *L'oreille de l'autre*. Montreal: V1b Editeur, 1982.

De Torre, Guillermo. "Memorias, autobiografias y epistolarios." *Doctrina y estilistica literaria*. Madrid; Guadarrama, 1970, 595–614.

Dikshina, N. "Nevydumannaja proza. O sovremennoj dokumental'noj literature."

Zhanrovo-stilevye iskanija sovremennoj prozy. Edited by L. M. Poljak and V. E. Kovskij. Moscow: Nauka, 1971.

Discussion sponsored by *Innostrannaja literatura.* "Literatura. Dokument. Fakt." *Innostrannaja literatura* (Moscow) 8 (1966).

Discussion sponsored by *Novyj mir.* "K sporam o khudozhestvennom dokumente." *Novyj mir* (Moscow) 8 (1968).

Doležel, Lubomir. "The Typology of the Narrator: Point of View in Fiction." *To Honor Roman Jakobson* 1. The Hague: Mouton, 1967, 541–52.

Dostoevsky, Fedor M. *Zapiski iz podpol'ja. Sobranie sochinenij.* Leningrad: Nauka, 1973.

Duchene, Roger. *Madame de Sévigné et la Lettre d'amour.* Paris: Editions Bordas, 1970.

―――. "Réalité vécue et réussite littéraire: Le statut particulier de la lettre." *Revue d'histoire littéraire de la France* 2 (1971) 177–94.

Dupuy, Aimé. *Un personnage nouveau du roman français: L'enfant.* Paris: Editions Hachette, 1931.

Durandin, Guy. *Les Fondements du mensonge.* Paris: Editions Flammarion, 1972.

Eakin, Paul John. *Fictions in Autobiography.* Princeton: Princeton University Press, 1985.

Ebner, Dean. *Autobiography in Seventeenth Century England: Theology and the Self.* The Hague: Mouton, 1971.

Edel, Leon. *Literary Biography.* New York, 1959.

Egan, Susanna. *Patterns of Experience in Autobiography.* Chapel Hill: University of North Carolina Press, 1984.

Eikhenbaum, Boris. *The Young Tolstoy.* Ann Arbor: Ardis Publishers, 1972.

Elbaz, Robert. *The Changing Nature of the Self.* Iowa City: University of Iowa Press, 1987.

Ellis, Madeleine. *Rousseau's Venetian Story: An Essay upon Art and Truth in* Les Confessions. Baltimore: Johns Hopkins University Press, 1966.

Elsworth, J. D. *Andrey Bely: A Critical Study of the Novels.* Cambridge: Cambridge University Press, 1983.

Erlich, Victor, ed. *Twentieth Century Russian Literary Criticism.* New Haven: Yale University Press, 1982.

Fanger, Donald. "Conflicting Imperatives in the Model of the Russian Writer: The Case of Tertz/Sinyavsky." In *Literature and History: Theoretical Problems and Russian Case Studies*, edited by Gary S. Morson. Stanford, Calif. Stanford University Press, 1986.

Felman, Shoshana. *Literature and Psychoanalysis: The Question of Reading Otherwise.* Baltimore: Johns Hopkins University Press, 1977.

Field, Andrew. *Nabokov: His Life in Art.* London: Hodder and Stoughton, 1967.

―――. *Nabokov: His Life in Art.* New York: Viking Press, 1977.

Fleishman, Avrom. *Figures of Autobiography.* Berkeley: University of California Press, 1983.

Fleishman, Lazar S. "Iz kommentariev k 'Kukkhe'. Konkrektor Obezvelvolpala." *Slavica Hierosolymitana* (Jerusalem) 1 (1977): 185–93.

Fleishman, Lazar S. "Bely's Memoirs." In *Andrey Bely: The Spirit of Symbolism*, edited by John Malmstad. Ithaca: Cornell University Press, 1987.

Fletcher, Angus, ed. *The Literature of Fact: Selected Papers of the English Institute*. New York: Columbia University Press, 1976.

Formen der Selbstdarstellung. Festgabe für Fritz Neubert. Berlin: Duncker und Humbolt, 1956.

Foucault, Michel. *L'ordre du discours*. Paris: Gallimard, 1971.

Fowler, Alistair. "The Life and Death of Literary Forms." *New Literary History* 2, no. 2 (Winter 1971): 199–216.

———. *Kinds of Literature: An Introduction to the Theory of Genres and Modes*. Cambridge, Mass.: Harvard University Press, 1982.

Frame, Donald. *Montaigne: A Biography*. New York: Harcourt, Brace and World, 1965.

Freidin, Grigory. "The Whisper of History and the Noise of Time." *Russian Review* 37, no. 4 (1978): 421–37.

———. "Mandel'shtam's Ode to Stalin: History and Myth." *Russian Review* 41, no. 4 (1982): 400–26.

———. *A Coat of Many Colors: Osip Mandelstam and His Mythologies of Self-Presentation*. Berkeley: University of California Press, 1987.

Freud, Sigmund. *The Standard Edition of the Complete Psychological Works of Sigmund Freud*. London: Hogarth Press, 1953.

———. *The Concordance to the Standard Edition of the Complete Psychological Works of Sigmund Freud*. Boston: G. K. Hall, 1980.

———. "Creative Writers and Day-Dreaming." In *20th Century Literary Criticism: A Reader*, edited by David Lodge, 36–43. London: Longman, 1972.

———. *The Interpretation of Dreams*. New York: Modern Library, 1950.

———. *The Psychopathology of Everyday Life*. New York: Norton, 1966.

———. *Three Essays on the Theory of Sexuality*. New York: Basic Books, 1975.

Freedman, Ralph. *The Lyrical Novel*. Princeton: Princeton University Press, 1963.

Friedman, Norman. "Point of View in Fiction." *PMLA* (1955): 1160–84.

Fumaroli, Marc. "Les mémoires du XVIIe siècle au carrefour des genres en prose." *XVIIe Siècle* 94–95 (1972): 7–37.

Garraty, John A. *The Nature of Biography*. New York, 1964.

Genette, Gérard. *Figures III*. Paris: Editions du Seuil, coll. Poétiques, 1972.

———. *Narrative Discourse: An Essay in Method*. Part of *Figures III*, translated by J. E. Lewin. Ithaca: Cornell University Press, 1980.

Gershtejn, Emma. *Novoe o Mandel'shtame*. Paris: Atheneum, 1986.

Ginzburg, Lidija. "Vjazemskij–literator." *Russkaja proza*. Leningrad: Academia, 1926: 102–34.

———. *Byloe i dumy Gertsena*. Leningrad: GIXL, 1957.

———. *O lirike*. Leningrad: Sovietskij pisatel', 1964. Revised and expanded edition. 1974.

———. *O psikhologicheskoj prose*. Leningrad: Sovetskij pisatel', 1971. Second edition. Leningrad: Khudozhestvennaja literatura, 1977. *Psychological Prose*. English translation by J. Rosengrant. Princeton: Princeton University Press, 1989.

———. *O literaturnom geroe*. Leningrad: Sovetskij pisatel', 1979.

———. *O starom i novom*. Leningrad: Sovetskij pisatel', 1982.

———. *Zapiski blokadnogo cheloveka*. *Neva* 1 (1984): 84–108.

———. *Notes from the Leningrad Blockade*. English translation by Jane G. Harris [forthcoming].

———. *Literatura v poiskakh real'nosti*. Leningrad: Sovetskij pistael', 1987.

———. "I zaodno s pravoporjadkom." *Tynjanovskij sbornik*. Tret'i Tynjanovskie chtenija. Riga, 1988.

Girard, Alain. *Le journal intime*. Paris: PUF, 1963.

Girard, René. *Deceit, Desire, and the Novel: Self and Other in Literary Structure*. Translated by Y. Freccero. Baltimore: Johns Hopkins University Press, 1965.

Glowinski, Michal. "On the First Person Novel." *New Literary History* 9, no. 1 (Autumn 1977): 103–15.

Goebiowski, Bronislaw. *Pamiętnikarstwo i literatura*. Warsaw: Ludowa Spodzielnia Wydawnicza, 1973.

Godenne, René. "Les débuts de la nouvelle narrée à la première personne (1645–1800)." *Romanische Forschungen* 82, no. 3 (1970): 253–67.

Goldberg, Jonathan. "Cellini's 'Vita' and the Conventions of Early Autobiography." *Modern Language Notes* 89, no. 1 (1974): 71–83.

Goscilo Helena. "Guilded Guilt: Confession in Russian Romantic Prose." *Russian Literature* 14, no. 2 (15 August 1983): 149–82.

Grayson, Jane. *Nabokov Translated*. Oxford: Oxford University Press, 1977.

Grigor'ev, A., and N. Petrova. "O. Mandel'shtam—Materialy k biografii." *Russian Literature* 15, no. 1 (January 1984): 1–27.

Group μ. *A General Rhetoric*. Translated by Paul B. Burell and Edgar M. Slotkin. Baltimore: Johns Hopkins University Press, 1981.

Gunn, Janet V. *Autobiography: Toward a Poetics of Experience*. Philadelphia: University of Pennsylvania Press, 1982.

Gusdorf, Georges "Conditions et limites de l'autobiographie." In *Formen der Selbstdarstellung. Festgabe fur Fritz Neuberg*, 105–23. Berlin: Duncker und Humbolt, 1956: English translation in Olney, *Autobiography: Essays*, 28–48.

———. *La Découverte de soi*. Paris: PUF, 1948.

———. *Mémoire et personne*. 2 vols. Paris: PUF, 1950.

———. "De l'autobiographie initiatique à l'autobiographie genre littéraire." *Revue d'histoire littéraire de la France* 6 (1975): 957–94.

Haight, M. R. *A Study of Self-Deception*. Humanities Press, 1980.

Hallowell, John. *Fact and Fiction: The New Journalism and the Nonfiction Novel*. Chapel Hill: University of North Carolina Press, 1977.

Hamlin, Cyrus. "The Poetics of Self-Consciousness in European Romanticism: Holderlin's *Hyperion* and Wordsworth's *Prelude*." *Genre* 6, no. 2 (June 1973): 142–77.

Haranin, L. Ja. *Memuarnyj zhanr sovetskoj literatury*. Minsk: Nauka i tekhnika, 1986.

Harkins, William. "The Theme of Sterility in Olesha's *Envy*." *Slavic Review* 3 (Sept 1966): 444–57.

Harris, Jane G. "The Impulse and the Text." In *Mandelstam: The Complete Critical Prose and Letters*, edited by Jane G. Harris. Ann Arbor: Ardis Publishers, 1979.

———. "Between Source and Pattern: The Meediating Function of the Autobiographical Mode in Joyce, Mandelstam, Schulz." *American Contributions to the IXth International Congress of Slavists, Kiev 1983*. Columbus, Oh.: Slavica, 1985.

―――. "Autobiographical Theory and Contemporary Soviet and American Narrative Genres." *American Contributions to the Xth International Congress of Slavists, Sofia 1988*. Columbus, Ohio: Slavica, 1988.

―――. *Osip Mandelstam*. Boston: G. K. Hall, 1988.

Hart, Francis R. "Notes for an Anatomy of Modern Autobiography." *New Literary History* 1, no. 3 (Spring 1970): 485–511.

―――. "Boswell and the Romantics: A Chapter in the History of Biographical Theory. *English Literary History* 27 (1960): 44–65.

Hartman, Geoffrey. *The Unmediated Vision*. New Haven: Yale University Press, 1954.

Håstad, Disa. *Samtal med sovjetiska författare* 32. Stockholm, 1979.

Heilbrun, Carolyn. *Writing a Woman's Life*. New York: Norton, 1988.

Heldt, Barbara. *Terrible Perfection: Women and Russian Literature*. Bloomington: Indiana University Press, 1987.

Hoggart, Richard. "A Question of Tone: Problems in Autobiographical Writings." *Speaking to Each Other*, 2: 174–200. London: Chatto and Windus, 1970.

Holland, Norman N. *The Dynamics of Literary Response*. New York: Oxford University Press, 1968.

Holquist, J. Michael. " 'Bad Faith' Squared: The Case of M. M. Bakhtin." *Russian Literature and Criticism*, edited by E. Bristol. Selected Papers from the Second World Congress for Soviet and East European Studies: Garmisch-Partenkirchen, 1980. Berkeley Slavic Specialties, 1982.

―――, ed. and trans., with Caryl Emerson. *M. M. Bakhtin: The Dialogic Imagination*. Austin: University of Texas Press, 1981.

Horowitz, Irving L. "Autobiography as the Presentation of Self for Social Immortality." *New Literary History* 9, no. 1 (Autumn 1977): 173–81.

Howarth, William L. "Some Principles of Autobiography." *New Literary History* 5, no. 2 (Winter 1974): 363–81. Reprint in Olney, *Autobiography: Essays*, 84–115.

Iser, Wolfgang. *The Implied Reader*. Baltimore: Johns Hopkins University Press, 1974.

Jakobson, Roman. *Selected Writings*. 7 vols. Amsterdam: Mouton, 1966–85.

―――. *Roman Jakobson: A Complete Bibliography of His Writings: 1912–1982*. Edited by Stephen Rudy. New York–Amsterdam: Mouton de Gruyter, 1987.

―――. *Language, Poetry and Poetics: The Generation of the 1890s: Jakobson, Trubetzkoy, Majakovskij; Proceedings of the First Roman Jakobson Colloquium at MIT, October 5–6, 1984*. Edited by K. Pomorska et al. New York–Amsterdam, 1987.

―――. *Verbal Art, Verbal Sign, Verbal Time*. Edited by K. Pomorska and S. Rudy. University of Minnesota Press, 1985.

―――. "What Is Poetry?" *Semiotics of Art. Prague School Contributions*, edited by L. Matejka and I. Titunik. Cambridge, Mass.: Harvard University Press, 1976.

―――. *A Tribute to Roman Jakobson, 1896–1982*. Berlin: Mouton, 1983.

Jakobson, Roman, and Krystyna Pomorska. *Dialogues*. Cambridge, Mass.: MIT Press, 1983.

Janacek, Gerald, ed. *Andrey Bely: A Critical Review*. Lexington: University of Kentucky Press, 1978.

———. *The Look of Russian Literature: Avant-Garde Visual Experiments, 1900–1930*. Princeton: Princeton University Press, 1984.

Jauss, Hans Robert. "Literary History as a Challenge to Literary Theory." *New Literary History* 2, no. 1 (Autumn 1970): 7–37.

Javchunovskij, Jakov I. *Dokumental'nye zhanry*. Saratov: Saratovskij gos. universitet, 1974.

Jay, Paul. *Being in the Text*. Ithaca: Cornell University Press, 1984.

Jelinek, Estelle C. *The Tradition of Women's Autobiography from Antiquity to the Present*. Boston: G. K. Hall, 1986.

Jensen, Peter Alberg. *Nature as Code: The Achievement of Boris Pilnjak: 1915–1924*. Copenhagen: Rosenkilde and Bagger, 1979.

Jung, C. G. *Collected Works of C. G. Jung*. Princeton: Princeton University Press.

Kaplan, Louis. *A Bibliography of American Autobiographies*. Madison: University of Wisconsin Press, 1962.

Karanfilov, Efrem. *Pisateli i memoaristi*. Sofia: Voen, Izd., 1980.

Kaulbach, Zoreslava. "The Life and Works of V. V. Rozanov." Ann Arbor: University Microfilms, 1973.

Kazin, Alfred. "Autobiography as Narrative." *Michigan Quarterly Review* 3 (1964): 210–16.

Kendall, Paul Murray. *The Art of Biography*. London: George Allen and Unwin, 1965.

Klaiber, T. *Die Deutsche Selbstbiographie*. Stuttgart, 1921.

Kodrjanskaja, N. *Aleksej Remizov*. Paris, 1959.

———. *Remizov v svoikh pis'makh*. Paris, 1977.

Konstenchik, N. K. "Zhanr i sjuzhet sovremennoj pisatel'skoj khudozhestvennoj avtobiografii." *Zhanr i Kompozitsija literaturnogo proizvedenija*, edited by A. M. Garkavi et al. Mezhvuzovskij sbornik. Vyp 2. 131–42. Kaliningrad: Kaliningradskij gos. universitet, 1976.

Kozhinov. V. V. "Problema avtora i put' pistatelja." *Kontekst* 40 (1977).

Kratkaja literaturnaja entsiklopedija. Moscow, 1962.

Kuzin, Boris S. "Ob O. E. Mandel'shtame." *Vestnik Russkogo khristianskogo dvizhenija* (Paris) 140 (1983): 99–129.

Kuznetsov, M. "Memuarnaja proza." *Zhanrovo-stilevye iskanija sovremennoj sovetskoj prozy*, edited by L. M. Poljak and V. E. Kovskij. Moscow: Nauka, 1971.

Lampl, Horst. "Additions to the Sinany *Bibliographie des oeuvres de Alexis Remizov*." *Wiener slawistischer Almanach* (Vienna) 2 (1978): 301–26.

Lecarme, Jacques. "L'autobiographie." *La Littérature en France depuis 1945*. Bordas, 1974, 311–23, 871–76.

Lecercle, Jean-Louis. *Rousseau et l'Art du roman*. Paris: Editions A. Colin, 1969.

Lehtonen, Maija. "Les Avatars du moi. Réflexions sur la technique de Sainte-Beuve, *Le lys dans la vallée* de Balzac, et *La confession d'un enfant du siècle* de Musset." *Neuphilologische Mitteilungen* 3 (1973): 387–411 and 4 (1973): 746–59, and 1 (1974): 164–78.

Lejeune, Philippe. *L'Autobiographie en France*. Paris: Editions A. Colin, coll. U2, 1971.

Lejeune, Philippe. *Le pacte autobiographique*. Paris: Editions du Seuil, 1975.

———. *Lire Leiris, autobiographie et langage*. Klincksieck, 1975.

———. *Je est un autre: L'autobiographie*. Paris: Editions du Seuil, 1980.

———. "Autobiography in the Third Person." *New Literary History* 9, no. 1 (Autumn 1977): 27–50.

———. *Bibliographie des études en langue française sur la littérature personnelle et les récits de vie*. Nanterre, Centre de sémiotique textuelle: Université de Paris 10, 1984–86.

———. *Moi aussi*. Paris: Editions du Seuil, 1986.

———. *On Autobiography*. Minneapolis: University of Minnesota Press, 1988.

Lillard, Richard. *American Life in Autobiography: A Descriptive Guide*. Stanford, Calif.: Stanford University Press, 1956.

Limonov, Eduard. *Eto ja—Edichka*. New York: Index Publishers, 1982. *It's Me, Eddie: A Fictional Memoir*. English translation by S. L. Campbell. New York: Random House, 1983.

———. *Podrostok Savenko*. Paris: Sintaksis, 1983. *The Adolescent Savenko*. English translation by Judson Rosengrant. New York: Grove Press, forthcoming.

———. *Molodoj negodjaj*. Paris: Sintaksis, 1986.

———. *Stikhotvorenija i poemy*. Moscow–Leningrad: Biblioteka poeta, 1964.

———. "My natsional'nyj geroj." In *Apollon-77*, edited by Mikhail Shemiakin. Paris: Les Arts grafiques de Paris, 1977.

Lobet, Marcel. *Ecrivains en aveu, essai sur la confession en aveu*. Bruxelles: Brepols, 1962.

———. *La Ceinture de feuillage; Essai sur la confession déguisée*. Bruxelles: La Renaissance du livre, 1966.

Lodge, David. *The Modes of Modern Writing: Metaphor, Metonomy, and the Typology of Modern Literature*. London: E. Arnold, 1977.

———. *Modernism, Antimodernism and Postmodernism*. Birmingham: University of Birmingham Press, 1977.

———. *Twentieth Century Literary Criticism*. London: Longman, 1972.

Lovejoy, Arthur O. *The Great Chain of Being*. Cambridge, Mass.: Harvard University Press, 1973.

Maksudov, S. "*Spokojnoj nochi* s Dobrym Utrom." *Strana i mir* 10 (1984).

Malmstad, John E., ed. *Andrey Bely: The Spirit of Symbolism*. Ithaca: Cornell University Press, 1987.

Mandel, Barrett. "The Autobiographer's Art." *The Journal of Aesthetics and Art Criticism* 26 (1968–69): 215–26.

———. "Full of Life Now." In *Autobiography: Essays Theroetical and Critical*, edited by J. Olney. Princeton: Princeton University Press, 1980, 49–72.

Mandelstam, Nadezhda Jakovlevna. *Hope Against Hope*. Translated by Max Hayward. New York: Atheneum, 1970. *Vospominanija*. New York: Chekhov Publishing House, 1970.

———. *Hope Abandoned*. Translated by Max Hayward. New York: Atheneum, 1974. *Vtoraja kniga*. Paris: YMCA Press, 1972.

Mandelstam, Osip. *Sobranie sochinenij*. Edited by Gleb Struve and Boris Filipoff.

Vols. 1–3. New York: Inter-Language Literary Associates, 1967–71; Vol 4. Supplementary. Paris: YMCA Press, 1981.

———. *The Complete Critical Prose and Letters*. Edited by Jane Gary Harris. Translated by J. G. Harris and Constance Link. Ann Arbor: Ardis Publishers, 1979.

———. *The Noise of Time: The Prose of Osip Mandelstam*. Edited and translated by Clarence Brown. San Francisco: North Point Press, 1986.

Markov, Vladimir. "Neizvestnij pisatel' Remizov." *Aleksej Remizov: Approaches to a Protean Writer*. Proceedings of International Symposium on Alexej Remizov. UCLA Slavic Studies 16. Los Angeles: Slavica, 1987.

Mashinskij, S. "O Memuarno-avtobiograficheskom zhanre." *Voprosy literatury* (Moscow) 6 (1960): 129–45.

Matich, Olga. "The Moral Immoralist: Eduard Limonov's *Eto ja—Edichka!*" *Slavic and East European Journal* 4 (1986): 526–40.

Maurois, André. *Aspects de la biographie*. Paris: Editions Grasset, 1930.

Mauss, Marcel. "Une Catégorie de l'esprit humain: La notion de personne, celle de 'moi.' " In *Sociologie et Anthropologie*, 331–62. Paris: PUF, 1950.

May, Georges. *Le Dilemne du roman au XVIIIe siècle*. Paris: PUF, 1963.

———. *L'Autobiographie*. Paris: PUF, 1979.

———. "Autobiography and the 18th Century." In *The Author and His Work*, 317–33. New Haven: Yale University Press, 1978.

McLean, Hugh. "Belated Sunrise: A Review Article." *Slavic and East European Journal* 18 (1974): 406–10.

Mehlman, Jeffrey. *A Structural Study of Autobiography: Proust, Leiris, Sartre, Levi-Strauss*. Ithaca: Cornell University Press, 1974.

Meletinskij, E. M. "Nizkij geroj volshebnoj skazki." *Geroj volshebnoj skazki*. Moscow: Nauka, 1958.

Meletinskij, E. M., S. Ju. Nekljudov, E. S. Novik, and D. M. Segal. "Problemy strukturnogo opisanija volshebnoj skazki." *Trudy po znakovym sistemam* (Tartu) 4 (1969).

"Mémoires et création littéraire." *XVIIe Siècle* 94–95 (1972.)

Merlant, Joachim. *Le roman personnel de Rousseau à Fromentin*. Paris: Editions Hachette, 1905.

Meyerhoff, Hans. *Time in Literature*. Berkeley: University of California Press, 1955.

Misch, Georg. *Geschichte der Autobiographie*. 8 vols. Frankfurt am Main: Schulte und Bulmke, 1949–69.

———. *A History of Autobiography in Antiquity*. 2 vols. Translation of part of above. Westport, Conn.: Greenwood Press, 1973.

Momiliano, E. *The Development of Greek Biography*. Cambridge, Mass.: Harvard University Press, 1971.

Monglond, André. "Confessions et lyrisme intérieur." *Le Préromantisme français*, 2: 241–312. Paris: Jose Corti, 1966.

Monsman, Gerald. *Walter Pater's Art of Autobiography*. New Haven: Yale University Press, 1980.

Montaigne, Michel de. *Essais. Oeuvres complètes*. Paris: Louis Canard, 1924.

Morris, John N. *Versions of the Self: Studies in English Autobiography from John Bunyan to John Stuart Mill*. New York: Basic Books, 1966.

Mukařovský, Jan. *The Word and Verbal Art*. Edited and translated by J. Burbank and P. Steiner. New Haven: Yale University Press, 1977.

Nabokov, Vladimir. *Speak, Memory: A Memoir*. London: Gollancz, 1951.

———. *Drugie Berega*. Russian translation of the 1951 edition of *Speak, Memory*. New York: Chekhov Publishing House, 1954.

———. *Speak, Memory: An Autobiography Revisited*. Revised edition. New York: Putnam, 1966.

———. *Strong Opinions*. London: Weidenfeld & Nicholson, 1974.

———. *The Real Life of Sebastian Knight*. Norfolk, Conn.: New Directions, 1941.

———. *Bend Sinister*. New York: Henry Holt, 1947.

———. *Pnin*. New York: Doubleday and Company, 1957.

———. *Lolita*. New York: Putnam, 1955.

———. *The Gift*. New York: Putnam, 1963.

———. *Ada*. New York: McGraw-Hill, 1969.

Neumann, Bernard. *Identität und Rollenzwang. Zur Theorie der Autobiographie*. Frankfurt am Main: Athenaum Verlag, 1970.

Olesha, Jurij. *Ni dnja bez strochki*. Moscow: Sovetskaja Rossija, 1965.

———. *No Day without a Line*. English translation by Judson Rosengrant. Ann Arbor: Ardis Publishers, 1979.

———. *Povesti i rasskazy*. Moscow: Khudozhestvennaja literatura, 1965.

———. *Envy*. Translated by Clarence Brown in *The Portable Twentieth Century Russian Reader*. New York: Viking Penguin Inc., 1985.

Olney, James. *Metaphors of Self: The Meaning of Autobiography*. Princeton: Princeton University Press, 1972.

———, ed. *Autobiography: Essays Theoretical and Critical*. Princeton: Princeton University Press, 1980.

———, ed. *Studies in Autobiography*. New York: Oxford Univ Press, 1988.

Pascal, Roy. "The Autobiographical Novel and the Autobiography." *Essays in Criticism* 9 (April 1959): 134–50.

———. *Design and Truth in Autobiography*. Cambridge, Mass.: Harvard University Press, 1960.

———. *The Dual Voice*. Manchester: University of Manchester Press, 1977.

Pasternak, Boris. "Okhrannaja gramota." *Proza 1915–1958*. Ann Arbor: University of Michigan Press, 1961. English translation. *Safe Conduct: An Autobiography and Other Writings*. New York: New Directions, 1958.

Peterson, Linda H. *Victorian Autobiography*. New Haven: Yale University Press, 1986.

Pevear, Richard. "On the Memoirs of Nadezhda Mandelstam." *Hudson Review* 24, no. 3 (1971).

Peyre, Henri. *Literature and Sincerity*: Yale University Press, 1963.

Pifer, Ellen, *Nabokov and the Novel*. Cambridge, Mass.: Harvard University Press, 1980.

Pike, Burton. "Time in Autobiography." *Comparative Literature* 28 (1976): 326–42.

Pilling, John. *Autobiography and Imagination: Studies in Self-Scrutiny*. London: Routledge and Kegan Paul, 1981.

Pomorska, Krystyna. *Themes and Variations in Pasternak's Poetics*. Lisse: The Peter de Ridder Press, 1975.

———. "The Utopian Future of the Russian Avant-Garde." *American Contributions to the IXth International Congress of Slavists* 2 (Kiev, September 1983). Columbus, Ohio: Slavica, 1983.

———. "Roman Jakobson—Lingua, arte e scienza d'avanguardia." *Roman Jakobson: Magia della parola,* edited by K. Pomorska, 155–77. Bari, 1980.

Pomorska, Krystyna et al., eds. *Language, Poetry and Poetics: The Generation of the 1890s: Jakobson, Trubetzkoy, Majakovskij. Proceedings of the First Roman Jakobson Colloquium, M.I.T., Oct. 5–6, 1984*. Amsterdam: Mouton de Gruyter, 1987.

Porter, Roger J., and H. R. Wolf. *The Voice Within: Reading and Writing Autobiography*. New York: Alfred A. Knopf, 1973.

Pratt, Sarah, ed. "Lidija Ginzburg's Contribution to Literary Criticism." *Canadian-American Slavic Studies* 19, no. 2 (Special Issue) (Summer 1985).

Proffer, Carl. *Keys to* Lolita. Bloomington, Ind.: Indiana University Press, 1968.

———. *The Widows of Russia and Other Writings*. Ann Arbor: Ardis Publishers, 1987.

Prince, Gerald. "Introduction à l'étude du narrataire. *Poétique* (Paris) 14 (1973): 178–96.

Propp, V. Ja. *Morfologija skazki*. Moscow: Nauka, 1969.

Proust, Marcel. *Le temps retrouvé*. Paris: Bibliothèque de la Pléiade, 1956.

Pryce-Jones, A. "The Personal Story." *The Craft of Letters in England*. London, 1955.

Questionnaire sponsored by *Voprosy literatury* (Moscow) 9 (1966).

Raimond, Michel. *La Crise du roman. Des lendemains du naturalisme aux années vingt*. Paris: José Corti, 1967.

———. *Le Roman depuis la Révolution*. Paris: Editions A. Colin, 1967.

Rannaud, Gerald. "Le moi et l'histoire chez Chateaubriand et Stendhal." *Revue d'histoire littéraire de la France* (Paris) 6 (1975).

Remizov, Alexey M. *Iveren'. Modern Russian Literature and Culture: Studies and Texts* 7. Edited by Olga Raevsky-Hughes. Berkeley: Berkeley Slavic Specialties, 1986.

———. *Kukkha*. Berlin: Z. I. Grzhebina. 1923.

———. *Vzvikhrennaja Rus'*. Paris: Tair, 1927.

———. *Po karnizam*. Belgrade: Russkaja biblioteka, 1929.

———. *Podstrizhennymi glazami*. Paris: YMCA Press, 1951.

———. *V rozovom bleske*. New York: Chekhov Publishing House, 1952.

———. *Myshkina dudochka*. Paris, 1953.

———. *Martyn Zadeka*. Paris: Opleshnik, 1954.

———. *Krug Schast'ja*. Paris: Opleshnik, 1957.

———. *Peterburgskij buerak*. Paris: La Presse Libre, 1983.

———. *Prud*. 1908.

———. *Uchitel' muzyki*. Paris: La Presse Libre, 1983.

———. *Vstrechi*. Paris: Lev, 1981.

———. *Ogon' veschej*. Paris: Opleshnik, 1954.

Remizov, Alexey M. "Avtobiografija. 1913." Fair copy. Remizov Archive in the State Public Library, Leningrad. GPB, fond 634, no. 1.

Renza, Louis. "The Veto of the Imagination: A Theory of Autobiography." *New Literary History* 9, no. 1 (Autumn 1977): 1–26.

Rest, B. "Golubaja kniga: Na dispute v Leningradskom diskussionnom klube prozaikov." *Literaturnaja gazeta* (15 March 1936).

Riggan, William. *Picaros, Madmen, Naifs, and Clowns: The Unreliable First Person Narrator*. Oklahoma University Press, 1981.

Rinehart, Keith. "The Victorian Approach to Autobiography." *Modern Philology* 51 (3 February 1954): 177–86.

Romberg, Bertil. *Studies in the Narrative Technique of the First Person Novel*. Stockholm–Lund: Almquist and Wiksell, 1962.

Ronen, Omry. *An Approach to Mandel'shtam*. Jerusalem: The Magnes Press, 1983.

Rose, Phyllis. *Parallel Lives*. New York: Alfred A. Knopf, 1983.

Rousseau, Jean-Jacques. *The Confessions*. Translated by John Grant. London: Dent, 1943.

Rousset, Jean. "Une forme littéraire, le roman par lettres." In *Forme et Signification, essais sur les structures littéraires de Corneille à Claudel* Paris: José Corti, 1964.

———. *Narcisse romancier, essai sur la première personne dans le roman*. Paris: José Corti, 1973.

Rowe, W. W. *Nabokov's Deceptive World*. New York: New York University Press, 1971.

Rozanow, Wassilij. *Ausgewahlte Schriften*. Munich: A. Neimanis, 1970.

Rustin, Jacques. "Mensonge et vérité dans le roman français du XVIII siècle." *Revue d'histoire littéraire de la France* (January–February 1969): 13–38.

———. "L'histoire véritable dans la littérature romanesque du XVIII siècle français." *Cahiers de l'Association internationale des études françaises* 18 (March 1966): 89–102.

Sayre, Robert F. "Autobiography and Images of Utopia." *Salmagundi* 19 (1972): 18–37.

———. *The Examined Self: Franklin, Adams, James*. Princeton: Princeton University Press, 1964.

———. "Autobiography and the Making of America." In *Autobiography: Essays Theoretical and Critical*, edited by J. Olney, 146–68. Princeton: Princeton University Press, 1980.

Scholes, Robert, and Robert Kellogg. *The Nature of Narrative*. New York and Oxford: Oxford University Press, 1966.

Scrivano, Riccardo. *Biografia e autobiografia*. Rome: Bulzoni, 1976.

Segal, Dmitry. "Voprosy poeticheskoj organizatsii semantiki v proze Mandel'-shtama." In *Russian Poetics: Proceedings of the International Colloquium at UCLA, Sept. 22–26, 1975*, edited by T. Eekman and D. Worth. UCLA Slavic Series 4. Los Angeles: University of California Press, 1983.

Shane, Alex M. "An Introduction to Alexei Remizov." In *The Bitter Air of Exile: Russian Writers in the West: 1922–1972*, edited by Simon Karlinsky and Alfred Appel, Jr. Berkeley: University of California Press, 1977.

————. *The Life and Works of Evgenij Zamjatin*. Berkeley and Los Angeles: University of California Press, 1968.

Shapiro, Stephen. "The Dark Continent of Literature: Autobiography." *Comparative Literature Studies* 5 (1968): 421–54.

Shklovskij, Viktor. *Zoo, ili pis' ma ne o liubvi.* In *Sobranie sochinenij v trekh tomakh* 1. Moscow, 1973.

————. *Rozanov.* Petrograd, 1921.

Shumaker, Wayne. *English Autobiography: Its Emergence, Materials and Form.* University of California Press, 1954.

Sinany-Mcleod, Hélène. *Bibliographie des oeuvres de Alexis Remizov.* Paris: Institut d'études slaves, 1978.

————. "Strukturnaja kompozitsija *Vzvikhrennoj Rusi.*" In *Aleksej Remizov: Approaches to a Protean Writer.* UCLA Slavic Studies 16. Los Angeles: Slavica, 1987.

Sinyavsky, Andrey [Abram Tertz]. *A Voice from the Chrous.* Translated by Kyril Fitzlyon and Max Hayward. New York: Farrar, Straus and Giroux, 1976.

————. *Kroshka Tsores.* Paris: Syntaksis, 1980.

————. *Spokojnoj nochi.* Paris: Syntaksis, 1984.

————. *Opavshie list' ja Rozanova.* Paris: Syntaksis, 1982.

Slobin, Greta Nachtailer. *Remizov's Fictions: 1900–125.* Forthcoming.

Slonimskij, Mikhail. "Mikhail Zoshchenko." In *Kniga vospominanij,* 145–70. Moscow: Sovetskij pisatel', 1966.

Smith, Sidonie. *A Poetics of Women's Autobiography.* Bloomington: Indiana University Press, 1987.

Smith, Valerie. *Self-discovery and Authority in Afro-American Narrative.* Cambridge, Mass.: Harvard University Press, 1987.

Somov, O. M. *Byli i nebylitsy.* Moscow: Sovetskaja Rossija, 1984.

Spacks, Patricia. *Imagining a Self: Autobiography and Novel in 18th Century England.* Cambridge, Mass.: Harvard University Press, 1976.

————. "Stages of Life: Notes on Autobiography and the Life Cycle." *Hudson Review* 30 (1977): 29–46.

Spengemann, William C. *The Forms of Autobiography.* New Haven: Yale University Press, 1979.

Spengemann, William C., and L. R. Lundquist. "Autobiography and the American Myth." *American Quarterly* 17 (Autumn 1965): 92–110.

Sprinker, Michael. "Fictions of the Self: The End of Autobiography." In *Autobiography: Essays Theoretical and Critical,* edited by J. Olney. Princeton: Princeton University Press, 1980.

Starobinski, Jean. *Jean-Jacques Rousseau. La transparence et l'obstacle.* Paris: Editions Gallimard, 1971.

————. *L'Oeil vivant.* Paris: Editions Gallimard, 1961.

————. Le Style de l'autobiographie." *Poétique* 3 (Paris, 1970): 257–65. English translation in Olney, *Autobiography: Essays Theoretical and Critical,* 73–83. Princeton: Princeton University Press, 1980.

Stauffer, Donald. *The Art of Biography in Eighteenth Century England.* Princeton: Princeton University Press, 1941.

Stempel, Wolf-Dieter. "Pour une description des genres littéraires." *Actele celui de-al XII-lea Congres international de linguistica si filologie romanica*. Bucarest: Editura Academiei Republicii Socialiste Romania, 1971, 565–70.

Stewart, Philip. *Imitation and Illusion in the French Memoirs-Novels, 1700–1750; The Art of Make-Believe*. New Haven: Yale University Press, 1969.

Stone, Albert. "Autobiography and American Culture." *American Studies: An International Newsletter* 9, no. 2 (January–March 1973): 26–37.

Struve, Gleb. *Russian Literature Under Lenin and Stalin, 1917–1953*. Norman, University of Oklahoma Press, 1971.

Stuart, Dabney. "The Novelist's Composure: *Speak, Memory* as Fiction." *Modern Language Quarterly* 36 (June 1975): 189–95.

Sturrock, John. "The New Model Autobiographer." *New Literary History* 9, no. 1 (Autumn 1977); 51–64.

Subbotin, V., and L. Lazarev. "Dialog." *Literaturnaja gazeta* (Moscow) (8 May 1967).

Szavai, Janos. "La place et le role de l'autobiographie dans la littérature." *Acta Littereria Academiae Scientiarium Hungaricae* (Budapest) 18. Akademiai Kiado (1976): 398–414.

———. *The Autobiography*. Budapest: Akademiai Kiado, 1984.

Taranovsky, Kiril. *Essays on Mandelstam*. Cambridge, Mass.: Harvard University Press, 1976.

Tertz, Abram. *See* Sinyavsky, Andrey.

Titunik, Irwin. "Vasilij Trediakovskij and Eduard Limonov: Erotic Reverberations in the History of Russian Literature." In *Russian Literature and American Critics: Papers in Slavic Philology* 4, edited by Kenneth Brostrom, 393–404. Ann Arbor: Department of Slavic Languages, University of Michigan (1984).

Todorov, Tzvetan. *The Poetics of Prose*. Translated by R. Howard. Ithaca: Cornell University Press, 1977.

———. "Les genres littéraires." *Introduction à la littérature fantastique*. Paris: Editions du Seuil, 1970, 7–27.

———. "The Notion of Literature." *New Literary History* 5, no. 1 (Autumn 1973): 5–16.

———. *The Fantastic*. Translated by R. Howard. Cleveland: Case Western Reserve Press, 1973.

———. *Mikhail Bakhtin and the Dialogical Principle*. Translated by Wlad Godzich. Theory and History of Literature Series 13. Minneapolis: University of Minnesota Press, 1984.

Trifonov, Jurij. *Povesti*. Moskva, 1978.

———. *Starik*. Moscow: Sovetskij pisatel', 1980. *The Old Man*. English translation by Jacqueline Edwards and Mitchell Schneider. New York: Simon and Schuster, 1984.

———. *Vremja i mesto*. Druzhba narodov 9–10 (1981).

———. *Another Life. The House on the Embankment. Novellas (from Povesti)*. Translated by Michael Glenny. New York: Simon and Schuster, 1986.

Tynianov, Jurij N. *Poetika, Istorija literatury, Kino*. Edited and notes by E. A. Toddes, A. P. Chudakov, and M. O. Chudakova. Moscow: Nauka, 1977.

————. "On Literary Evolution." In *Readings in Russian Poetics*, edited by L. Matejka and K. Pomorska. Cambridge, Mass.: MIT Press, 1971.

Urban, Adol'f. "Khudozhestvennaja avtobiografija i dokument." *Zvezda* (Leningrad) 2 (1977): 192–208.

Vaksel', Olga. "O Mandel'shtame (Iz dnevnika)." In *Chast' rechi: Almanakh literatury i iskusstva* 1:251–62. New York: Serebrjannij vek, 1980.

Vance, Eugene. "Le moi comme langage: Saint Augustin et l'autobiographie." *Poétique* (Paris) 143 (1973): 163–77.

————. "Augustine's *Confessions* and the Grammar of Selfhood." *Genre* 6, no. 1 (March 1973): 1–28.

Vatnikova-Prizel, Zoya. *O russkoj memuarnoj literature: kriticheskie analizy i bibliografija*. East Lansing, Mich.: *Russian Language Journal* publication, 1978.

Vercier, Bruno. "Le mythe du premier souvenir et sa place dans le récit: Pierre Loti, Michel Leiris." *Revue d'histoire littéraire de la France* (Paris) 6 (1975).

Vinokur, G. *Biografiia i kul'tura*. Moscow: Trudy Gos. Akademii Khudozhestvennykh Nauk, Filosofskoe otdelenie, Vyp. 2, 1927.

Vitz, Evelyn. "Type et individu dans 'l'autobiographie' médiévale." *Poétique* 24 (1975).

Vladiv, Slobodanka B. *Narrative Principles in Dostoevskij's Besy: A Structural Analysis*. Bern: European University Papers, Series 16, Slavonic Languages and Literatures 10, 1979.

Voisine, Jacques. "Naissance et évolution du terme littéraire 'autobiographie.' " In *La Littérature comparée en Europe orientale*, Budapest conference October 26–29, 1962, 278–86. Budapest: Akademiai Kiado, 1963.

————. "De la confession religieuse à l'autobiographie et au journal intime: entre 1760 et 1820." *Néohélicon* 3–4 (1974): 337–57.

Weinrich, Harald. *Le Temps*. Paris: Editions du Seuil, coll. Poétique, 1973.

Weinstein, Arnold. *Fictions of the Self: 1550–1800*. Princeton: Princeton University Press, 1981.

Weintraub, Karl Joachim. *The Value of the Individual: Self and Circumstance in Autobiography*. Chicago: University of Chicago Press, 1982.

————. "Autobiography and Historical Consciousness." *Critical Inquiry* 1, no. 4 (June 1975): 821–48.

Wilden, A. G. *The Language of the Self*. Baltimore: Johns Hopkins University Press, 1968.

Williams, Huntington, *Rousseau and Romantic Autobiography*. Oxford: Oxford University Press, 1983.

Zeraffa, Michel. *Personne et Personnage; Le romanesque des années 1920 aux années 1950*. Klincksieck, 1969.

Zimmerman, T. C. Prince. "Confession and Autobiography in the Early Renaissance." In *Renaissance Studies in Honor of Hans Baron*, edited by A. Molho and J. A. Tedeschi, 119–40. Urbana-Champaign: Illinois University Press, 1971.

Zoshchenko, Mikhail. *1935–1937: Rasskazy, povesti, fel'etony*. Leningrad: Khudozhestvennaja literatura, 1937.

————. *Pered voskhodom solntsa*. New York: Chekhov Publishing House, 1973.

————. *Before Sunrise*. Translated by Gary Kern. Ann Arbor: Ardis Publishers, 1974.

Zoshchenko, Mikhail. *Vozvrashchennaja molodost'*. Moscow: Sovetskij pisatel', 1935.

———. *Povest' o razume*. *Zvezda* 3 (1972).

———. "O sebe, ob ideologii, i eshche koe o chem." *Literaturnye zapiski* 3 (August 1922).

———. *Izbrannoe* (Odnotomnik). Leningrad: Izd. pisatelej v Leningrade, 1934.

———. *Izbrannoe v dvukh tomakh*. Leningrad: Khudozhestvennaja literatura, 1978.

———. *Rasskazy, sentimental'nye povesti, komedii, fel'tony*. Moscow: Sovetskaja Rossija, 1977.

"Zoshchenko, Mikhail Mikhajlovich." In *Sovetskie pisateli: Avtobiografii* 3, edited by B. Ja. Brajnina and A. N. Dmitrieva, 278–87. Moscow: Khudozhestvennaja literatura, 1966.

Zoshchenko, Vera. *Neizdannyj Zoschchenko*. Edited by Vera von Wiren. Ann Arbor: Ardis Publishers, 1977.

———. "Tak nachinal M. Zoshchenko." *Voprosy literatury* 10 (1975): 244–66.

Zumthor, Paul. "Autobiographie au Moyen Age?" *Langue, Texte, Enigme*, 165–80. Paris: Editions du Seuil, 1975.

Index

Acmeists, 79n.30

affective disorders, 144n.23

Akhmatova, Anna: and Lydia Ginzburg, 207, 211, 215; and Nadezhda Mandelstam, 196–200, 205n.17

Aksakov, Sergey, 20

Alther, Lisa, 187n.32

Andreyev, Leonid: and "vulgar, tawdry symbolism" (Mandelstam), 108, 129n.28

Appel, Alfred, 169nn. 53 and 56

Augustine, Saint, 4n.3, 6n.10, 41, 46; and Zoshchenko and conversion narrative, 143–44, 147, 213, 239–40

autobiographer: beliefs of, 7; and contemporaneity, 15–16; conventions associated with, 7; and dual nature of autobiography, 24–25; identity of, 7, 16, 23; and impulse to create, 16; information and events associated with, 7; as mediator in continuing dialogue, 24; and philosophical and psychological problems of self-knowledge, 12, 16; reader expectations of, 8, 9, 23; and subject of creation, 16. *See also* autobiographical act; autobiographical narrator; autobiographical self; autobiography; self, the

autobiographical act: aesthetic properties of, 16; definition of, 10; and moral testimony, 15; and multiple identities, 30–31; and time consciousness, 15

autobiographical consciousness, 5; and autobiographical imagination, 26; definition of (Mandel), 11. *See also* recollection, experience of; self, the; self-consciousness; self-reflexion

autobiographical discourse: and the addressee, 31; aesthetic tension of, and time consciousness, 15–16, 27; as art of mediation, 25; as autobiographical act, 10; as autobiographical statement, 10–12; and conventions violated, 12; definitions of, 3–4, 7–12, 17, 24–26; and "dissimilarity between identity and discourse" (Jay), 30; diversity and flexibility of forms in, 9–11; and dual role of autobiographer, 22–23; and fiction, 12, 16; and historical and social dimension,

6, 14–15, 31; mannerisms of, 10; meaning and, 11–12; and memoir and feminist theory, 194–97; and memory and paradox, 5; modalities of, 10; as organizing principle of the text, 12, 24; and other factors, 5, 9–12; parallelism in, 5; poetics of, 9, 11–12; purpose or function of, 12; and quest for new forms, 13–14; and quest motif, 31; range of formal features and textual strategies of, 10–11, 17, 26; recurrent forms and styles in, 10, 12; as self-reflexive process, 5; signs of, 10, 17, 25–26; as source of human value, 6, 14–15, 31; structure of, 5, 10–12, 16–17, 25–26; thematic patterns in, 10, 17, 26; as twentieth-century phenomenon, 9–10, 13–14; and typology of discourse (Todorov), 17–18

autobiographical mode of perception, 5, 27

autobiographical narrative: aesthetic meaning of, 6; dual origins of, 14; organizing principle of, 25; and transformation of the self, 17. *See also* autobiographical discourse; autobiography

autobiographical narrator: dual role of, 7, 22, 24; identity of, 7, 28; memoir and Russian female writers, 194–97; and relationship to materials (Javchunovsky), 22; and subjective and objective narration, 22, 24. *See also* autobiographer; autobiographical discourse; autobiographical self; self, the

autobiographical self: existence of, in text only, 8–9; vs. insignificant "I," 8; and language, 9; and time consciousness, 15–16; transformation of, 17. *See also* autobiographer; self, the; self-consciousness; self-reflexion

autobiographical situation: and significance of cultural dimension, 9, 12, 15

autobiographical statement: aesthetic coherence of, 24; aesthetic properties of, 10, 15–16, 24, 27; aesthetic tension of, 32; affirmative nature of, 32; and autobiographical discourse, 10 (*see also* autobiographical discourse); and conventional and nonconventional autobiography, 10, 134; defini-

Studies of the Harriman Institute

Soviet National Income in 1937 by Abram Bergson, Columbia University Press, 1953.

Through the Glass of Soviet Literature: Views of Russian Society, Ernest Simmons Jr., ed., Columbia University Press, 1953.

Polish Postwar Economy by Thad Paul Alton, Columbia University Press, 1954.

Management of the Industrial Firm in the USSR: A Study in Soviet Economic Planning by David Granick, Columbia University Press, 1954.

Soviet Politics in China, 1917–1924 by Allen S. Whiting, Columbia University Press, 1954; paperback, Stanford University Press, 1968.

Literary Politics in the Soviet Ukraine, 1917–1934 by George S. N. Luckyj, Columbia University Press, 1956.

The Emergence of Russian Panslavism, 1856–1870 by Michael Boro Petrovich, Columbia University Press, 1956.

Lenin on Trade Unions and Revolution, 1893–1917 by Thomas Taylor Hammond, Columbia University Press, 1956.

The Last Years of the Georgian Monarchy, 1658–1832 by David Marshall Lang, Columbia University Press, 1957.

The Jápanese Thrust into Siberia, 1918 by James William Morley, Columbia University Press, 1957.

Bolshevism in Turkestan, 1917–1927 by Alexander G. Park, Columbia University Press, 1957.

Soviet Marxism: A Critical Analysis by Herbert Marcuse, Columbia University Press, 1958; paperback, Columbia University Press, 1985.

Soviet Policy and the Chinese Communists, 1931–1946 by Charles B. McLane, Columbia University Press, 1958.

The Agrarian Foes of Bolshevism: Promise and Defeat of the Russian Socialist Revolutionaries, February to October, 1917 by Oliver H. Radkey, Columbia University Press, 1958.

Pattern for Soviet Youth: A Study of the Congresses of the Komsomol, 1918–1954 by Ralph Talcott Fisher, Jr., Columbia University Press, 1959.

The Emergence of Modern Lithuania by Alfred Erich Senn, Columbia University Press, 1959.

The Soviet Design for a World State by Elliot R. Goodman, Columbia University Press, 1960.

Settling Disputes in Soviet Society: The Formative Years of Legal Institutions by John N. Hazard, Columbia University Press, 1960.

Soviet Marxism and Natural Science, 1917–1932 by David Joravsky, Columbia University Press, 1961.

Russian Classics in Soviet Jackets by Maurice Friedberg, Columbia University Press, 1962.

Stalin and the French Communist Party, 1941–1947 by Alfred J. Rieber, Columbia University Press, 1962.

Sergei Witte and the Industrialization of Russia by Theodore K. Von Laue, Columbia University Press, 1962.

Ukranian Nationalism by John H. Armstrong, Columbia University Press, 1963.

The Sickle under the Hammer: The Russian Socialist Revolutionaries in the Early Months of Soviet Rule by Oliver H. Radkey, Columbia University Press, 1963.

Comintern and World Revolution, 1928–1943: The Shaping of Doctrine by Kermit E. McKenzie, Columbia University Press, 1964.

Weimar Germany and Soviet Russia, 1926–1933: A Study in Diplomatic Instability by Harvey L. Dyck, Columbia University Press, 1966.

Financing Soviet Schools by Harold J. Noah, Teachers College Press, 1966.

Russia, Bolshevism, and the Versailles Peace by John M. Thompson, Princeton University Press, 1966.

The Russian Anarchists by Paul Avrich, Princeton University Press, 1967.

The Soviet Academy of Sciences and the Communist Party, 1927–1932 by Loren R. Graham, Princeton University Press, 1967.

Red Virgin Soil: Soviet Literature in the 1920's by Robert A. Maguire, Princeton University Press, 1968; paperback, Cornell University Press, 1987.

Communist Party Membership in the U.S.S.R., 1917–1967 by T. H. Rigby, Princeton University Press, 1968.

Soviet Ethics and Morality by Richard T. DeGeorge, University of Michigan Press, 1969; paperback, Ann Arbor Paperbacks, 1969.

Vladimir Akimov on the Dilemmas of Russian Marxism, 1895–1903 by Jonathan Frankel, Cambridge University Press, 1969.

Soviet Perspectives on International Relations, 1956–1967 by William Zimmerman, Princeton University Press, 1969.

Krondstadt, 1921 by Paul Avrich, Princeton University Press, 1970.

Class Struggle in the Pale: The Formative Years of the Jewish Workers' Movement in Tsarist Russia by Ezra Mendelsohn, Cambridge University Press, 1970.

The Proletarian Episode in Russian Literature by Edward J. Brown, Columbia University Press, 1971.

Labor and Society in Tsarist Russia: The Factory Workers of St. Petersburg, 1855–1870 by Reginald E. Zelnik, Stanford University Press, 1971.

Archives and Manuscript Repositories in the USSR: Moscow and Leningrad by Patricia K. Grimsted, Princeton University Press, 1972.

The Baku Commune, 1917–1918 by Ronald G. Suny, Princeton University Press, 1972.

Mayakovsky: A Poet in the Revolution by Edward J. Brown, Princeton University Press, 1973.

Oblomov and his Creator: The Life and Art of Ivan Goncharov by Milton Ehre, Princeton University Press, 1973.

German Politics Under Soviet Occupation by Henry Krisch, Columbia University Press, 1974.

Soviet Politics and Society in the 1970's, Henry W. Morton and Rudolph L. Tokes, eds., Free Press, 1974.

Liberals in the Russian Revolution by William G. Rosenberg, Princeton University Press, 1974.

Famine in Russia, 1891–1892 by Richard G. Robbins, Jr., Columbia University Press, 1975.

In Stalin's Time: Middleclass Values in Soviet Fiction by Vera Dunham, Cambridge University Press, 1976.

The Road to Bloody Sunday by Walter Sablinsky, Princeton University Press, 1976; paperback, Princeton University Press, 1986.

The Familiar Letter as a Literary Genre in the Age of Pushkin by William Mills Todd III, Princeton University Press, 1976.

Russian Realist Art. The State and Society: The Peredvizhniki and Their Tradition by Elizabeth Valkenier, Ardis Publishers, 1977.

The Soviet Agrarian Debate by Susan Solomon, Westview Press, 1978.

Cultural Revolution in Russia, 1928–1931, Sheila Fitzpatrick, ed., Indiana University Press, 1978; paperback, Midland Books, 1984.

Soviet Criminologists and Criminal Policy: Specialists in Policy-Making by Peter Solomon, Columbia University Press, 1978.

Technology and Society under Lenin and Stalin: Origins of the Soviet Technical Intelligentsia by Kendall E. Bailes, Princeton University Press, 1978.

The Politics of Rural Russia, 1905–1914, Leopold H. Haimson, ed., Indiana University Press, 1979.

Political Participation in the USSR by Theodore H. Friedgut, Princeton University Press, 1979; paperback, Princeton University Press, 1982.

Education and Social Mobility in the Soviet Union, 1921–1934 by Sheila Fitzpatrick, Cambridge University Press, 1979.

The Soviet Marriage Market: Mate Selection in Russian and the USSR by Wesley Andrew Fisher, Praeger Publishers, 1980.

Prophecy and Politics: Socialism, Nationalism, and the Russian Jews, 1862–1917 by Jonathan Frankel, Cambridge University Press, 1981.

Dostoevsky and The Idiot: *Author, Narrator, and Reader* by Robin Feuer Miller, Harvard University Press, 1981.

Moscow Workers and the 1917 Revolution by Diane Koenker, Princeton University Press, 1981; paperback, Princeton University Press, 1986.

Archives and Manuscript Repositories in the USSR: Estonia, Latvia, Lithuania, and Belorussia by Patricia K. Grimsted, Princeton University Press, 1981.

Zionism in Poland: The Formative Years, 1915–1926 by Ezra Mendelsohn, Yale University Press, 1982.

Soviet Risk-Taking and Crisis Behavior by Hannes Adomeit, George Allen and Unwin Publishers, 1982.

Russia at the Crossroads: The 26th Congress of the CPSU, Seweryn Bialer and Thane Gustafson, eds., George Allen and Unwin Publishers, 1982.

The Crisis of the Old Order in Russia: Gentry and Government by Roberta Thompson Manning, Princeton University Press, 1983; paperback, Princeton University Press, 1986.

Sergei Aksakov and Russian Pastoral by Andrew A. Durkin, Rutgers University Press, 1983.

Politics and Technology in the Soviet Union by Bruce Parrott, MIT Press, 1983.

The Soviet Union and the Third World: An Economic Bind by Elizabeth Kridl Valkenier, Praeger Publishers, 1983.

Russian Metaphysical Romanticism: The Poetry of Tiutchev and Boratynskii by Sarah Pratt, Stanford University Press, 1984.

Ruling Russia: Politics and Administration in the Age of Absolutism, 1762–1796 by John P. LeDonne, Princeton University Press, 1984.

Insidious Intent: A Structural Analysis of Fedor Sologub's Petty Demon by Diana Greene, Slavica Publishers, 1986.

Leo Tolstoy: Resident and Stranger by Richard Gustafson, Princeton University Press, 1986.

Workers, Society, and the State: Labor and Life in Moscow, 1918–1929 by William Chase, University of Illinois Press, 1987.

Andrey Bely: Spirit of Symbolism, John Malmstad, ed., Cornell University Press, 1987.

Government and Peasant in Russia, 1861–1906: The Prehistory of the Stolypin Reforms by David A. J. Macey, Northern Illinois University Press, 1987.

The Making of Three Russian Revolutionaries: Voices from the Menshevik Past, edited by Leopold H. Haimson in collaboration with Ziva Galili y García and Richard Wortman, Cambridge University Press, 1988.

Revolution and Culture: The Bogdanov-Lenin Controversy by Zenovia A. Sochor, Cornell University Press, 1988.

A Handbook of Russian Verbs by Frank Miller, Ardis Publishers, 1988.

1905 in St. Petersburg: Labor, Society, and Revolution by Gerald D. Surh, Stanford University Press, 1989.

Iuzovka and Revolution. Volume 1, *Life and Work in Russia's Donbass, 1869–1924* by Theodore H. Friedgut, Princeton University Press, 1989.

Alien Tongues: Bilingual Russian Writers of the "First" Emigration by Elizabeth Klosty Beaujour, Cornell University Press, 1989.

The Menshevik Leaders in the Russian Revolution: Social Realities and Political Strategies, by Ziva Galili, Princeton University Press, 1989.